TRANSCENDENT GOD, RATIONAL WORLD

Edinburgh Studies in Islamic Scripture and Theology
Series Editor: Ramon Harvey

Published and forthcoming titles

Muḥammad ibn Ismāʿīl al-Bukhārī
Belal Abu Alabbas

Hadith Commentary: Continuity and Change
Edited by Joel Blecher, Stefanie Brinkmann and Ali Zaherinezhad

Transcendent God, Rational World: A Māturīdī Theology
Ramon Harvey

The Integrity of the Qur'an: Sunni and Shi'i Historical Narratives on Falsification
Kara Seyfeddin

edinburghuniversitypress.com/series/esist

TRANSCENDENT GOD, RATIONAL WORLD

A Māturīdī Theology

RAMON HARVEY

EDINBURGH
University Press

For my grandad, Harry Hughes, who invited me to the life of the mind

Edinburgh University Press is one of the leading university presses in the UK. We publish academic books and journals in our selected subject areas across the humanities and social sciences, combining cutting-edge scholarship with high editorial and production values to produce academic works of lasting importance. For more information visit our website: edinburghuniversitypress.com

Edinburgh University Press Ltd
TheTun–HolyroodRoad
12 (2f) Jackson's Entry
Edinburgh EH8 8PJ

First published in hardback by Edinburgh University Press 2021

Typeset in 11/13 Minion Pro by
IDSUK (DataConnection) Ltd

A CIP record for this book is available from the British Library

ISBN 978 1 4744 5164 2 (hardback)
ISBN 978 1 4744 5165 9 (paperback)
ISBN 978 1 4744 5166 6 (webready PDF)
ISBN 978 1 4744 5167 3 (epub)

Contents

Foreword by Bruce R. Reichenbach vii
Preface xi
Acknowledgements xiii

Introduction 1

1 Tradition and Reason 10

2 Rational Reality 56

3 Natural Theology 103

4 Divine Nature 124

5 Omniscience and Wisdom 159

6 Creative Action 175

7 Divine Speech and the Qur'an 191

Conclusion 222

Glossary of Arabic Terminology 237
Bibliography 239
Index 269

Foreword by Bruce R. Reichenbach

Ramon Harvey undertakes the daunting task of bringing classical Islamic thought not only into the twenty-first century but enjoining it as a meaningful dialectician and helpful contributor to contemporary philosophical conversation. He proposes to join the fray by reinvigorating the arguments, insights and concerns of the fourth/tenth-century Sunnī Islamic theologian Abū Mānṣūr al-Māturīdī in ways that enhance and enlighten the current discussion. He chooses Edmund Husserl and the phenomenological tradition as philosophical mates to al-Māturīdī, while incorporating the significant contributions of analytic philosophers of religion and ethics such as Alasdair MacIntyre, Alvin Plantinga, Nicholas Wolterstorff, Linda Zagzebski and Brian Leftow. These, he contends, have sufficient similarities to facilitate and enlighten a tradition-contemporary debate regarding questions posed by Western philosophical theology.

He notes that the contemporary Christian view of philosophy of religion is decidedly pluralistic, with both foundationalists and non-foundationalists proclaiming their wares. Harvey sides with the non-foundationalists and treats al-Māturīdī as proposing a non-foundationist position in the *kalām* tradition that – when brought into the contemporary discussion, as he puts it – leaves it 'receptive to overt dialogue and development' (p. 5). Thus, he embarks on a voyage through the treacherous waters of the tradition-reason debate in justifying theological beliefs, consciously embedding himself in Islamic tradition while extending the rational dialogue beyond that tradition. The prospects for success are greater than one might expect, considering that both traditions share common intellectual ancestry in Platonic, Neoplatonic and Aristotelian thought.

To expound his theology, Harvey reverses the ontological role that commences with a creator God, instead rooting it in human concepts reaching toward the Transcendent. Guided by tradition, enveloped within the arms of reason, he reaches toward an understanding that at once brackets the ordinary while subjecting the conceptual grounding of the Transcendent

Absolute to the investigation of human reason. The teleology of the world makes rational investigation possible, without limiting the Transcendent to linguistic univocity. And rational investigation is possible only under the presumption that the world is rational – that is, open to exploration by consciousness, as it teleologically explores that to which it connects phenomenally. Here Harvey reaches out to creatively connect the teleology of al-Māturīdī's Islamic thought, Husserlian transcendentalism and the Copenhagen interpretation of quantum physics, to focus on the primacy of the subject in the epistemic investigation of both the world and the Transcendent.

When Harvey turns to the concept of God, he walks the thin line between anthropomorphism and *via negativa*. Clinging to the latter alone would leave us without any knowledge of God's nature, only that he is some sort of particular being. To cling to the former confuses the space-time creation with the Creator. He brings them together: 'to exist is to have a given nature, and conversely, to have a given nature is to exist' (p. 79). The difficulty is how to flesh out the analogical relationship from our limited and human-oriented epistemological perspective.

Harvey is equally at home discussing set theory as theology, Islamic metaphysics and contemporary ontology, truthmakers and tropes. All of this he directs to moving the reader from an understanding of the material world phenomenologically considered to the Transcendent to which, he thinks, it points teleologically. With dialectical skill that parses the arguments, he defends his form of nominalism against any form of Platonism, all the while skirting the idealism of essences that remains after Husserl's phenomenological bracketing, intentionally conceived.

As to God's existence, Harvey expresses substantial agreement with current formulations of the *kalām* cosmological argument (with what one might consider an in-house although important disagreement over the status of the actual infinite), while with his Islamic counterpart he countenances versions of the teleological argument to flesh out the nature of the metaphysically necessary being. He focuses specifically on the contention that the teleological argument works best when it appeals to the premise that certain features (such as actualising quantum potentialities) cannot arise apart from intelligent causes.

Harvey's nominalism comes into focus when he addresses the question of God's nature, especially given the limits of human language. The problem of the temporal particularity with respect to God's knowledge leads Harvey to find a conception of time that not only invokes both A and B theories of time, but also allows God who is outside time to act immanently in it. Part of the heavy work is done by rejecting a realist sense of tensed time and holding that the objective reality of time is constituted by human consciousness, which itself is a divine creation, as is each event in the B sequence. In effect, God knows (events in) time through his creation of human consciousness that verifies temporal events. Time is, in short, ideal.

Affirming God's metaphysical but not logical necessity, Harvey follows al-Māturīdī in holding that the attributes of God's nature are essential and eternal. This follows from his view of a timeless God and leaves one to wonder whether in His relation to the world, God has non-eternal, accidental attributes. Harvey rules this out by definition, in that God's 'properties form a complete and consistent set: they cannot be removed or altered' (p. 157), a set that constitutes his nature. At the same time, rejecting divine simplicity, Harvey makes room for analogical predication of God's different attributes. God is conceived of as a concrete particular whose nature is comprised of a bundle of distinct attributes that are to be understood analogically.

Omniscience is one of those attributes. Harvey discusses divine knowledge from the perspective of both non-propositional wisdom and propositional knowledge. The function of the former is to ground the modal notions relating to metaphysical and actuality necessity. God is omniscient in the sense that 'He directly and intuitively verifies each proposition via His intimate acquaintance with its object of knowledge, its lack thereof, or its indeterminacy' (p. 167). The unity of God's knowledge is found in that it is all occurrent, not derived sequentially. God is thus omniscient in that he can know all propositions that it is possible to know. That God can know events in time, such as now, is due to 'His direct eternal knowledge of this proposition as indexed to my particular consciousness at this time' (p. 167).

Crucial to much of his presentation is the denial of the Law of Excluded Middle. In doing so, he allows for a significant amount of indeterminacy. This, in turn, enhances his non-foundationalism and enables him to address a variety of problems in metaphysics, logic and epistemology.

Divine creation is an eternal attribute of God, even if its effects are temporal. He addresses the pesky problem of evil by maintaining that, since God's creative action is an eternal attribute, even though the evils that arise in creation are the effects of God's action, they are properly ascribed to creation. Harvey invokes the concept of middle knowledge, whereby God knows all possibilities, including the free choices of potential individuals, and employs this knowledge in his act of creating the actual world against other possible worlds that he could create. While he writes of God's act of creation as an attribute, it is obvious from his discussion that this term really comprises a multitude of creative actions. From God's timelessness, everything is created simultaneously; from the subjective or ideal human consciousness, they are time-indexed.

Finally, he addresses the attribute of divine speech, where God's speech is an eternal divine action, manifested in a plurality of speech acts. It is a divine action that is not tied to any particular language, or a specific, ordered composition (although he holds that the relation between revelation and divine speech is clearer in the Qur'an than in the Biblical writings), but at the same time is not heard directly by humans. What is conveyed are the underlying meanings understood by us as created locutions. Harvey invokes the speech act theory advanced by Wolterstorff to help convey an understanding of both God's illocutionary speech acts and our understanding of their meaning; in this they are analogous to human speech acts but lack any hint of temporality.

This brief survey cannot fully convey the richness of Harvey's arguments and his careful and detailed location of the themes in the Māturīdī tradition. Before integrating the insights of al-Māturīdī's thought into the current debate, he carefully and extensively attends to its sources, discusses diverse interpretations of it and traces its subsequent, complex and not always consistent development. In this discussion, which plays more than an auxiliary role in the text, the invoked tradition is not only clarified but developed and assessed as to its viability and suggestiveness for engaging in the theological and philosophical debate. Whether one agrees or disagrees with the contention that God can be, in part, rationally comprehended by using human categories, that God is timeless and that this is consistent with God's actions in the world, and with his bundle theory of the divine nature, his arguments and unity of perspective cannot be ignored. Thus, in detailing the contributions of al-Māturīdī and subsequent commentators, as well as in bringing this venerable tradition into dialogue with Western philosophical thought and exchanging insights, Harvey has performed a significant service to both Islamic thought and contemporary philosophical theology.

Preface

Belief in revelation is a curious thing. On the one hand, it may provoke the believer to desist from systematic rational elaboration of the world and God. Why take the trouble when you believe that God has sent down the Qur'an 'as an explanation for everything (*tibyānan li-kulli shay*ʾ) (Q. 16:89)'? On the other hand, it may propel believers to greater heights of reflection, along the lines expressed in the Christian tradition as faith seeking understanding. The steep mountain trail of theological investigation is not one that all people want, nor need, to climb. Yet for those walking in its foothills, those who feel called to make the ascent, it becomes an irresistible pull. One gathers one's supplies and sets out to navigate the sheer cliffs and treacherous ravines. Often in such an endeavour one faces no hope of progress without following the tracks left by a great master who has gone on ahead, perhaps, one hopes, further than any other. No one knows for sure who has gone furthest, which of the forerunners may have reached the peak, and if such an end point is even within the bounds of human capacity.

Nonetheless, we climb. Along the way, we write accounts that detail the unique path we have taken amidst the terrain of concept and argument, over the footprints of those who have preceded us long ago and those who still climb with us. Maybe these scrawlings will be useful for others facing the same dangers, those who yearn for the path, or those who are comfortable at home but look up at the mountain from time to time and wonder. This book is such an account, and the master behind whom I march is a fourth/tenth-century Samarqandī theologian known as Abū Manṣūr al-Māturīdī. Many thousands of scholars have followed his path, and I can see the signs of some of the more prominent ones around his trail. Sometimes, they have diverged and discovered routes to new vistas. Yet his way, faded and difficult to climb, was somehow still the most bold, deft and original in its approach – it needed to be, because it was made during an era in which the very ground beneath the feet was shifting. Perhaps that time has come around again, and so I trace his steps as I forge on.

Ramon Harvey
26 Rabīʿ al-Ākhir 1441/23 December 2019
London

Acknowledgements

For their boundless love and support for my writing, I am so grateful to my three children, Safiya, Leila and Yusuf, my wife Shukri and my family, especially my mum, dad and sisters. I love you all.

While writing this book, I have been based at Ebrahim College in London and worked as a visiting lecturer at the Cambridge Muslim College. I thank all my colleagues and students in both institutions for sharing their good company, knowledge and questions. I thank the Aziz Foundation, which has funded my academic position and has been incredibly supportive of my work. I also thank the John Templeton Foundation for awarding a grant for the research project that I lead, *Beyond Foundationalism: New Horizons in Muslim Analytic Theology (2020–23)*, which is in collaboration with the Aziz Foundation and hosted by the Cambridge Muslim College. The present text was the starting point for the epistemological questions asked in the project and is its first published output.

I am grateful to a wider network of friends, colleagues and contacts that reaches via the internet all over the world. In thinking through and shaping the ideas that comprise this book, I have benefitted greatly from the discussions, resources and companionship that this loose, good-natured group has provided. You know who you are.

There are two individuals whom I would like to single out for their great support in this project. Harith Bin Ramli, now at Edge Hill University, is a true friend. Discussion with him about aspects of my previous book was important for turning me towards the world of theology, while our private reading sessions on *Kitāb al-tawḥīd*, before I ever envisaged this book, deepened my appreciation for the complexity of early *kalām*. More recently, he has helped me chew over many of the deepest problems in the text and has provided his critical reflections on my drafts. Kayhan Özaykal at Istanbul University has been exceptionally generous with his time and expertise. From discussing translation problems in *Kitāb al-tawḥīd*, to sending me Māturīdī primary sources from Istanbul, referencing key parts of the Turkish literature and commenting on my manuscript, he has helped this book develop and prevented its isolation from the important scholarship in Turkey.

I would like to recognise several other colleagues for their assistance. David Vishanoff provided many valuable remarks on my manuscript. Arnold Yasin Mol reviewed the text and offered excellent suggestions for revision. Kamaluddin Ahmed read an early draft and gave comments and encouragement. Safaruk Chowdhury read early chapters and has benefitted me with his philosophical knowledge. Philip Dorroll has shared his own work and other useful resources. Mustafa Bilal Öztürk has kindly procured for me digitised manuscripts of extant texts by al-Māturīdī's student Abū al-Ḥasan al-Rustughfanī. Najah Nadi, my colleague at Cambridge Muslim College, generously shared her doctoral dissertation on Saʿd al-Dīn al-Taftāzānī. Salman Younas has provided early Ḥanafī and *ahl al-ḥadīth* references. Sohaib Saeed has discussed questions relating to the Qur'an and exegesis. Asim Islam commented on my treatment of quantum mechanics in Chapter 2. Joshua Ralston invited me to the University of Edinburgh to present a paper on the divine nature, based on Chapter 4, and has been enthusiastic in sharing his knowledge of Christian and Islamic theology. The reviewers working on behalf of Edinburgh University Press have been exemplary in helping me frame the work as a whole. I would also like to extend my special gratitude to Bruce Reichenbach, Professor Emeritus at Augsburg University, for his support, his critical comments on my manuscript and his erudite foreword. The book is much richer for all the above interactions.

Finally, I would like to thank the entire team at Edinburgh University Press and especially my commissioning editor Nicola Ramsey. Her vision and professional excellence have not only made it possible for this title to appear at all, but for it to be one of the first publications in Edinburgh Studies in Islamic Scripture and Theology, a new series that I am editing for the press.

‘It is not possible that the world in which reason is foundational is based on other than wisdom or is futile’.

Abū Manṣūr al-Māturīdī[1]

‘And since *the rationality* which the fact-world shows is not in any sense such as the essence demands, there lies concealed in all this a wonderful *teleology*’.

Edmund Husserl[2]

1 Al-Māturīdī, *Kitāb al-tawḥīd*, p. 67.
2 Husserl, *Ideas*, pp. 112–13.

Introduction

The intellectual activity named *ʿilm al-kalām* in Arabic is broadly equivalent to the English term philosophical theology.[1] This translation is useful because it presupposes that there can be a coherent combination of philosophy – the use of rational argument to clarify, or justify, truth – and theology in the sense of systematic discourse about the divine.[2] The function of such a theology is to articulate the truths of theism in a language appropriate to a civilisation's intellectual milieu. The credibility of this project was taken for granted during the long medieval period,[3] with its diverse contributions from Muslim, Christian and Jewish scholars.

1 The early use of the word *kalām* for a specific method of dialectical dispute (hence the alternative translation dialectical theology) can be distinguished from the subject of theology more broadly conceived. See van Ess, 'Early Development of *Kalām*', p. 113. Traditional answers for how *kalām*, which literally means speech, came to be a term of art include the notion that it refers to an exposition on a given topic or to the centrality of debate about the theological status of the Qur'an – God's divine speech – in the early generations. Abdel Haleem, 'Early *kalām*', pp. 71–72. Alexander Treiger proposes a potential origin for the word meaning both disputation and theology in the context of first/seventh-century Christian-Muslim debates but concludes that this reconstruction is inconclusive. Treiger, 'Origins of *Kalām*', pp. 33–34.

2 Dimitri Gutas has provocatively argued for the incoherence of this pairing within the *kalām* tradition on the grounds that a true philosophy is scientific and cannot have a theological agenda informed by revealed scripture. He proposes the term 'paraphilosophy'. Gutas, 'Avicenna and After', p. 43. I think that the term 'philosophical' in the phrase is properly used for highlighting an approach that takes philosophical argument seriously while remaining within certain boundaries dictated by the requirements of theology. Christian Lange has critiqued the prevailing contemporary approach to the history of classical Islamic theology for its textual focus and privileging of *kalām*. Lange, 'Power, Orthodoxy, and Salvation in Classical Islamic Theology', pp. 136–37. There are certainly merits to this argument, although the current study with its specific constructive theological ambitions is the wrong place to pursue it.

3 The medieval period, or Middle Ages, has sometimes been understood as the nearly thousand-year stretch from *ca* 500 CE, the fall of the Roman Empire in the West, to *ca* 1453 CE, the fall of Constantinople. Stevenson, *Shorter Oxford English Dictionary*,

Nevertheless, theologians from these traditions have long had an ambivalent relationship with philosophical thought, often both drawing from its tools and reviling its 'excesses'.[4] In the *kalām* tradition, while members of the Ashʿarī and Māturīdī Sunnī theological schools were always invested in Aristotelian-Neoplatonic philosophical techniques to some extent, albeit circumscribed to varying degrees, there is a palpable sense in recent centuries that the pendulum has swung towards a distrust of this mode of discursive theology.[5] Even in Sunnī circles that in theory are not opposed to its study, the discipline of *kalām* has stalled, remaining stagnantly fixated either on scholastic arguments developed centuries ago or on the learning and scriptural defence of creed.[6]

The challenges posed by contemporary thought are profound. Developments in the foundations of mathematics and logic impacted the conception of rational activity and led to the emergence of analytic philosophy in the twentieth century. This is paralleled by the phenomenological movement within so-called continental philosophy, which interrogated the significance of tradition in the constitution of any reasoned reflection upon the world.[7] Meanwhile, breakthroughs in physics exemplified by quantum mechanics heralded a re-evaluation of earlier scientific pictures of reality with deep potential philosophical and theological implications.

vol. 1, p. 1777. Although any such periodisation has its limitations, it has the advantage of encompassing in a single phrase the formative and classical development of the Islamic tradition, the Augustinian and scholastic periods of Christian theology and post-Talmudic Rabbinical scholarship. Garth Fowden has argued for the cogency of the first millennium for the emergence of Rabbinical Judaism, Christianity and Islam, along with their canonical scriptures and consolidated creeds. See Fowden, *Before and After Muḥammad*, pp. 55–57. Al-Māturīdī lived at the end of this time span.

4 In Islam, Abū Ḥāmid al-Ghazālī (d. 505/1111) is the most famous case in point. Despite the popular conception that he defeated philosophy and entrenched traditionalism, contemporary scholarship demonstrates that he was a significant filter for the emergence of a revised Avicennism. Wisnovsky, 'One Aspect of the Avicennian Turn in Sunnī Theology', p. 65. But as Chapter 1 will show, Muslim philosophy is also an important part of the genealogy of *kalām* in the formative centuries, including that of al-Māturīdī.

5 See Özervarli, 'Attempts to Revitalize *Kalām* in the Late 19th and Early 20th Centuries', pp. 100–2; Gardet, 'Allāh'.

6 Wielandt, 'Main Trends', p. 710. The Shīʿī tradition has generally remained more interested in dynamic rational thought, particularly through continued engagement with Mulla Sadra (d. 1050/1640). See Rizvi, '"Only the Imam Knows Best"', pp. 487–88.

7 I use the term 'world' to refer to everything except God, as found in the *kalām* tradition. See Dgheim, *Mawsūʿa muṣṭalaḥāt ʿilm al-kalām al-islāmī*, vol. 1, p. 758. Also see the definition of Husserl: 'The World is the totality of objects that can be known through experience, known in orderly theoretical thought on the basis of direct present experience'. Husserl, *Ideas*, p. 10. This idea of 'universal experienceability' is important for some of the philosophical and theological positions that I advance. See pages 64, 130, 188.

These conditions would seem to require a unique and renewed programme of philosophical theology. Yet at least in the first half of the twentieth century, the confidence that one could speak about God and His attributes was largely lost within Western philosophy.[8] A number of reasons can be given for this: the prominence of atheism, especially after the horrors of war; the demand of logical positivism for meaning to be defined by what can be measured empirically; and a post-Kantian preoccupation with the limits of human thought.[9] In many ways, such scepticism reflected the slow loss of confidence in the comprehensive metaphysical systems that undergirded the investigations of earlier thinkers.[10]

In Islamic thought, for over a century there have been calls to develop a *kalām jadīd* (renewed theology), which is fit for the conditions of modernity.[11] Arguably, however, a significant part of this movement has aimed to provide accessible theological writing suitable for wider consumption by a modern literate public.[12] Laudable as such educational efforts may be, they do not deal with the more fundamental question of reconciling the premodern *kalām* tradition in all of its subtlety with the considerable resources of modern theological and philosophical thought, as represented by the mainly European and North American tradition. An attempt to achieve such a synthesis is found in Muhammad Iqbal's *The Reconstruction of Religious Thought in Islam* (1930). The exceptional nature of that text points to the rarity of such integrative approaches by Muslim thinkers.

While my own project differs in many ways from that of Iqbal, I am convinced that there remains a real need for theological work that returns to the basic questions of epistemology, metaphysics, God's nature and His attributes from the twin lights of a robust *kalām* tradition and modern thought. But my present effort to put forward a contemporary Islamic philosophical

8 Flint and Rea, 'Introduction', pp. 1–2. In this book, I write God for the proper name Allāh and use the grammatically masculine translation and capitalisation of His pronouns. I judge this to be the most effective way to communicate my theological ideas to a broad audience, while retaining a close rendering of scriptural language.

9 See Murray and Rea, 'Philosophy and Christian Theology'; Wolterstorff, 'How Philosophical Theology Became Possible', p. 157.

10 David Trenery provides the following useful definition for the concept of a comprehensive metaphysical system: 'A set of ontological and ethical presuppositions which are taken to encompass and explain the nature of the universe of which our species is a part, and which also provide a framework for human practical reasoning and action.' See Trenery, *Alasdair MacIntyre, George Lindbeck, and the Nature of Tradition*, p. 1.

11 For a recent expression of this idea, see al-Ghursī, *Taḥqīq masāʾil muhimmāt min ʿilm al-tawḥīd wa-l-ṣifāt*, pp. 25–27. Despite his words, al-Ghursī's text remains within the theological categories of the late classical tradition.

12 Aspects of the background to this phenomenon are considered in Kurzman, 'Introduction', pp. 8–10.

theology is placed in a double bind by the reservations within Western philosophy and Islamic theology. I need to argue for the relevance of Islamic theology to the philosophy of religion as well as the acceptance of the tools of contemporary philosophy within *kalām*.

The astonishing recent flourishing of Christian philosophical theology within the Western analytic tradition has opened the door wide for the first of these.[13] As Nicholas Wolterstorff argues, while the earlier mode of analytic philosophy depended on a stance of classical foundationalism – that any belief, to be rationally held, must be justified by reference to indubitable truths[14] – such a perspective is beset with difficulties.[15] In fact, it is difficult to establish the foundationalist theory of justification itself on this basis.[16] The field remains in what Wolterstorff terms a state of 'dialogic pluralism', in which philosophers, whether theists, atheists, or others, are free to treat their starting commitments as rationally held first principles.[17] Recent work in Christian philosophical theology has not just considered questions of God's nature that are largely shared with other theists, but have dealt philosophically with religiously specific doctrines, such as incarnation and atonement.[18] There has also been a return to taking seriously the medieval Christian theological tradition as a philosophically fruitful source for thinking about God.[19] There is no principled argument available to preclude Muslim scholars from joining this conversation on equivalent grounds. That so few have done so must reflect mainly non-philosophical factors.

The point of departure for this book is the exploration of one such kind of enquiry.[20] I take a distinct tradition of *kalām*, the school of thought inaugurated by the Transoxianan theologian Abū Mānṣūr al-Māturīdī

13 The continental tradition, while never embracing atheism as enthusiastically as early-twentieth-century analytic philosophy, seems to remain wary about theology that does not stay within the phenomenologically accessible world of the human being. Flint and Rea, 'Introduction', pp. 2–3.

14 A more technical definition of foundationalism can be provided as follows: an epistemological system in which all non-basic propositions are inferred from basic propositions for the purpose of providing certainty. See Williams, 'Is Aquinas a Foundationalist?', p. 33.

15 Wolterstorff, 'How Philosophical Theology Became Possible', pp. 160, 163.

16 See Hasan and Fumerton, 'Foundationalist Theories of Epistemic Justification'; Oppy, 'Natural Theology', pp. 24–25.

17 Wolterstorff, 'How Philosophical Theology Became Possible', pp. 165–66. See also Ross, *Philosophical Theology*, p. 32.

18 Flint and Rea, 'Introduction', p. 4.

19 Freddoso, 'Introduction', pp. 1–2.

20 The *Shorter Oxford English Dictionary* distinguishes between enquiry (to ask) and inquiry (to investigate) in British English. Stevenson, *Shorter Oxford English Dictionary*, vol. 1, p. 1391. I follow Alasdair MacIntyre in using enquiry in a semi-technical sense of systematic reasoned investigation, a usage presumably borrowed from David Hume's *An Enquiry Concerning Human Understanding*.

(d. 333/944),[21] and through a close reading of his epistemological writing argue that, unlike later members of the theological school bearing his name, he should not be understood as a foundationalist. I see him as a non-foundationalist, presaging modern philosophers such as Edmund Husserl, Hans-Georg Gadamer and especially Alasdair MacIntyre, whom I use to argue for the significance, or even necessity, of self-consciously constituting one's rational activity within a tradition of thought and to justify my focus on the Māturīdī school for my own theological proposals.

The theological consequences of al-Māturīdī's epistemic position explain why I see his work as so useful for my own project of *kalām jadīd*. I propose that, in meta-epistemological terms, we can draw the distinction between an open model of theology and a closed one. An open theology is characterised by a receptiveness to diverse sources in its theological structure, prioritising meaning above systematic, foundationalist proof. This is exemplified by al-Māturīdī's reception of the prevailing rational discourses of his day and constitutes a methodology that I follow in the present text with respect to contemporary thought.[22] A closed theology excludes concepts that cannot be justified foundationalistically, sacrificing total theological meaning to secure its system. This, I will suggest, is the programme in which classical-era Māturīdīs were engaged and explains why they filtered out some of al-Māturīdī's distinctive concepts and methods – ones that I think are crucial to revisit today.[23] Moreover, the continuance of this aspect of the classical foundationalist approach in modernity can help to explain why the *kalām jadīd* movement has been underwhelming and why constructive philosophical theology has not seemed relevant to many Muslim theologians. Once it is shown that there is room to work from a non-foundationalist epistemology, the door is opened to a conception of the *kalām* tradition that is self-reflective about its own contingency and thus receptive to overt dialogue and development.[24]

This is not the only time that a reader of this book will find my interpretation of al-Māturīdī's position diverging from the received opinion of

21 Transoxiana, in Arabic *mā warāʾ al-nahr* (lit. what lies beyond the river), is the name for a region of Central Asia east of the Oxus River centred on modern-day Uzbekistan. The name al-Māturīdī denotes someone from Māturīd (or Māturīt), a village in or near Samarqand, a major city of the region. See al-Damanhūrī, *Sadd al-thughūr bi-sīrat ʿalam al-hudā*, p. 101. For maps of Samarqand and Transoxiana that indicate the extent of settlement in the fourth/tenth century, see Kennedy, *An Historical Atlas of Islam*, pp. 40–41.

22 This can be compared to Christian constructive theology, such as that proposed by Gordon D. Kaufman. See, for instance, his book *The Theological Imagination: Constructing the Concept of God* (1981).

23 I am grateful to Arnold Yasin Mol whose comments have contributed greatly to my expression of this point.

24 See Arkoun, *The Unthought in Contemporary Islamic Thought*, pp. 39–40.

later figures in his tradition. My approach to a given theological question in the pages that follow is always to return first to the difficult, yet rewarding, words of al-Māturīdī before branching out to consider select later figures and how their ideas may confirm, explain, develop or even conflict with his. The power of al-Māturīdī's fundamental method for theologising about God and its centrality for the present project deserve further comment here. The core theological problem raised within this book is how finite human beings within the world can use language to speak rationally about the transcendent divine. Al-Māturīdī's insight is to argue that God must be discussed through analogy with the creation in certain circumstances, for instance, when affirming substantive attributes such as His knowledge and speech, while applying strict limits to avoid anthropomorphising Him. This procedure preserves the possibility of human language, and therefore revelation, to speak about the divine nature. Yet in other cases, God's utter transcendence is affirmed, such that He is spoken of in contrast to the created order.[25] Crucially, within al-Māturīdī's system the world is always amenable to a rational analysis that provides indications towards God through one of these two kinds of inference. This is what makes a systematic theology possible.

The scholars that followed in al-Māturīdī's wake brought new arguments and, in some places, even adjusted his conclusions, but the boundaries of their enquiries were shaped by his analysis. It is my intention to place this constellation of ideas from the Māturīdī tradition in conversation with contemporary philosophical and theological thought, to see how well it holds up and what further modifications may be required. As MacIntyre has so keenly pointed out, it is only through continued testing and verification against the best that rivals can offer that a tradition of enquiry retains its vibrancy.[26]

Both the historical and philosophical dimensions of the book should be framed in the light of the specific audiences whom I seek to address. In one sense this book is a work of intellectual history. Within the specific theological themes that I cover, I aim to build on existing modern scholarship, such as that of Ulrich Rudolph, Mustafa Cerić and J. Meric Pessagno, to provide advances in the reconstruction of al-Māturīdī's system on its own terms.[27] I also pay attention to related discourses in the subsequent centuries and so contribute, albeit in a necessarily constrained way, to the study of the development of the Māturīdī tradition, especially in the centuries immediately following al-Māturīdī.

25 See the discussion on pages 74–76.

26 See page 53.

27 Rudolph points to his own work as a necessary precondition for this kind of historical project. See Rudolph, *Al-Māturīdī and the Development of Sunnī Theology*, pp. 17–18.

For ease of expression, I use the term 'Māturīdī tradition' as inclusive of all figures after Abū Manṣūr al-Māturīdī who receive the particular tradition of fourth/tenth-century Samarqandī Ḥanafī theology of which he is the most famous representative. I recognise, however, that this moniker was only adopted by members of the tradition much later and that well into the classical era scholars typically saw themselves either as Ḥanafīs or belonging to the *ahl al-sunna wa-l-jamāʿa* (people of precedent and the community). When discussing the fourth/tenth century, I make use of terms such as 'Samarqandī Ḥanafī' to avoid glaring anachronism, while reserving 'Ḥanafī-Māturīdī' for the entire sweep of the theological tradition, before al-Māturīdī and after him. The number and range of Arabic Māturīdī texts of which I make use, including unpublished manuscripts, reflect my recognition of the tradition as a formidable intellectual endeavour that deserves rigorous philological study from its primary sources. Furthermore, in interpreting this tradition, I consider as much secondary scholarship as I can in a range of languages.

Although the historical study of Māturīdism is itself a valuable activity, in this book it serves an auxiliary role to the constructive theological project that I have already introduced. Thus, the function of the above investigations in premodern Islamic theological discourse is to excavate and refine ideas for use in contemporary philosophical theology. Here I engage with recent Islamic theological work from the *kalām jadīd* approach where available, philosophical theology (mainly Christian) and philosophy of religion that includes critical and even sceptical voices. Within specific philosophical areas – such as epistemology, ontology and the philosophy of science and mathematics – I reference work that, even though it may not have been written with a theological application in mind, I feel may be profitably drawn into my project. Such interdisciplinary forays cannot hope to be comprehensive and are not necessarily intended as interventions into their respective fields proper, although I hope that they are respectable. Each such topic, or just one approach to it, is regularly the focus of specialised articles and monographs, which often make only incremental gains on the previous literature. I am attempting to take a synoptic view that will allow me to sketch a way to navigate these various discussions. It may be – and experience tells me it is likely – that further focused study of them would lead to shifts in, and refinements of, my theological position.

The book's structure is loosely symmetrical. It starts with a historical perspective towards theological enquiry and epistemology in Chapter 1, justifying locating my work within a tradition and paying attention to the genesis and development of Māturīdism. I also introduce the major cast of historical characters and some of the important themes to be addressed throughout the book. Attention then shifts in Chapter 2 to the idea of reason in the world and the elements of epistemology and ontology through which enquiry can be directed towards the transcendent divine. Chapter 3 considers rational arguments for God's existence in the field of natural theology, while Chapter 4, the theological heart of the book, discusses the divine nature as timelessly eternal, metaphysically necessary and possessing substantive attributes. Chapters 5, 6 and 7 look at God's omniscience (*ʿilm*) and wisdom (*ḥikma*), His creative action (*takwīn*), and His speech (*kalām*) and the Qur'an. I there apply the foregoing theological principles to attributes that manifest God's interaction with the world. In the case of wisdom and creative action, I pay attention to eternal attributes that are emphasised by the Māturīdī tradition.

This structure also reflects in some respects the logical order of *kalām* manuals, none more so than al-Māturīdī's *Kitāb al-tawḥīd.* He too begins with reflections upon theological tradition and epistemology, before turning to the world, arguments for God, and His nature and attributes. The latter half of al-Māturīdī's text deals with anthrocentric themes, such as prophecy, fate, faith and human action.[28] In my case, although there is a turning back towards the creation in my study of God's attributes, analysis of the human being falls outside the scope of my investigation. Despite the perpetual significance of questions of theological anthropology and the common practice within contemporary philosophy of religion to discuss them alongside the divine attributes that I cover, I have decided it is best to leave them for later treatment. I am also aware of the implications that this project has for constructive ethics, especially as this book arose from reflections begun in my previous work *The Qur'an and the Just Society.* As premodern Muslim scholars writing in the fields of *kalām* and *uṣūl al-fiqh* were aware, Islamic ethics derives its meaning and justification from its theological grounding. Hence, the renewal of theology is a precondition for ethics. Such questions cross back over into the territory of hermeneutics that was a major part of my prior book, but they emerge here only tangentially. My focus is on the elaboration of a contemporary Māturīdī theology, and that is task enough for a single monograph.

A few notes for the reader are in order. I reference the Arabic text of the Qur'an according to the Cairo edition and use the translation of M. A. S. Abdel Haleem, unless the portion quoted is very short or the context requires a different interpretation. Honorifics for the Prophet Muḥammad and other revered figures within the Islamic tradition should be taken as implicit. This book is best read linearly from beginning to end, perhaps with occasional

28 There are some similarities with the arrangement of Aquinas' *Summa theologiae*. See McGinn, *Thomas Aquinas's* Summa theologiae, p. 68.

jumping around to follow up on cross-references (written as 'see page . . .', rather than 'p.' for citations). But those mainly interested in contemporary philosophical theology may want to focus on the latter parts of each chapter and section where these discussions are usually located (historians of *kalām* may want to do the opposite). The arguments in each chapter are designed to build on those that have come before (often the philosophical discussions in Chapter 2), and while I try to recap, I avoid unnecessary repetition. If a reader finds a theological argument in Chapters 3–7 unclear, it may be helpful to turn to my first introduction of the key concepts. Be aware, too, that I do not always understand the terms of *kalām* according to their classical usages within the Māturīdī tradition, and the main text, notes and glossary provide specific explanations when this is the case. One of my arguments in this book is that *kalām* in the hands of al-Māturīdī and the early school of Samarqand is not identical to that later popularised under the name Māturīdī. My own constructive work will often, though not always, favour the approach of the former, while benefitting from the latter, and then arrive at a new distinct theological position after taking modern thought into account.

CHAPTER 1

Tradition and Reason

The binary of 'tradition' and 'reason' as the source of opposing theologies is an old canard in studies of Islamic intellectual history. A sober look at the various schools of thought reveals that each is distinctively invested in both its inherited traditions and a practice of rational elaboration. In an important intervention, Sherman Jackson has argued that Muslim rationalism in its familiar guise of *kalām* reflects an ideological effort to ensconce a specific Aristotelian-Neoplatonic formation of reason as paradigmatic. It thus represents merely a different tradition of reason than its traditionalist rival, which in turn is not innocent from possessing its own first principles, selections and accretions.[1] The lesson that can be drawn here will be a keynote for this chapter: revelation is always heard, understood, interpreted and transmitted by human beings whose sense of reasonableness is embodied in their histories.[2] As Rowan Williams observes:

> Appealing to tradition and community without some reflection on history can be a way of avoiding uncomfortable critical questions about legitimate authority – just as appealing to timeless metaphysical argument can be a way of avoiding the specifics of human practice and habit.[3]

This chapter takes seriously my claim to be adding to a historically grounded tradition of Islamic theology, the Māturīdī school. The textual excavations presented here introduce many of the theologians whom I reference in the remainder of the book. Thematically, the discussion revolves around the epistemology of al-Māturīdī's theological system and my goal to develop it in *kalām jadīd*. Section I works through al-Māturīdī's conceptualisation of his

1 Jackson, *On the Boundaries of Theological Tolerance*, pp. 19–20. Cf. Frank, 'Elements in the Development of the Teaching of al-Ashʿarī', pp. 143–44.
2 Jackson, *On the Boundaries of Theological Tolerance*, p. 16.
3 Williams, *The Edge of Words*, p. 3.

own epistemic commitments and critically contrasts its non-foundationalist approach with later school figures. Section II gauges the implicit grounding of his work within a range of pre-existing philosophical ideas and theological discourses. Section III examines the development of the Māturīdī tradition through formative, classical, late classical and modern phases, its interaction with Ashʿarism and the impact of Avicennism. Finally, Section IV turns towards Western philosophy since Kant, situating my project within a historical frame able to draw from both continental and analytic approaches and to take a meta-theoretical stance towards tradition and reason.

I. Tradition and Reason in Māturīdī Epistemology

Al-ʿAqīda al-Nasafiyya is one of the most important creedal texts within the Sunnī theological tradition. It was written in the early classical period of the Māturīdī school by the Transoxanian theologian Abū Ḥafṣ al-Nasafī (d. 537/1142) to summarise its tenets. The creed attracted commentaries, and the treatise penned by Saʿd al-Dīn al-Taftāzānī (d. 793/1390) is the most famous of these, a subject for further super-commentaries (*ḥawāshī*) that is still studied in madrasas today.[4] A distinctive quality of this short creed is its opening section, which presents what could be called a foundationalist position of epistemic justification.[5] It starts with the following sentence: 'The People of Truth state that the realities of things are established and knowledge of them is realised, in opposition to the sophists (*qāla ahlu al-ḥaqqi ḥaqāʾiqu al-ashyāʾi thābitatun wa-l-ʿilmu bi-hā mutaḥaqqiqun khilāfan lil-sūfasṭāʾiyya*)'. The author then outlines three means (*asbāb*) to knowledge (*ʿilm*): healthy senses (*al-ḥawāss al-salīma*), the truthful report (*al-khabar al-ṣādiq*) and the intellect (*al-ʿaql*).[6]

Abū Ḥafṣ al-Nasafī here summarises his teacher Abū al-Muʿīn al-Nasafī (d. 508/1114), the major consolidator of the classical Māturīdī school tradition. In his large theological work *Tabṣirat al-adilla*, Abū al-Muʿīn states that knowledge is only achieved by rational enquiry into evidence and that this must be founded on the epistemic sources of the senses and necessary knowledge (*badāha fī al-ʿuqūl*).[7] But the explicit defence of *kalām* for gaining certain knowledge is given its first extended Māturīdī expression in the

4 Calder et al., *Classical Islam*, p. 155.

5 While I acknowledge that one may question whether such contemporary philosophical terms are anachronistic, I think that it is helpful to use them to clarify latent positions within the tradition and to retrieve premodern positions for my constructive project. Thanks to Harith Bin Ramli for raising this point.

6 Al-Nasafī, 'Matn al-ʿaqīda al-Nasafiyya', p. 51.

7 Al-Nasafī, *Tabṣirat al-adilla*, vol. 1, p. 138. For a discussion of *badāha*, see Dgheim, *Mawsūʿa muṣṭalaḥāt ʿilm al-kalām al-islāmī*, vol. 1, p. 279.

Talkhīṣ al-adilla of Abū Isḥāq al-Ṣaffār (d. 534/1140), a contemporary of Abū Ḥafṣ.[8] Al-Ṣaffār writes of the three means to knowledge as 'the proof leading to certainty (*al-dalīl al-muwaṣṣil ilā al-yaqīn*)'.[9]

The source of these distinctive epistemological introductions in Māturīdī *kalām* manuals is the school's eponym, Abū Manṣūr al-Māturīdī, at the beginning of his only surviving theological text, *Kitāb al-tawḥīd*.[10] After some initial remarks on this book, which is the single most significant source for the present monograph, I will engage in an excavation of al-Māturīdī's major arguments in his epistemological introduction, aiming to show that, while he proposes a correspondence theory of knowledge, in which different aspects of the world reach the human being via a number of means, his justificatory system is non-foundationalist.[11] Instead, al-Māturīdī highlights the centrality of tradition itself in constituting any epistemic activity, a position that implies its grounding within a comprehensive metaphysical system. This is a crucial second-order level of discussion that has been missed by the later school in seeking to establish its classical foundationalist position.

Only one extant manuscript is known to exist of *Kitāb al-tawḥīd*, which is currently housed in the main library of the University of Cambridge and

8 Demir, 'Māturīdī Theologian Abū Ishāq al-Zāhid al-Saffār's Vindication of the Kalām', pp. 447–48.

9 Al-Ṣaffār, *Talkhīṣ al-adilla*, vol. 1, p. 35. See also his entire discussion on pp. 28–38.

10 See Wisnovsky, 'One Aspect of the Avicennian Turn in Sunnī Theology', p. 66. Rudolph argues that al-Māturīdī works from a model provided by the Muʿtazilī Muḥammad b. Shabīb (d. 230/840). Rudolph, *Al-Māturīdī and the Development of Sunnī Theology*, pp. 228–29. Epistemological preliminaries are also discussed by al-Māturīdī's contemporary Abū Muṭīʿ Makḥūl al-Nasafī. See al-Nasafī, *Kitāb al-radd ʿalā ahl al-bidaʿ wa-l-ahwāʾ*, pp. 54–57. A short creed is ascribed to al-Māturīdī, with commentary provided by Tāj al-Dīn al-Subkī (d. 771/1370) in the text *Al-Sayf al-mashhūr fī sharḥ ʿaqīdat Abī Manṣūr*. This can be identified with the manuscript in Oxford titled 'Kitāb al-uṣūl'/'Uṣūl al-dīn' in Bodleian MS. Marsh 629, fols 1v–15r, which begins with 'the things that provide knowledge are three (*al-ashyāʾ allatī yaqaʿu bi-hā al-ʿilmu thalātha*)'. See Nicoll, *Bibliothecæ Bodleianæ Codicum Manuscritorum Orientalium*, vol. 2, p. 579. The same work can be found in Riyadh, as listed in al-Zayd, *Fahras al-makhṭūṭāt fī markaz al-malik Fayṣal*, vol. 1, p. 48, and in Istanbul in Şeşen, *Fahras makhṭūṭat maktaba Kūbrīlī*, vol. 3, p. 113. The content of the text, including discussion of the Ashʿarīs, demonstrates that al-Māturīdī is not the author. See also Rudolph, *Al-Māturīdī and the Development of Sunnī Theology*, p. 329. The same is true for *Sharḥ al-fiqh al-akbar*, see page 32, note 114. Seven lost treatises by al-Māturīdī refuting other theological groups are listed in Cerić, *Roots of Synthetic Theology in Islam*, p. 45. His heresiography, *Kitāb al-maqālāt*, is also missing. See page 75, note 120.

11 This parallels a contemporary discussion about the epistemology of Aquinas. See Williams, 'Is Aquinas a Foundationalist?'.

has been fully digitised.[12] To compound the difficulty of working with a single manuscript source, the text may represent unedited notes, suffers from an awkward, cryptic Arabic style and seems to have been copied by a scribe sometimes unsure of the intended meaning.[13] As Josef van Ess points out, at any given point the question under investigation is not laid out clearly but presupposed, so that the reader must supply the appropriate theological context and premises.[14] Despite these limitations, the close reader of *Kitāb al-tawḥīd* finds surprising theological solutions to familiar

12 The manuscript consists of 206 folios with twenty-one lines to the page and according to its library listing was written in the eleventh/seventeenth or the twelfth/eighteenth century. See https://cudl.lib.cam.ac.uk/view/MS-ADD-03651/1, accessed 25 July 2018. But it seems that the year 1150 (1737) written on the front of the manuscript refers to a time when it was purchased, putting its transcription at an unknown date before this. Özervarlı, 'The Authenticity of the Manuscript of Māturīdī's Kitāb al-Tawḥīd', pp. 27–28. Van Ess and Madelung point out indications that the scribe collated the text from at least two manuscripts. Van Ess, review of *Kitāb al-tawḥīd*, by Abū Manṣūr al-Māturīdī, ed. Fathalla Kholeif, p. 557; Madelung, review of *Kitāb al-tawḥīd*, by Abū Manṣūr al-Māturīdī, ed. Fathalla Kholeif, p. 151. Although acquired by the University of Cambridge from a Dr Sethian in 1900 and mentioned by Ignaz Goldziher in 1904 and Edward Granville Browne in 1922, it did not receive much attention until its significance was pointed out by Joseph Schacht in a 1951 lecture in Brussels that was later published in *Studia Islamica*. See Schacht, 'New Sources for the History of Muhammadan Theology', pp. 24 and 41; Rudolph, *Al-Māturīdī and the Development of Sunnī Theology*, p. 13. Schacht noted that he was preparing an edition but seems not to have completed it. One did not appear until the 1970 publication by Fathalla Kholeif. While acknowledging that producing any edition of this book is an achievement, Hans Daiber provided nearly ten pages of suggested emendations to Kholeif's text and van Ess added several pages more. See Daiber, 'Zur Erstausgabe von al-Māturīdī, *Kitāb al-Tauḥīd*', pp. 303–12; van Ess, review of *Kitāb al-tawḥīd*, by Abū Manṣūr al-Māturīdī, ed. Fathalla Kholeif, pp. 561–65. A superior version was published by Bekir Topaloğlu and Muḥammad Aruçi in 2003 and is now into its third edition. Note that my references are to the second edition, as I acquired the latest edition after completing a significant amount of work and as it appears to differ only in its typesetting, headings and the addition of a Turkish introduction. Topaloğlu also produced an impressive explanatory Turkish translation of *Kitāb al-tawḥīd* in 2002. J. Meric Pessagno worked on a full English translation and commentary of the text, but it has never appeared. See Pessagno, '*Irāda, Ikhtiyār, Qudra, Kasb*', p. 177; Rudolph, *Al-Māturīdī and the Development of Sunnī Theology*, p. 16. Recently, Sulaiman Ahmed has self-published an English translation of the first half of the text. Unfortunately, it is not a scholarly work. Ahmed is excessively polemical in the introduction; he relies solely on Kholeif's Arabic edition with no reference to the original manuscript and is seemingly unaware of the contributions of Topaloğlu and Aruçi; he does not provide citations to relevant primary or secondary literature; and he makes repeated errors in understanding the text. See al-Māturīdī, *The Book of Monotheism*, trans. Sulaiman Ahmed.

13 Van Ess, review of *Kitāb al-tawḥīd*, by Abū Manṣūr al-Māturīdī, ed. Fathalla Kholeif, pp. 556–57; Thomas, *Christian Doctrines in Islamic Theology*, pp. 80, 93. Also see al-Bazdawī, *Uṣūl al-dīn*, p. 14.

14 Van Ess, review of *Kitāb al-tawḥīd*, by Abū Manṣūr al-Māturīdī, ed. Fathalla Kholeif, p. 556.

kalām problems, from epistemology and metaphysics to the divine attributes, and starts to see different possibilities at a key juncture of the formative period of *kalām*. As will follow in Section II of this chapter, the originality of al-Māturīdī's system can partly be explained by the multiple, diverse and disruptive theological discourses of his era. In many ways, that time is a closer relative to the current age than are the scholastic certainties of the long medieval period. One of my larger arguments in this book is that a critical rereading of al-Māturīdī is often more useful than the settled consensus of the later school for engaging contemporary questions of philosophical theology from the standpoint of Islamic tradition.

Al-Māturīdī addresses the question of the relationship between tradition and reason three times at the beginning of *Kitāb al-tawḥīd*, circling around so as to draw out different aspects of the problem.[15] First, he deals with the diversity of religions and sects and the need to reach a firm conclusion about the truth; second, he proposes that this can only be secured through an interplay of both tradition and reason; third, he shows how this can be applied through an epistemic theory with three paths to knowledge: the senses, reports and rational enquiry.[16]

After the opening invocations, al-Māturīdī begins his book as follows:

> We find people of differing sectarian schools of thought agreeing despite their differences in religion upon a single principle. This is that their own [belief] is the truth and that of others is falsehood, based on their collective agreement that each of them has predecessors who are followed. So, it is established that the one who merely follows authority is not spared from finding the like of it against him due to there being a great number [of authorities], unless there is for one of those whose statements reach him rational evidence by which the truthfulness of his claims is known – a proof that leads the fair-minded to alight upon the truth.[17]

Al-Māturīdī first asserts, based on empirical observation, that the one thing that all religious groups agree on is the rightness of their own faction and the erroneousness of others. For the person within such a group, the truthfulness of their own tradition is a given that undergirds any claims they make. Al-Māturīdī responds to the relativistic threat that traditional

15 Rudolph, 'Ratio und Überlieferung in der Erkenntnislehre al-Ashʿarī's und al-Māturīdī's', p. 79.

16 Rudolph, 'Ratio und Überlieferung in der Erkenntnislehre al-Ashʿarī's und al-Māturīdī's', pp. 79–84.

17 Al-Māturīdī, *Kitāb al-tawḥīd*, pp. 65–66.

authority is equally available to everyone by declaring the need in public debate to supplement one's tradition with rational evidence to justify truth claims.[18] Thus, the position developed by al-Māturīdī affirms the legitimacy of members of religious traditions both to hold certain truths as first principles and to justify them.

He proceeds to mention how members of the (presumably Muslim) community are to rationally justify their belief:

> The one [i.e. prophet] who is referred to in religion, such that he obligates its validation, possesses the truth. And it is incumbent upon everyone to know the truth about their religion, just as he who practised it [first] has surrounded them with the evidence of his truthfulness and his testimony for it. Thus, the ultimate point of the evidence possessed by them is to compel their intellects to submit to it, were it to be acquired. Indeed, it is manifest for the person whom I have mentioned [above]. It is not possible that similar evidence is manifest for his opponent in religion, as this would mean a conflict in rational evidence after [the first set] is already preponderant. In this way, the falsity of confusion is manifest in other than him.[19]

This passage is open to two interpretations. A common approach is to read it as a continuation of the general point that only rational argument is able to decide between competing traditions.[20] As Cerić observes, this reading appears to lead to a complete rejection of the authorities of tradition (*taqlīd*) in favour of rational proof, although he acknowledges that such a position is complicated by al-Māturīdī's further discussion of epistemology.[21] As I have shown in the above translation, a second reading is

18 Al-Māturīdī, *Kitāb al-tawḥīd*, pp. 65–66. Compare with Ibn Saʿdī's description of an interreligious *majlis al-kalām* in late-fourth/tenth-century Baghdad in which '[t]he use of citations from one's own Scriptures was not permissible since these Scriptures were not accepted as authoritative by all present'. Sklare, 'Responses to Islamic Polemics by Jewish Mutakallimūn in the Tenth Century', p. 140.

19 Al-Māturīdī, *Kitāb al-tawḥīd*, p. 66.

20 Cerić, *Roots of Synthetic Theology in Islam*, pp. 67–68; Pessagno, 'Intellect and Religious Assent', pp. 19–20; Daccache, *Le Problème de la Création du Monde*, pp. 102–3.

21 Cerić, *Roots of Synthetic Theology in Islam*, p. 68. This interpretation was reinforced by the section heading added by Kholeif in his edition of *Kitāb al-tawḥīd*: 'The Invalidity of Following Authority and the Necessity of Knowing Religion by Proof (*ibṭāl al-taqlīd wa-wujūb maʿrifat al-dīn bi-l-dalīl*)'. Al-Māturīdī, *Kitāb al-tawḥīd*, ed. Fathalla Kholeif, p. 3. The phrase '*ibṭāl al-taqlīd*', which is not used here by al-Māturīdī, is dropped by Topaloğlu and Aruçi. Al-Māturīdī, *Kitāb al-tawḥīd*, p. 65. This understanding of al-Māturīdī was also likely influenced by al-Ashʿarī's rejection of *taqlīd*. See Frank, 'Elements in the Development of the Teaching of al-Ashʿarī', pp. 150–53.

possible, in which al-Māturīdī can be taken as referring to a prophet (and alluding to the Prophet Muḥammad) as the paradigm of the truthful and rationally justifiable source of traditional authority mentioned in the first quotation.[22] Al-Māturīdī seems to have made a stylistic choice throughout his introductory section to speak in a neutral tone even when discussing Islam, which suggests a wish to reach beyond a purely Muslim audience. This can be compared to his contempory al-Fārābī (d. 339/950–51) who adopts a similar strategy in his *Kitāb ārāʾ ahl al-madīna al-fāḍila*.[23]

Al-Māturīdī does not repudiate the value of tradition but proposes a schema for how members of his own tradition are to face the polemical challenge raised by others possessing their own authoritative teachings. He argues that the Prophet brought manifest evidence that the intellect is able to accept upon enquiring into it and, in a subsequent section, he explains that foremost is the Qur'an, 'which humanity and the jinn are incapable of producing the like thereof'.[24] Unlike the later Māturīdī (and Ashʿarī) tradition, the justificatory basis of this truth is not premised on indubitable propositions, but on al-Māturīdī's tradition-reason dyad. The Prophet's proofs were convincing to the first community in the context of their lives, and in the change his message brought to the existing tradition of the people that he called. While there may be numerous reasons that his companions accepted his message as truth, for the present enquiry the important insight is that these may be conveyed as rational pieces of evidence that are preponderant over those of rivals.[25] This process of justification does not exist in the abstract, but must itself be delivered through

22 The inference that this refers to the Prophet Muḥammad is made in a marginal note on the manuscript. Al-Māturīdī, 'Kitāb al-tawḥīd', fol. 1v. It is not possible to know the provenance of such notes, other than that they postdate the manuscript's production. Some of the ones discussed in this study seem to reflect later theological contexts; see, for example, page page 74, note 109 and page 91, note 221. Nevertheless, they may be useful clues towards the resolution of puzzles in *Kitāb al-tawḥīd*, representing some of the only explicit premodern commentary we have on the text. The same identification is made by al-Damanhūrī, *Naẓariyyat al-maʿrifa ʿinda ahl al-sunna wa-l-jamāʿa*, p. 130, n. 2. There is an interesting similarity to al-Ashʿarī on this point in his *Risāla ilā ahl al-thaghr* (if it is correctly ascribed to him). See Frank, 'Al-Ashʿarī's Conception of the Nature and Role of Speculative Reasoning in Theology', p. 137.

23 Rudolph comments on the parallels between this work of al-Fārābī and al-Māturīdī's *Kitāb al-tawḥīd*, and other *kalām* texts from a similar era. See Rudolph, 'Reflections on al-Fārābī's *Mabādiʾ ārāʾ ahl al-madīna al-fāḍila*', pp. 5, 7–8, 13–14.

24 Al-Māturīdī, *Kitāb al-tawḥīd*, p. 73. This idea is elaborated within the theological tradition by the notion of *iʿjāz* (inimitability), usually closely linked to the way in which the Qur'an is understood as God's speech. See the discussion in Chapter 7 on pages 204–5.

25 Cf. MacIntyre's conception of rational vindication between rival traditions. MacIntyre, 'Moral Relativism, Truth and Justification', pp. 216–20. See page 53.

a tradition, especially via the mechanism known as *tawātur* (continuous mass transmission) that al-Māturīdī discusses as part of his theory of knowledge (see below).[26]

My constructive interpretation of al-Māturīdī's position is comparable to important debates in contemporary epistemology. The classical foundationalism of twentieth-century evidentialism was profoundly criticised by the movement of Reformed Epistemology, which argued that religious beliefs could be rationally held without requiring inferential grounding on other more basic beliefs. Prominent figures such as Alvin Plantinga and Nicholas Wolterstorff proposed that the 'warrant' of such beliefs could be granted externally by a human being's natural faculties working correctly or by socialisation in a tradition in which they are taken for granted.[27] Stephen Wykstra develops the rival concept of 'sensible evidentialism', giving the example of the belief in the existence of electrons. While this belief is rationally justified for individuals without inferential grounding, there has to be some link in the community to a specialist who can provide this function.[28] Furthermore, Wykstra argues that the evidentialist is able to bring the same kind of externalist warrant to inferential dispositions that the Reformed epistemologist provides for basic beliefs.[29]

I propose that revised evidentialism is a good fit to the picture that al-Māturīdī presents.[30] He acknowledges that most people within a given tradition will never question the beliefs handed down by authority. But, given that rival beliefs are held by others in the same way, it must be possible for some members of the community – theologians such as al-Māturīdī no less – to rationally justify their own religious truths. Yet that process of justification is not foundationalist but includes a wide array of inferential methods themselves drawn from tradition.

26 Contrast this with al-Ashʿarī whose conception of tradition relevant to the vindication of religion is solely that comprised of revelation. For al-Ashʿarī, the authority of the Prophet is grounded on revealed rational proofs. Thus, while there is a reciprocity in the simultaneous use of reason and revelation, it occurs within a specific inflexible framework. See Frank, 'Al-Ashʿarī's Conception of the Nature and Role of Speculative Reasoning in Theology', pp. 143–47. Frank points out the rigidity of al-Ashʿarī compared to al-Māturīdī in this regard on p. 154, n. 92. See also the remarks in Rudolph, 'Ratio und Überlieferung in der Erkenntnislehre al-Ashʿarī's und al-Māturīdī's', p. 86.

27 Wolterstorff, 'Reformed Epistemology', pp. 50–52; Plantinga, 'Reason and Belief in God', p. 33.

28 Wykstra, 'On Behalf of the Evidentialist', pp. 75–76.

29 Wykstra, 'On Behalf of the Evidentialist', pp. 80–81.

30 Anthony Booth refers to al-Kindī, who is an important intellectual predecessor of al-Māturīdī, as an evidentialist. See Booth, *Analytic Islamic Philosophy*, pp. 54–55.

From this meta-level of discourse, al-Māturīdī sketches a political philosophy.[31] His thesis is that the dual foundation (*aṣl*) of tradition (*samʿ*) and reason (*ʿaql*) mandates society to be based on religion and human beings to seek aid from it. His starting point again is that there is no escape from standing within a tradition. He comments that this is no less true for the person who calls to the prophetic message and to wisdom than it is for kings who seek to unite the hearts of their subjects – a point in which he subtly anticipates Ibn Khaldūn's (d. 808/1406) notion of *ʿaṣabiyya* (group identity)[32] – or for the person who organises the various types of crafts.[33] This also undercuts foundationalism insofar as the process of knowledge acquisition assumes a set of background assumptions in social context, language and so on.[34] This point will be developed in Section IV of this chapter, through discussion of the modern philosophers Edmund Husserl, Hans-Georg Gadamer and Alasdair MacIntyre.

Al-Māturīdī draws on a Platonic philosophical tradition by mentioning that 'the philosophers term [the human being] the microcosm (*wa-huwa alladhī sammathu al-ḥukamāʾu al-ʿālama al-ṣaghīr*)',[35] proposing that both the world at the macro level and the human being at the micro level contain diverse natures (*ṭabāʾiʿ*) that tend to pull apart.[36] In later sections, al-Māturīdī is explicit in using this observation as an argument for the existence of a wise creator who sustains these aspects of creation.[37] In the present section, his focus is on society. He highlights that human beings must behave correctly

31 See Cerić, *Roots of Synthetic Theology in Islam*, p. 83.

32 See Ibn Khaldūn, *Muqaddima*, pp. 156–57.

33 Al-Māturīdī, *Kitāb al-tawḥīd*, pp. 66–67.

34 See MacIntyre, *The Tasks of Philosophy*, pp. 8–9.

35 Al-Māturīdī, *Kitāb al-tawḥīd* p. 67. This is ultimately a reference to Plato's *Timaeus*, which was available in Arabic translation from early in the third/ninth century and attracted a great deal of attention from Muslim philosophers during the lifetime of al-Māturīdī. Rescher, *Studies in Arabic Philosophy*, pp. 16–17. See Plato, *Timaeus*, pp. 451–52, 461; Nader El-Bizri, 'The Microcosm/Macrocosm Analogy', pp. 5–6. In particular, al-Māturīdī's formulation may have been paraphrased from al-Kindī who writes that 'those of the ancient philosophers possessing discrimination who did not speak our language termed the human being the microcosm (*tusammā dhawū al-tamyīzi min ḥukamāʾi al-qudamāʾi min ghayri ahli lisāninā al-insāna ʿālaman ṣaghīran*)'. Al-Kindī, *Rasāʾil al-Kindī al-falsafiyya*, vol. 1, p. 260. It is also comparable to the couplet famously attributed to ʿAlī: 'You reckon yourself a small body but wrapped inside you is the macrocosm (*taḥsubu annaka jirmun ṣaghīrun – wa-fīka inṭ awā al-ʿālamu al-akbar*)'. See al-Kayyālī, *Al-Nafaḥāt al-rabbāniyya*, p. 125.

36 For discussion of the *ṭabāʾiʿ* in al-Māturīdī's thought, see pages 90–93. Other aspects of his metaphysical system and proposals for a contemporary perspective are also explored in Chapter 2.

37 Al-Māturīdī, *Kitāb al-tawḥīd*, pp. 84, 211. See pages 93 and 120.

to avoid falling into social corruption and rejecting the divinely guided wisdom that is integral to their existence.[38] Thus, there must be a means, religion, that enables them to fulfil their higher purpose to know God.[39]

This conclusion has two corollaries. First, if the proper function of religion in society is established, then so is its obligation for human beings, given their needs.[40] Hence, he provides a rational argument for why human beings are obliged to accept the dictates of religion, including divine law. Second, as human beings are needy, they require someone to explain religion to them and lead them.[41] Although al-Māturīdī does not state it explicitly here, it seems that he again has in mind the Prophet Muḥammad. He also refers to an earlier explanation, which is likely the paragraph identified above as alluding to the Prophet.[42]

The next question that al-Māturīdī tackles in the first pages of *Kitāb al-tawḥīd* is how the good can be known. He considers four candidates: personal intuition, spiritual insight, drawing lots, or physiognomy. On the first, he argues that, if determining the good at the social level was as simple as everyone just following their hearts, there would be no differences between religions. Of course, the same lack of verifiability applies to alleged *ilhām* (spiritual insight).[43] Returning to his opening theme, his argument is that there is not just a need to happen upon the truth personally, but to be able to justify it to others within the public sphere.[44] Note, too, that this is the background to the rejection of *ilhām* as a source of knowledge in the

38 See pages 70–71.

39 Al-Māturīdī, *Kitāb al-tawḥīd*, pp. 67–68, 166–67.

40 Al-Māturīdī, *Kitāb al-tawḥīd*, p. 68.

41 Al-Māturīdī, *Kitāb al-tawḥīd*, p. 68.

42 Al-Māturīdī expands this idea considerably in his section on prophecy, arguing for the rational necessity that God sends messengers to humanity due to His wisdom. See al-Māturīdī, *Kitāb al-tawḥīd*, pp. 248–52. This civilisational aspect of his thinking about prophecy deserves more treatment than can be provided here. It is also a point picked up by later proponents of the Māturīdī tradition. See, for example, Bāshā, *Al-Munīra fī al-mawāʿiẓ wa-l-ʿaqāʾid*, p. 46.

43 Al-Māturīdī, *Kitāb al-tawḥīd*, p. 69. These two categories could target Muʿtazilī and Sufi groups, respectively. The comments on *ilhām* might also be a specific response to the famous philosopher Abū Bakr al-Rāzī (d. 313/925 or 323/935) who, in his debate with the Ismāʿīlī missionary Abū Ḥātim al-Rāzī (d. 322/934), argued that the superior expression of God's wisdom would be to provide everyone with *ilhām*, rather than just individual prophets. See al-Rāzī, *Rasāʾil falsafiyya*, p. 296. For further discussion and translation of the debate, see Pines, 'A Study of the Impact of Indian, mainly Buddhist, Thought on Some Aspects of Kalām Doctrines', p. 8; Crone, 'Post-Colonialism in Tenth-Century Iran', pp. 3–4.

44 See page 15.

subsequent Māturīdī tradition.[45] Furthermore, al-Māturīdī rejects drawing lots in order to determine the good, as things drawn out at random are mutually contradictory,[46] as well as following the pronouncements of a physiognomist (*qāʾif*).[47] This leads him to his famous statement, which formed the kernel for later Māturīdī epistemology, that 'the path to reach knowledge of the reality of things is perception (*ʿiyān*), reports (*akhbār*) and enquiry (*naẓar*)'.[48]

Rudolph demonstrates how al-Māturīdī's commitment to this triad of sources is sustained in his method of construction for theological arguments. He frequently attempts to simultaneously justify his position from at least two of them; in effect, he builds fail-safes into his system.[49] The very fact that he provides so many arguments from as many different sources as he is able – sensory, traditionary and rational – is a clue that he does not see these arguments as individually providing absolute certainty but working together to secure epistemic warrant.

If al-Māturīdī is not using these sources of knowledge as routes to indubitable justificatory foundations, as assumed by the later authors with whom I started this section, then what is he doing? I suggest that he is sketching a correspondence theory of knowledge, in which the 'paths' in question securely connect the nature of the world to the experiences of the

45 This is famously summarised in *Al-ʿAqīda al-Nasafiyya* by Abū Ḥafṣ al-Nasafī who comments that spiritual insight (*ilhām*) is not considered a means of perception (*maʿrifa*). Al-Nasafī, 'Matn al-ʿaqīda al-Nasafiyya', p. 52. Al-Taftāzānī explains that this rejection of *ilhām* is because it is not a means of knowledge for the generality of the creation. Although it may evince personal knowledge, it is not suitable for obligating other people. Otherwise, it is backed by evidence in scripture and the actions of the early generations of Muslims, and other types of non-definitive evidence are generally held to be included within the category of knowledge. Al-Taftāzānī, *Sharḥ al-ʿaqīda al-Nasafiyya*, p. 25. The super-commentator al-Çūrī adds that these other types of *ẓannī* (probabilistic) knowledge are to be contrasted with *ilhām*, which is *yaqīnī* (certain), but not accessible to everyone. Al-Çūrī, *Ḥāshiyat al-Çūrī ʿālā sharḥ al-ʿaqāʾid*, p. 35. Al-Taftāzānī's revision of this point within the text on which he is commenting may reflect his Ashʿarī leanings, although I think it is more likely that the incongruity of al-Nasafī's reference to *ilhām* comes from its origin in the passage from *Kitāb al-tawḥīd*, now displaced and shorn of its earlier meaning, which al-Taftāzānī is able to reconstruct. There is evidence for the transition between al-Māturīdī and Abū Hafṣ al-Nasafī in the texts of Abū al-Yusr al-Bazdawī and Abū al-Muʿīn al-Nasafī. See al-Bazdawī, *Uṣūl al-dīn*, p. 20; al-Nasafī, *Tabṣirat al-adilla*, vol. 1, p. 151. See also al-Samarqandī, *Mīzān al-uṣūl*, vol. 2, p. 1027.

46 Drawing lots (*iʿlām al-qurʿa*) possibly echoes the superstitious pre-Islamic practice of divining with arrows (*azlām*) condemned in Q. 5:3 and 5:90.

47 Al-Māturīdī, *Kitāb al-tawḥīd*, p. 69; al-Māturīdī, *Taʾwīlāt al-qurʾān*, vol. 1, p. 80. See al-Azharī, *Muʿjam tahdhīb al-lugha*, vol. 3, pp. 2858–59.

48 Al-Māturīdī, *Kitāb al-tawḥīd*, p. 69.

49 Rudolph, *Al-Māturīdī and the Development of Sunnī Theology*, p. 232; Rudolph, 'Ratio und Überlieferung in der Erkenntnislehre al-Ashʿarī's und al-Māturīdī's', pp. 84–85.

human being. Abū al-Muʿīn al-Nasafī summarises al-Māturīdī's definition of knowledge as follows (although he points out that his predecessor did not mention it in this exact form): 'a quality that, by it, the thing mentioned is realised for the one whom it is established within (*sifatun yatajalli bihā li-man qāmat hiya bihi al-madhkūr*)'.[50]

Al-Māturīdī treats the senses as providing a consistent picture of empirical reality between human beings, which furnishes 'knowledge that cannot be opposed with ignorance'.[51] As he works from a position of sense realism, his discussion is mainly aimed at showing the incoherence of the denial of knowledge about the external world exhibited by various types of sophists (again the influence on *Al-ʿAqīda al-Nasafiyya* is very obvious). This includes the agnostic who neither argues for, nor entirely rejects, the external existence of things.[52] Al-Māturīdī recommends the denier be trapped in paradox by being asked, 'Do you know what you reject?' or – with gallows humour – suggests that he be subjected to intense pain by cutting off his limbs to stop his obstinacy.[53]

Reports are a second epistemological category, one considered by al-Māturīdī as so basic for human life that they also cannot be consistently rejected.[54] They are of two types: those that are transmitted via *tawātur* and are not conceivably erroneous, and those that require individual assessment of the veracity of their narrators.[55] Although this has general use as an epistemological theory, it is clear that he is primarily interested in its application to the revealed teachings of the Prophet Muḥammad.[56] He writes:

> The reports that reach us from the messengers pass via those who it is conceivable are in error, or lie, and those who do not have evidence for their truthfulness, nor proof for their protection from error. So, they require investigation. If it is such that deceit is impossible, then [the report] which is received in this way obligates that the statement has been truthfully witnessed from one [i.e. the Prophet] for

50 Al-Nasafī, *Tabṣirat al-adilla*, vol. 1, pp. 136–37. I provide a rereading of this theory in Chapter 2.

51 Al-Māturīdī, *Kitāb al-tawḥīd*, p. 70. Cf. Husserl, *Ideas*, p. 73.

52 Al-Māturīdī, *Kitāb al-tawḥīd*, p. 70. See Cerić, *Roots of Synthetic Theology in Islam*, p. 98. It is unclear whether the sceptical positions that al-Māturīdī refutes were really held in his time; they may merely reflect particularly infamous arguments. There are interesting parallels with the view attributed to the sophist Gorgias, 'that nothing exists, that if anything did exist it could not be known and that if anything could be known it could not be communicated.' Taylor and Lee, 'The Sophists'.

53 Al-Māturīdī, *Kitāb al-tawḥīd*, p. 70.

54 Al-Māturīdī, *Kitāb al-tawḥīd*, pp. 70–71.

55 Al-Māturīdī, *Kitāb al-tawḥīd*, pp. 71–72.

56 Al-Māturīdī, *Kitāb al-tawḥīd*, p. 72.

> whom proofs clarify his protection from error. That is the quality of the mass transmitted report: all [of the transmitters] – even if there is no proof for their protection from error – if the report from them meets that definition, its truth becomes manifest. Its protection from error is established, even if it is possible that other than it could be established from them taken singly.[57]

The *tawātur* report is transmitted in such numbers that, though it is conceivable that the narrators may individually fall into error or lie, these doubts are overwhelmed by the sheer level of corroboration. This is established by a process of investigation: once the number of supporting testimonies reaches a mentally compelling point, certainty is established. In fact, I would add, in paradigm cases of *tawātur*, such as the transmission of the ʿUthmanī *rasm* (consonantal skeleton) of the Qur'an[58] or the existence of Mecca,[59] it is impossible to enumerate all of the transmitters, which is rather the point.[60]

To illustrate this, al-Māturīdī draws on the example of jurists who, while individually fallible, secure certainty for those rules upon which they agree. It is, he argues, God's kindness (*luṭf*) that allows these jurists to find consensus despite their differing desires.[61] How should this comparison be interpreted? Or to put the question in another way: why would an *ijmāʿ* (consensus) of jurists have the same epistemological status as the *mutawātir* (continuous mass-transmitted) report? The approach taken by ʿAlāʾ al-Dīn al-Samarqandī (d. 539/1144) is that, in order for the consensus of jurists to be universal, it must be based on an originally mass-transmitted report that was later not explicitly passed on.[62] But this ignores the criterion that the mass-transmitted report must be testimony

57 Al-Māturīdī, *Kitāb al-tawḥīd*, pp. 71–72.

58 The mass transmission of the ʿUthmānī *rasm* is from the regional exemplars, which have a pattern of slight variations that can be reconstructed into different possible stemmas. See Cook, 'The Stemma of the Regional Codices of the Koran', pp. 89–98. Hythem Sidky uses early Qur'anic manuscripts to refine Cook's conclusions, arguing that the text of the regional Medinan tradition is the archetype from which Syrian and Iraqī texts were copied. Hythem Sidky, 'On the Regionality of Qurʾānic Codices' (forthcoming). Marijn van Putten shows that the consistency of two ways of spelling the phrase *niʿmat allāh* in extant manuscripts points to a single exemplar text and continuous written transmission. Van Putten, '"The Grace of God" as Evidence for a Written Uthmanic Archetype', pp. 279–80.

59 Al-Bazdawī, *Maʿrifat al-hujaj al-sharʿiyya*, p. 118.

60 See Zysow, *The Economy of Certainty*, p. 21.

61 Al-Māturīdī, *Kitāb al-tawḥīd*, p. 72.

62 Al-Samarqandī, *Mīzān al-uṣūl*, vol. 2, pp. 807–8. This parallels arguments by figures such as al-Ghazālī. See Zysow, *The Economy of Certainty*, pp. 118–21.

of something perceived, while consensus is based on the internal judgement of jurists.[63] Moreover, in the present case, al-Māturīdī is arguing that the mass-transmitted report is akin to consensus, not the converse.

Another way to interpret al-Māturīdī's argument – and one that may appear to have more explicit support from his writing – emphasises his reference to God's grace and His means to make manifest His truth. It would have been impossible for all jurists to come to agreement, and by extension for the certainty of mass-transmitted reports to be known, except by the special favour that God bequeaths to his chosen community. As pointed out by Aron Zysow, this became a standard reading within the Ḥanafī tradition with respect to the doctrine of *ijmāʿ* and was defended by reference to verses of the Qur'an, prophetic traditions and rational arguments.[64] Dale Correa has taken a similar line of interpretation towards al-Māturīdī's comparison in her work on his epistemology, arguing that the mass-transmitted report furnishes certain knowledge because of the supernatural protection that God grants to the truth.[65]

I think that a different reading is possible when considering the basic problem with which al-Māturīdī is grappling, and the underlying dialectic in which he is engaged. His worry seems provoked by the influential third/ninth-century Muʿtazilī theologian al-Naẓẓām (d. 221/836) who is infamous for rejecting both the *mutawātir* report and the doctrine of *ijmāʿ* on the basis that the addition of multiple probabilities cannot furnish a result of certainty.[66] This discussion may be a response to Ibn Shujāʿ al-Thaljī (d. 266/879), a prominent Ḥanafī who apparently followed him on this question,[67] and engagement with the epistemological ideas of Ibn Shabīb (d. 230/840), one of al-Naẓẓām's Muʿtazilī students.[68]

Al-Māturīdī recognises that, for epistemic truth, mass-transmitted reports and juristic consensus to a great extent stand or fall together, so he appeals to divine kindness to ward off a sceptical conclusion. This strategy would be rhetorically effective against a Muʿtazilī interlocutor of the Baghdadī school tradition who concedes God's grace towards human

63 Cf. Zysow, *The Economy of Certainty*, p. 9, n. 8.

64 Zysow, *The Economy of Certainty*, pp. 115–16.

65 Correa, 'The Vehicle of Tawātur in al-Māturīdī's Epistemology', pp. 379–80.

66 Al-Bazdawī, *Uṣūl al-dīn*, p. 21; al-Samarqandī, *Mīzān al-uṣūl*, vol. 2, pp. 617–18. See Zysow, *The Economy of Certainty*, pp. 14, 118, n. 10; Vishanoff, *The Formation of Islamic Hermeneutics*, pp. 71–73. Cf. John Locke's argument that the probability of a given testimony declines at each stage of its transmission due to the increased possibility for error. Coady, *Testimony*, p. 209.

67 Zysow, *The Economy of Certainty*, p. 14.

68 Rudolph, *Al-Māturīdī and the Development of Sunnī Theology*, pp. 162, 229; Pessagno, 'The Reconstruction of the Thought of Muḥammad Ibn Shabīb', p. 453.

beings as a basic premise.[69] My contention, however, is that it would go against al-Māturīdī's fallibilism (see below) and shared emphasis with the Muʿtazila on human free will for his reference to grace to be a kind of supernatural event, or quasi-miracle, that confirms the truth. Instead, I suggest that he sees this grace as operating in the way that God has endowed human beings with mental abilities that allow them to reach epistemic certainty on various aspects of their shared social world.

Looking back at how al-Māturīdī frames the discussion, he proposes that, once it is determined that the narrators of a given report reach a sufficient number, it becomes impossible that they have accidently or purposefully made an error in its transmission. Such proof of veracity in reporting only provides certain truth of the content of the statement when it comes from a prophet due to their protection from error (*ʿiṣma*). But according to al-Māturīdī's premises, any report can be mass transmitted and become certain in its transmission, provided that it fulfils the requisite condition for its narrators; there is no special requirement that the report corresponds to truth as such.[70] For example, the lying statement of a miserly ruler that he was actually generous could be mass transmitted. The later Māturīdī tradition makes explicit this general application of the epistemological position – for instance, *Al-ʿAqīda al-Nasafiyya* gives the example of 'the knowledge of bygone kings in ancient times and distant lands'.[71]

Although the concept of *tawātur* is not original to al-Māturīdī,[72] when placed within his wider framework, it leads to a conclusion insufficiently taken up in the later creedal tradition: reports are only mass transmitted within the context of traditions, at least ones with a certain amount of linguistic and social continuity. It is through one's place within, or at least contact with, a continuous tradition extending back to the time of the report in question that one gains certainty about it.[73] Take the English King

69 See page 163.

70 This is also the reading in Rudolph, 'Ratio und Überlieferung in der Erkenntnislehre al-Ashʿarī's und al-Māturīdī's', p. 83.

71 Al-Nasafī, 'Matn al-ʿaqīda al-Nasafiyya', p. 51.

72 Zysow argues that *tawātur* was used in juristic circles before it became prevalent in theological ones. The earliest references that he adduces, however, are to theological debates involving the Muʿtazila and Shīʿa. Zysow, *The Economy of Certainty*, pp. 12–13. His inference to an older juristic doctrine to which these figures were responding is speculative and seems improbable, especially considering that discursive theology in the second/eighth century preceded the emergence of legal theory. Hansu convincingly locates the origins of *tawātur* in the early Muʿtazilī tradition. Hansu, 'Notes on the Term *Mutawātir* and its Reception in *Ḥadīth* Criticism', pp. 389–90. Also see Laher, *Twisted Threads*, pp. 24–26.

73 This is a similar point in some respects to Saul Kripke's causal picture of reference. See Kripke, *Naming and Necessity*, p. 91.

Henry VIII. I cannot recall the first time I heard about him, his succession of wives and various exploits, but these things have been corroborated from so many channels that I have no doubt whatsoever about his existence. For many other kings I have no such knowledge, although if I began to check, I could doubtless reach a similar conclusion. This restates the point that one must investigate until the narrators of reports become sufficient in number to preclude a need to assess their probity. The conclusion is that, while some *tawātur* knowledge may appear to come immediately to the mind, it is relative to the cumulative experiences of a person's life and their embedding in a society and tradition.[74]

The case of juristic consensus is different as it is not based on corroboration in transmitting a discrete report, but on reaching a meaning through *ijtihād* that justifiably corresponds to truth. How can the impossibility of agreeing on a mistaken ruling be explained on the human level without appealing to a special divine compulsion in the juristic process? I suggest that one also cannot read al-Māturīdī on this question without relating it to his wider theological concerns. When he states that God's grace facilitates (*yuwaffiqu*) the jurists' agreement on the truth despite their differing desires,[75] this should not be construed as a suspension of their free choice in *ijtihād* and a compulsion to choose a single ruling.[76] Like his understanding of *tawātur*, it must mean that God has constituted human beings in such a way that the concurrence of their natural faculties on a question of juristic reasoning justifiably overwhelms the individually probabilistic nature of their enterprise.[77] Due to al-Māturīdī's fallibilism, however, if one jurist takes a different position, even at a later time, it becomes conceivable that truth is in either of the two camps, but not both.[78] Such a conception of *ijmāʿ*

74 Compare with the contemporary philosophical idea of epistemic necessity. See Kment, 'Varieties of Modality'. This reading of *tawātur* is a form of *a posteriori* necessity. See Kripke, *Naming and Necessity*, pp. 38–39. It would seem that the more distant a given event is from one's personal linguistic and social continuity, the harder it is to gain certainty about its occurrence. The mass emergence of the internet as a phenomenon during approximately the last thirty years has led to reducing linguistic and social distance between geographically distant users and thus arguably has increased the opportunity (if used rationally) for certainty about more of global history.

75 Al-Māturīdī, *Kitāb al-tawḥīd*, p. 72.

76 See also al-Māturīdī, *Kitāb al-tawḥīd*, p. 307.

77 Al-Damanhūrī similarly interprets al-Māturīdī's comparison as such jurists gaining confidence due to reaching the same result despite their different methodologies (*uṣūl*), which is part of God's grace towards His creation. Al-Damanhūrī, *Naẓariyyat al-maʿrifa ʿinda ahl al-sunna wa-l-jamāʿa*, p. 139, n. 4.

78 When discussing the interpretation of the Qur'an in *Kitāb al-tawḥīd*, al-Māturīdī argues that every group holds its own interpretation of decisive (*muḥkam*) verses to be correct and those that oppose it to be wrong. Al-Māturīdī, *Kitāb al-tawḥīd*, p. 302. In his *Taʾwīlāt al-qurʾān*, he explores evidence on both sides of the well-known question of whether

can only furnish certainty during the time that agreement remains. While al-Māturīdī is primarily making a claim of epistemology, it has implications for legal authority: a concurrence of views in one generation is not binding for future generations. In his *Ta ʾwīlāt al-qur ʾān*, he argues that consensus indicates the presence or absence of the underlying cause (*ma ʿnā*) for a given ruling.[79] According to this principle, if the *ma ʿnā* were to disappear due to a change in social or other circumstances, one would expect this to lead to the consensus on the topic breaking down and the rule changing.

In light of his views on tradition, such agreement not only reflects shared rational deliberation but a commonly constituted intellectual culture. Here al-Samarqandī's point that *ijmā ʿ* reflects an earlier *mutawātir* report is echoed in a different way. When a shift in an agreed position occurs, it is prompted not by the rational decisions of abstracted mind, but those of embodied reason within history.

Human enquiry (*naẓar*) is the linchpin of al-Māturīdī's epistemological system. Although he seems to follow Aristotle in assuming that human enquiry utilises sense perception for its initial raw materials, he makes it the ultimate arbiter of truth over both sense data and reports.[80] This is because many things are remote or too subtle for the senses to apprehend, while reports need to be scrutinised according to their narrators (or need sufficient reflection to determine whether they reach

'every jurist is correct (*kull mujtahid muṣīb*)', when commenting on Q. 21:79 in which Prophet Solomon solves a legal problem ahead of his father David. Al-Māturīdī comments that Abū Yūsuf and al-Shaybānī hold that every jurist is correct, such that whatever they determine is the ruling according to God. Abū Ḥanīfa and Bishr (al-Marīsī) say that only one jurist can be correct but that those who are incorrect are excused. Al-Māturīdī, *Ta ʾwīlāt al-qur ʾān*, vol. 9, p. 306. In another place, he indicates that he follows the latter opinion. Al-Māturīdī, *Ta ʾwīlāt al-qur ʾān*, vol. 15, p. 77. ʿAlā ʾ al-Dīn al-Samarqandī clarifies a further subtlety within this position: for both al-Māturīdī and himself, the jurist whose *ijtihād* fails to determine the truth also fails in their efforts (and so does not deserve reward for them). The other Samarqandī scholars, who follow al-Māturīdī's student al-Rustughfanī, hold that such a jurist succeeds in their efforts (and so is rewarded). Al-Samarqandī, *Mīzān al-uṣūl*, vol. 2, p. 1132. See Zysow, *The Economy of Certainty*, p. 271. Note that Zysow cites inconsistent views from al-Marīsī based on reports in classical-era texts: that he did not accept the validity of *ijtihād* at all and that he held that the incorrect jurist was liable to punishment (p. 265). It seems likely that al-Māturīdī, who references al-Marīsī more proximately and as a member of his own tradition, is accurate. For further discussion of the fallibilist-infallibilist divide between Māturīdī Ḥanafīs in Central Asia and Mu ʿtazilī Ḥanafīs in Iraq, see Zysow, 'Mu ʿtazilism and Māturīdism in Ḥanafī Legal Theory', pp. 239–47.

79 Al-Māturīdī, *Ta ʾwīlāt al-qur ʾān*, vol. 15, p. 125. See Harvey, 'Al-Māturīdī on the Abrogation of the Sharī ʿa in the Qur'an and Previous Scriptures', p. 522.

80 Al-Māturīdī, *Kitāb al-tawḥīd*, pp. 72, 74.

the condition of *tawātur*).[81] Enquiry is also required for distinguishing the miracles of prophets from the falsehoods of sorcerers and for understanding the miraculous inimitability of the Qur'an.[82] Al-Māturīdī adduces scriptural evidence for the obligation and efficacy of reasoned reflection to truly know reality: 'So we will show them Our signs in the horizons [and themselves until it is made clear to them it is the truth] (Q. 41:53)'; 'Do they not ponder the camel,[83] [how it is created]? (Q. 88:17)'; 'Indeed in the creation of the heavens and the earth [. . . are signs for a people who think] (Q. 2:164)'; 'And [signs for certain people] are within themselves. Do you not perceive? (Q. 51:21)'.[84]

Like sense perception and reports, reasoned enquiry cannot be rejected without self-contradiction.[85] The centrality of such enquiry for al-Māturīdī is underlined by his statement that '[its necessity is indicated by] the inescapable knowledge of those aspects of the creation comprising wisdom, as it is impossible that its like was made without purpose'.[86] Moreover, in al-Māturīdī's view, human enquiry is able to proceed from the rational necessity of wisdom underlying the creation to an inference of the self-subsistence of the Creator and His eternality.[87]

Enquiry also plays a central part in al-Māturīdī's ethics. Having already rejected four invalid ways to know the good, al-Māturīdī completes his epistemological discussion by arguing that rational enquiry is the only way in which human beings can pass the divine test as those that God has distinguished with management over the creation.[88] A person is composed of both a material nature (*ṭabīʿa*) and intellect (*ʿaql*). This nature will tend to desire what the intellect rejects, so only by enquiring into each matter can one ascertain its reality and choose the right way.[89]

The point of departure for this investigation into al-Māturīdī's epistemology was the contention that he cannot be read as a foundationalist in the sense understood by his successors within the Māturīdī school tradition.

81 Al-Māturīdī, *Kitāb al-tawḥīd*, p. 72. Al-Māturīdī does not mention that *tawātur* requires enquiry in his section on reason, but it is implied by his discussion of *mutawātir* reports. See pages 21–22.

82 *Al-Māturīdī, Kitāb al-tawḥīd*, pp. 72–73.

83 The word *ibl* (camel) can also mean 'rain cloud', an interpretive option taken by some modern translators. See Asad, *The Message of the Qur'ān*, p. 948; Abdel Haleem, *The Qur'an*, p. 593. Al-Māturīdī reads it as camel. See al-Māturīdī, *Taʾwīlāt al-qurʾān*, vol. 17, pp. 181–82.

84 Al-Māturīdī, *Kitāb al-tawḥīd*, p. 73.

85 Al-Māturīdī, *Kitāb al-tawḥīd*, p. 73.

86 Al-Māturīdī, *Kitāb al-tawḥīd*, p. 73.

87 Al-Māturīdī, *Kitāb al-tawḥīd*, p. 73. See Chapters 2–4.

88 Al-Māturīdī, *Kitāb al-tawḥīd*, p. 73; Harvey, *The Qur'an and the Just Society*, pp. 12–14.

89 Al-Māturīdī, *Kitāb al-tawḥīd*, p. 74 See page 91.

In my reading, although his tripartite scheme of sense perception, reports and enquiry provide means (*asbāb*) to reach publicly justifiable knowledge, with the exception of some things known via the senses, they cannot ground each inferred proposition as indubitable according to the conditions of a foundationalist theory.[90]

Moreover, the complex activities of the transmission of reports and rational enquiry operate within the contingent categories of human tradition and reason, with which they should not be conflated.[91] In other words, al-Māturīdī seems to implicitly acknowledge that human beings are never free from the existing tradition in which they stand and through which reports are accessed and enquiry made. While the propositions of theology reached via these means can be justified, they cannot be entirely divorced from the tradition in which they emerge. A prominent example in his own introductory section is his use of the philosophical discourse of the *ṭabāʾiʿ* as a valid starting point for his arguments, without grounding it via one of the three means of knowledge.

A non-foundationalist rereading of al-Māturīdī's project paves the way to use contemporary philosophical approaches to tradition and constuctively build upon his theological ideas. It also leads us to the general conclusion, apparently not developed explicitly by al-Māturīdī, that the systematic use of reason is itself always drawn from the modes of discourse characteristic of a particular tradition.[92] Like other Muslim theologians of his time, a significant part of al-Māturīdī's regime of reason emerges from the Aristotelian-Neoplatonic tradition.[93] In fact, it is clear from his above reference to the *ḥukamāʾ* (philosophers) that he is more comfortable acknowledging this pedigree than many of his contemporaries.[94] Before returning to the development of the Māturīdī tradition and relevant modern perspectives on tradition and reason, I will delve

90 Rudolph comments that, while al-Māturīdī tries to show that any given argument can be based on one or more of these sources, he does not actually argue back to them. Instead, he makes use of several other premises. Rudolph, *Al-Māturīdī and the Development of Sunnī Theology*, pp. 232–33. See also his analysis on pp. 236–42.

91 Cf. Cerić, *Roots of Synthetic Theology in Islam*, pp. 85–87, 91.

92 MacIntyre, *The Tasks of Philosophy*, p. 12. See pages 50–54 below.

93 Jackson, *On the Boundaries of Theological Tolerance*, p. 20. Also see his caveats on p. 75, n. 51. Jackson does not identify al-Māturīdī specifically in this book but discusses both him and his school in a later work. See Jackson, *Islam and the Problem of Black Suffering*, pp. 99–117.

94 Notwithstanding al-Māturīdī's implicit approval for some of the philosophers' conceptual apparatus, he also mentions the term *ḥukamāʾ* when criticising them. Examples include his rebuttal of their argument that there is a cause (*ʿilla*) for God's creation and his assertion of their inferiority to prophets in certain areas of knowledge. See, respectively, al-Māturīdī, *Kitāb al-tawḥīd*, pp. 165, 254. See also Frank, 'Notes and Remarks on the Ṭabāʾiʿ in the Teaching of al-Māturīdī', pp. 148–49.

deeper into the history and nature of the philosophical assumptions underlying his system.

II. The Genealogy of al-Māturīdī's Theology

What was the intellectual environment in which al-Māturīdī thought? Muslims within the early centuries of Islam encountered, in the words of Gustave von Grunebaum, . . .

> [M]ore fully developed edifices of thought erected with the help of a logical technique of extraordinary subtlety, a rational science, a larger and more varied accumulation of texts to serve as authoritative basis for deductive reasoning, a wider range of admissible and assimilated experience, and quite generally a higher level of training and sophistication. This sophistication was manifest not least in acute awareness of the implications and problems of a given philosophical or religious position; and it may be argued that the foremost effect of the plunge into the milieux of ancient Hellenization was a rise in self-consciousness regarding the meaning of the Muslim postulates and an inner compulsion of increasing force to think through, articulate and harmonize the accepted religious data.[95]

Al-Māturīdī's theological system, like that of others in the early centuries of Islam, can be understood as emerging from this encounter. In developing his new synthesis,[96] he simultaneously drew on several main sources: the incipient local Samarqandī Ḥanafī *kalām* tradition; intra-Muslim debate with Baghdadī Muʿtazila; inter-religious polemic with Zoroastrian, Christian, Buddhist and other disputants in Transoxiana; and the growing corpus of Arabic Hellenic philosophy.[97]

Like Ḥanafism, the roots of the Muʿtazila go back to the second/eighth century, although the famous Baghdadī and Basran school traditions were consolidated in the third/ninth.[98] During this century, there was an organic link with the tradition associated with the Kufan scholar Abū Ḥanīfa (d. 150/767), especially in Iraq, by which many Muʿtazilī theologians

95 Von Grunebaum, 'The Sources of Islamic Civilization', p. 15. See also Dhanani, *The Physical Theory of Kalām*, p. 1.

96 This is the context in which Cerić uses the term 'synthetic' in the title of his work on al-Māturīdī. See Cerić, *Roots of Synthetic Theology in Islam*, pp. 70, 234.

97 Cf. Rudolph, 'Ḥanafī Theological Tradition and Māturīdism', p. 288.

98 See Watt, *The Formative Period of Islamic Thought*, pp. 217–24. Van Ess traces an early connection between Ḍirār b. ʿAmr and the circle of Abū Ḥanīfa. Van Ess, *Theology and Society in the Second and Third Centuries of the Hijra, Volume 3*, p. 37.

adopted the nascent juristic school (and Ḥanafī jurists adopted Muʿtazilī theology).[99] This can be contrasted with the Transoxanian Ḥanafī tradition, which branched off directly from its Kufan founding figures and developed for the most part outside the purview of Muʿtazilī thinking in Balkh and Samarqand.[100] By the lifetime of al-Māturīdī, the views of especially the Baghdadī Muʿtazila had filtered into Transoxiana through outposts such as Rayy in Persia. Closer to home, the figure of Abū al-Qāsim al-Kaʿbī (al-Balkhī) (d. 319/931), who was originally from the region, had returned to take up a teaching position in Nasaf after studying in Baghdad with the Muʿtazilī Abū al-Ḥusayn al-Khayyāṭ (d. *ca* 300/913).[101] Al-Māturīdī maintains an open mind to the rich Muʿtazilī intellectual tradition within his theological writing. He appropriates some aspects as models for rational argumentation, like the figure Ibn Shabīb who may have written an earlier text with the title *Kitāb al-tawḥīd*,[102] while rebutting the ideas of others, such as Ibn Shabīb's teacher al-Naẓẓām, as well as al-Kaʿbī.[103]

There is circumstantial evidence that regional Ḥanafī engagement with the question of the divine attributes goes back to at least the first half of the third/ninth century. Rudolph mentions a Ḥanafī school in Rayy, of which the key teachings belong to the Basran al-Ḥusayn al-Najjār (d. *ca* 230/845) and some hints of a deeper *kalām* strand within the Samarqandī tradition in the same century.[104] Al-Najjār, who drew from the ideas of Ḍirār b. ʿAmr (d. *ca* 200/815), is interesting for developing a systematic Ḥanafī theological position outside of Muʿtazilī thought.[105] Al-Māturīdī is more positive towards al-Najjār than to the Muʿtazila, although, as Rudolph points out, this is expressed not just through open reference but also silent adoption of his doctrines.[106] Furthermore, it can be argued that the controversial views

99 Zysow, 'Muʿtazilism and Māturīdism in Ḥanafī Legal Theory', pp. 235–36.

100 Madelung, 'The Early Murjiʾa in Khurāsān and Transoxania and the Spread of Ḥanafism', pp. 37–39.

101 Van Ess, 'Abuʾl-Qāsim al-Kaʿbī', p. 1381.

102 Pessagno, 'The Reconstruction of the Thought of Muḥammad Ibn Shabīb', pp. 446, 448; Rudolph, *Al-Māturīdī and the Development of Sunnī Theology*, pp. 162–63. Rudolph speculates that, while al-Māturīdī was able to use the Ḥanafī tradition exemplified by *Al-Fiqh al-absaṭ* for the themes within the second half of his book connected to human faith and action, he relied on Ibn Shabīb's model for the first half on divine attributes. Rudolph, *Al-Māturīdī and the Development of Sunnī Theology*, pp. 228–30. See also the discussion of epistemology on page 23 above.

103 Daccache, *Le Problème de la Création du Monde*, pp. 39–41.

104 Rudolph, 'Ḥanafī Theological Tradition and Māturīdism', pp. 285–86. See also van Ess, *Theology and Society in the Second and Third Centuries of the Hijra, Volume 2*, p. 633.

105 Rudolph, *Al-Māturīdī and the Development of Sunnī Theology*, pp. 164–65.

106 Rudolph, *Al-Māturīdī and the Development of Sunnī Theology*, pp. 1645–46. See pages 163–64 and page 89 respectively for examples of explicit and implicit use of al-Najjār's ideas.

of Ibn Karrām (d. 255/869) on divine attributes are variations on a recognisable Ḥanafī genealogy, which were part of the inherited Transoxianan tradition.[107]

The Ḥanafī *kalām* tradition from which al-Māturīdī's thought emerged did not focus on the nature of God's attributes, which was usually a central concern for Muslim theologians of the period.[108] Instead, Ḥanafīs continued to highlight faith, its relation to action and its implication for community membership, questions that were central to the origins of theological dispute in the first/seventh century.[109] This can partly be explained by the theological activity of Abū Ḥanīfa. A notable letter that he wrote to his Basran contemporary ʿUthmān al-Battī (d. 143/760) centres on these questions, as does the dialogue recorded between him and his student Abū Muqātil al-Samarqandī (d. 208/823) in *Kitāb al-ʿālim wa-l-mutaʿallim*. Only a text written by another student, Abū Muṭīʿ al-Balkhī (d. 199/814), known as *Al-Fiqh al-akbar* (later called *Al-Fiqh al-absaṭ*) contains material germane to the theology of divine attributes.[110]

In his study of early Ḥanafī history, Rudolph draws a neat line of development from selective and explorative theological thinking in the letter, a process of development in the Transoxianan tradition, and finally a flowering of Sunnī theology in the fourth/tenth or, at best, late-third/ninth centuries.[111] This approach goes back to Shiblī Nuʿmānī and A. J. Wensinck who argued that other more sophisticated creeds attributed to Abū Ḥanīfa must be dated to a time period after his death.[112] Wensinck dates *Kitāb al-waṣiyya* later than his lifetime, but before Aḥmad b. Ḥanbal (d. 241/855).[113] He places another text named *Al-Fiqh al-akbar* (he calls it *Al-Fiqh al-akbar II*), the most famous theological text ascribed to Abū Ḥanīfa, not before the

107 See Rudolph, *Al-Māturīdī and the Development of Sunnī Theology*, pp. 77–78; Madelung, *Religious Trends in Early Islamic Iran*, pp. 41–42.

108 Rudolph, 'Ḥanafī Theological Tradition and Māturīdism', p. 286.

109 Rudolph, 'Ḥanafī Theological Tradition and Māturīdism', pp. 284–85. See van Ess, 'Kalām', p. 906.

110 See Rudolph, *Al-Māturīdī and the Development of Sunnī Theology*, pp. 28–71; van Ess, *Theology and Society in the Second and Third Centuries of the Hijra, Volume 1*, pp. 219–43.

111 Rudolph, *Al-Māturīdī and the Development of Sunnī Theology*, p. 317.

112 Nuʿmānī, *Imam Abu Hanifah*, pp. 83–84.

113 Wensinck, *The Muslim Creed*, p. 187. Watt puts *Kitāb al-waṣiyya* no earlier than about 235/850, which leaves only a five-year window between their datings. Watt, *Islamic Creeds*, p. 57. A text from al-Māturīdī's student al-Rustughfanī suggests that it was written after the mid-fourth/tenth century. See pages 203–4, note 64. *Kitāb al-waṣ iyya* does not seem to be attested early in the Ḥanafī tradition, and the contemporary scholar ʿInāyat Allāh Iblāgh states that he has failed to come across a chain of transmission for it. Iblāgh, *Al-Imām al-Aʿẓam Abū Ḥanīfa al-Mutakallim*, p. 124. But its precise dating needs further study to be settled.

early-fourth/tenth century in the time of Abū al-Ḥasan al-Ashʿarī (d. 324/935–36), omitting discussion of al-Māturīdī.[114] William Montgomery Watt argues that *Al-Fiqh al-akbar II* appears to be a late-fourth/tenth-century composition, an assessment with which I concur, although it did not have an impact on the Māturīdī tradition until the eighth/fourteenth century.[115] The important point for the current enquiry is that this text, though claimed to be written by Abū Ḥanīfa, in fact postdates al-Māturīdī, highlighting his own contribution to the school's distinctive theological solutions.

Al-Māturīdī's engagement with non-Islamic religious ideas such as Zoroastrianism, Christianity and Buddhism is significant, albeit far from comprehensive.[116] David Thomas points out that, while he was evidently literate with the core polemical discussions of his day, he was mainly content within *Kitāb al-tawḥīd* to attack what he saw as the most egregious

114 Wensinck, *The Muslim Creed*, pp. 245–46. He extracted ten points from *Sharḥ al-fiqh al-akbar* and named this 'decalogue' *Al-Fiqh al-akbar I*. But, as shown by van Ess and Rudolph, this reconstructed short creed of Abū Ḥanīfa never existed. Van Ess, *Theology and Society in the Second and Third Centuries of the Hijra, Volume 1*, pp. 237–41; Rudolph, *Al-Māturīdī and the Development of Sunnī Theology*, pp. 56–58. The commentary on the text of al-Balkhī is published with an ascription to al-Māturīdī, but this is widely discredited. Hans Daiber suggests it is a work of Abū al-Layth al-Samarqandī (d. 373/983) based on manuscript and internal evidence. Daiber, *The Islamic Concept of Belief in the 4th/10th Century*, pp. 5–10. Rudolph argues that it may have been written about one hundred years later, in the era of al-Bazdawī during the fifth/eleventh century. See Rudolph, *Al-Māturīdī and the Development of Sunnī Theology*, pp. 325–28. Züleyha Birinci has shown that the earliest manuscript ascription is to the obscure figure ʿAṭāʾ b. ʿAlī al-Jūzjānī who lived before 565/1170. See Birinci, 'Ebû Mutîʿ Rivâyetli', pp. 71–72. I agree with these later datings and will refer to 'the author of *Sharḥ al-fiqh al-akbar*' in recognition of the difficulty. Wensinck gave the title *Al-Fiqh al-akbar II* to the creed allegedly transmitted by Abū Hanīfa's son Ḥammād, and I will keep this name for clarity and to distinguish it from al-Balkhī's *Al-Fiqh al-akbar* (*Al-Fiqh al-absaṭ*). It is this latter text that contains the phrase 'the greatest understanding (*al-fiqh al-akbar*)' as a term originally intended to signal correct answers to disputed polemical questions, but later interpreted as a synonym for *uṣul al-dīn* or *ʿilm al-kalām*. Abū Ḥanīfa, *Al-ʿĀlim wa-l-mutaʿallim*, ed. Muḥammad Zāhid al-Kawtharī, p. 40; al-Ṣaffār, *Talkhīṣ al-adilla*, vol. 1, p. 65. The treatise was only renamed *Al-Fiqh al-absaṭ* in the late classical period due to its relative length after *Al-Fiqh al-akbar II* became very popular. The new name is found in works such as al-Bayāḍī, *Ishārāt al-marām*, p. 21.

115 Watt, *The Formative Period of Islamic Thought*, p. 133. See a forthcoming article by the present author for a detailed discussion.

116 Select views of Zoroastrians (*al-majūs*), Christians (*al-naṣārā*) and Buddhists (*al-sumaniyya*) are discussed in al-Māturīdī, *Kitāb al-tawḥīd*, pp. 263–66, 288–94 and pp. 221–22. There are also some possible connections between al-Māturīdī's theology and Indian schools of thought, especially Buddhism. See Pines, 'A Study of the Impact of Indian, mainly Buddhist, Thought on Some Aspects of Kalām Doctrines', pp. 12–14, 17; Xiuyuan, 'The Presence of Buddhist Thought in Kalām Literature', pp. 960–61. Also see page 60, note 23.

theological errors where they intersected with his articulation of Islamic doctrine, rather than present them on their own terms.[117] The value of citing these foreign teachings was to support the arguments that he wished to make about the veracity of Islamic teachings on select topics.[118] Nevertheless, naturalised philosophical ideas from these sources are significant in the conceptual formations of the *kalām* tradition to which al-Māturīdī is indebted.[119]

Centuries earlier, the Jewish Platonist Philo of Alexandria (d. 50 CE)[120] laid down eight presuppositions for theistic adoption of the rational methods of Hellenic thought. These were the existence of God; His unity; the creation of the world; divine providence; the unity of the world; the existence of Platonic Forms; the revelation of the Law; and its eternity.[121] Harry Wolfson argues that, with the exception of the unity of the world, which is assumed but not treated as a religious question, Muslim theologians only outright rejected the eternity of the Law, as they understood it to be revealed and applied within time.[122] But two of these principles were finessed in order to be accommodated within the Islamic *Weltanschauung*. The unity of God was understood by Philo to consist of four aspects: the denial of polytheism, God's self-sufficiency, unique eternality and absolute simplicity. While Muslim theologians accepted most of these conditions, the question of divine simplicity was the site of dispute, with the Muʿtazila and some others accepting this idea and claimants to the title of *ahl al-sunna wa-l-jamāʿa* rejecting it.[123] The Islamic conception of a personal God, known from scripture, was transcendent, yet possessed attributes. For the Muʿtazila, these attributes must be in some sense identical with God, while for others that amounted to their denial. The discussion also relates to the final modified doctrine in Philo's list, the existence of Platonic Forms, which, although formally repudiated, finds an equivalent of sorts in the divine attributes, especially divine knowledge, wisdom and speech.[124] In contrast, there was

117 Thomas, *Christian Doctrines in Islamic Theology*, pp. 92–93.
118 Thomas, *Christian Doctrines in Islamic Theology*, p. 93.
119 Islamic theological articulations were also significant in the development of distinctively Christian and Jewish *kalām* traditions within the Arabic milieu. See Griffith, 'Faith and Reason in Christian Kalām', pp. 5–6; Sklare, 'Muʿtazili Trends in Jewish Theology', pp. 145–47.
120 See Dillon, *The Middle Platonists*, pp. 139–44.
121 Wolfson, *The Philosophy of the Kalam*, p. 74.
122 Wolfson, *The Philosophy of the Kalam*, pp. 75–76.
123 Wolfson, *The Philosophy of the Kalam*, p. 75. Medieval Christian theologians also differed on the question of simplicity with the dominant view acceptance of it. See pages 141–42.
124 Wolfson, *The Philosophy of the Kalam*, p. 76. See Chapters 5 and 7.

near-universal condemnation of Jahm b. Ṣafwān (d. 128/745–46) who developed a negative theology denying the attribution of any properties to God.[125]

Muslim theologians were not then reinventing the wheel but applying rational techniques already well-adapted to previous revelations that shared the same basic conceptual presuppositions. As pointed out by von Grunebaum, Late Antiquity furnished a familiarity with a series of philosophical binaries that easily accommodated particular Islamic expressions: substance and accident, eternity and creation, spiritual descent into the material world and ascending return.[126] To a certain extent, Hellenic and other existing modes of thought entered Muslim theology when 'converts would come to Islam "thinking" on the data of revelation in the best way they knew how',[127] as well as conversation in the melting pots formed through Muslim settlements in the new lands of empire. Nowhere was more fruitful for this than the twin garrison towns of Kufa and Basra in Iraq, as well as, at the dawn of the Abbasid era in the second/eighth century, the new capital, Baghdad. It was here that the most intensive 'translation movement' of Greek philosophical texts into Arabic took place, often via the intermediary of Syriac.

Dimitri Gutas suggests that from the outset such translations were understood as 'part of research processes stemming from intellectual currents in Baghdad and as such creative responses to the rapidly developing Arabic scientific and philosophical tradition'.[128] Furthermore, the different 'complexes' undertaking these translations had their own particular characteristics and methodologies.[129] One of the most philosophically important, the complex centred around the circle of al-Kindī (d. *ca* 259/873), the 'Philosopher of the Arabs', has been analysed in detail. The conclusion is that, rather than attempting to render philosophical texts in a literal – or neutral – manner, there is an obvious tendency for Neoplatonic interpretations, yet ones that attempt to remove elements deemed inimical to monotheistic *tawḥīd* (unicity), such as the divine hypostases of the One, the Intellect and the Soul mentioned by Plotinus (d. 270 CE).[130]

An example with great resonance for Muslim theology can be found within the circle's translation of the *Enneads* of Plotinus, the very popular text known as the *Theology of Aristotle*. The original Greek phrase meaning

125 Schöck, 'Jahm b. Ṣafwān (d. 128/745–46) and the 'Jahmiyya' and Ḍirār b. ʿAmr (d. 200/815)', pp. 57–58; Küng, *Islam*, pp. 284–85.

126 Von Grunebaum, 'The Concept and Function of Reason in Islamic Ethics', p. 16.

127 Jackson, *On the Boundaries of Theological Tolerance*, p. 16.

128 Gutas, *Greek Thought, Arabic Culture*, p. 150.

129 Gutas, *Greek Thought, Arabic Culture*, p. 146.

130 Gutas, *Greek Thought, Arabic Culture*, p. 146.

'The One is all things and no one of them' is rendered as 'The pure One is the cause of all things and is not like any of them',[131] which recalls Qur'anic verses, such as Q. 42:11, 'There is nothing like Him . . .' and Q. 112:41–4, 'Say, "He is God, singular. God, eternally besought by all. He does not beget, nor was He begotten. And there is nothing at all like Him"'.

In al-Kindī's original philosophy, too, there are signs that he worked with an active awareness of the concerns of the Muʿtazila, the most prominent Muslim theologians around him. Thus in his *Fī al-falsafa al-ūlā* (*First Philosophy*), he states that God may be called 'one' essentially (*bi-l-dhāt*).[132] Peter Adamson argues that, although al-Kindī does not draw the following general conclusion, the underlying philosophical principle with which he works could be stated as follows: 'for any divine attribute F, God is truly F because He is essentially F and in no respect not-F'.[133] Formulated like this, his approach would seem to admit the method adopted by al-Māturīdī in essential attributes, such as God's wisdom, which he treats as eternally describing Him and free from any defect.[134] The defining point of difference between those theologians who understand God to have distinct eternal attributes, such as al-Māturīdī, and those who do not, such as the Muʿtazila, is thus not necessarily in respect of the essentiality of attributes, but can be in their different presuppositions regarding God's simplicity.[135]

One need not probe the prior tradition to appreciate al-Māturīdī's engagement with Hellenic philosophy. In his *Kitāb al-tawḥīd*, al-Māturīdī quotes Aristotle by the name Arisṭāṭālīs.[136] The context, important in determining his reception of the philosopher, is a refutation of the position of *al-dahriyya* (materialists) that the world is eternal.[137] Al-Māturīdī states that a certain group claims that the raw material (*ṭīna*) of the world is eternal prime matter (*hayūlā*), which is devoid of any accidental qualities, such as length, weight, heat, or movement.[138] He then lists Aristotle's ten categories as substance (*ʿayn*), location (*makān*), quality (*ṣifa*), time (*waqt*), quantity (*ʿadad*), relatives (*muḍāf*), having (*dhū*), positionality (*niṣba*), acting (*fāʿil*) and acted upon (*mafʿūl*), from a book identified as *Al-Manṭiq* (*The Logic*).

131 Adamson, 'The Theology of Aristotle'.
132 Adamson, 'Al-Kindī and the Muʿtazila', p. 50.
133 Adamson, 'Al-Kindī and the Muʿtazila', pp. 55–56.
134 See the discussion on page 162. Rudolph suggests that the student of al-Kindī, Abū Zayd al-Balkhī (d. 322/934), may have been the conduit of the Neoplatonic resonances within the thought of al-Māturīdī, although the evidence is lacking to make more than a circumstantial case. Rudolph, *Al-Māturīdī and the Development of Sunnī Theology*, p. 277.
135 See Chapter 4.
136 Al-Māturīdī, *Kitāb al-tawḥīd*, p. 215.
137 See al-Māturīdī, *Kitāb al-tawḥīd*, pp. 209–20. See page 108, note 27.
138 Al-Māturīdī, *Kitāb al-tawḥīd*, p. 215.

This is an obvious reference to the *Organon*, which contained the *Categories*, one of the earliest Greek texts to be translated into Arabic, in the mid second/eighth century, by Ibn al-Muqaffaʿ (d. *ca* 139/756) or his son.[139] Al-Māturīdī appears to refer approvingly to the ten categories, adding that 'no one is able to mention anything outside of them'.[140] Apparently his argument is that the exhaustiveness of the categories outlined by Aristotle precludes the existence of eternal prime matter that cannot fit within any one of them.

Frank A. Lewis comments on Aristotle's method in this context:

> In the *Categories*, we classify an individual substance, Socrates (say), by the fact that he Is (a) man. A parallel system of classification is at work in the nonsubstance categories: each nonsubstance too Is some predicable that exists above it in the same category. Invariably, then, there is an answer to the question 'What is it?' not only in the case of items in the category of substance, but also for nonsubstances as well. In contrast to all of this, there is no *x* from any category such that (prime) matter IS *x*. In the case of (prime) matter, there is no answer to the question 'What is it?' from any of the categories. But nothing can be a member of a category, yet not Be some predicable within that category. Accordingly, (prime) matter falls outside the system of categories altogether.[141]

The point here is not to determine the correct reading of Aristotle's approach to prime matter, nor deny that his view may have changed in works written after the *Categories*.[142] But we are able to appreciate why al-Māturīdī apparently sees Aristotle as a voice against the theory of eternal

139 Al-Māturīdī, *Kitāb al-tawḥīd*, pp. 215–16. For an edition of a surviving Arabic translation of the *Categories* by Isḥāq b. Ḥunayn, see Zenker, 'Kitāb Arisṭūṭālis al-musammā qāṭīghūriyyā ay al-maqūlāt', p. 5. Also see Cerić, *Roots of Synthetic Theology in Islam*, pp. 99–100; D'Ancona, 'Greek Sources in Arabic and Islamic Philosophy'. Van Ess gives a clue towards a textual link between the second/eighth-century translation and al-Māturīdī's reception in their common use of the term *ʿayn* for substance. Van Ess, review of *Kitāb al-tawḥīd*, by Abū Manṣūr al-Māturīdī, ed. Fathalla Kholeif, p. 559. The later al-Sālimī, despite not mentioning al-Māturīdī in his *Al-Tamhīd*, produces a similar argument without naming its provenance, listing nine kinds of accidents that accompany substance, which he terms *jawhar*. Al-Sālimī, *Al-Tamhīd fī bayan al-tawḥ īd*, p. 80. Al-Māturīdī also uses the similar phrase *ṣāḥib al-manṭiq* in his voluminous *tafsīr* to claim Aristotle's authority on the definition of certainty, probabilistic knowledge and doubt. Al-Māturīdī, *Taʾwīlāt al-qurʾān*, vol. 1, p. 117.

140 Al-Māturīdī, *Kitāb al-tawḥīd*, p. 216.

141 Lewis, *Substance and Predication in Aristotle*, pp. 297–98.

142 Lewis, *How Aristotle Gets By in* Metaphysics Zeta, pp. 1–2.

prime matter and considers citation of the ten categories metaphysically relevant to his arguments.[143]

Along with this mention of Aristotelian philosophical methods, al-Māturīdī draws from the early *kalām* approach to logic that emphasises dialectic in line with the Stoic tradition.[144] The 'science of what is true and false' developed by the Stoic logicians dealt with inference between propositions, unlike the Peripatetic system that focused on terms.[145] The Stoics are sometimes portrayed as very keen to hold on to a strict bivalency in their logic, accepting only true or false to be asserted of each proposition, even in cases where it may have been easier to drop this criterion.[146] But Mueller concludes in his reconstruction that there is no reason to include within the fundamental principles of Stoic logic the Law of Excluded Middle (LEM), the principle that, if a given proposition is not true, then it is false (and *vice versa*).[147] Likewise, it seems that some Stoics were ready to 'solve' the Liar Paradox by asserting it to be neither true nor false.[148] The possible reception of some of these logical ideas in al-Māturīdī's theological system will be explored further in Chapter 4.[149]

A strength of al-Māturīdī's thought is his ability to fashion existing Ḥanafī *kalām* with other philosophical and theological material into a new paradigm.[150] In presenting this aspect of his theological genealogy I have argued that the dominant mode of reason in al-Māturīdī's synthesis derives from the Aristotelian-Neoplatonic tradition. Normatively speaking, I see this pedigree neither as a shameful secret, nor an alien intrusion within the 'pristine purity' of Islamic revelation, but indicative of the perennial viability for philosophical theology to provide a systematic articulation of scriptural truths. Al-Māturīdī's achievement lies in harvesting a new tradition from these seeds, one able to rationally justify itself against rivals within its

143 In his Turkish translation, Topaloğlu understands al-Māturīdī to be critiquing Aristotle by inferring references to him in subsequent paragraphs that continue the refutation of the *dahriyya*. See al-Māturīdī, *Kitâbü't-Tevhîd*, pp. 232–33; al-Māturīdī, *Kitâbü't-Tevhîd*, p. 216, n. 9. I do not see any evidence for these inferences. As I have indicated, I read the passage as al-Māturīdī citing Aristotle to rebut those who believe in the existence of prime matter, not to include him with them. I thank Kayhan Özaykal for bringing Topaloğlu's interpretation to my attention and translating the relevant parts.

144 For a discussion on Stoic dialectic and early *kalām*, see van Ess, 'The Logical Structure of Islamic Theology', pp. 26–29.

145 Barnes, 'Introduction', pp. 66, 77.

146 Brunschvig, *Papers in Hellenistic Philosophy*, pp. 75–76.

147 Mueller, 'The Completeness of Stoic Propositional Logic', p. 215.

148 Van Ess, 'The Logical Structure of Islamic Theology', p. 31.

149 See page 152.

150 Rudolph, *Al-Māturīdī and the Development of Sunnī Theology*, p. 316; Cerić, *Roots of Synthetic Theology in Islam*, pp. 105–6.

milieu including those with a shared history. The acceptability of his school as a recognisable expression of Sunnī Islam comes not just from its Ḥanafī origins and certain distinctive doctrines, but from its meaning, coherence and openness to the best thinking of its age. These should be criteria for any contemporary Islamic theology. But what of Māturīdism in the centuries after al-Māturīdī? Where does it fit in the story?

III. The Māturīdī Tradition after al-Māturīdī

We have already come across several later Māturīdī figures when discussing the question of epistemology. In this section, I provide a general synopsis of the formation and development of the school up to modern times. I divide this history into four stages, although some of the periods overlap, as earlier approaches coexist with later ones:

1. Early – from al-Māturīdī in the early fourth/tenth century until the end of the fifth/eleventh century.
2. Classical – from the end of the fifth/eleventh century until the eighth/fourteenth century.
3. Late classical – from the eighth/fourteenth century until the end of the thirteenth/nineteenth century (and still in many madrasas).
4. Modern – from the end of the thirteenth/nineteenth century until the present day.

In the early period, al-Māturīdī's distinctive synthesis was not immediately widely adopted in Samarqand and its environs, even though he became head of the madrasa Dār al-Jūzjāniyya and students began to transmit his teachings.[151] The more significant among them are Abū al-Ḥasan al-Rustughfanī (d. *ca* 345/956), author of a number of influential books,[152] though only one and extracts of its legal and theological responsa survive;[153] and – known

151 See Rudolph, *Al-Māturīdī and the Development of Sunnī Theology*, pp. 319–20; Dorroll, 'The Universe in Flux', p. 122.

152 His most important theological treatise was *Al-Irshād* (or *Irshād al-muhtadī*). Al-Nasafī, *Tabṣirat al-adilla*, vol. 1, pp. 240, 556. See Rudolph, *Al-Māturīdī and the Development of Sunnī Theology*, pp. 142–43.

153 See al-Rustughfanī, 'Al-As'ila wa-l-ajwiba', fol. 154v; al-Rustughfanī, 'Bāb al-mutafarriqāt min fawā'id', MS Yeni Cami 547, fols 285v–307v; al-Rustughfanī, 'Bāb al-mutafarriqāt min fawā'id', MS Veliyüddin Efendi 1545, fols 276v–302v. Rudolph considered his writings lost and Muhammed Aruçi stated he was unable to confirm if they were extant. Rudolph, *Al-Māturīdī and the Development of Sunnī Theology*, pp. 143–44; Aruçi, 'Rüstüfağnî'. Şükrü Özen is preparing an edition of his *Kitāb al-zawā'id wa-l-fawā'id fī aṣnāf al-'ulūm*. For more on al-Rustughfanī's literary legacy and significance to the early school, see a forthcoming article by the present author.

for his piety – Abū Aḥmad al-ʿIyāḍī, the son of al-Māturīdī's teacher Abū Naṣr al-ʿIyāḍī.[154] Abū Aḥmad represents a more traditionalist wing of the Samarqandī school, along with his brother Abū Bakr al-ʿIyāḍī (d. 361/972) who wrote the extant public testament *Al-Masāʾil al-ʿashar al-ʿIyāḍiyya.*[155] Also associated with this tendency is the famous al-Ḥakīm al-Samarqandī (d. 342/953), author of *Al-Sawād al-aʿẓam.*[156] Abū Salama al-Samarqandī, a student of Abū Naṣr and Abū Aḥmad,[157] wrote a concise summary of *Kitāb al-tawḥīd* titled *Jumal min uṣūl al-dīn*, which is still extant.[158]

The commentary on *Jumal min uṣūl al-dīn* that follows it in the same manuscript appears anonymous due to the absence of its early portion.[159] But the author identifies himself as the son and student of a disciple of Abū Naṣr named [Abū][160] Zakariyyā Yaḥyā b. Isḥāq.[161] Recent scholarship has linked him to the known early Samarqandī scholar Abū al-Ḥusayn Muḥammad b. Yaḥyā al-Bashāgharī.[162] He relates from his father and teacher that he heard Abū al-Ḥasan (al-Rustughfanī) speak in praise of Abū Salama's knowledge,[163] making it probable that both of them should be placed in the more rationally inclined circle in Samarqand known as the Jūzjāniyya to which al-Māturīdī belonged.[164] Ibn Yaḥyā al-Bashāgharī quotes time and again from Abū Zakariyyā, whom he usually refers to as 'the Shaykh, may God be pleased with him', as well as al-Māturīdī,

154 Kholeif, 'Al-Imām Abū Manṣūr al-Māturīdī', p. 241; Rudolph, *Al-Māturīdī and the Development of Sunnī Theology*, pp. 137–44. ʿAbd al-Karīm al-Bazdawī, the great-grandfather of Abū al-Yusr al-Bazdawī, is also important as a student of al-Māturīdī and transmitter of his teachings. See al-Bazdawī, *Uṣūl al-dīn*, p. 14; al-Nasafī, *Al-Qand fī dhikr ʿulamāʾ al-Samarqand*, p. 311.

155 See Özen, 'IV. (X.) Yüzyılda Māverāünnehirʾde Ehl-i Sünnet-Muʿtezile Mücadelesi ve Bir Ehl-i Sūnnet Beyannamesi'.

156 Dorroll, 'The Universe in Flux', p. 123.

157 See al-Samarqandī, *Jumal min uṣūl al-dīn wa-yalīhu sharḥuhu*, p. 36; Rudolph, *Al-Māturīdī and the Development of Sunnī Theology*, p. 139.

158 A single manuscript in the Süleymaniye Library in Istanbul dated to 677/1279 contains first Abū Salama's text over sixteen folios and then its commentary over 152 folios. See al-Samarqandī, *Jumal min uṣūl al-dīn wa-yalīhu sharḥuhu*, pp. 7, 13, 40 and 231. The text was published as *Jumal uṣūl al-dīn* in Istanbul in 1989 and republished as *Jumal min uṣul al-dīn* in Beirut along with the commentary in 2015.

159 See al-Samarqandī, *Jumal min uṣūl al-dīn wa-yalīhu sharḥuhu*, p. 40.

160 The manuscript says Ibn, but this is likely a transcription error given the rest of the name. See Kuegelgen and Muminov, 'Mâturîdî Döneminde Semerkand İlahiyatçıları (4./10. Asır)', pp. 279–80. The author also refers to him as al-Shaykh Zakariyyā in one place. Al-Samarqandī, *Jumal min uṣūl al-dīn wa-yalīhu sharḥuhu*, p. 182.

161 Al-Samarqandī, *Jumal min uṣūl al-dīn wa-yalīhu sharḥuhu*, p. 224.

162 Arıkaner, 'Şerhu Cümeli usûli'd-dîn'in Ebü'l-Hüseyin Muhammed b. Yahyâ el-Beşâğarî'ye Aidiyeti Meselesi', pp. 59–60.

163 Al-Samarqandī, *Jumal min uṣūl al-dīn wa-yalīhu sharḥuhu*, p. 218.

164 Dorroll, 'The Universe in Flux', p. 123.

al-Rustughfanī and al-Ḥakīm al-Samarqandī, in order to explicate Abū Salama's theological points.

Despite the presence of this tightly knit group, in the first century after al-Māturīdī's death, greater renown fell to scholars who upheld the more traditionalist and creed-focused Ḥanafī theological tradition, such as Abū al-Layth al-Samarqandī.[165] Moreover, even as late as the second half of the fifth/eleventh century the Samarqandī figure Abū al-Shakūr al-Sālimī does not mention al-Māturīdī at all,[166] coming close to a number of Ashʿarī positions, while still declaring that others, such as their approach to God's creative action, amount to disbelief.[167] This development was due to Ashʿarī presence in Nishapur: the school tradition of Ibn Fūrak (d. 406/1015) and Abū Isḥāq al-Isfarāyīnī (d. 418/1027), followed by the Transoxianan Abū Bakr al-Fūrakī (d. 478/1085).[168]

Abū al-Yusr al-Bazdawī (d. 493/1099) responded to Ashʿarī competition by adopting al-Māturīdī as the central focus of the school, naming him one of the leaders of the *ahl al-sunna wa-l-jamāʿa* and a worker of saintly miracles.[169] Throughout his book, *Uṣūl al-dīn*, and within the copious works of Abū al-Muʿīn al-Nasafī (d. 508/1114), the figure of al-Māturīdī takes on a prominence that outstrips any other Samarqandī theologian, even though the earlier tradition remains immensely important as a pool of theological wisdom.[170] But it seems that the difficulty of al-Māturīdī's *Kitāb al-tawḥīd*, a point explicitly made by al-Bazdawī,[171] meant that he was often referenced through informal records of his theological doctrines

165 For a discussion of Abū al-Layth al-Samarqandī's theological output, which was directed more to creedal matters than rational theology, see Mangera, *A Critical Edition of Abū 'l-Layth al-Samarqandī's* Nawāzil, pp. 40–41; Aldosari, *Ḥanafī Māturīdism*, pp. 171–72.

166 Rudolph, *Al-Māturīdī and the Development of Sunnī Theology*, p. 321.

167 Al-Sālimī, *Al-Tamhīd*, pp. 136–37. Also see Brodersen, 'New Light on the Emergence of Māturīdism'. For examples of al-Sālimī's adoption of Ashʿarī ideas, see pages 146, 148 and 164–65.

168 Madelung, relying on Manfred Götz and followed in turn by Rudolph, claims that al-Fūrakī was the first member of a rival school to refer to Māturīdī doctrine. See Madelung, 'The Spread of Māturīdism and the Turks', pp. 110–11; Rudolph, *Al-Māturīdī and the Development of Sunnī Theology*, p. 320. But Aldosari argues convincingly that the position in question, God's status as creator in pre-eternity, is far too widespread amongst all Ḥanafī groups, as well as early traditionists, to uniquely pick out Māturīdism. See Aldosari, *Ḥanafī Māturīdism*, p. 221.

169 Al-Bazdawī, *Uṣūl al-dīn*, p. 14.

170 The pattern is established by one of al-Nasafī's first major discussions on the definition of knowledge, in which he rejects the doctrines of various Muʿtazilīs and Ashʿarīs before presenting an anonymous view of his own group and then the opinion of 'al-Shaykh al-Imām Abū Manṣūr al-Māturīdī' as correct. Al-Nasafī, *Tabṣirat al-adilla*, vol. 1, pp. 136–37.

171 Al-Bazdawī, *Uṣūl al-dīn*, p. 14.

and arguments, rather than a textual tradition based on study of his written work.[172] It was thus the figures of this second period, above all Abū al-Muʿīn al-Nasafī, who became the key authors for the development of the Māturīdī literary legacy. Al-Nasafī's influential works provided the definitive paradigm for the organisation of *kalām* manuals within the classical tradition, the set of doctrines to be defended and the rational tools to be used in doing so.[173] The longevity of *Al-ʿAqīda al-Nasafiyya*, the creed of his student Abū Ḥafṣ al-Nasafī, demonstrates the success of his approach.

The first two periods of the Māturīdī tradition follow the model of dialectical *kalam*, in which scriptural data and rational argumentation are used to substantiate a preferred theological interpretation over that of rivals. The *mutakallim* would argue in accordance with the challenge of a given opponent, such that shared premises would be taken for granted and the refutation of the other's position would often take precedence over the support of one's own.[174] A second shift occurred in the wake of the Transoxianan *munāẓarāt* (debates) engaged in by Fakhr al-Dīn al-Rāzī (d. 606/1209), who brought into play within the Māturīdī milieu a sophisticated *kalām* conceptually indebted to the philosophy of Ibn Sīnā (Avicenna) (d. 429/1037).[175] His Ḥanafī opponents in these debates were figures such as Nūr al-Dīn al-Ṣābūnī (d. 580/1184) who were committed to the classical method as exemplified by Abū Muʿīn al-Nasafī.[176] Al-Rāzī claims that, at the end of his debates with al-Ṣābūnī, the Ḥanafī confessed:

> Sir, I have read the *Kitāb Tabṣirat al-Adillah* by Abū l-Muʿīn al-Nasafī and I believe that nothing excels that book in accuracy and perfection, but now that I have seen you and heard your argument, I realize that if I wanted to learn this science, I would have to go back to the beginning, and learn the science as the beginner does . . . [177]

In part through the intervention of al-Rāzī, the Avicennan method became central to the teaching of *kalām* in the madrasa, whether in eager adoption or critical response.[178] The new approach began to be adopted by Ḥanafīs

172 Aldosari, *Ḥanafī Māturīdism*, p. 153.

173 Aldosari, *Ḥanafī Māturīdism*, pp. 184–85.

174 Van Ess, 'The Logical Structure of Islamic Theology', pp. 23–26.

175 I use Ibn Sīnā for the proper noun but Avicennan for adjectival constructions.

176 For a translation of al-Rāzī's stinging account of his debate with al-Ṣābūnī, in which he claims to have humiliated him, see Kholeif, *A Study on Fakhr al-Dīn al-Rāzī*, pp. 36–43, 45–46.

177 Kholeif, *A Study on Fakhr al-Dīn al-Rāzī*, p. 46.

178 Endress, 'Reading Avicenna in the Madrasa', pp. 398–99; Gutas, 'Avicenna and After', pp. 50–51. For a broader view of Ibn Sīna's historical impact on Islamic intellectual history, see Gutas, 'Avicenna and After', pp. 35–36.

such as Shams al-Dīn al-Samarqandī (d. 722/1322)[179] in his *Al-Ṣaḥā'if al-ilāhiyya* and Ṣadr al-Sharī'a al-Maḥbūbī (d. 747/1348), who was well-versed in the works of Ibn Sīnā and wrote *Ta'dīl al-'ulūm*, which combined logic, *kalām* and astronomy.[180] Kamāl al-Dīn al-Andukānī (Andījānī) (d. after 777/1375–76) critically addressed the ideas of Ibn Sīnā directly in his *Ṣidq al-kalām fī 'ilm al-kalām*, while adapting the direction in *kalām* pioneered by al-Rāzī to a Māturīdī framework.[181] More famous figures were to follow in al-Sayyid al-Sharīf al-Jurjānī (d. 816/1413), author of *Sharḥ al-mawāqif*, and Sa'd al-Dīn al-Taftāzānī, author of *Sharḥ al-'aqīda al-Nasafiyya* and *Sharḥ al-maqāṣid*, his competitor at the Timurid court in Samarqand.[182] It is questionable whether all of these scholars can truly be considered within the Māturīdī tradition proper. At least al-Samarqandī and al-Jurjānī may be better characterised as Ash'arīs, due to the centrality of the thought of al-Rāzī in their work.[183] Nonetheless, they are an important part of the Māturīdī story for their presence in the Transoxianan Māturīdī heartlands and for their impact on subsequent Māturīdī *kalām*.

Epistemologically, this strand of theology is characterised by its reliance on the conceptual tools of Ibn Sīnā, which meant prefacing treatises with *al-umūr al-'āmma* (universal matters), including the logical terms by which arguments of demonstration (*burhān*), rather than dialectic (*jadal*) could be composed.[184] Such demonstrative arguments were held to enable valid syllogisms to be built on true propositions leading to true truth-apt assent, in contrast to prior dialectical ones leading to truth-apt assent that is merely the subject of common consent (*'umūm al-i'tirāf*).[185] Yet while the claim to build certain arguments from indubitable premises was certainly rhetorically impactful, the new methods were arguably just a different form of dialectic[186] – one that was not as effective for the practice of

179 For the preference of this date to the usual 690/1291, see El-Rouayheb, *The Development of Arabic Logic (1200–1800)*, p. 66.

180 Dallal, *An Islamic Response to Greek Astronomy*, pp. 8–10. See also Kalaycı, 'Projections of Māturīdite-Ḥanafite Identity on the Ottomans', p. 12.

181 See, for instance, the conceptual discussion of God's existence in al-Andukānī, 'Sidq al-kalām fī 'ilm al-kalām', fols 56r–57r.

182 Endress, 'Reading Avicenna in the Madrasa', pp. 416, 420.

183 For example, al-Samarqandī mentions a dispute over whether God has seven or eight attributes; yet the eighth one he mentions is the Ash'arī permanence (*baqā'*), not the Māturīdī creative action (*takwīn*). Al-Samarqandī, *Al-Ṣaḥā'if al-ilāhiyya*, p. 302. Harith Bin Ramli has remarked to me on this point: 'Even the term Ash'arī is complicated – always, and definitely at this stage in this group of scholars'. For comments on al-Taftāzānī, see page 44, note 193.

184 Walbridge, *God and Logic in Islam*, pp. 117–19. See also El-Rouayheb, 'Theology and Logic', p. 413.

185 Street, 'Arabic and Islamic Philosophy of Language and Logic'.

186 Abderrahmane, *Su'āl al-lugha wa-l-manṭiq*, p. 28.

theology as the old *kalām*[187] – and the shift to them a higher-order dialectical response to certain intellectual conditions.[188] Their adoption among Māturīdī theologians was never complete. The compromise that seems to have been reached is that the new approach would be used in commentary on major creedal primers, most famously *Al-ʿAqīda al-Nasafiyya*, thereby preserving the basic doctrinal positions elaborated in classical-era *kalām* manuals.

This turn towards a shared demonstrative programme was one part of a broader trend for Māturīdīs and Ashʿarīs to be brought closer together during the late classical era. In response to external political pressures, such as the repercussions of the Mongol invasions and Crusades, the Mamlūk and Ottoman dynasties that arose in the seventh/thirteenth and eighth/fourteenth centuries promoted a shared Sunnī unity. This led to an increased tendency for theologians of the two schools to either downplay their differences or to choose eclectically from the positions of either one.[189] The former approach is represented well on the Māturīdī side by Ibn Kamāl Bāshā (d. 940/1534), the polymath Shaykh al-Islām serving under the Ottoman Sultan Suleiman the Magnificient (r. 926/1520–974/1566). In his *Masāʾil al-ikhtilāf bayna al-Ashāʿira wa-l-Māturīdiyya*, he affirms twelve differences between the two schools.[190] This is close to the position of the Ashʿarī Tāj al-Dīn al-Subkī (d. 771/1370) who earlier proposed that they only differ on thirteen questions, of which six are meaningful and the remainder merely verbal.[191] Some Māturīdī theologians were unhappy with the perception that reconciliation typically occurred in favour of the Ashʿarī standpoint. The Ottoman Muḥammad b. Walī al-Qīrshahrī al-Izmīrī (d. 1165/1752) mentions at the beginning of his lengthy *Sharḥ masāʾil al-khilāfiyyāt fī mā bayna al-Ashʿariyya wa-l-Māturīdiyya* that, due to the prevalence of books based on the principles of the Ashʿarīs and the mischief of philosophers, he will work from the solid foundations of Māturīdī thought. Nevertheless, like his predecessors in this debate, he indicates that he will highlight the verbal nature of some disagreements.[192]

This increased harmonisation also led to theologians treating the two traditions as housing a common stock of Sunnī theological formulations

187 Gutas, 'Avicenna and After', pp. 46–47.

188 Wisnovsky, 'On the Emergence of Maragha Avicennism', pp. 272–73. See the discussion of MacIntyre on page 53.

189 Rudolph, *Al-Māturīdī and the Development of Sunnī Theology*, pp. 9–11.

190 Foudeh, *Masāʾil al-ikhtilāf bayna al-Ashāʿira wa-l-Māturīdiyya*, p. 19.

191 See al-Jābī, *Al-Masāʾil al-khilāfiyya bayna al-Ashāʿira wa-l-Māturīdiyya*, p. 57; Rudolph, *Al-Māturīdī and the Development of Sunnī Theology*, pp. 8–9.

192 Al-Izmīrī, 'Sharḥ masāʾil al-khilāfiyyāt fī mā bayna al-Ashʿariyya wa-l-Māturīdiyya', fol. 1v. See Haidar, *The Debates between Ash'arism and Māturīdism in Ottoman Religious Scholarship*, pp. 180–81.

that could be picked up and used as needed. Al-Taftāzānī was an influential figure in the late classical Sunnī theological tradition whose commentary on *Al-ʿAqīda al-Nasafiyya* incorporated positions from both Ashʿarī and Māturīdī schools and became the central text to receive super-commentary up to the modern period.[193] An example of the long-term vibrancy of such texts in the late classical period is the work of the Iranian Kurdish scholar Ḥasan b. al-Sayyid al-Çūrī (d. 1904). He both provides his own super-commentary on *Sharḥ al-ʿaqīda al-Nasafiyya* and additional marginal notes on the super-commentary of a theologian from nearly five centuries before him, Aḥmad b. Mūsā al-Khayālī (d. 861/1457).

Philip Dorroll notes the subtlety of such syncretistic thought within Māturīdī theology of the later Ottoman period in his study of texts discussing the question of human free will by Muḥammad b. Aḥmad al-Gumuljinawī (d. *ca* mid-twelfth/eighteenth century) and Dāwūd al-Qārṣī (d. 1169/1756). He concludes:

> While these two theologians may have been broadly syncretistic and pan-Sunnī in their intellectual outlook, they were not uncritically so. Ottoman theologians' understanding of Sunnī kalām debates therefore evinces a level of extraordinary sophistication and development, to the point of being able to draw fine distinctions among a variety of divergent theological traditions, within a single theological problem.[194]

Although a strong tide, this approach precipitated a minor countercurrent of Māturīdī thought that sought a return in some respects to earlier authorities. An example is the Ottoman theologian Kamāl al-Dīn al-Bayāḍī (d. 1097/1687) who wrote *Ishārāt al-marām min ʿibārāt al-imām Abī Ḥanīfa al-Nuʿmān fī uṣūl al-dīn*. As intimated by the title, al-Bayāḍī in one sense seeks to undercut the shared Ashʿarī-Māturīdī project of his era by revisiting the roots of

193 For a summary of the apparent positioning of al-Taftāzānī within the two schools and in relation to al-Nasafī, see al-Taftāzānī, *A Commentary on the Creed of Islam*, pp. xxiv–xxxi. Hamza el-Bekri argues that al-Taftāzānī, and other scholars in his milieu, would often comment on texts primarily according to their author's school of thought. See Hamza el-Bekri, '*Sharḥ al-ʿaqāʾid al-dars 1*' (Lecture, Sultanahmet Medresesi, Istanbul, 13 October 2018), <https://www.youtube.com/watch?v=3pNNnvP5GEA&list=PLnXQtAauTV70v2qcjnGC5d-slGiLFqLzk>, accessed 4 August 2020. He suggests that al-Taftāzānī alludes to this in his introductory phrase 'and verification for the questions after affirmation (*wa-taḥqīqun li-l-masāʾili ghibba taqrīr*)'. Al-Taftāzānī, *Sharḥ al-ʿaqīda al-Nasafiyya*, p. 8. Najah Nadi Ahmad remarks that al-Taftāzānī's focus on verification (*taḥqīq*) ahead of reconciliation (*tawfīq*) helps to explain his eclecticism. Ahmad, *Theorising the Relationship between* Kalām *and* Uṣūl al-Fiqh, p. 24.

194 Dorroll, 'Māturīdī Theology in the Ottoman Empire', p. 235.

Māturīdī thought in the theological teachings of Abū Ḥanīfa. He therefore declares as delusion (*wahm*) the idea that the differences between the two schools are merely verbal, although he is careful to observe that they concern subsidiary matters that do not result in deviation (*tabdī*ʿ).[195] But al-Bayāḍī displays significant influence from al-Rāzī and those who followed his method, meaning that his direct exegesis of the texts ascribed to Abū Ḥanīfa sometimes seems more of an attempt to bypass the classical Māturīdī tradition than to vindicate it.[196]

The present period of Māturīdī theology can be termed modern or part of the broad movement of *kalām jadīd*. The challenges of modernity, including the colonial and post-colonial experiences of Muslims, have provoked attempts to rethink, revise and reformulate traditional theological positions. The end of the nineteenth and beginning of the twentieth century heralded a call for theological works to address new questions or to look again at familiar ones in the light of contemporary Western philosophy. This included in some cases leaving Arabic for the vernacular languages of the non-Arabophone regions in which Māturidism has historically thrived. Figures important in the first wave of this movement include Muḥammad ʿAbduh (d. 1905) in Egypt; Shiblī Nuʿmānī (d. 1914) in India; and ʿAbd al-Laṭīf al-Kharpūtī (d. 1916) in Turkey.[197]

Although a student of Jamāl al-Dīn al-Afghānī (d. 1897) who was versed in the illuminationist and Sadrian philosophical theology popular in Iran, Muḥammad ʿAbduh mainly developed his *kalām* along familiar Sunnī lines. Rotraud Wielandt argues that the claim that ʿAbduh was a neo-Muʿtazilī is not accurate, especially on the key position of the createdness of the Qur'an as God's speech (*kalām allāh*).[198] But Nasr Abu Zayd claims that the Muʿtazilī position was only dropped in the second edition of the text.[199] In his *Risālat al-tawḥīd*, which is based on school lessons he delivered in Beirut, ʿAbduh emphasises God's attribute of *ḥikma* (wisdom) and the concept of *ikhtiyār* (choice) in human free will, and he declares good and bad knowable via human reason in language reminiscent of al-Māturīdī.[200] The influence of Māturīdism on ʿAbduh's thought

195 Al-Bayāḍī, *Ishārāt al-marām*, p. 23. See Bruckmayr, 'The Spread and Persistence of Māturīdī Kalām and Underlying Dynamics', pp. 69–70.

196 For instance, see his claim that Abū Ḥanīfa's alleged words substantiate a late classical position on divine speech in al-Bayāḍī, *Ishārāt al-marām*, p. 179.

197 The Turkish theologian İzmirli İsmail Hakkı (d. 1946) is another significant figure. See the discussion in Özervarli, 'Attempts to Revitalize *Kalām* in the Late 19th and Early 20th Centuries', pp. 94–100.

198 Wielandt, 'Main Trends', p. 723.

199 Abu Zayd, 'The Dilemma of the Literary Approach to the Qur'an', p. 40.

200 ʿAbduh, *Risālat al-tawḥīd*, pp. 55–58, 65–72. See Wielandt, 'Main Trends', pp. 723–24. MacDonald noticed this at an early date. See MacDonald, 'Māturīdī'.

can potentially be traced back to his earlier years in Cairo where he studied *Al-ʿAqīda al-Nasafiyya* at Al-Azhar.[201] It is, however, very unlikely that he had direct access to al-Māturīdī's *kalām*: he railed against the absence of his works and those of other early scholars in the libraries of Muslims. Meanwhile, the last known manuscript of *Kitāb al-tawḥīd* found its way to Cambridge during his lifetime.[202]

Though ʿAbduh's contribution to new theological ideas in his *Risālat al-tawḥīd* is modest, the direction is significant. His anonymising interpretation of al-Māturīdī's concepts is in some respects a return to the approach of the early Samarqandī school. This is combined with a theology of history that emphasises Islam as a rational progression from earlier revealed dispensations and seems to draw on the ideas of Auguste Comte (d. 1857) or previous Enlightenment thinkers.[203] The important point is not the specifics of his appropriation of aspects of European thought, but his openness to entertain such a synthesis between traditions at all.

Nuʿmānī, a central figure in the 1894 founding of Nadwatul Ulema as a reformed madrasa in Lucknow, India, was more circumspect in his appreciation of the Māturīdī tradition. He remarks in puzzlement that, despite Māturīdī Ḥanafīs outnumbering other theological affiliations among common Muslims, the majority of Ḥanafī scholars in his day are Ashʿarī, reflecting the greater fame and prolific output of that school's scholars.[204] This observation demonstrates the effect of the late classical harmonisation of the two schools. By the beginning of the twentieth century, the difference between them was seen to be minimal, and it had become unproblematic for Hanafī ulema to entirely adopt Ashʿarism. Although drawing more on Ashʿarī figures such as al-Ghazālī than their Māturīdī counterparts, Nuʿmānī is sceptical about what he sees as anti-rationalist tendencies within *kalām*. Also, like ʿAbduh, Nuʿmānī emphasises the need to avoid the intricate philosophical discussions of the late classical period and to present an accessible theology that can deal with contemporary concerns.[205]

Similar calls for a *kalām jadīd* were made in the twilight years of Ottoman Turkey. ʿAbd al-Laṭīf al-Kharpūtī, who unlike Nuʿmānī had studied in

201 Kholeif, 'Al-Imām Abū Manṣūr al-Māturīdī', p. 235.

202 El Shamsy, *Rediscovering the Islamic Classics*, p. 34. See page 13, note 12.

203 Wielandt, 'Main Trends', pp. 720–21.

204 Nuʿmānī, *ʿIlm al-kalām al-jadīd*, p. 86. The Arabic translation combines two Urdu works: *ʿIlm al-kalām*, a historical introduction, and *Al-Kalām: yaʿnī ʿilm-i kalām-i jadīd*, a theological study, originally published in 1903 and 1904, respectively. See Wielandt, 'Main Trends', p. 761.

205 Özervarli, 'Attempts to Revitalize *Kalām* in the Late 19th and Early 20th Centuries', pp. 99–100.

a traditional madrasa, proposes in his Arabic-language text *Tanqiḥ al-kalām fī ʿaqāʾid ahl al-islām* that the way to respond to new deviations and heresies is 'a revision (*tanqīḥ*) of the principles of our Islamic creed from the authentic theological books'.[206] Although al-Kharpūtī's *kalām* manual follows a familiar structure and summarises standard creedal positions and arguments, his thought is distinguished by a historical awareness of the periods through which Muslim theology had already passed, as well as the possibility of heralding a new age.[207] For instance, with respect to the definition of *ʿilm al-kalām*, he declares that, whereas earlier figures had treated it as research into the essence, attributes and actions of God with respect to the first and last things, their successors focused their efforts on epistemological certitude in creed.[208] In other words, al-Kharpūtī identifies the transition to foundationalism discussed earlier in this chapter.

In *Tanqīḥ al-kalām*, he consistently contrasts the views of the philosophers (*ḥukamāʾ*) with those of the theologians, whether earlier or later, Ashʿarī or 'our group (*maʿsharinā*) the Māturīdīs' – as he says when affirming *takwīn* as the eighth established attribute (*ṣifa thubūtiyya*).[209] His self-identification with Māturīdism, while drawing broadly from both schools, shows his continuity with the late classical Ottoman tradition. Yet this is tempered with a preference in some places to return to scriptural arguments, rather than philosophical demonstration.

For example, in his discussion of the existence of God, he explains that there are two methods in *kalām*: that of possibility (*imkān*), followed by the philosophers and the verifiers (*muḥaqqiqīn*) of the theologians, and temporality (*ḥudūth*), followed by the majority of theologians.[210] The former is what is known in modern philosophy as the 'Leibnizian cosmological argument', that the merely possible things in the world require ultimate reliance on a necessary existent, God, as famously articulated by Ibn Sīnā.[211] The latter is the *kalām* cosmological argument propounded by the Muʿtazilī Abū al-Hudhayl (d. 227/841–42) and many after him, including al-Māturīdī.[212] Yet he adds poetically:

206 Al-Kharpūtī, *Tanqiḥ al-kalām fī ʿaqāʾid ahl al-islām*, p. 9.
207 See Özervarli, 'Attempts to Revitalize *Kalām* in the Late 19th and Early 20th Centuries', p. 95.
208 Al-Kharpūtī, *Tanqiḥ al-kalām fī ʿaqāʾid ahl al-islām*, p. 10.
209 Al-Kharpūtī, *Tanqiḥ al-kalām fī ʿaqāʾid ahl al-islām*, p. 74.
210 Al-Kharpūtī, *Tanqiḥ al-kalām fī ʿaqāʾid ahl al-islām*, p. 61.
211 See page 109.
212 Al-Kharpūtī does not provide these names. Al-Kharpūtī, *Tanqiḥ al-kalām fī ʿaqāʾid ahl al-islām*, pp. 61–63. See Davidson, *Proofs for Eternity, Creation, and the Existence of God*, p. 134; van Ess, *Theology and Society in the Second and Third Centuries of the Hijra, Volume 3*, pp. 249–50. See pages 108–111.

> Regarding the affirmation of the creator of the world, there is a third method. The one who turns his sight to this visible world, reflecting extensively; seeing in its height the planets established effortlessly with perpetual orbits; especially the luminous sun in its specific course and from which results the difference of night and day; and the changing of seasons in the poles; and the clouds subservient in the sky; and the water that descends from them; and he sees beneath the earth and what is upon it of oceans and rivers; and land containing trees and fruits; and the regions with cities and capitals; and types of creation: mineral, plant and animal; especially those perfected by their conscious knowledge – I mean the truth of the human condition – and regard closely their natural state, becoming certain about the wondrous lessons and beneficial wisdoms that have been placed and enfolded therein, as well as the accompanying blessings; he is compelled to judge that this perfected order and important complete system cannot do without the existence of a power that brings it into being, a wise creator to arrange it. This method belongs to the prophets and the saints.[213]

This looks like a textbook example of a teleological argument, which as al-Kharpūtī himself goes on to elaborate, draws closely on Qur'anic material. But the argument in this passage goes beyond a paraphrase of the Qur'an. His discussion of natural phenomena suggests a familiarity with scientific discussions, and so it is not surprising that he wrote an article in Ottoman Turkish reconciling scripture and astronomical findings.[214] Moreover, the passage may be better classified as what Alvin Plantinga calls a 'design discourse', which consists of looking at something and, by a kind of perception, not inference, forming the belief that it is designed.[215] The author, like other proponents of *kalām jadīd* at the beginning of the twentieth century, was interested in a return to theological argument unencumbered by late classical epistemological baggage. His focus on reflective conscious knowledge as the basis for human perfection, as well as the natural state (*fiṭra*) and the wise order of the world as proofs for their creator, touches on themes familiar from al-Māturīdī's *Kitāb al-tawḥīd.*[216]

These early notable attempts to articulate a *kalām jadīd* within major Muslim intellectual contexts tied to the Māturīdī tradition have given way at the end of the twentieth and beginning of the twenty-first century to a new era of studies within the modern university. The theology of al-Māturīdī

213 Al-Kharpūtī, *Tanqiḥ al-kalām fī ʿaqāʾid ahl al-islām*, p. 63.

214 Özervarli, 'Attempts to Revitalize *Kalām* in the Late 19th and Early 20th Centuries', p. 94.

215 Plantinga, *Where the Conflict Really Lies*, p. 245.

216 See pages 119–20.

has become an important touchstone in contemporary Turkish scholarship, with both the school legacy and his personal authority deployed as part of a resurgent Islamic national identity. Moreover, there has been a widespread tendency to claim him as ethnically Turkic.[217] Whereas a group of scholars working under the late Bekir Topaloğlu at Marmara University have been instrumental in publishing definitive editions of al-Māturīdī's two surviving texts and shedding light on their difficult phrasing, others, such as Sönmez Kutlu and Hanifi Özcan, have worked to articulate contemporary theological positions.[218] In Anglophone Western scholarship, there has been a more tentative movement towards a resurgent Māturīdī theology. The most important figure is the prominent Bosniak imam Mustafa Cerić who, in his *Roots of Synthetic Theology in Islam* (1995), provides a reading of important themes in al-Māturīdī's *Kitāb al-tawḥīd*, while highlighting the suitability of al-Māturīdī's work for further modern theological engagement.[219]

The present book can be placed within the same trajectory of thought, though I draw from a wider range of philosophical influences in both attempting to show their relevance to a Māturīdī *kalām jadīd* and its contribution to broader academic discussions. The task remaining in this chapter is to provide an overview of modern philosophers who are most significant to this work. This will allow me to provide a more rigorous theoretical grounding for the notion of tradition that I am utilising in my efforts to synthesise Māturīdī *kalām* with the conceptual tools of the philosophy and theology of the present age.

IV. Tradition and Reason in Contemporary Thought

Of all the European philosophers who broke with the Christian scholastic theologians in forming modern Western thought, Immanuel Kant (d. 1804) casts the longest shadow. Though frustrated by the initial lukewarm reception of his magnum opus, the *Critique of Pure Reason*,[220] he was well aware of the radical power of his ideas, comparing his project to that of Copernicus who 'tried to see whether he might not have greater success by making the spectator revolve and leaving the stars at rest'.[221] The key

217 Dorroll, *Modern by Tradition*, pp. 218–20.
218 Dorroll, *Modern by Tradition*, pp. 229–32.
219 Cerić, *Roots of Synthetic Theology in Islam*, pp. 234–35. Also see Chapter 2 of Harvey, *The Qur'an and the Just Society*. Scholars such as Pessagno and Rudolph, despite the importance of their contributions, do not situate their work within the Māturīdī theological tradition.
220 Kant, *Critique of Pure Reason*, p. xxvii.
221 Kant, *Critique of Pure Reason*, p. 18.

Kantian insight is that *a priori* categories of thought set the preconditions by which each phenomenon, or object of possible experience, is constituted for the human subject.[222] In raising the question of whether it was possible for human knowledge to move from the level of the phenomenon to the noumenon, or thing-in-itself, Kant set much of the agenda for debates about the place of reason until today.[223]

One of the most important figures to respond to Kant's ideas is Edmund Husserl who was not only a first-rate philosopher of mathematics and logic, but also the founder of phenomenology. Husserl uses the Greek term *epochē* to refer to a bracketing process central to what he calls the phenomenological reduction, whereby metaphysical assumptions about the nature of noumenal reality are set aside in order to know the phenomenal world and the categories of mind that constitute it.[224] His debt to Kant on this point should be obvious. In his mature thought, he argues that there is no hidden noumenal reality behind the objects of possible experience. Husserl's deployment of intentionality, a concept he adapted from Bernard Bolzano (d. 1848), makes the phenomenal world one of human-directed meanings. To ask about the thing-in-itself outside of any conceivable phenomenological awareness is to commit the naturalist fallacy and become incoherent. This is because he defines truth through verification, and noumena are, by definition, non-verifiable.[225]

Husserl sees the world as intersubjective, meaning that, despite the importance of the phenomenological first-person perspective, it is conceived as a shared reality that is mutually constituted.[226] Here he introduces the notion of the life-world, his concept for the everyday context within which the human experience is constantly enveloped and from which all theoretical enquiry must inevitably emerge. Thus, he takes Kant to task for not questioning his presupposition of the very world in which he lives.[227] He gives the example of Einstein's use of previous experiments, including their human investigator, apparatus and room, in an ordinary prescientific way, which presupposes the life-world of common experience.[228] But the assumed nature of the life-world can lead to what Husserl calls traditionalisation or sedimentation, the closing off of meaning through the constant presupposition of 'constructions, concepts, propositions, theories'.[229]

222 Kant, *Critique of Pure Reason*, pp. 166–67.
223 See Kant, *Critique of Pure Reason*, p. 261, 452–53.
224 See Moran and Cohen, *The Husserl Dictionary*, pp. 106–11.
225 There is further discussion of these points in Chapter 2.
226 See MacIntyre, *Edith Stein*, p. 20.
227 Husserl, *Crisis*, p. 104.
228 Husserl, *Crisis*, pp. 125–26.
229 Husserl, *Crisis*, p. 52.

The centrality of Husserl to my theological project in the present book will become clear in the chapters to come. I use his insights about the structure of ideal consciousness to broach a conversation with the Māturīdī *kalām* tradition that provides important conceptual resources for its contemporary articulation.[230] Furthermore, as Husserl's thought encompasses both the formal rigour and logical concerns of analytic philosophy and the phenomenological life-world of continental philosophy, I see him as a key figure in the much-needed rapprochement between the two trends.

Phenomenological ideas relevant to the concerns of this book are further extended by Hans-Georg Gadamer, who in his *Truth and Method* (1960) focuses on hermeneutics. His investigation of the reason-tradition binary in Western aesthetics and (theological) hermeneutics has the aim, no less, of formulating a general theory of understanding grounded within contingent history. Returning to Kant, he argues that the effect of another major work, the *Critique of the Power of Judgement*, was to limit the concept of knowledge to that of reason in its theoretical and practical dimensions.[231] The only model of enquiry – 'method' – becomes that of the natural sciences, which is used to conceptualise the human ones, making it impossible to acknowledge the 'truth claim of traditionary materials'.[232] Gadamer challenges the position that truth is only found in conceptual knowledge, by using the obvious case of the experience of art, which can be conceivably extended to scripture. He shows that there needs to be a way for the human sciences to transcend their conceptual self-awareness and take account of their being, or facticity. It is here that he brings in the philosophical contribution of Husserl's star student, Martin Heidegger, as a model that allows him to interrogate the being of historical understanding, applying it to hermeneutics.[233] On Gadamer's reading, Heidegger's return to the ancient Greek debate on the status of being develops a 'teleology in reverse', looking backwards to contingent human history.[234] This implies that human understanding necessarily happens within a tradition regardless of its particular content.[235] Gadamer extends this point to challenge the Enlightenment's rejection of tradition-based 'prejudice' and 'authority'. The rejection of all prejudice is itself the greatest prejudice,[236] and hence the reality of human standing within traditions must be properly acknowledged. Therefore the

230 See pages 63–65.
231 Gadamer, *Truth and Method*, p. 37.
232 Gadamer, *Truth and Method*, p. 38.
233 Gadamer, *Truth and Method*, pp. 90–91.
234 Gadamer, *Truth and Method*, p. 257. See Knight, 'After Tradition?', pp. 33–34.
235 Gadamer, *Truth and Method*, p. 264.
236 Gadamer, *Truth and Method*, p. 283.

reason-tradition binary is illusionary: all reason is grounded in tradition, and all tradition is grounded in reason.[237]

This way of theorising tradition has been considerably extended by Alasdair MacIntyre.[238] Building on Gadamer's work, as well as the idea of paradigms developed by Thomas Kuhn,[239] he shifts the ground from hermeneutics to systematic intellectual investigation in general, through his notion of a 'tradition of enquiry'. This is a body of discursive activity that rationally justifies and develops the beliefs and normative practices institutionalised within human society.[240] Such traditions progress via rational deliberation using criteria embedded within their own historical contingency.

MacIntyre's fidelity to the central Heideggerian-Gadamerian ontological insight is demonstrated by his position that advanced human reasoning only ever happens from the grounded perspective of one tradition or another.[241] He makes this point in a particularly audacious way after over one hundred pages of apparently neutral discussion of the positions of 'encyclopaedic' Enlightenment rationality and various other perspectives in his *Three Rival Versions of Moral Enquiry*:

> It is at this point in the argument that it becomes evident that in characterizing the variety of standpoints with which I have been and will be concerned, I too must have been and will be speaking as a partisan. The neutrality of the academic is itself a fiction of the encyclopaedist, and I reveal my antiencyclopaedic partisanship by calling it a fiction. It is not that the adherent of one particular standpoint

237 Gadamer, *Truth and Method*, p. 293.

238 This has also been taken in an anthropological direction by Talal Asad with his idea of a 'discursive tradition'. Nevertheless, I find MacIntyre's concerns to be more suitable for the type of philosophical theology with which I am engaged. See Asad, 'The Idea of an Anthropology of Islam', pp. 19–24.

239 See his comments in MacIntyre, *The Tasks of Philosophy*, pp. vii–viii. MacIntyre's debt to Kuhn's concept of scientific paradigm shifts in formulating his own theory of tradition-constituted enquiry is particularly obvious in his example of Galileo versus Aristotelian representatives of the late medieval impetus theory. See MacIntyre, *Three Rival Versions of Moral Enquiry*, pp. 118–20; Kuhn, *The Structure of Scientific Revolutions*, pp. 123–25. He critiques and reformulates Kuhn's ideas in MacIntyre, 'Epistemological Crises, Dramatic Narrative and the Philosophy of Science', pp. 463–71.

240 MacIntyre, 'Practical Rationalities as Forms of Social Structure', pp. 120–21. See also Trenery, *Alasdair MacIntyre, George Lindbeck, and the Nature of Tradition*, pp. 184–85.

241 MacIntyre, 'On Not Having the Last Word', p. 158. This view has been challenged by critics, but coherently defended by MacIntyre. See Harvey, 'Whose Justice? When Māturīdī Meets MacIntyre' (forthcoming). Compare with Kuhn's statement: 'Once it has achieved the status of paradigm, a scientific theory is declared invalid only if an alternate candidate is available to take its place.' Kuhn, *The Structure of Scientific Revolution*, p. 77.

> cannot on occasion understand some rival point of view both intellectually and imaginatively, in such a way and to such a degree that he or she is able to provide a presentation of it of just the kind that one of its own adherents would give. It is that even in so doing the mode of presentation will inescapably be framed within and directed by the beliefs and purposes of one's own point of view.[242]

MacIntyre does not hold that anyone can start enquiry from whatever assumptions they prefer, but contends that one is always already circumscribed by certain linguistic and social particularities.[243] Within such a model, starting from the authority of religious scripture is not problematic, as long as it is acknowledged that the justificatory and interpretive frameworks of the rational appeal to divine communication are open to revision.[244] The beliefs and practices that survive through the process of tradition-constituted enquiry described by MacIntyre are not vindicated by their grounding in publicly available certainties, but by their survival over time as the best rational formulations available, according to the most suitable methods for developing them.[245]

MacIntyre informally outlines six stages, the first three necessary to be considered a tradition properly speaking, the second three representing its mature development. These can be summarised as follows:[246]

1. Authority – grounded in natural or revealed beliefs, institutions and practices.
2. Questioning – generated by internal interpretation or external ideas and circumstances.
3. Reformulation – responding to these questions.
4. Verification – continually subjecting these reformulations to dialectical challenge.
5. Methodology – institutionalising these practices of enquiry.
6. Theory – a meta-account of tradition-constituted enquiry, such as that provided by MacIntyre himself.

MacIntyre's theory for the justification of knowledge stands decisively against both foundationalism that seeks epistemic grounding in indubitable truths

242 MacIntyre, *Three Rival Versions of Moral Enquiry*, p. 117.

243 MacIntyre, *Whose Justice? Which Rationality?*, pp. 360–61.

244 MacIntyre, *Whose Justice? Which Rationality?*, p. 355.

245 MacIntyre, *Whose Justice? Which Rationality?*, p. 360; MacIntyre, *Three Rival Versions of Moral Enquiry*, p. 116.

246 MacIntyre, *Whose Justice? Which Rationality?*, pp. 354–55, 358–59; MacIntyre, *Three Rival Versions of Moral Enquiry*, p. 116. See Harvey, 'Whose Justice? When Māturīdī Meets MacIntyre' (forthcoming).

and coherentism that looks to the coherence of a given set of beliefs. His achievement is to unite the phenomenological insight of historical particularity with the analytic focus on logical consistency,[247] thus producing a model for enquiry that can be adapted for use by varied traditions of thought. The major criticism levelled at his approach is relativism with respect to truth. But it seems that, by distinguishing truth from its systematic justification, he is able to successfully counter the charge, even if it is possible that rival traditions are left in a position of intractable dispute due to incommensurable standards of rationality.[248]

MacIntyre's tradition-constituted enquiry is more theoretically thoroughgoing than either Wolterstorff's notion of dialogic pluralism,[249] or al-Māturīdī's undeveloped acknowledgement of an ineliminable tradition-grounded intellectual starting point,[250] although it does not necessarily conflict with either position. For the purposes of this book, the conception of my project as an extension of a historically constituted Muslim theological tradition makes it natural to look towards thinkers who appreciate such contingency. Moreover, I see my work as equally in the tradition of 'Western' philosophy, a reflection both of my personal history and intellectual context. More pragmatically, this book's genesis is in an extension of certain concerns from *The Qur'an and the Just Society*, in which various ideas of MacIntyre, and to a lesser extent Gadamer, were behind the scenes, even if the nature of that work meant they were not ready to fully take the stage.

I therefore argue that, by adopting a MacIntyrean meta-theory, I marry my commitment to a Māturīdī theological stance with my appreciation of the tools of both analytic and continental philosophy. I acknowledge that the theological formulations of the Ḥanafī-Māturīdī tradition cannot be frozen at any stage in their history but must receive continual verification. One of the principal values of MacIntyre to this study is to challenge the rational frameworks of both *kalām* and contemporary philosophy to justify their validity and usefulness. The theoretical and methodological opportunities that contemporary thought, especially Husserl and analytic philosophy of religion, offer to rationally explicate truth from an Islamic perspective should not be squandered for dogmatic reasons.

The broad shape of the constructive argument so far has been an attempt to undercut the epistemology of classical *kalām* foundationalism. I have

247 See Trenery, *Alasdair MacIntyre, George Lindbeck, and the Nature of Tradition*, p. 129.
248 See the discussion in Harvey, 'Whose Justice? When Māturīdī Meets MacIntyre' (forthcoming).
249 See page 4.
250 See pages 14–17.

suggested that an implicit orientation within al-Māturīdī's *Kitāb al-tawḥīd* can be theoretically extended by the MacIntyrean notion of tradition-constituted enquiry. This means that the embedding of theological discourse within traditions of thought must be presupposed. Yet acknowledging this grounding does not hinder the development of a systematic theology. That is the project to which I now turn.

CHAPTER 2

Rational Reality

The theist affirms that God's nature precedes the created world, which in turn underlies their own personal existence and ability to form concepts.[1] Nevertheless, when embarking on a discursive investigation in philosophical theology, the direction is reversed: concepts describe the human experience of the world and indicate the nature of God.[2] That a conception of the divine – specifically the personal God who speaks in the Qur'an – can be aimed towards as the *telos* of enquiry reflects the basic grounding in tradition that al-Māturīdī refers to as *samʿ*.[3] Without this starting point, the philosopher would not be a theologian and would not know in which direction to set out. With it, one becomes able to continually refine the adequacy of their conceptions in correspondence to the nature of the world and ultimately God.[4] A similar idea is expressed by the Christian phrase 'faith seeking understanding'.[5]

The postulate that the universe possesses a rational structure comprehensible to human thought goes at least as far back as the Greek philosophical concept of *logos*.[6] One of the earliest philosophers to discuss this idea was the pre-Socratic Heraclitus (d. *ca* 500 BCE). G. S. Kirk explains his development of it in the following words:

> [A]n *a priori* demand for an underlying unity in the world, together with a consideration of the regularity of large-scale natural changes,

1 See al-Māturīdī, *Kitāb al-tawḥīd*, p. 93. The discussion should not be framed according to what Husserl calls the 'natural attitude', the naïve assumption of an external world outside of potential phenomenological grasp, but by the life-world. See Husserl, *Ideas*, p. xxvii.

2 See Abdelsater, *Shiʿi Doctrine, Muʿtazili Theology*, p. 52.

3 See page 18.

4 Cf. MacIntyre, *Whose Justice? Which Rationality?*, pp. 356–57.

5 See Migliore, *Faith Seeking Understanding*, p. 2. There is a lot to recommend the interpretation of this concept sketched in Alston, *Divine Nature and Human Language*, p. 8.

6 Cassin, *Dictionary of Untranslatables*, p. 585; Walbridge, *God and Logic in Islam*, p. 19.

> led him to 'distinguish each thing according to its constitution', and to find the universal formula operating in the behaviour of even the smallest objects.[7]

Dorroll has astutely drawn the connection between Heraclitus – whose idea of *logos* provides order, unity and wisdom to a chaotic, fluctuating world – and al-Māturīdī, who gives similar ideas a Qur'anic rationale with his notion of God's wisdom.[8] Not only does it explain why the world is rational, it also ensures – following Aristotle – that God is knowable through human concepts.[9] One of the most important modern philosophers to pick up on the idea of the rationality of reality and relate it to both knowledge of the world and of God is Husserl. He argues that there is no reason to expect the world to exhibit the rational consistency that it does, stating, as quoted in the epigraph to this book, 'since *the rationality* which the fact-world shows is not in any sense such as the essence demands, there lies concealed in all this a wonderful *teleology*'.[10]

The application of Husserlian insights to Islam has a precedent in Muslim scholarship, notably in the work of Hassan Hanafi who even goes as far as to write: 'The Qur'an sometimes uses a language that sounds as if it may have been written by Husserl himself'.[11] The centrality of Husserl in the

7 Heraclitus, *The Cosmic Fragments*, p. 43.

8 Dorroll, *Modern by Tradition*, pp. 110–11. See Harvey, *The Qur'an and the Just Society*, pp. 28–29. Also see page 63. Refer to Chapter 5 for a more detailed investigation into this divine attribute.

9 See Walbridge, *God and Logic in Islam*, p. 76.

10 Husserl, *Ideas*, pp. 112–13. See Bello, *The Divine in Husserl*, pp. 25–26. A concept of the rationality of the world can also be reached via the Christian *imago dei* (image of God), drawing from Genesis 1:27 in which God made Adam in His image. The idea is not found in the Qur'an but does appear in the Hadith literature on the authority of Abū Hurayra: 'God created Adam in His image (*khalaqa allahu ādama ʿalā ṣūratihi*)'. Al-Bukhārī, *Ṣaḥīḥ*, vol. 3, pp. 1267–68. This provoked theological controversy among those opposed to anthropomorphism and was either read allegorically or unconvincingly as 'in [Adam's] image'. See Melchert, 'God Created Adam in His Image', pp. 118–19. To me, this hadith – like other reports of Abū Hurayra on similar themes – appears to have its origin in lore gathered by early Muslims from Jewish and Christian converts and contacts. Aquinas does not interpret the *imago dei* as an anthropomorphic concept, but primarily as the human capacity for knowledge, which in some sense is akin to that of God. See Dauphinais, 'Loving the Lord Your God', p. 251. In this respect it bears comparison to al-Māturīdī's idea that God's attributes can be understood analogically with those of humanity. See pages 144–45. Hassan Hanafi writes, 'If the person is the image of God, then God is the person endlessly remote'. Hanafi, *Taʾwīl al-ẓāhiriyyāt*, p. 393.

11 Hanafi, 'Phenomenology and Islamic Philosophy', p. 319. Hanafi wrote a doctoral dissertation at the Sorbonne in the 1960s, titled *L'exegèse de la phénoménologie* in which he used a Husserlian phenomenological method to reconstruct classical Islamic disciplines. Hanafi, 'Phenomenology and Islamic Philosophy', p. 320. In this book, I reference his own more recent Arabic translation titled *Taʾwīl al-ẓāhiriyyāt*.

genealogy of the modern thought that I engage in this book, as well as his emphasis on the rationality of the world, which he shares with al-Māturīdī, puts him centre stage in my attempt to bridge the divide between *kalām* and contemporary philosophy. Both al-Māturīdī and Husserl attempt to articulate comprehensive and original systems with which to explain reality. I have already commented on the extent to which al-Māturīdī builds on an Aristotelian-Neoplatonic framework. Likewise, Husserl, in the words of Leo Strauss, sees 'with incomparable clarity that the restoration of philosophy or science – because he denies that that which today passes as science is genuine science – presupposes the restoration of the Platonic-Aristotelian level of questioning'.[12]

Take an apple. It has a certain roughly spherical shape, a green colour, smooth texture, sweet taste and so on. This is the level of analysis at which we can recognise and describe the concrete particular as an apple. The phenomenological insight is that this description of the object is not reducible to an allegedly more real quantitative level of analysis. We may indeed provide more technical descriptions of its various properties, its exact dimensions, mass, density and so on, but they are yet new varieties of phenomenological analysis that use instruments to enhance our human faculties. This is shown by what happens when we dig down to the deepest measurement of its subatomic structure and replace it with pure symbol. We find, according to the Copenhagen interpretation of quantum mechanics, that this description cannot be divorced from our conscious choices in measurement.[13] Ultimately, it seems that the properties of a concrete particular cannot be assayed without deciding at what level our minds are to constitute it as an object of knowledge.[14] Despite the wondrous power of scientific analysis, we are back, in one sense, at the level of the everyday in thinking about the nature of reality and hence philosophical (not physical) arguments about its constituents.

To proceed in my enquiry, I will take inspiration from Husserl in discussing rationality within a series of levels, each transcended by the one in which it is enveloped. Husserl argues that his method of the *epoché* allows him to bracket the question of the transcendence of God, so that he reaches his position of transcendental phenomenology on rational grounds alone.[15] But despite this procedure, he acknowledges a 'divine' Being beyond the world:

12 Emberley and Cooper, *Faith and Political Philosophy*, p. 17.

13 See pages 67–69.

14 See Barrett, review of *The Wave Function: Essays on the Metaphysics of Quantum Mechanics*, by Alyssa Ney and David Z. Albert (eds.). Also, consider the description of analysis as the function of science in Bergson, *An Introduction to Metaphysics*, pp. 7–9.

15 Husserl, *Ideas*, pp. 112–13.

> [This] existence should not only transcend the world, but obviously also the 'absolute' Consciousness. It would thus be an 'Absolute' in a totally different sense from the Absolute of Consciousness, as on the other hand it would be a transcendent in a totally different sense from the transcendent in the sense of the world.[16]

For Husserl, the essential rationality of the universe is what allows the pure 'I' of human consciousness to both transcend itself in moving outwards towards the world in its intentional constitution of 'things' and be transcended by the world, which grounds it as the ontological basis of what it verifies. Finally, God transcends both self and world in a different, absolute way.[17]

The structure of the present chapter reflects this 'moving outwards' in crucial respects. Section I discusses in more detail the theological and philosophical relationship between the mind, the world and God, including some consideration of the philosophical interpretation of quantum mechanics. Section II discusses ideas of essence and existence, proposing a conception of truth to act as the basis for logic, and provides the language for an appeal to set theory as a scheme of mental structure, or formal ontology. Section III articulates a corresponding structure for objects in the world, or material ontology.[18] Each section interweaves a reading of al-Māturīdī's theology with constructive argument.

I. The Mind, the World and God

The rationality of the world is the basic presupposition for an important principle within the *kalām* tradition known as *qiyās al-ghāʾib ʿalā al-shāhid* (the veiled is analogous to the manifest). Theologians use it to assert that human knowledge of the world can lead to valid inferences about God.[19] Al-Māturīdī dedicates a short section in *Kitāb al-tawḥīd* to discuss this principle, which he calls *dalālat al-shāhid ʿalā al-ghāʾib* (the manifest indicates the veiled).[20] His terminological expression underscores

16 Husserl, *Ideas*, pp. 113.

17 Husserl, *Ideas*, pp. 113, 98–99. This follows the interpretation in Bello, *The Divine in Husserl*, pp. 25–27.

18 See Smith, '"Pure" Logic, Ontology, and Phenomenology', p. 141.

19 Van Ess points out that dialectical thought has a characteristic predilection for analogy. See van Ess, 'Disputationspraxis in der islamischen Theologie', p. 930. For relevant brief comments on the use of analogy by al-Jubbāʾī (d. 303/915–16) and his erstwhile student al-Ashʿarī, see Frank, 'The Kalām, an Art of Contradiction-Making or Theological Science? Some Remarks on the Question', p. 297, n. 4.

20 Al-Māturīdī, *Kitāb al-tawḥīd*, p. 92. This principle has been previously analysed by Cerić and Rudolph. See Cerić, *Roots of Synthetic Theology in Islam*, pp. 102–5; Rudolph, *Al-Māturīdī and the Development of Sunnī Theology*, pp. 266–68.

his modification of the earlier philosophical formulation of this idea. The *falāsifa* (philosophers) followed Aristotle in asserting the eternality of the world and drew a likeness between what is visible and veiled that extends to its howness (*kayfiyya*) and whatness (*mā ʾiyya*).[21] Such a viewpoint, al-Māturīdī argues, makes the visible world the foundation (*aṣl*) and the veiled realm its derivative (*far ʿ*); yet he avers, this is the wrong way around. The world that we know is grounded in the divine reality, which makes it possible to use indications from the former to understand the latter.[22] Al-Māturīdī allows his process of *dalāla* (indication) to work in two modes, analogy (*mithl*) and transcendence (*khilāf*), of which he considers transcendence to be the clearer (*awḍaḥ*) of the two.[23]

Al-Māturīdī denies that there can be a complete match between the manifest and the veiled in analogical inference. This relates to a wider theme in his epistemological system: that the human being is unable to grasp all aspects of the world simultaneously.[24] As will be discussed in the next section, when it comes to the elaboration of God and His attributes, analogy allows particular existence, or isness, to be affirmed,

21 This position is rebutted in al-Māturīdī, *Kitāb al-tawḥīd*, p. 93, and the identification of the opponents is made in Cerić, *Roots of Synthetic Theology in Islam*, pp. 103–4. Although essence is arguably a valid translation for *mā ʾiyya*, I have found that al-Māturīdī's pre-Avicennan usage combined with the common rendering of the distinct concept *dhāt* as essence makes the word opaque. I judge that the literal term 'whatness', albeit clumsy, better illuminates the meaning. See Cassin, *Dictionary of Untranslatables*, p. 1137. While the problem is less acute, I think howness also gives more clarity to *kayfiyya* than more refined alternatives, such as modality. Al-Māturīdī mentions *mā ʾiyya* far more often than *kayfiyya*, including in contexts in which al-Ashʿarī uses the latter term. Also, see Frank, 'Elements in the Development of the Teaching of al-Ashʿarī', p. 156, n. 35. I discuss al-Māturīdī's approach to *mā ʾiyya* in detail on pages 73 and 75–76.

22 Al-Māturīdī, *Kitāb al-tawḥīd*, pp. 92–93. He may also be subtly critiquing the Muʿtazila for using a human scale of ethical values to judge the actions of God. See Rudolph, *Al-Māturīdī and the Development of Sunnī Theology*, p. 267. See page 163.

23 Al-Māturīdī, *Kitāb al-tawḥīd*, p. 92. The concepts of *mithl* and *khilāf* have an interesting similarity to the two types of *anumāna* (inference) in Hindu philosophy and the two kinds of *sēmion* (sign or signal), known as *hypomnestika* (commemorative) and *endeiktika* (indicative), in Stoic thought. See Pines, 'A Study of the Impact of Indian, mainly Buddhist, Thought on Some Aspects of Kalām Doctrines', pp. 5–7. Pines did not make this connection with respect to al-Māturūdī, despite discussing other terms in his epistemology on pp. 12–14. Identifying these concepts within al-Māturīdī's system provides a solution to a puzzle set by van Ess, who named them as one of the few aspects of Stoic philosophy to which he could not find parallels within *kalām*. Van Ess, 'The Logical Structure of Islamic Theology', pp. 33–34.

24 Al-Māturīdī, *Kitāb al-tawḥīd*, p. 224. See Dorroll, 'The Universe in Flux', pp. 129–32. This idea has striking similarities to the Heisenberg uncertainty principle and more broadly Bohr's idea of complementarity. See pages 67–69. Also, see the concept of noematic and noetic multiplicities in Husserl, *Ideas*, pp. 209–10.

but not whatness.[25] In other cases of unknown things (in the world or perhaps relating to the Hereafter), al-Māturīdī accepts that if one knows the howness of the witnessed thing and has been informed about it with respect to the veiled one, it is possible to make an inference based on this aspect.[26] He gives the examples of fire and body, in which a person may extend their knowledge from perceived to unperceived instances.[27]

This side to al-Māturīdī's theology would seem to belong to the class of inductive inferences that reason from the observed to the unobserved. If this is the case, it would fall under the 'problem of induction', famously formulated by David Hume, which contends that induction lacks justified grounds. This potential flaw in al-Māturīdī's system has been pointed out by Dorroll who suggests that he does not address the difficulty in drawing general conclusions from the particular data of experience.[28] The main thrust of Hume's contention is that arguments require justification via *a priori* or *a posteriori* evidence, but neither is able to support the assumption of a fundamental regularity to the world needed by inductive inference. This regularity can be called the Uniformity Principle (UP). A summarised modern reconstruction of Hume's argument is as follows:[29]

25 Compare with Ibn Taymiyya, who rejects the principle of *qiyās al-ghāʾib ʿalā al-shāhid* as used in analogical reasoning for the existence of things (*thubūt*), their reality (*ḥaqīqa*) and howness (*kayfiyya*). Thus, he only accepts revealed reports or sense data as means for knowing them. See El-Tobgui, *Ibn Taymiyya on Reason and Revelation*, pp. 278–80. Although there are terminological and conceptual distinctions in Ibn Taymiyya's system that cannot be engaged here, it would seem that the most important difference between the two thinkers on this point is that al-Māturīdī allows inference from the world to establish the existence of God and His attributes. This leads al-Māturīdī to an analogical theory of reference, in which properties of the world can be used to reason about the attributes of God, as opposed to Ibn Taymiyya's univocal theory by which only the language of revelation can refer to them (according to common linguistic usage) but cannot be the basis for further inference. See El-Tobgui, *Ibn Taymiyya on Reason and Revelation*, p. 192. Also see pages 144–45.

26 Al-Māturīdī's sentence 'you are informed about this howness with respect to the hidden world (*wa-ukhbirta bi-tilka al-kayfiyyati li-ghāʾib*)' presumably can refer to information that comes from a revealed source. Al-Māturīdī, *Kitāb al-tawḥīd*, p. 93. On this point with respect to analogy, see Hall, *Knowledge, Belief, and Transcendence*, pp. 119–20. See page 145.

27 Al-Māturīdī, *Kitāb al-tawḥīd*, p. 93. Although there is no hint of an intentional link in the text, the examples chosen thematically reflect the polemics of al-Māturīdī's age, in which the resurrection of bodies and therefore the literal fire of Hell were understood to be rejected by the same class of *falāsifa* who argued for the eternality of the world. See Genequand, 'Metaphysics', p. 797.

28 Dorroll, *Modern by Tradition*, pp. 113–15. As van Ess comments, a purely empiricist approach cannot reason to God from the functioning of nature. Van Ess, '60 Years After', p. 12.

29 This argument is adapted from Henderson, 'The Problem of Induction'.

P1. All arguments are justified on either an *a priori* or *a posteriori* basis (known as Hume's fork).
P2. The inductive inference is based on UP.
P3. UP cannot be known by the necessary (analytic) relations between ideas.
C1. UP cannot be justified on an *a priori* basis (from P3).
P4. Knowledge of UP through empirical experience presupposes UP.[30]
C2. UP cannot be justified on an *a posteriori* basis (from P4).
C3. As UP cannot be justified, neither can the inductive inference (from P1, P2, C1 and C2).

One of the first, and arguably most effective, attempts to counter this argument was made by Kant. He focused his attention on P3 and proposed that the human mind has basic categories through which experience is always filtered, including the presupposition of the world's fundamental regularity in cause and effect. He thus argued that there exists a synthetic *a priori* principle that justifies UP and hence induction.[31] Al-Māturīdī draws a similar distinction when he writes:

> Each thing that is existent on the basis of another, according to rationality (*ʿalā ṭarīqat al-ʿaql*), is external from the substance of [the other] in the visible world; such as building, writing and every kind of action and statement that is other than that [thing] due to which it exists. It is not conceivable that [reason] encloses them within the substance and quality [of their causes].[32]

Al-Māturīdī argues that reason organises experience in such a way as to distinguish between the respective substances of causes and their effects.[33]

30 In other words, experience cannot be used to justify the regularity found within experience without circularity. See Russell, *History of Western Philosophy*, p. 647.

31 De Pierris and Friedman, 'Kant and Hume on Causality'. See Kant, *Critique of Pure Reason*, pp. 116–17. W. V. Quine influentially criticised the analytic-synthetic distinction in his 1951 article 'Two Dogmas of Empiricism', leading many to abandon it. As powerfully argued by Robert Hanna, he did not refute the distinction, and thus it remains philosophically crucial. See Hanna, *Cognition, Content, and the A Priori*, pp. 153–77. Quentin Meillassoux attempts to undermine Kant's argument for the necessity of UP by showing that it is based on an invalid inference that, 'if it were possible for natural laws to change without reason, they would do so frequently'. Meillassoux, *After Finitude*, p. 94. This fails to address Kant's own main arguments for the necessity of UP in the possibility of experience. In his Transcendental Deduction, Kant argues that aspects of our experience such as causation only arise due to a type of mental processing, 'synthesis', and that this must be predicated on the necessity of the categories. See Pereboom, 'Kant's Transcendental Arguments'.

32 Al-Māturīdī, *Kitāb al-tawḥīd*, p. 93.

33 Al-Māturīdī's similarity to Kant in the joint role of sense and reason for knowing the world is noted in Özcan, *Matüridi'de Bilgi Problemi*, pp. 67–68.

His introduction of its ability to filter the temporal flux of particulars in the world is situated within discussion of his second class of indicants, those characterised by *khilāf*, or transcendence, between the two realms of knowledge.

Still in polemical dispute with those who profess the eternality of the world, he argues that the difference between things is what points to their temporality and their causes differing from their effects.[34] As in the case of *mithl*, or analogy, only a single aspect of a cause can be inferred from its effect: 'Therefore, writing points towards a writer but not to its howness or analogue: it is not permissible to [determine whether] it is an angel, a human being or a jinn'.[35] Al-Māturīdī does accept that different aspects allow separate inferences to the veiled realm, which he emphasises in reasoning about God. His is the wise intelligence that has provided human beings with the tools to read the relevant signs in the worldly phenomena of which He is the source, and to which He is profoundly different.[36] Al-Māturīdī summarises this point as follows:

> The foundational principle is that the indication of the world is in conflict based on its different aspects: its possibility of change, its cessation, and combination of opposites in a particular thing and state point to its temporality. Then [the world's] ignorance about its foundation and its incapacity to rectify its corruption indicate that it is not self-sufficient. Its gathering of opposite states and knitting together the substances of creation into order indicates that the arranger and originator of everything is one. Also, the knitting together, ordering and preserving the opposites in a substance points to the power, wisdom and knowledge of its arranger.[37]

In contrast to al-Māturīdī, Kant rejects cosmological and teleological arguments for the existence of God (he also rejects ontological arguments, which al-Māturīdī does not make). An assessment of al-Māturīdī's natural theology and its validity in contemporary post-Kantian philosophy will be presented in Chapter 3. For now, it is more important to address the objection that arises when proposing that phenomenal reality is approached

34 Al-Māturīdī, *Kitāb al-tawḥīd*, p. 93.

35 Al-Māturīdī, *Kitāb al-tawḥīd*, p. 93. See also Rudolph, *Al-Māturīdī and the Development of Sunnī Theology*, p. 268.

36 Al-Māturīdī, *Kitāb al-tawḥīd*, p. 94. The idea is summarised in al-Bazdawī, *Uṣūl al-dīn*, p. 20. Also see Daccache, *Le Problème de la Création du Monde*, pp. 172–73; van Ess, 'The Logical Structure of Islamic Theology', p. 27. Refer to the discussion of reasoning to the infinite from the finite on pages 85–86 and in the context of the cosmological argument on page 107.

37 Al-Māturīdī, *Kitāb al-tawḥīd*, p. 94.

through mental categories: do we arrive at an idealism for which the true nature of the world is unknowable, as Kant arguably held with his concept of noumena?[38]

A potential way to answer this concern is creative appropriation of Husserl's phenomenological stance. Like Kant, Husserl at times uses the term transcendental idealism, sharing with him the focus on consciousness as constitutive of the experienced world, although differing in the method by which it is secured.[39] But he thinks reality must be open to verification, so that there cannot be a mind-independent noumenal world to which we lack access.[40] He argues that things that the mind cannot grasp in principle (even if they are never actually known)[41] are by definition non-verifiable and therefore absurd.[42] David Woodruff Smith calls this position 'universal experienceability'.[43] Through such a move, Husserl rejects the Kantian level of noumena and makes phenomena the whole of worldly reality. This does not mean that Husserl sees the world as merely a phenomenalist projection of mind. He states:

> Our phenomenological idealism does not deny the positive existence of the real world and of Nature – in the first place as though it held it to be an illusion. Its sole task and service is to clarify the meaning of this world, the precise sense in which everyone accepts it, and with undeniable right, as really existing.[44]

His principle of the phenomenological reduction leads him to at first bracket the 'natural attitude', or original phenomenal assumption of humankind, meaning that he proposes that one stands within it while suspending it to seek the basic structure of conscious experience.[45] He ultimately reaches what he terms pure consciousness, in a manner knowingly reminiscent of Descartes,[46] but his bracketing, rather than doubt, of reality makes it intentionally directed at the objects of the world. As Husserl puts it, 'the whole

38 Kant, *Critique of Pure Reason*, pp. 260–61.
39 Staiti and Clarke, 'Introduction', p. 3.
40 Zahavi, *Husserl's Legacy*, p. 69.
41 Husserl, *The Idea of Phenomenology*, pp. 20–21.
42 Husserl, *Ideas*, pp. 92–93. Al-Māturīdī appears to make a similar distinction when he states about the objects of God's knowledge, power and will that 'the times of the occurrence of these things are mentioned, as their pre-eternity cannot be conceived (*li-alā yutawahhama qidamu tilka al-ashyāʾ*)'. Al-Māturīdī, *Kitāb al-tawḥīd*, p. 111. See pages 126–27. Cf. Williams, *The Edge of Words*, p. 32.
43 Smith, *Husserl*, p. 167.
44 Husserl, *Ideas*, p. xlii.
45 Husserl, *Ideas*, pp. 55–60.
46 Husserl, *Cartesian Meditations*, pp. 5–6.

being of the world consists in a certain "meaning" which presupposes absolute consciousness as the field from which the meaning is derived'.[47] This leads him to Kant's insight of the fundamental categories of mind that structure experience; yet Husserl argues that, whereas Kant discarded the categorial as psychological, he acknowledges it as the ideal correlate to the material.[48] Thus, mind and world become mutually interdependent, such that truth is determined by the verified correlation that obtains between the two.[49] In the words of Robert Sokolowski, 'Consciousness necessarily demands the world as its correlative; this is as apodictic in phenomenology as the claim that the sense of the world requires consciousness as a correlative supplement to itself'.[50]

This interdependence is connected to Husserl's non-representational theory of intentionality: the subject does not look at images in the mind that represent mind-independent objects, but makes its intentional objects manifest as what they are.[51] Dan Zahavi argues that for Husserl a 'proper philosophical exploration of reality does not consist in inventorying the content of the universe, but in accounting for the conditions under which something can appear as real'.[52] As reality is a socially shared space, this takes account of the intersubjective meanings that can be expressed in language.[53] There must not just be a concern with human concept formation, but with concepts possible to grasp when formulated in language, which is a precondition for their expression to others. Husserl comments: 'so far as it is intersubjective, all the criticism from which the rationally true should emerge employs language and, in the end, leads always to statements'.[54]

Husserl here stresses that stating truth in propositional form only emerges as a response to the requirements of social discourse. Whether formulated verbally or in writing, the purpose of propositions is to convey meaning to others. Moreover, there exist certain discourses about which human beings value making truth claims, such as theology. The discursive history of *kalām* demonstrates that such propositions are translatable, in the sense that the key claims are usually understandable within different traditions of thought. But the ability of their representatives to rationally

47 Husserl, *Ideas*, p. 108.
48 See Husserl, *Ideas*, pp. 118–20. Smith is keen to defend Husserl's 'perspectivism', by which he means that consciousness of any given object must involve an intentional perspective on it. Smith, *Husserl*, p. 166.
49 Zahavi, *Husserl's Legacy*, pp. 84, 114.
50 Sokolowski, *The Formation of Husserl's Concept of Constitution*, p. 220.
51 Zahavi, *Husserl's Legacy*, p. 96.
52 Zahavi, *Husserl's Legacy*, p. 68.
53 Zahavi, *Husserl's Legacy*, p. 123.
54 Husserl, *Formal and Transcendental Logic*, p. 19. See also Zahavi, *Husserl's Legacy*, p. 21.

justify the truth of propositions is another question altogether, as mentioned in Chapter 1.[55]

The transcendental, or phenomenological, idealism that Husserl adopts may be understood as transcending the metaphysical realism-idealism dichotomy.[56] Realism, used here in the sense of physicalism, seeks to ground consciousness within matter, leading to the so-called 'hard problem' of consciousness. As pointed out by Bernardo Kastrup, a major contemporary proponent of idealism, this problem is conjured up by trying to explain what is qualitatively primary to our experience, consciousness, through the explanatory abstractions that populate our physical theories.[57] Kastrup's alternative is to explain the world as excitations within a single mind that through a process of disassociation appears to house a multitude of consciousnesses.[58] From the Husserlian point of view, both materiality and a single universal mind are inaccessible constructs. Our experience is that of one consciousness of many within a shared world, and so it is this intersubjective level that should be taken as metaphysically primary.[59]

Husserl's stance on the mind, which accepts but transcends the natural attitude, may evince incredulity. Arguably, however, such a reaction to his perspective reflects the modern phenomenon that Charles Taylor speaks of as the 'buffered self'. This is a self that approaches the world of objects as if insulated and detached from it in a way not necessarily felt by members of pre-enlightenment societies who had a more immersive, 'porous' experience. Taylor gives the example of the fear of demonic possession and the popular cure of beating the suffering host, in order to make the site uncomfortable for the evil spirit.[60] As Taylor points out, beliefs like this have become open to question today, not just because they are labelled as superstition, but due to a violation of the self. There is something obscene to the modern mind about a breakdown of its boundaries with the 'outside' world. But common-sense wisdom can also lag behind the contemporary state of scientific knowledge. While the naturalist assumption accords with classical Newtonian physics, it does not necessarily agree with the findings of quantum mechanics.

55 See page 54. Also see the detailed discussion in Harvey, 'Whose Justice? When Māturīdī Meets MacIntyre' (forthcoming).

56 Zahavi, *Husserl's Legacy*, p. 61.

57 Kastrup, *The Idea of the World*, p. 35.

58 See Kastrup, *The Idea of the World*, pp. 49–50, 63–71.

59 Zahavi, 'Husserl's Intersubjective Transformation of Transcendental Philosophy', pp. 235–36.

60 Taylor, *A Secular Age*, p. 35. I will not discuss the question of the belief in jinn possession within Islam, other than to note in passing that al-Māturīdī's student al-Rustughfanī declares its impossibility. See page 164, note 35.

On broaching this topic in the philosophy of science, I should note that, although contemporary physicists agree on the mathematical formalism that underpins the physical calculations of quantum mechanics, there is no consensus on its correct interpretation. A philosophical stance that draws its main support from any one such interpretation is in a weak position.[61] For this reason, none of the central theological arguments in this book rely on any specific interpretation of quantum mechanics. Nonetheless, I think it is valuable to show how theological conversation may engage and cohere with significant scientific findings; in this vein, I do indicate my philosophical preferences and make use of certain ideas for a few subsidiary arguments.[62]

Since early in the twentieth century, physicists have been aware that Newton's laws of motion break down at the smallest level of reality. A basic insight of quantum mechanics is that the dynamics of any system are unknown before they are measured. One of the most significant results is the uncertainty principle discovered by Werner Heisenberg in 1927, which further demonstrates that, unlike classical physics, both the position and velocity of any given subatomic particle cannot be known with certainty.[63] Heisenberg describes this as follows:

> It has been stated in the beginning that the Copenhagen interpretation of quantum theory starts with a paradox. It starts from the fact that we describe our experiments in the terms of classical physics and at the same time from the knowledge that these concepts do not fit nature accurately.[64]

The term 'Copenhagen interpretation' was coined by Heisenberg in the 1950s to express ideas worked out by physicists collaborating with the key figure Niels Bohr in Denmark thirty years earlier. It is increasingly recognised, however, that its invention was part of a rhetorical move to defend the distinct, yet similar, positions of Heisenberg, Bohr and others against alternative emerging interpretations of quantum mechanics.[65] I will treat Bohr's ideas in their own right and use the term Copenhagen interpretation to refer to the family of ideas developed by Bohr's students, which has been dominant in the field during the last century. My special focus on Bohr's epistemological interpretation is explained by my judgement that,

61 Pugliese, 'Quantum Mechanics and an Ontology of Intersubjectivity', pp. 333–34.

62 See Plantinga, *Where the Conflict Really Lies*, pp. 120–21.

63 Heisenberg, *Physics and Philosophy*, p. 85.

64 Heisenberg, *Physics and Philosophy*, p. 56.

65 Faye, 'Copenhagen Interpretation of Quantum Mechanics'. The two main contenders are the pilot-wave theory of David Bohm (anticipated by Louis de Broglie), and the many-worlds theory of Hugh Everett III.

in both its philosophical genealogy and substantive position, it is closest to Husserlian phenomenology.[66] But arguably this philosophical connection can be maintained even in the absence of Bohr's specific formulation. As Marc Pugliese has suggested, the undisputed mathematical and scientific facts of quantum mechanics reveal 'an ontology of intersubjectivity', which is based around subject-like activity and the relation between discrete events.[67]

Bohr's interpretation hinges on the principle that 'the mathematical formalism of quantum mechanics and electrodynamics merely offers rules of calculation for the deduction of expectations about observations obtained under well-defined experimental conditions specified by classical concepts'.[68] This means that quantum mechanics allows scientists to correctly describe the correlations of their conscious knowledge about the world, rather than the world in itself.[69] His insight is thus that quantum mechanics, like all physics, is context dependent, providing a symbolism that must be pegged to the phenomenological data of the world.[70]

Catherine Chevally argues that, in order to understand Bohr, it is necessary to situate him in the post-Kantian philosophical tradition. She reads Kant as proposing that human intuitive experience is split into two modes of presentation: schematic presentation occurs when the understanding applies its categories to whatever is presented in pure intuition, like mathematics, or empirical intuition, such as classical physics; symbolic presentation occurs when there is no direct intuition available, so that instead a symbol stands in its place. The symbolic presentation is then based on an analogy with schematic concepts.[71] For instance, we cannot directly intuit the concept of sovereignty via a schematism, but we can intuit the concept of a crown based on our experience. The analogy proceeds as follows: the schematic concept of a crown is to an actual crown as the symbolic concept of a crown is to sovereignty.[72]

Post-Kantian philosophers argue that purely symbolic thought, without reference to any schematic concept drawn from experience, should be considered part of intuition.[73] Husserl in particular highlights the notion of ideal meaning in his conception of a general 'theory of theories' that

66 See Lurçat, 'Understanding Quantum Mechanics with Bohr and Husserl, p. 231–34.

67 Pugliese, 'Quantum Mechanics and an Ontology of Intersubjectivity', pp. 334–37.

68 Bohr, *Essays 1958–1962*, p. 60.

69 Stapp, *Mindful Universe*, p. 11; Altaie, *God, Nature, and the Cause*, p. 97.

70 Faye, 'Copenhagen Interpretation of Quantum Mechanics'. See Husserl, *Ideas*, p. 75.

71 Chevally, 'Niels Bohr's Words', pp. 43–44.

72 Note that the similarity of this idea to the *kalām* concept of *qiyās al-ghā'ib 'alā al-shāhid* is striking and deserves further reflection. Also, see in this context Alston, *Divine Nature and Human Language*, p. 22.

73 Chevally, 'Niels Bohr's Words', p. 48.

defines a theory as a system of propositions referring to a certain domain; a proposition as an ideal meaning, expressible by a complete sentence; and meaning as the content of intentional experience directed at a given object.[74] For Husserl, then, scientific theorising rests on phenomenological experience.

Chevally concludes that Bohr is implicitly thinking within the post-Kantian tradition when insisting on substituting symbols for concepts in his interpretation of quantum mechanics.[75] He does not conceive of the uncertainty principle as placing a limit on what can be known about a noumenal reality,[76] but argues that the practice of science allows us to clarify what we can say about reality, as beings 'suspended in language'.[77] Crucially, the abstract mathematical formula of the wave function given by the Schrödinger equation at the heart of quantum mechanics is a symbolisation, which can only be interpreted in the intersubjective context of a given experimental setup.[78] This setup provides the conditions under which concepts such as position, momentum, time and energy can be applied to the quantum phenomena.[79] Within his mature thinking after the challenge of the EPR (Einstein, Podolsky and Rosen) paper of the mid-1930s, Bohr held that the choice of experimental setup for measuring properties of space-time (position and time) was complementary to measuring causality (conservation of momentum and energy). Yet between them, these aspects exhaust all properties of an object.[80]

Science does not give us an ontology. It is the task of philosophy to provide a metaphysical interpretation of the empirical data.[81] Bohr was both a scientist and a philosopher. Although he did not commit to a specific ontology, he provided a pragmatic epistemology by which quantum mechanics reveals that human observational choice is implicated in the constitution of phenomenal reality.[82] I propose that Bohr's interpretation of quantum mechanics, albeit contested and often misunderstood, places the categories of the human mind and the intersubjective activity of scientific enquiry at the centre of the world. Heisenberg, and others, such as John Archibald Wheeler and Henry Stapp, who have developed Bohr's ideas under the name of the Copenhagen interpretation, went a step further to argue that

74 Smith, *Husserl*, p. 93. See Husserl, *The Shorter Logical Investigations*, pp. 76–81.
75 Chevally, 'Niels Bohr's Words', p. 49.
76 Favrholdt, 'Niels Bohr and Realism', p. 87–88.
77 Favrholdt, 'Niels Bohr and Realism', p. 83. See Heisenberg, *Physics and Philosophy*, pp. 107–8.
78 Bohr, *Essays 1958–1962*, pp. 3–7.
79 Faye, 'Copenhagen Interpretation of Quantum Mechanics'.
80 Faye, 'Copenhagen Interpretation of Quantum Mechanics'.
81 Lewis, *Quantum Ontology*, p. 1.
82 Stapp, *Mindful Universe*, pp. 85–87.

this reveals a fundamental place for consciousness that is squeezed out by a mechanistic Newtonian description of reality.[83] I argue that drawing from this tendency in the philosophy of science provides some degree of empirical validation for the transcendental idealism that Husserl establishes on phenomenological grounds.

A couple of questions may arise with respect to my present project. First, a pertinent theological one: does the indeterminacy apparently brought into the world by quantum mechanics pose a threat to God's omniscience? In Chapter 5, I will argue that it does not.[84] Second, if human consciousness is centred, what can be said about the world, or any of its aspects, in the absence of an observer? The same question arises with respect to the transcendental idealism of Husserl and so can be profitably answered from the perspective of his thought. He does not uphold a crude idealism in which concrete objects pop out of existence when one's back is turned. What he does is to consider the ontological coextensive with the phenomenological: everything that exists in the universe can, in principle, be an object of consciousness. This returns to his focus on ideal meaning and the basic rationality of reality.[85]

Such a perspective that puts consciousness centre stage in our understanding of the universe, instead of as a peripheral, even accidental, phenomenon, is teleological in a way unfamiliar to modern thought but a commonplace of the premodern theistic tradition. Al-Māturīdī makes a related teleogical argument in his introduction to *Kitāb al-tawḥīd* when discussing the necessity of religion for human beings, which allows them to sustain and not perish:[86]

> As for reason, it dictates that the nature of the world being specifically to perish would not be wise. Every rational agent abhors their action leaving the path of wisdom. So, it is not possible that the world in which reason is foundational is based on other than wisdom or is futile. This establishes that the world was made to sustain not to perish.[87]

For the world to perish (*fanāʾ*) in this context means that it would lack the basic stability to sustain in existence and thereby support human life

83 Stapp, *Mindful Universe*, p. 7. See Pugliese, 'Quantum Mechanics and an Ontology of Intersubjectivity', pp. 330–32.

84 See pages 169–70.

85 For more discussion of ontology, see Section III.

86 See pages 18–19.

87 Al-Māturīdī, *Kitāb al-tawḥīd*, p. 67. See al-Māturīdī, *Taʾwīlāt al-qurʾān*, vol. 8, p. 109. Compare with Husserl, *The Basic Problems of Phenomenology*, pp. 27–28.

for its purpose. This is a metaphysical parallel to the stabilising effects that al-Māturīdī sees religion bringing to human society. It is useful to reconstruct it as a deductive argument along with its assumed premises:

P1. Every rational agent abhors unwise action.
P2. God is a rational agent.[88]
P3. Reason is foundational to the created world.
P4. A rational agent will not do what is abhorrent with respect to those things for which reason is foundational.
C1. The world cannot be based on other than wisdom or be futile (from P1, P2, P3 and P4).
P5. For the world to perish would be unwise.
C2. It is impossible for the world to perish (from P1, P2, P3, P4 and P5).

This argument draws an integral link between God's wisdom, human reason and the purpose of the world. The nature of God means that it is metaphysically necessary that the world is not chaotic or purposeless.[89] If reason is foundational to the world, human rationality must not only be able to comprehend it but in some important respects be pegged to it. Moreover, reason – by virtue of its fruits – is the *telos* for the stable existence of the world.

The quantum physicist most ready to contemplate an application of the Copenhagen interpretation of quantum mechanics to a similar end is John Archibald Wheeler. He highlights that what the observer chooses to ask about the quantum world – for example, the polarisation of a photon – forms an integral aspect of what would conventionally be understood as having happened in the past.[90] Following Bohr (and Husserl), this amounts to an intersubjective phenomenological description, one that is communicable between human beings.[91] It is the basis for what has been called the Participatory Anthropic Principle (PAP),[92] which is encapsulated in Wheeler's statement: 'the observer is as essential to the creation of the universe as the universe is to the creation of the observer'.[93]

The concept of the Anthropic Principle deserves further comment. As formulated by Brandon Carter, the Strong Anthropic Principle (SAP)

88 Al-Māturīdī does not state this premise, but I think that it is the best way to make sense of his argument.
89 The connection between the attribute of wisdom and metaphysical modality will be explored in Chapters 4 and 5. See pages 139 and 172.
90 Wheeler, 'Genesis and Observership', pp. 24–25.
91 Wheeler, 'Genesis and Observership', pp. 25–26; Bohr, *Essays 1958–1962*, pp. 11–12.
92 See Bostrom, *Anthropic Bias*, p. 49.
93 Wheeler, 'Genesis and Observership', p. 27. See Nesteruk, 'A "Participatory Universe" of J. A. Wheeler'.

reads as follows: 'the Universe (and hence the fundamental parameters on which it depends) must be such as to admit within it the creation of observers within it at some stage'.[94] Carter's SAP has been famously misread by Barrow and Tipler as supporting the teleological argument.[95] Yet it actually acts as an objection to traditional teleological arguments for the existence of God or their contemporary fine-tuning equivalents.[96] The basic idea is of selection bias: it should not be surprising to us that the universe has observers; if it did not, we would not be in the position to observe it in the first place.[97] Various versions of the Anthropic Principle have been criticised for merely showing that the existence of observers in the universe is tautological.[98] It can, in fact, be rewritten as the analytic proposition: 'an internally observed universe contains observers'.

John Earman is scathing in his criticism of Wheeler's PAP. He argues that, even on an interpretation of quantum mechanics whereby the centrality of observership is granted, 'it does not follow that without conscious observers the world would not have being, existence, reality, or actuality, but only that certain kinds of changes would not take place in it'.[99] His point is that, before an observer makes a measurement to actualise a possibility of the quantum state, there is already a world in existence, and it is one that does not require that observation to exist. I think this misses an interesting implication of Wheeler's PAP, which is not subject to the critique of selection bias. While quantum indeterminacy does not hold that there is a necessity for observership to arrive, it does mean that, at least on one construal of the Copenhagen interpretation, the universe can be conceived as pure potentiality waiting for observers to actualise it.[100] This is the sense in which Wheeler's reciprocal relationship between world and observer should be understood. Moreover, such a perfect fit between the universe and conscious observership is not the inevitable result of selection bias, but the surprising result of empirical measurement. It therefore invites teleological thinking about the existence of human consciousness. Although PAP is not in itself a teleological argument for the existence of God, it may be taken in that direction, as will be shown in Chapter 3.

The present discussion has brought together the teleological approach of Māturīdī *kalām*, the transcendental phenomenology of Husserl and the Bohr-Copenhagen interpretation of the empirical findings of quantum mechanics to shift the human being to the centre of the cosmos. As

94 Carter, 'Large Number Coincidences and the Anthropic Principle in Cosmology', p. 294.
95 Friederich, 'Fine-Tuning'.
96 See pages 119–23.
97 Friederich, 'Fine-Tuning'; Bostrom, *Anthropic Bias*, p. 48.
98 Bostrom, *Anthropic Bias*, pp. 44–46.
99 Earman, 'The SAP Also Rises', p. 313.
100 Wheeler, 'Beyond the Black Hole', pp. 354–59.

al-Māturīdī approvingly mentions, the human being is the microcosm.[101] If the significance of the idea of the human mind looking outwards to the world and to God has been adequately justified, then the next step is to dig deeper into the conceptual foundations of rational activity used in the remainder of this book.

II. Knowledge of Material and Categorial 'Things'

Rowan Williams observes that 'the concept of the thing is what is presupposed in the very concept of a perceived world'.[102] The category of 'thing' is basic to our preconceptual ability to see a world of change and individuation at all. When trying to know the concrete things in the world, or mathematical entities, we can mentally come to grips with certain distinctions. The difference that we invoke between 'what' something is, on the one hand, and 'that' it is at all, on the other, is often discussed as respectively that of its essence and existence. The key problematic to be explored is whether this language reflects an ontic[103] distinction or is a product of our conceptions about entities. I will first highlight al-Māturīdī's position and contribution to this question before considering the unarguable influence of Avicennan philosophy in the development of these ideas within the late classical *kalām* tradition.

Recall the definition of knowledge attributed to al-Māturīdī: 'a quality that, by it, the thing mentioned is realised for the one whom it is established within'.[104] In his discussion of perception, which he considers the most immediate form of knowledge, he mentions that there is debate over the whatness (*mā'iyya*) or the isness (*hastiyya*) of things.[105] The term *mā'iyya* originates in the Arabic translation *mā huwa* (what it is) of Aristotle's Greek phrase for essence *τὸ τί ἦν εἶναι* (lit. what it is to be a thing).[106] It is attested as a technical term in al-Kindī's major treatise *Fī al-falsafa al-ūlā*.[107] Al-Māturīdī defines it as a question: '"What is it? (*mā huwa*)" means, "From what is its whatness known in the creation?"'[108] The word

101 Al-Māturīdī, *Kitāb al-tawḥīd*, p. 67. See page 18.

102 Williams, *On Christian Theology*, p. 150. See also Husserl, *Ideas*, pp. 73–74.

103 I use ontic in its linguistic sense of that pertaining to 'existence in reality' and ontological for the domain of ontology. The reader should not infer Heidegger's technical usage of the terms.

104 See page 21.

105 Al-Māturīdī, *Kitāb al-tawḥīd*, p. 70.

106 Wisnovsky, *Avicenna's Metaphysics in Context*, p. 150; Cassin, *Dictionary of Untranslatables*, p. 1133. See also al-Sālimī, *Al-Tamhīd fī bayan al-tawḥīd*, pp. 111–12; Cohen, 'Aristotle's Metaphysics'. The closely related form *māhiyya* is also found in the *kalām* tradition. Wisnovsky, *Avicenna's Metaphysics in Context*, p. 150.

107 Adamson and Pormann, *The Philosophical Works of al-Kindī*, p. 30.

108 Al-Māturīdī, *Kitāb al-tawḥīd*, p. 174.

hastiyya comes from the Persian *hast* (is), thus meaning isness or particular existence.[109]

I will interpret al-Māturīdī's understanding of these terms through his theological use of them. While the rationality of reality allows language to refer to God, it can only be applied within certain limits. His method of *mithl* and *khilāf* seeks a middle path between anthropomorphism (*tashbīh*) and nullification of attributes (*ta ʿṭīl*), which he calls verification (*taḥqīq*) or affirmation (*ithbāt*).[110] Al-Māturīdī argues that God is a concrete particular, or substance (*ʿayn, jawhar*), because His existence is affirmed,[111] and he thinks that the term *hastiyya* is more accurate for His isness than the alternative *shay ʾiyya* (thingness).[112] Yet we do not know God's whatness, so He is termed a 'thing unlike [other] things (*shay ʾun lā ka-l-ashyā ʾ*)'.[113] The scriptural support for this is Q. 42:11, 'There is nothing like Him (*laysa ka-mithlihi shay ʾ*), yet He is the hearing, the seeing'.[114] One of his main uses of this key principle is to negate a body or accidents to God, as 'they are the explanation of the likeness of things (*humā ta ʾwīlā shibhi al-ashyā ʾ*)'.[115] As al-Māturīdī argues, having a likeness allows things to fall under the concept of number, whereas having an opposite makes them liable to extinction when the opposite is destroyed. This makes similarity and opposition the basis for plurality, non-existence and contingent form, all of which God transcends in His unicity.[116]

109 A marginal note on the manuscript of *Kitāb al-tawḥīd* interprets these two terms as the mental and external existence of a thing respectively, although this gloss seems likely to reflect post-Avicennan developments in the tradition. Al-Māturīdī, 'Kitāb al-tawḥīd', fol. 3r. Van Ess explains *hastiyya* as 'what exists and therefore can be experienced'. Van Ess, review of *Kitāb al-tawḥīd*, by Abū Manṣūr al-Māturīdī, ed. Fathalla Kholeif, p. 560. Also, see Wisnovsky, *Avicenna's Metaphysics in Context*, p. 157.

110 In the *kalām* tradition, this is more commonly termed *tanzīh*. See Cerić, *Roots of Synthetic Theology in Islam*, pp. 157–58.

111 I use substance and concrete particular as synonymous translations for the term *ʿayn* or *jawhar*, preferring the former for al-Māturīdī's theology and the latter for my contemporary project. In either of these contexts, it should not be understood as any kind of atomic substrate or divine substratum/essence.

112 Al-Māturīdī, *Kitāb al-tawḥīd*, pp. 105–6. Wisnovsky discusses a possible fourth/tenth-century origin for *shay ʾiyya*. See Wisnovsky, *Avicenna's Metaphysics in Context*, p. 157. But it is already in use in the third/ninth-century writing of the Zaydī theologian al-Qāsim b. Ibrāhīm al-Rassī (d. 246/860). See Ali, *Substance and Things*, pp. 69–70.

113 Al-Māturīdī, *Kitāb al-tawḥīd*, p. 105; al-Māturīdī, *Ta ʾwīlāt al-qur ʾān*, vol. 13, p. 173. See page 144. Cf. van Ess, *Theology and Society in the Second and Third Centuries of the Hijra, Volume 4*, pp. 484–85.

114 See al-Māturīdī, *Kitāb al-tawḥīd*, pp. 89, 105, 121, 138, 160, 311, 315; al-Māturīdī, *Ta ʾwīlāt al-qur ʾān*, vol. 13, pp. 172–73. In his *Ta ʾwīlāt al-qur ʾān*, he also approvingly cites Ibn Mas ʿūd's reading of the verse as, 'Nothing is His likeness (*laysa mithlahu shay ʾun*)'. Al-Māturīdī, *Ta ʾwīlāt al-qur ʾān*, vol. 1, pp. 253–54.

115 Al-Māturīdī, *Kitāb al-tawḥīd*, p. 89.

116 Al-Māturīdī, *Kitāb al-tawḥīd*, p. 89.

In an illuminating passage, he explains in more detail how the unique existence of God makes it impossible to verify the whatness of Him or His attributes via the corporeal and accidental creation:

> Then the meaning of our statement 'a thing unlike things' is an annulment of the whatness (*māʾiyya*) of things [from God]. [A thing] is of two kinds: a substance (*ʿayn*), which is a body (*jism*), and a quality (*ṣifa*), which is an accident (*ʿaraḍ*). So, it is necessary with respect to Him to annul the whatnesses of the substances, which are bodies, and qualities, which are accidents. When we remove the meaning of body from the substances, we negate the associated name, just as when we remove the anthropomorphic meaning from the affirmation and reject nullification of attributes, we negate the position [of anthropomorphism].[117]

This conclusion flows directly from his principle of analogy in his theological method *dalālat al-shāhid ʿalā al-ghāʾib*. Observing the world, we see substances, things, which possess qualities. We are therefore able to draw an inference that God is a concrete particular and has qualities. Yet we cannot infer that He has the whatnesses that we are familiar with from the world, which are the spatially extended body and its temporal accidents.[118]

This position apparently goes back to Abū Ḥanīfa who is reported to have believed that God has a *māʾiyya* that human beings cannot know during their worldly lives.[119] Abū al-Muʿīn al-Nasafī quotes from al-Māturīdī's *Kitāb al-maqālāt*, one of his lost books,[120] to show that this report is baseless,

117 Al-Māturīdī, *Kitāb al-tawḥīd*, p. 105. For contemporary discussion of arguments rejecting the concept of body from God, see Wainwright, 'God's Body', pp. 73–76.

118 Elsewhere al-Māturīdī comments that 'the world is not free from accidents and bodies'. Al-Māturīdī, *Kitāb al-tawḥīd*, p. 314. The rejection of substantiality to God accords with the philosophical view of al-Kindī who may have taken it from the Neoplatonic tradition. See Netton, *Allāh Transcendent*, p. 53. For more on this point, see Berruin, *The Concept of Substance in the Philosophy of Yaʿqūb al-Kindī and Avicenna (Ibn Sīnā)*, p. 183.

119 Van Ess, *Theology and Society in the Second and Third Centuries of the Hijra, Volume 1*, p. 242. The idea of annulling the whatness of God within theological discourse is a feature also shared with Ḍirār b. ʿAmr, even though, unlike al-Māturīdī, he took it to imply that only negative theological statements about God's attributes could be made. Van Ess, '60 Years After', p. 12.

120 Brockelemann cites it as MS Körprülü 856. Brockelmann, *History of the Arabic Written Tradition, Supplement Volume 1*, p. 348. Yet this manuscript's catalogue listing is for al-Ashʿarī's *Maqālāt al-islāmiyyīn*, while its opening lines identify it as *Mujarrad Maqālāt al-Ashʿarī* by Ibn Fūrak. See Şeşen, *Fahras makhṭūṭāt maktaba Kūbrīlī*, vol. 1, p. 420; Ibn Fūrak, *Maqālāt al-shaykh Abī al-Ḥasan al-Ashʿarī*, p. 2. Note that this citation by al-Nasafī belies the claim of Keith Lewinstein that 'Nasafī (along with the rest of the Ḥanafī tradition) neglects to provide even a single quotation from the book'. Lewinstein, 'Notes on Eastern Ḥanafite Heresiography', p. 585, n. 14. Nevertheless, it does seem to be the sole instance.

and if it is not, then *mā ʾiyya* cannot mean *mujānasa* (similarity), the coming under the genus of something else, and thus *tashbīh*.[121] In the passage that al-Nasafī relates, al-Māturīdī argues that to claim God's *mā ʾiyya* is not known is to deny that His *hastiyya* – His isness, or particular existence – is similar to other things.[122] This is reinforced by a statement in *Kitāb al-tawḥīd*: 'There is not in the affirmation of the names and verification of the attributes a similarity [to the creation] due to the nullification from Him of the realities of the creation, such as [its] isness (*hastiyya*) and substantiality (*thabāt*)'.[123]

Where does this leave us in thinking about al-Māturīdī's approach to the question of essence and existence? I suggest he is saying that, from the standpoint of human knowledge, to speak about a thing's isness is to affirm that it exists, while to speak about its whatness is to affirm what its qualities resemble in the contingent world. Anything that we find within the world has a contingent isness, meaning that its whatness can be known due to its similarity to other things on the same ontological level. It is only God who has a unique, eternal isness, such that His whatness cannot be known due to its dissimilarity to all other things. When human beings perceive something in the world, they can distinguish between its particular existence and the abstraction of its qualities through their worldly resemblances. Whatness and isness are categories used in the verification of concrete particulars in human knowledge and al-Māturīdī's distinction between them is thereby conceptual, not existential.[124] These points will be significant in section III below.

As a segue to the development of this topic in *kalām*, I shall turn to al-Māturīdī's rejection of the well-known Muʿtazilī doctrine that the non-existent is a thing (*al-maʿdūm shayʾ*).[125] If this was the case, then it would possess a *shayʾiyya* that precedes its entry into existence. But according to al-Māturīdī's metaphysical postulates, this would mean both having an isness and not having one at the same time, which is a contradiction. The Muʿtazilī position was arguably derived from the Stoics[126] and implies that some kind of particularity about a thing transcends its existence or,

121 Al-Nasafī, *Tabṣirat al-adilla*, vol. 1, pp. 320–21.

122 Al-Nasafī, *Tabṣirat al-adilla*, vol. 1, p. 321.

123 Al-Māturīdī, *Kitāb al-tawḥīd*, p. 91.

124 See also al-Māturīdī's comment regarding the dying of temporal things: 'there is no distinction between the extinction of a [body's] life and of its nature (*lā farqa bayna ḥayātin tafnā wa-bayna dhātihi*)'. Al-Māturīdī, *Kitāb al-tawḥīd*, p. 78.

125 Al-Māturīdī, *Kitāb al-tawḥīd*, pp. 151–52. Although separated from al-Māturīdī's epistemological introduction in *Kitāb al-tawḥīd*, the topic of *al-maʿdūm shayʾ* is given its logical place in the section on knowledge in al-Nasafī, *Tabṣirat al-adilla*, vol. 1, pp. 128–29. For further discussion of this doctrine, including distinctions between different Muʿtazilīs, see Dhanani, *The Physical Theory of Kalām*, pp. 27–29, n. 34.

126 Rescher, *Studies in Arabic Philosophy*, pp. 69–70.

in Robert Wisnovsky's words, 'existent is subsumed extensionally but not intensionally under thing'.[127] As I have shown for al-Māturīdī (and the same is true for al-Ashʿarī), the two terms are the same extensionally and intensionally: to be an existent is to be a thing, and *vice versa*.[128] A similar idea is found in al-Fārābī who argues that existence in actuality is nothing apart from a given thing. There is no additional predicate, and it is only on a logical basis within the intellect that one may distinguish between a thing and its existence.[129] This is opposed to the view of Ibn Sīnā, for whom a thing's *shayʾiyya* is only one of several terms for its essence (*dhāt*, *ṭabīʿa*, *shayʾiyya*, or *māhiyya*). This essence is not 'ontologically neutral' but has a degree of primacy that implies its intrinsic possible or necessary existence outside of the mind.[130]

Fakhr al-Dīn al-Razi is the point of transmission for these ideas in the subsequent *kalām* tradition. He imports Avicennan distinctions into the theological discourse and adds his own elements, most importantly the superaddedness of existence to essence (*ziyādat al-wujūd ʿalā al-māhiyya*).[131] This represents an ontic distinction between the two concepts. Whereas God is needed as a cause to bring existence to a merely possible essence, His own essence is the necessary cause for His existence.[132]

Within the Ḥanafī tradition, this position is adopted at an early date by Shams al-Dīn al-Samarqandī.[133] According to his general practice, he does not mention al-Māturīdī, but states that al-Ashʿarī held essence and existence to be the same.[134] But one must be careful in taking such comparisons entirely at face value. Heidrun Eichner comments:

> Applying Avicennian terminology and analytical categories to the interpretation of the position of authors – most notably theologians – predating Avicenna is an anachronism typical of how the amalgamation of theological and philosophical positions in the thirteenth century takes place.[135]

127 Wisnovsky, *Avicenna's Metaphysics in Context*, p. 152.
128 Wisnovsky, *Avicenna's Metaphysics in Context*, p. 153.
129 Rescher, *Studies in Arabic Philosophy*, pp. 71–72; Wisnovsky, *Avicenna's Metaphysics in Context*, pp. 150–51.
130 Lizzini, 'Ibn Sina's Metaphysics'. See Campanini, *An Introduction to Islamic Philosophy*, pp. 85–86.
131 Wisnovsky, 'On the Emergence of Maragha Avicennism', pp. 276–77.
132 Wisnovsky, 'Essence and Existence in the Eleventh- and Twelfth-Century Islamic East (*Mashriq*)', pp. 40–43. This builds on the prior theological concept of a divine substratum-essence (*dhāt*). See pages 146–47.
133 Al-Samarqandī, *Al-Ṣaḥāʾif al-ilāhiyya*, p. 79. See Wisnovsky, 'Essence and Existence in the Eleventh- and Twelfth-Century Islamic East (*Mashriq*)', p. 47.
134 Al-Samarqandī, *Al-Ṣaḥāʾif al-ilāhiyya*, p. 78.
135 Eichner, 'Essence and Existence', p. 132.

As argued by Murat Kaş, Ibn Sīnā's innovative philosophical concepts made possible new theoretical questions about mental existence.[136] The idea at first blush is that the Avicennan distinction of essence from existence allows a given essence to be realised in knowledge via a merely mental existence (*iʿtibarī*), as opposed to a concrete one (*khārijī*). Kaş refers to two basic principles that must hold between the world and the mind to make this possible: the conservation of essence and the variation of existence.[137] For Ibn Sīnā, the essence of an object is known mentally as an accident, just with a different aspect of existence than when out in the world. This provoked a reaction from al-Rāzī. Despite also holding that knowledge is an accident, he argued that only a corresponding symbol, not an object's essence, could be present to the mind. The mental existence of essences did not accord with his principle that existence is superadded to essence.[138]

While some figures, such as al-Samarqandī, followed al-Rāzī's position,[139] others like the Ashʿarī Athīr al-Dīn al-Abharī (d. *ca* 663/1265) borrowed ideas from al-Suhrawardī (d. 587/1191) to justify a position that identity between essence and existence in the external world can be combined with an Avicennan notion of a different kind of existence for essences in the mind.[140] Moreover, he accuses al-Rāzī of making the same mistake as the Muʿtazila with respect to the superaddedness of existence.[141]

This debate over the conceptualisation of essence provided new resources for thinking about knowledge and the ontology of logical and mathematical objects. Thus al-Taftāzānī, in his *Sharḥ al-maqāṣid*, draws on al-Rāzī, whom he simply calls 'the leader (*al-imām*)', to define knowledge as either a mental conceptualisation (*taṣawwur*), or the confirmation (*taṣdīq*) of one, by means of a judgement (*ḥukm*).[142] Confirmation here acts to correspond mental conceptions with the world of experience. Al-Samarqandī, at the beginning of his *Al-Ṣaḥāʾif al-ilāhiyya*, states:

> Everything of which the mind conceives (*yataṣawwaru*) with respect to the external world is either necessary, impossible, or possible. That is because, if its essence must have existence in the external world, then it is necessary. If not, then if it must lack existence therein, it is impossible. [Whereas] if neither of the two are required, then it is possible.[143]

136 Kaş, 'Mental Existence Debates in the Post-Classical Period of Islamic Philosophy', p. 50.
137 Kaş, 'Mental Existence Debates in the Post-Classical Period of Islamic Philosophy', p. 53.
138 See Kaş, 'Mental Existence Debates in the Post-Classical Period of Islamic Philosophy', pp. 59–60.
139 Al-Samarqandī, *Al-Ṣaḥāʾif al-ilāhiyya*, pp. 82–83.
140 Eichner, 'Essence and Existence', p. 129.
141 Eichner, 'Essence and Existence', p. 132.
142 Al-Taftāzānī, *Sharḥ al-maqāṣid*, vol. 1, p. 199.
143 Al-Samarqandī, *Al-Ṣaḥāʾif al-ilāhiyya*, p. 67.

As every conception about the external world must accept one of these three logical terms, it is implicit that the status of these terms themselves is mental. The easiest way to see this is in the case of the impossible. It is something that by definition lacks existence outside of the mind, as mentioned by al-Sayyid al-Sharīf al-Jurjānī in his *Sharḥ al-mawāqif*.[144] Whether or not it is termed a 'mental existence', it cannot be other than purely conceptual. Likewise, for al-Jurjānī, mathematical objects do not exist within external reality, although the judgements based on them for facts about the world are certain.[145] The tendency within the *kalām* tradition to uphold a correspondence theory of truth and to treat logical and mathematical entities as mental constructions is a significant background for the contemporary philosophical position that I will adopt on this question. For the moment, it will suffice to reject the superaddedness of existence to essence; instead, I will view the distinction as a conceptual tool that allows the following formulation: to exist is to have a given nature, and conversely, to have a given nature is to exist.[146]

Turning to the modern tradition, I will pick up a point from Husserl who uses the language of intentionality to approach the same problem of bridging the divide between essence and existence. His vision of phenomenology is a science of essences; yet these are extracted from the world of experience by a process of phenomenological bracketing. Though Husserl accepts the ordinary 'natural attitude' talk of objects as existent, he argues that under the conditions of such bracketing they must be understood as intentional objects. He thus defines existence as the verification of an intentional object within a given belief context.[147] To take a prosaic example, to say that 'the pen exists' is to say that it is true that the intentional object 'the pen' is verified within the context of waking reality. On this criterion, categorial objects, such as mathematical ones, must be constructible (see below), while material ones must be verifiable in principle by consciousness. Note that this is not the empirical verification of logical positivism,

144 Al-Jurjānī, *Sharḥ al-mawāqif*, p. 129.

145 Fazlıoğlu, 'Between Reality and Mentality', pp. 20–21.

146 Affirming the distinction between the whatness and isness of things as conceptual decentres the question of their Being. This move reflects my choice to adopt a Husserlian formulation of phenomenology and not a Heideggerian one. Gadamer shows that Husserl developed a robust counter to Heidegger's claim that phenomenology must be grounded in the facticity (isness) of Dasein (Being-in-the-world). Husserl argued that, while transcendental subjectivity is grounded historically at the point of the phenomenological reduction, as the ideal consciousness from which all possible phenomena are constituted, it reveals the meaning of any facticity, including its own, as an *eidos* (whatness). See Gadamer, *Truth and Method*, pp. 255–56.

147 Pietersma, 'Husserl's Concept of Existence', pp. 323–24.

which falls into many difficulties, but the ideal verification of transcendental phenomenology.[148]

Drawing from the *kalām* tradition and Husserl, let us now consider a generic correspondence theory of truth. This holds that there must be a corresponding link between a 'truthbearer' and the thing to which it refers, its 'truthmaker'.[149] If we want to say, for instance, that the proposition 'ravens are black' is true, we say that the sentence corresponds by linguistic convention to a certain species of bird found out in the world. It is the adequacy of the colour of this animal as truthmaker to pick out the proposition 'ravens are black' as truthbearer that we call truth. One could say that we are always traversing the hermeneutic circle in trying to make our concepts more adequate in corresponding to reality. Refusing to make truth a primitive notion also profoundly affects the philosophy of logic and mathematics that underlies any rational articulation of theology.

Michael Dummett shows that that such an approach to truth is a departure from classical logic in the inferences that can be drawn from the value of propositions.[150] He suggests that any theory that defines truth by the verification of something cannot accept the principle of bivalence,[151] which stipulates that every proposition must be either true or false.[152] Dummett argues that this point about truth conditions can be extended to inference, implying rejection of the Law of Excluded Middle (LEM).[153] Nullifying the validity of LEM in the context of a correspondence theory of truth amounts to an acknowledgement that our concepts cannot pick out definite truths within certain fields of reality. Thus, if something is known not to be true, it is not logically necessary that it is false (and *vice versa*). As Graham Priest comments, 'each applied logic provides, in effect, a theory about how the domain of application behaves'.[154]

148 See Swinburne, *The Coherence of Theism*, revised edn, pp. 22–23; Swinburne, *The Coherence of Theism*, 2nd edn, pp. 40–43; Creath, 'Logical Empiricism'; Smith and McIntyre, *Husserl and Intentionality*, pp. 270–71. Also see page 64.

149 David, 'The Correspondence Theory of Truth'. In this section, I follow Husserl in considering truthbearers to be propositions of ideal meaning, while reserving judgement on the ontology of truthmakers until Section III below. Other possibilities for the nature of propositions are mentioned in Koons and Pickavance, *The Atlas of Reality*, p. 16. I note that, even though I use the language of truthmakers for a correspondence theory, it can be a neutral terminology for other theories. See Leftow, *Time and Eternity*, pp. 6–7.

150 See Dummett, *The Logical Basis of Metaphysics*, p. 61.

151 Dummett, *The Logical Basis of Metaphysics*, p. 318.

152 See Horn, 'Contradiction'.

153 Dummett, *The Logical Basis of Metaphysics*, p. 318. The disagreement over whether LEM can be held in the absence of bivalence is a live philosophical dispute. Haack argues they can be treated as independent. Haack, *Deviant Logic*, p. 67. Wright suggests otherwise. Wright, 'How High the Sky?', p. 2076.

154 Priest, 'Revising Logic', p. 215.

The most significant rejection of LEM in a school of modern logic is the intuitionism of L. E. J. Brouwer, which was proposed at the beginning of the twentieth century and later formalised by Arend Heyting. Brouwer restricted the rules of logical inference based on a principled stance about the nature of mathematical reality and truth. Using the intuition of time as a foundation for number, he argued that logic was dependent on mathematics as conceived by human beings.[155] This meant that he saw mathematical objects and their properties as ideal mental constructions that must be established via proof.[156] For a proposition to be true, it must adequately describe a mathematical construction and could not be inferred by the falsity of its negation.[157] Brouwer did accept the validity of LEM in certain areas of mathematics that dealt with finite domains and constructions, but considered it absolutely unreliable in the field of natural science, due to the problem of induction, and mysticism, which he called 'wisdom', due to the dissolution of time consciousness.[158]

Brouwer's intuitionism, which is a type of constructivism, led to his rejection of bivalence. An example that Brouwer used to illustrate his perspective is the unproven Goldbach Conjecture that every even integer (greater than 2) is the sum of two prime numbers, a version of which was first proposed in 1742.[159] Whereas a mathematical realist, or Platonist, would affirm that this conjecture is either true or false (even if we may never know which), Brouwer contended that, as no constructive mathematical proof has been found for it, it is neither true nor false. Given the possibility that a proof for or against the conjecture will one day be found, he also found a method to extend his argument to any open problem.[160]

Brouwer's intuitionistic programme can be interpreted within the general model of Husserl who placed time consciousness at the deepest level of his phenomenological reduction.[161] Mark van Atten provides eleven properties in common between Brouwer's understanding of the

155 Franchella, 'Philosophies of Intuitionism', p. 74. It seems Brouwer was initially motivated by Kant's idea of the *a priori* nature of time (although rejecting it for space). Later, he distanced himself from the Kantian perspective, as he saw that logical intuition could be applied to time to treat potential infinities as constructible objects. See van Atten, *Essays on Gödel's Reception of Leibniz, Husserl, and Brouwer*, pp. 262–63. See page 116.

156 Van Dalen, 'Intuitionistic Logic', p. 2.

157 Van Atten, *Essays on Gödel's Reception of Leibniz, Husserl, and Brouwer*, p. 241, n. 8.

158 Van Atten and Sundholm, 'L. E. J. Brouwer's "Unreliability of the Logical Principles"', pp. 4, 7.

159 Wang, *The Goldbach Conjecture*, p. 1.

160 See the supplement 'Weak Counterexamples' in van Atten, 'Luitzen Egbertus Jan Brouwer'. Dummett develops a further constructivist defence for the rejection of bivalence. See Wright, 'How High the Sky?', p. 2073.

161 Husserl, *Ideas*, pp. 165–66.

constructability of mathematical objects and Husserl's constitution of purely categorial objects.[162] This puts van Atten's position in stark contrast to those, like Guillermo Haddock, who understand Husserl as a Platonist with respect to mathematical entities.[163] Yet Husserl's famous rejection of psychologism in his development of transcendental phenomenology is a negation of founding mathematics on particular psychological states, rather than of the ideal nature of mathematical entities. Husserl himself took pains to rebut a Platonistic understanding of his position by the 'most frequent type of superficial reader who foists on the author his own wholly alien conceptions'.[164] Husserl makes the crucial distinction between a subject's construction of a particular 'number-presentation' – for instance, 'adding unit to unit' – which is a different psychological entity even if repeated identically, and the categorial idealisation of a given number, such as 2, within the number series.[165] Like Brouwer, the relevant subject here is an ideal one without contingent limitations on memory and time and thus represents the essential mathematical facility shared, in principle, by all human beings.[166]

On the question of LEM, the affinity of Husserl and Brouwer seems particularly clear: 'Husserl came to see the difference between the logic of non-contradiction and the logic of truth, and it is the latter, not the former, that governs formal ontology'.[167] In his *Formal and Transcendental Logic*, Husserl argues that LEM is only unavoidable when working with a pure logic that looks to the consequence of various judgements and their mutual non-contradiction without considering their truth value, as determined by reference to evidence of some kind.[168] While LEM claims that knowing the

162 Van Atten, *Essays on Gödel's Reception of Leibniz, Husserl, and Brouwer*, p. 247. The term 'categorial' when applied by Husserl to objects of thought refers to basic ontological categories, such as object, number, unit, plurality and relation, by which the human mind can understand the world. See Thomasson, 'Categories'; Husserl, *The Basic Problems of Phenomenology*, pp. 20–21.

163 Haddock, 'Platonism, Phenomenology, and Interderivability', pp. 26–27.

164 Husserl, *Ideas*, p. 40.

165 Husserl, *Ideas*, pp. 41–42.

166 Van Atten, *Essays on Gödel's Reception of Leibniz, Husserl, and Brouwer*, pp. 249–51. This interpretation is very close to the position of Richard Tieszen who reads Husserl as holding a 'constituted platonism', in which mathematical objects are understood as ideally constituted entities. See Tieszen, 'Mathematical Realism and Transcendental Phenomenological Idealism', pp. 13–14. Tieszen briefly compares him to Brouwer on p. 20.

167 Van Atten, *Essays on Gödel's Reception of Leibniz, Husserl, and Brouwer*, pp. 240–41. Contrast this with Wittgenstein who, while also rejecting LEM for statements like the Goldbach Conjecture, repudiates intuitionism as an invalid counterpart to Platonism. Steiner, 'Wittgenstein and the Covert Platonism of Mathematical Logic', p. 140.

168 Husserl, *Formal and Transcendental Logic*, pp. 330–33. Note that when the mathematics of quantum mechanics are translated into the language of logic, LEM does not hold. Heisenberg, *Physics and Philosophy*, pp. 181–82.

truth or falsity of a proposition leads to knowledge about its negation, Husserl argues that this is not adequately established as an indubitable law of thought:

> We all know very well how few judgments anyone can in fact legitimate intuitively, even with the best efforts; and yet it is supposed to be a matter of apriori insight that there can be no non-evident judgments that do not 'in themselves' admit of being made evident in [read: by] either a positive or a negative evidence.[169]

The affirmation within human thought of propositions that cannot be proved as true merely because their negation is false, or *vice versa* – so-called logical gaps – will prove useful when dealing with certain tricky notions in the ontology of the world and God. I hold that, whereas this law of thought can be coherently dispensed with, the Law of Non-contradiction and the Law of Identity cannot, as they are presupposed within rational thought.[170] The remainder of this section will develop these ideas through discussion of how they can apply to a fundamental rational tool, the idea of a collection, class, or set.

One of the best ways to approach the distinctive concept of a set is to contrast it with the concept of a fusion, which is nothing but the individuals that compose it, such that, unlike the set, it can be decomposed in any manner.[171] To see the difference, take a copy of the Torah as the set formed of the five books of Moses. This set has an individual identity, and if it is to be split up, it can only be done so into its five constituent books. The fusion of the five books can be divided in an indefinite number of ways, such as by chapter and verse, odd and even pages, or passages of dialogue and narration.

It is a metaphysical challenge to say in what sense a collection of any kind relates to its constituent members: it seems to be in some way an additional entity over them; yet it is not at all clear how this is so. David Lewis focuses on this problem through the singleton, which is an individual made into a set (or class in his terminology). He argues that what relationship there is between the member (for instance, my apple) and its singleton (the set of

169 Husserl, *Formal and Transcendental Logic*, p, 194.

170 Baggini and Fosl, *The Philosopher's Toolkit*, p. 40; MacIntyre, *Whose Justice? Which Rationality?*, p. 4. The argument for the Law of Non-contradiction can be found in Aristotle, *Metaphysics*, trans. Hugh Lawson-Tancred, pp. 89–90. There has been some recent work applying ideas of dialetheism, a paraconsistent logic that allows true contradictions, to Islamic theology. See, for instance, Zolghadr, 'The Sufi Path of Dialetheism'; Chowdhury, 'God, Gluts and Gaps'. Note also that Aristotle likewise argued for the necessity of LEM. Aristotle, *Metaphysics*, trans. Hugh Lawson-Tancred, pp. 107–8.

171 Potter, *Set Theory and its Philosophy*, p. 22.

my apple) is utterly mysterious.[172] His presentation assumes realism about the existence of singletons, giving the option that they are either outside of space-time and thus Platonic, or tied to the location of their members.[173]

Building on my discussion above, I propose that the mystery can be solved by adopting an intuitionistic point of view, whereby a set is an ideal categorial object with a relationship to other similar entities, such as numbers, or to ontic structures existing in the world (see Section III).[174] It seems more plausible to explain that the singleton of my apple is my mental bracketing of it, rather than the other available options. Lewis mentions an analogy proposed by Daniel Isaacson: that is, a singleton should be conceived akin to a person who intends to make an art collection but then runs out of money after the first painting. Yet he dismisses this due to the existence of the countless sets that he thinks must have been formed without human involvement.[175] In this, he seems to beg the question of the realist ontology of sets.

The intuitionistic rejection of LEM allows logical leeway for the ambiguity that emerges between a set and its members. One can stipulate without contradiction that the singleton set {1} is neither identical to its member, 1, nor other than it. This can be generalised as a principle and applied also to the empty set, of which there must be only one. As a mental encapsulation of nothing, it is neither nothing, nor other than it.[176]

Why should this apparently counterintuitive proposition be the case? I suggest that it is a consequence of the primitive notion of set membership itself. In mereology, fusions are exactly equal to the sum of their members; hence, this problem of set identity does not arise. Since Ernst Zermelo's axiomatic reformulation of set theory in 1908 to avoid the paradoxes of the naïve set theory of Gregor Cantor, the binary element $\in$ has been posited to capture the idea of set membership.[177] In fact, the concept of membership is

172 Lewis, *Parts of Classes*, pp. 31–35.

173 Lewis, *Parts of Classes*, pp. 31–32.

174 This is akin to Husserl's view in his early work *Philosophy of Arithmetic*. See Centrone, *Logic and Philosophy of Mathematics in the Early Husserl*, p. 9.

175 Lewis, *Parts of Classes*, pp. 30–31.

176 Cf. Abū al-Muʿīn al-Nasafī who comments: 'Two different things are two existent things whereby one can be conceptualised alongside the non-existence of the other'. He then gives the example of the number one-out-of-ten, which is neither the same as ten, nor different from it, due to the impossibility of conceptualising ten without it. Al-Nasafī, *Al-Tamhīd fī uṣūl al-dīn*, pp. 42–43. Critique of this point from Muʿtazilī sources and further responses are in al-Sighnāqī, 'Al-Tasdīd fī sharḥ al-tamhīd', pp. 178–79. See also al-Bazdawī, *Uṣūl al-dīn*, pp. 46–47; Spannaus, *Preserving Islamic Tradition*, p. 158. The context is the conceptualisation of God's attributes. Compare with the Kullābī formula on pages 150–51.

177 Hallett, 'Zermelo's Axiomatization of Set Theory'.

reciprocal with the notion of a collecting set: $a \in b$ (a is an element of set b) is the same as $b\{a\}$ (b is a set with element a).[178] Thus, an axiomatic set theory consistent with the principles outlined so far could be posited using the symbol $\in$ and the language of intuitionistic first-order logic.[179] I argue, drawing from Husserl, that the introduction of $\in$ as an 'ideological primitive'[180] is best interpreted as the symbolic expression of a categorial intuition of the mind. This categorial intuition adds no additional ontic structure to the aggregation that is not already there – compare the set of the Torah, which has in some sense an integral structure that I verify, with someone's collection of five favourite books that regularly changes in composition.[181] Nevertheless, it does alter how it is intentionally presented to the mind.

The normal use of set theory is as a powerful tool for the expression and exploration of mathematics. In the present enquiry, I am not concerned with the technical aspects of the theory when applied to mathematical entities, but its conceptual utility for the articulation of ontology. As John Bacon states, '[p]hysical structures and metaphysical structures both fall under the general theory of structure, which is set theory'.[182] My adoption of an intuitionistic version of set theory means that I am not a realist about sets as abstract entities, nor do I propose that logic and sets are used for 'cutting nature at its seams'.[183] Instead, I think they reflect basic categories for human knowledge about the structure of reality and the intentional constitution of its objects, ideal, physical and metaphysical.

To see how this is theologically significant, consider the beginning of Alain Badiou's *Being and Event*. Badiou introduces a philosophical contention he traces back to Plato's *Parmenides* that 'what *presents* itself is essentially multiple; *what* presents itself is essentially one'.[184] By this formulation, he argues that, though a given entity is presented to us as a multiplicity, its underlying being is a unity. Badiou then declares that 'the one is not'. This means that structure is not defined by an integral being, but the human subject counting a presented multiplicity as a unity. So far, his presentation is similar to the current section. Yet here he introduces the idea of the Great Temptation, which amounts to ultimately grounding the

178 Cf. Badiou, *Being and Event*, p. 61.
179 Crosilla, 'Set Theory: Constructive and Intuitionistic ZF'. See also Fraenkel et al., *Foundations of Set Theory*, pp. 334–35.
180 See Miller, 'Are All Primitives Created Equal?', pp. 275–76.
181 Husserl, *The Shorter Logical Investigations*, p. 177. There is some debate over whether a set can change membership without changing identity. Sharvy, 'Why a Class Can't Change Its Members', p. 314. See pages 99–100.
182 Bacon, *Universals and Property Instances*, p. 10.
183 See El-Rouayheb, 'Theology and Logic', p. 416.
184 Badiou, *Being and Event*, p. 23.

unity of contingent finite beings on a transcendent infinite Being.[185] His criticism of this theological move is redolent of Muhammad Iqbal's argument that 'the infinite reached by contradicting the finite is a false infinite, which neither explains itself nor the finite which is thus made to stand in opposition to the infinite'.[186]

Badiou's major innovation is that, whereas monotheistic traditions ground being in an infinite One, he claims that through set theory it can be grounded in the void. The fundamental principle of set membership, which is axiomatically assumed within the system, allows the creation of pure sets from nothing.[187] Specifically, the empty set is in a sense one, the set of the empty set is two and so on. While pre-Cantorian mathematics, including that of the *kalām* tradition, drew a sharp distinction between the potential infinities of the world and the transcendent infinity of God,[188] he contends that, in describing actual infinities of different cardinalities, set theory allows the grounding of ontology in an infinite brought into the world.[189] The axiomatic structure of the system, especially in its assumption of the membership relation, closes the gap between one and multiplicity by allowing multiplicities to be posited without reference to any defined unity.[190]

Badiou acknowledges his decision to adopt Cantorian set theory, to treat the resulting mathematics as ontology and to rely on the Zermelo-Fraenkel axiomatisation, as well as classical logic.[191] These choices flow from a stated anti-theological objective – to liberate the thought of being from the One. In his florid expression: 'By initiating a thinking in which the infinite is irrevocably separated from every instance of the One. Mathematics has, in its own domain, successfully consummated the death of God'.[192]

My aims are different, and consequently so are my theoretical decisions. As adumbrated in this chapter, I have embraced the well-worn theological move that Badiou's project is predicated on avoiding, explaining the multiplicity of the contingent world through an infinite God who transcendently grounds the existence of multiple contingent and finite beings.[193] This is precisely the aspect of negative theology adopted by al-Māturīdī in his appeal to the principle of *khilāf*,[194] which I will pick up for the cosmological

185 Badiou, *Being and Event*, p. 24.

186 Iqbal, *The Reconstruction of Religious Thought in Islam*, p. 23.

187 Baki, *Badiou's* Being and Event, pp. 102–3.

188 Wolfson, *The Philosophy of the Kalam*, p. 471.

189 Badiou, *Theoretical Writings*, p. 19. See Miller, review of *Being and Event*, by Alain Badiou, trans. Oliver Feltham.

190 Miller, review of *Being and Event*, by Alain Badiou, trans. Oliver Feltham, pp. 124–25.

191 See Badiou, *Theoretical Writings*, pp. 50, 58–60.

192 Badiou, *Theoretical Writings*, p. 39.

193 Badiou, *Theoretical Writings*, pp. 28–29.

194 See page 63.

argument in Chapter 3 and God's nature in Chapter 4. In my view, it is the contemporary constructivist approach to mathematics and logic that works best with this theology, as it preserves the relation of dependence between the actual infinity of God and the merely potential infinity, and therefore finitude, to be found within the world.[195] Badiou, I think, recognises this and reserves some of his fiercest criticism for intuitionism and its proponents' idea of the constructively valid.[196]

III. Ontology

If the structure of things corresponds to the sets that we are able to conceptualise, and if truth can be understood as the verification of propositions about them, then a question deferred earlier returns with greater force: what is the ontology of their truthbearers and truthmakers? A significant position within the *kalām* tradition holds that mental concepts are accidental in nature. Although sticking to the broad outlines of a classical correspondence theory, I have taken it in a Husserlian direction, whereby propositional truthbearers are ideal, intersubjective meanings. Truthmakers can be split into either categorial entities (as discussed in the previous section) or material ones; yet in both cases I suggest that what is verified are particular things and qualities. Thus, I will argue for a global ontology based on a phenomenological trope theory (see below). In this, I will also pick up on the suggestion that I made in *The Qur'an and the Just Society* that a trope theory might be a fruitful way to interpret al-Māturīdī's unusual *kalām* cosmology.[197] In fact, I will go further than this in Chapter 4 to show that the idea of divine tropes is an effective way to discuss God's attributes.

Taking the argument back a few steps, to hold that the world is rational in its conceptual verification means that there must be a link between human concepts and a consistent ontological picture. This is what explains why we apprehend it as non-chaotic. In the *kalām* tradition, three main avenues were explored for the world's ontology, as follows:[198]

1. Everything is composed of bodies (*ajsām*; sing. *jism*).
2. Everything is composed of accidents (*aʿrāḍ*; sing. *araḍ*).
3. Everything is composed of atoms (*jawāhir*; sing. *jawhar*, *al-juzʾ alladhī lā yatajazzaʾ*) and accidents.

195 See pages 116–19.

196 Badiou, *Theoretical Writings*, pp. 58–59.

197 Harvey, *The Qur'an and the Just Society*, pp. 34, 201, n. 77.

198 Dhanani, *The Physical Theory of Kalām*, pp. 4–5. Also see van Ess, '60 Years After', p. 10. As I am working from the early and classical *kalām* tradition, I leave to one side the *falāsifa*'s preference for synthesis between Aristotelian hylomorphism and Neoplatonic emanationism. See Pessin, 'Forms of Hylomorphism', pp. 197–200.

The theory that everything is composed of interpenetrating bodies is associated with Hishām b. al-Ḥakam (d. 179/795–96) who was not averse to giving it an explanatory role for prevailing Shīʿī ideas of a corporeal God.[199] By the early third/ninth century, it was adopted by the Muʿtazilī al-Naẓẓām who restricted it to the world alone and accounted for change by an idea of latencies (*kumūn*) hidden within bodies.[200] This explanation of the changing world proved counterintuitive and did not last long.

The second proposal makes accidents, or particular qualities, the fundamental ontology. As transmitted in the Aristotelian-Neoplatonic tradition, the accident has the sense of what must subsist within something yet may belong or not belong to any given thing.[201] The centrality of accidents was supported by al-Najjār and, more prominently, by Ḍirār b. ʿAmr who proposed a kind of bundle theory to explain bodies.[202] Afterwards, it too was mainly dropped by Muslim theologians. Nevertheless, I follow Rudolph in arguing that one of the distinctive aspects of al-Māturīdī's thought is his articulation of a version of this theory. I will also attempt to locate it within my constructive theological concerns later within this section. First, however, I will mention the third position above, so-called Islamic atomism, which became the dominant cosmological model within formative and classical *kalām*.

Atomism encompasses a range of theories and their proponents engaged in complex debate over their details. As it is not the main story of this book, it will suffice to sketch it rather than becoming bogged down in the intricacies of its provenance and development.[203] The idea of conceiving the world as structured from atoms in which accidents inhere[204] was first adopted around the turn of the third/ninth century by the prominent Basran Muʿtazilīs Muʿammar b. ʿAbbād (d. 215/830) and Abū al-Hudhayl.[205] In the cosmological tradition that followed, atoms were variously described as extended or unextended;[206] homogenous or diverse in nature;[207] and able or unable to exist without accidents.[208] In any of these formulations, including the version that later became dominant in the classical Ashʿarī and Māturīdī *kalām* traditions (homogenous unextended atoms requiring

199 Van Ess, '60 Years After', pp. 16–17.
200 See Wolfson, *The Philosophy of the Kalam*, pp. 498–514.
201 Cassin, *Dictionary of Untranslatables*, p. 835.
202 Sorabji, *Matter, Space and Motion*, p. 57; van Ess, *Theology and Society in the Second and Third Centuries of the Hijra, Volume 4*, p. 171.
203 For further discussion, see Pines, *Studies in Islamic Atomism*, pp. 1–19; van Ess, '60 Years After', pp. 10–16; Dhanani, *The Physical Theory of Kalām*, pp. 55–62.
204 Wolfson, *The Philosophy of the Kalam*, pp. 488–89.
205 Pines, *Studies in Islamic Atomism*, pp. 5–6; van Ess, '60 Years After', pp. 8–9.
206 Wolfson, *The Philosophy of the Kalam*, pp. 472–73.
207 Wolfson, *The Philosophy of the Kalam*, p. 491.
208 Wolfson, *The Philosophy of the Kalam*, p. 488.

accidents),[209] the ontological system of atom and accident leads directly to a substrate-attribute theory.

Although characteristically joined to make the larger bodies of substances, the people, tables and apples that we see in the world, atoms are ultimately the substrates in which accidents inhere. In other words, atoms are the kind of stuff that can hold qualities. As Frank illustrates, '[To be black] is not, in short, a real ontological attribute or qualification of the being of a thing, but simply the present accident in its presence and inherence in the material substrate: a physical disposition of the substrate'.[210] This left proponents of atomism with the notable difficulty of explaining how an entity composed of numerous atoms, each with its own individual accidents, nonetheless could be treated as a single unified being.[211] This problem is absent from a bundle theory that makes the substance directly possess its attributes instead of via a substratum, though such a theory has other questions to address.

I suggest that al-Māturīdī adopts the following ontological position:

1. A bundle theory in which every substance (*ʿayn, jawhar*), in the sense of a created body (*jism*), is formed from, and characterised by, accidents.
2. An absence of atomism.
3. A conception of natures (*ṭabāʾiʿ*) as the accidents that compose any body, which have specific dispositions to act, or in more general terms the nature dominant in any given substance.

For (1), see the discussion in the previous section, in which al-Māturīdī only defines the 'thing' as the *ʿayn*, a word he sometimes uses instead of *jawhar* for the Aristotelian category of substance, and its *ṣifāt*.[212] He seems to distinguish between the accidents that comprise the parts of a *jism* and those that characterise it: 'Power, as it is not from the parts of the body, is an accident in reality (*anna al-quwwata idh laysat hiya min ajzāʾi al-jismi fa-hiya ʿaraḍ un fī al-ḥaqīqa*)'.[213] This is close to the idea of *abʿāḍ* (sing. *baʿḍ*; parts or primary qualities) of Ḍirār b. ʿAmr and al-Najjār, which tend to be of opposites from which bodies are formed, as opposed to *aʿrāḍ* that characterise contrasting states.[214] Ḍirār's distinction between inseparable and separable

209 See al-Nasafī, *Al-Tamhīd fī uṣūl al-dīn*, pp. 19–20; al-Bāqillānī, *Kitāb al-tamhīd*, pp. 17–19; Fakhry, *Islamic Occasionalism*, p. 37; Hye, 'Ashʿarism', vol. 1, p. 240.

210 Frank, *Beings and Their Attributes*, p. 105.

211 Frank, *Beings and Their Attributes*, p. 40.

212 Al-Māturīdī, *Kitāb al-tawḥīd*, pp. 105, 215.

213 Al-Māturīdī, *Kitāb al-tawḥīd*, p. 346.

214 See Rudolph, *Al-Māturīdī and the Development of Sunnī Theology*, p. 253, 259–60; van Ess, *Theology and Society in the Second and Third Centuries of the Hijra, Volume 3*, pp. 41–43; Schöck, 'Jahm b. Ṣafwān (d. 128/745–46) and the 'Jahmiyya' and Ḍirār b. ʿAmr (d. 200/815)', pp. 68–72. Cf. al-Māturīdī, *Kitāb al-tawḥīd*, p. 78.

accidents may help to explain al-Māturīdī's position that bodies are only able to endure through time due to God giving them successive momentary accidents of endurance (*baqāʾ*).[215] It seems that the addition of *baqāʾ* allows the body and thereby its constituents, but not other momentary accidents such as *quwwa*, to continue in existence.[216]

The strongest evidence for (2) is that al-Māturīdī nowhere brings atoms into his ontological picture.[217] On (3), al-Māturīdī indicates that the *ṭabāʾiʿ* are either substances or accidents.[218] Nevertheless, interpretation of them as accidents seems the better inference from statements such as the following:

215 Al-Māturīdī, *Kitāb al-tawḥīd*, pp. 80–81, 346.

216 Al-Māturīdī, *Kitāb al-tawḥīd*, p. 346. There is an indication that al-Māturīdī followed Ḍirār's position because only accidents are perceptible in al-Nasafī, *Tabṣirat al-adilla*, vol. 1, pp. 189–90. Here al-Nasafī unconvincingly tries to argue that he did not really hold this view. See Rudolph, *Al-Māturīdī and the Development of Sunnī Theology*, p. 253; Yavuz, 'İmâm Mâtürîdî'nin Tabiat ve İlliyete Bakışı', pp. 56–57. For another reading of these points, see Bulgen, 'al-Māturīdī and Atomism', pp. 251–54.

217 See Rudolph, *Al-Māturīdī and the Development of Sunnī Theology*, p. 245. This is supported by Frank, 'Notes and Remarks on the Ṭabāʾiʿ in the Teaching of al-Māturīdī', p. 140, n. 12. Dhanani thinks al-Māturīdī combines the 'normative *kalām* view of atoms/bodies and accidents' with his idea of the *ṭabāʾiʿ*. Dhanani, 'Al-Māturīdī and al-Nasafī on Atomism and the Tabāʾiʿ', p. 72. I would argue, however, that Dhanani does not establish atoms and bodies to be equivalent in al-Māturīdī's system, nor show that he makes use of atoms at all. Mehmet Bulgen discusses the question of whether al-Māturīdī should be considered an atomist at length and gathers many of the relevant materials. See Bulgen, 'al-Māturīdī and Atomism', pp. 241–57. The texts Bulgen quotes are explicit that al-Māturīdī saw substances (or bodies) as composed of accidents alone, and I do not find his arguments inferring a possible implicit atomist position convincing. While Rudolph is right that al-Māturīdī does not outline an atomistic ontology, he is not entirely correct to assert that 'one seeks in vain in the *K. al-Tawḥīd* for the term *al-juzʾ alladhī lā yatajazza*''. Rudolph, *Al-Māturīdī and the Development of Sunnī Theology*, p. 245. I have found three occurrences of variants of this phrase: (1) Criticism of the 'fanciful' idea that bodies are divided into atoms, which could lead to the claim that the invisible parts could be joined together by other than God. Al-Māturīdī, *Kitāb al-tawḥīd*, pp. 155–56. (2) A discussion of divine and human action in which the idea of an indivisible part is used for the analogy of two people working together to carry an object. Al-Māturīdī, *Kitāb al-tawḥīd*, pp. 319–20. (3) A related point refuting al-Kaʿbī's claim that the human act cannot be a creation of God, as that would require the sharing of a single act, which is impossible to divide so that each party has a part. Al-Māturīdī, *Kitâbü't-Tevhîd*, p. 322. On points (2) and (3), see al-Māturīdī, *Kitâbü't-Tevhîd*, pp. 361–62, 365. I extend grateful thanks to Kayhan Özaykal for his translation of relevant sections of Topaloğlu's Turkish rendering and his own comments on the arguments.

218 Al-Māturīdī, *Kitāb al-tawḥīd*, p. 211. Frank rejects the idea that natures are accidents and instead treats them as bodies. His claim is based on a text that he interprets as al-Māturīdī excluding colour, taste and so on from the category of accidents. See Frank, 'Notes and Remarks on the Ṭabāʾiʿ in the Teaching of al-Māturīdī', p. 139.

> That every sensed thing is not free from being gathered from diverse opposed natures (*ṭabāʾiʿ*), the reality of which is to mutually repel and distance each other, establishes that their gathering is [achieved] by other than them; and in that is their temporality.[219]

Al-Māturīdī's most explicit reference to the position occurs in his refutation of *aṣḥāb al-ṭabāʾiʿ*, the name that he gives to a group of the *falāsifa* who thought that the *ṭabāʾiʿ* were eternal constituents of the material world.[220] In this context he says: 'we find heat rises by its nature (*bi-ṭabʿihā*) and cold descends and the two are gathered in a body'.[221] In other places, he is less specific, mentioning that the world is 'built upon different natures and opposed aspects',[222] that 'people are composed of divergent inclinations, diffuse natures, and desires that are dominant in their construction'[223] and that 'the human being is disposed to have a nature and an intellect, such that what the intellect finds good is not what the nature desires and what it finds bad is not what the nature is repelled from'.[224]

The passage in question is concerned with rejecting the possibility of human sight 'reaching' (*idrāk*) God when affirming the Beautific Vision (*al-ruʾya*), as this is based on the limits (*ḥudūd*) enveloping corporeal things. Al-Māturīdī mentions colour as one such limit, an aspect by which an object is perceived, and that all things other than God have such limits, 'even minds and accidents (*ḥattā al-ʿuqūli wa-l-aʿrāḍ*)'. Al-Māturīdī, *Kitāb al-tawḥīd*, pp. 145–46. He is not making a point about the status of colour but using a familiar example of a concrete object bounded by its coloured exterior to express that all created things, from the greatest to the simplest, have limits. Moreover, elsewhere al-Māturīdī indicates that colour is an accident (p. 81).

219 Al-Māturīdī, *Kitāb al-tawḥīd*, p. 78. See Rudolph, *Al-Māturīdī and the Development of Sunnī Theology*, pp. 254–56.

220 See al-Māturīdī, *Kitāb al-tawḥīd*, pp. 184–86; Frank, 'Notes and Remarks on the Ṭabāʾiʿ in the Teaching of al-Māturīdī', p. 146; Dhanani, 'Al-Māturīdī and al-Nasafī on Atomism and the Tabāʾiʿ', p. 69.

221 Al-Māturīdī, *Kitāb al-tawḥīd*, p. 184. See Frank, 'Notes and Remarks on the Ṭabāʾiʿ in the Teaching of al-Māturīdī', p. 139. Note that the argument that God must be one, so that He can balance between the 'four natures (*al-ṭabāʾiʿ al-arbaʿa*)' does appear in the margins of the manuscript of *Kitāb al-tawḥīd*. Al-Māturīdī, 'Kitāb al-tawḥīd', fol. 14v; al-Māturīdī, *Kitāb al-tawḥīd*, p. 93. This comment postdates the text.

222 Al-Māturīdī, *Kitāb al-tawḥīd*, p. 67.

223 Al-Māturīdī, *Kitāb al-tawḥīd*, p. 67.

224 Al-Māturīdī, *Kitāb al-tawḥīd*, p. 76. Rudolph thinks natures are probably to be identified with the four primary qualities of warm, cold, dry and damp, following al-Kaʿbī, due to scattered remarks in *Kitāb al-tawḥīd* and the presence of this doctrine in al-Sālimī (though without mention of al-Māturīdī). See Rudolph, *Al-Māturīdī and the Development of Sunnī Theology*, pp. 255–56, 259, 261–62. In a subsequent treatment, he acknowledges that further research is needed, pointing to al-Māturīdī's exegetical work *Taʾwīlāt al-qurʾān*. Rudolph, 'Ḥanafī Theological Tradition and Māturīdism', pp. 288–89.

Turning to his *Taʾwīlāt al-qurʾān* further complicates this picture. In his exegetical work, al-Māturīdī sometimes references the ancient elemental concept of *ṭabāʾiʿ*, while never personally endorsing it, nor preferring any version of the theory. Thus, he comments on Q. 23:14 – 'Blessed is God, the best of creators' – that a possible meaning is a refutation of those *falāsifa* who believe the world's foundation (*aṣl*) is the four qualities (*ṭabāʾiʿ*), or four or five [elements], such as water, earth and fire.[225] He also says in regard to Q. 76:2: 'We created humankind from a drop of mixed fluid', that 'some say [it is] the mixture of the four humours that humankind is disposed towards (*al-ṭabāʾiʿ al-arbaʿ allatī ʿalayhā jubila al-insān*)'.[226] In many more places within his *tafsīr*, al-Māturīdī uses the term *ṭabāʾiʿ* for the tendency or nature of a given thing to act. He mentions the medicinal properties of plants (*ṭabāʾiʿ al-nabāt*);[227] the instinctual nature of bees and other animals to seek good;[228] the wholesome nature of food;[229] the timid natures (*al-ṭabāʾiʿ al-nāfira*) encouraged by paraenetic speech;[230] and the nature averse to the spilling of blood.[231]

The best interpretation is that *ṭabāʾiʿ* is the name for a class of *aʿrāḍ*, or according to al-Māturīdī's preferred terminology, *ṣifāt*, upon considering their diverse propensities to act when bound together in bodies.[232] But as the term *ṭabāʾiʿ* highlights that these qualities have specific tendencies, it is also used in a more general sense for which of these natures is dominant in a given concrete entity.[233] Thus, even though al-Māturīdī does not seem completely opposed to utilising conceptions of the *ṭabāʾiʿ* that are drawn from the prevailing philosophical models of his time, he does not restrict himself to the defined system of four elemental qualities in delineating the natures of things. In fact, when writing about the specific tendencies of

225 Al-Māturīdī, *Taʾwīlāt al-qurʾān*, vol. 10, p. 16. Also see the refutation of *aṣḥāb al-ṭabāʾiʿ* in vol. 2, pp. 501–2, and vol. 8, p. 238.

226 Al-Māturīdī, *Taʾwīlāt al-qurʾān*, vol. 16, p. 316. The phrase and the Qur'anic context suggest the four humours (blood, black bile, yellow bile and phlegm) more than the primary qualities or elements.

227 Al-Māturīdī, *Taʾwīlāt al-qurʾān*, vol. 16, p. 185.

228 Al-Māturīdī, *Taʾwīlāt al-qurʾān*, vol. 8, p. 141.

229 Al-Māturīdī, *Taʾwīlāt al-qurʾān*, vol. 4, pp. 292–93.

230 Al-Māturīdī, *Taʾwīlāt al-qurʾān*, vol. 3, p. 206. This can also be read as *al-ṭabāʾiʿ al-nāqira* (argumentative natures), as found in one manuscript copy.

231 Al-Māturīdī, *Taʾwīlāt al-qurʾān*, vol. 17, p. 348.

232 See al-Māturīdī, *Kitāb al-tawḥīd*, p. 83; Rudolph, *Al-Māturīdī and the Development of Sunnī Theology*, p. 259.

233 If 'material' is replaced with 'qualitative' or 'accidental', to accord with the *ṣifa*, this is close to Frank's description of the *ṭabāʾiʿ* as 'the natural action of the material constituents of bodies, *i. e.*, their specific behaviour, active and passive, as is determined by and flows from the nature of their materiality'. Frank, 'Notes and Remarks on the Ṭabāʾiʿ in the Teaching of al-Māturīdī', p. 138.

diverse objects he appears to be reaching for what modern philosophical parlance calls dispositions.[234]

Although al-Māturīdī views things as having causal effects within the world, this is combined with a parallel insistence on God's power and creative activity.[235] His conceptual use of natures reflects their utility for his religious arguments as much as it does for his ontology. That the world is formed from fundamentally opposed and contradictory elements necessitates that it is brought into being and maintained by God.[236] Moreover, this is His intelligent choice. The world cannot have occurred blindly and is not kept in stasis, but fluctuates from state to state according to the divine design.[237] Analogously, the human being as microcosm is shaped by conflicting internal desires that require the regulation of God's great gift to humanity: the intellect.[238] Notwithstanding the classical tradition's rejection of al-Māturīdī's *ṭabāʾiʿ*, the doctrine had some impact on the early Ḥanafī Samarqandī school, for instance in Ibn Yaḥyā al-Bashāgharī's commentary on *Jumal min uṣūl al-dīn*. He presents the *dahriyya* (another name for *aṣḥāb al-ṭabāʾiʿ*) as believing that things in the world are composed of four elemental qualities of which one dominates, but adds that this supports his own stance that there must be a creator to cause this to occur.[239]

Al-Māturīdī's bundle theory of properties and dispositional reading of natures are not just of historical interest. As I have sought to demonstrate, these metaphysical positions play an important role in his theological system and deserve exploration with respect to their contemporary salience. Hence, I will reinterpret al-Māturīdī's ontological position in the light of a phenomenological trope theory.[240] A crucial insight that allows this move

234 Choi and Fara, 'Dispositions'. It is possible to interpret al-Māturīdī's account of dispositions as deflationary, so that they are nothing more than concepts for the properties of given concrete particulars as they act in certain regular ways in the world. See Armstrong, *A World of States of Affairs*, pp. 81–82. See also Muhtaroglu, 'Al-Māturīdī's View of Causality', p. 13.

235 See the discussion in al-Māturīdī, *Kitāb al-tawḥīd*, pp. 83–85. I suggest that a concurrentist position may best account for these two aspects of his thought. But I will save further discussion on this point for a future treatment of human and divine action, which is where it is theologically most significant. For a sketch, see Harvey, *The Qur'an and the Just Society*, pp. 32–34. Also consider points (2) and (3) on page 90, note 217. For an alternative occasionalist interpretation of al-Māturīdī, see Muhtaroglu, 'Al-Māturīdī's View of Causality', pp. 8–10.

236 Al-Māturīdī, *Kitāb al-tawḥīd*, p. 211.

237 Al-Māturīdī, *Kitāb al-tawḥīd*, p. 108. See Dorroll, 'The Universe in Flux', pp. 132–33.

238 Dhanani, 'Al-Māturīdī and al-Nasafī on Atomism and the Tabāʾiʿ', pp. 70–72.

239 Al-Samarqandī, *Jumal min uṣūl al-dīn wa-yalīhu sharḥuhu*, p. 65.

240 Tropes are also known by terms such as 'property (and relation) instances', 'abstract particulars', 'concrete properties', 'quality (and relation) bits', 'individual accidents' and, for Husserl, 'moments'. The word 'trope' was coined lightheartedly by D. C. Williams in 1953 and has become the dominant terminology. Bacon, 'Tropes'; Cassin, *Dictionary of Untranslatables*, p. 1157.

is to understand his conception of accidents as equivalent to such tropes. Notably, the term *ʿaraḍ*, which was used for accident in the formative period of *kalām*, originally refers to the perception of a phenomenon when an object presents itself.[241] To develop this argument further, I will examine some key developments in modern ontology.

For our purposes, we can look at trope theory as one way to deal with the question of how the concrete particulars of the world, such as its people, tables and apples, are to be related to their familiar properties, such as wise, flat and green. Since at least Plato, a common solution has been 'realism' about the existence of universal properties of wisdom, flatness and greenness and so on, that concrete particulars may exemplify or instantiate. Trope theory treats property instances as particulars, such as 'this greenness'[242] when seeing an apple, and usually eliminates universals as ontic realities.[243] There are various philosophical attractions to this nominalist metaphysics. Two of the common ones are its parsimony in reducing ontological kinds by removing the mysterious category of universals, and its utility in explaining the causal powers of concrete entities, as tropes are causally active particulars.[244] To this we may add theological attractions that do not normally arise in the analytic philosophy literature. I have already identified its consonance with al-Māturīdī's ontological thought, which is connected to its general utility as a language to speak about God. Moreover, it is useful for the articulation of specific theological arguments.[245]

241 Van Ess, '60 Years After', p. 9.

242 Although the property of colour is just a convenient example, common in the literature, I note that my phenomenological position rejects the distinction between primary and secondary qualities that could be used to dispute its cogency. See Byrne and Hilbert, 'Are Colors Secondary Qualities?', pp. 354, 358; Husserl, *Ideas*, pp. 74–75. There is a distinction made in recent literature between modifying and modular tropes. A modifying trope grounds a property in an object without itself having that property – for example, a greenness trope is the greenness of an apple but not itself green. A modular trope grounds a property in an object while having that property, so in this case the greenness of the apple would be considered green. Koons and Pickavance, *The Atlas of Reality*, p. 167. I think the latter position, which meta-qualifies tropes with further properties, is incoherent and likely to lead to a regress (see the discussion of *waṣf al-ṣifa* on pages 148–49). It is alleged that not allowing tropes to be qualified by a property makes them unsuitable for being causal relata or the objects of sense perception. Koons and Pickavance, *The Atlas of Reality*, pp. 167–68. I find this unconvincing: when I see a green apple, surely what I see is its greenness (amongst other properties). To say that greenness has to itself 'be green' seems a category mistake.

243 Campbell, *Abstract Particulars*, pp. 27–28. Armstrong suggests that it is possible to combine tropes with a theory of uninstantiated universals. He argues, however, that it is more plausible to either treat universals as instantiated only and therefore eliminate tropes or to replace them with resembling tropes. Armstrong, *Universals*, p. 132.

244 For a fuller list, see Ehring, *Tropes*, pp. 1–2.

245 See pages 156–58, 221.

So much for a brief introduction to trope theory. How does phenomenology come into the picture? Arguably, the specialisation of contemporary analytic philosophy has led to the abandonment of comprehensive philosophical systems and a silo effect in which metaphysicians work, for the most part, detached from broader questions of epistemology, logic and truth. This is what Badiou calls the replacement of the 'grand style' by the 'little style'.[246] Exotic ontological universes are proposed alongside an assumed naturalism about the strict separation of the mind from the world that is described by the theory. As discussed in the present chapter, the phenomenological position from which I am working, however, is that truth is not to be conceived as first and foremost a set of posited mind-independent 'facts', but the verification of intersubjective propositions in the world. Here is another respect in which the idea of tropes is attractive: they are precisely the intentional objects that are made to appear to the mind.[247]

I should state at this juncture that my contribution simultaneously draws from three traditions: al-Māturīdī's *kalām* ontology; prevailing analytic trope theory; and Husserlian phenomenology. Therefore, my ontological theory is not entirely representative of that articulated by Husserl. Though he makes use of trope-like entities, which he calls 'moments', he also has a place for universals in his system, which I reject.[248] Moreover, Husserl's method of the phenomenological reduction leads him to articulate his analyses of objects in a complex technical register, which would not advance my primarily theological rather than philosophical aims. If I were to adopt a more phenomenological idiom in what follows, instead of analysing objects as sets of tropes, I could discuss them as manifolds[249] by which their appearances are given to consciousness.[250] Nevertheless, I suggest that my formulation of objects phenomenologically constituted by tropes can apply relevant key insights from Husserl to resolve a more familiar series of ontological problems.

The next part of the enquiry is structured by three topics relating properties to their objects, each of which reveals a distinct theme of analysis for fleshing out a trope theory:[251]

246 Badiou, *Theoretical Writings*, p. 3.

247 Cf. Husserl, *The Idea of Phenomenology*, pp. 24–25.

248 See Smith, *Husserl*, p. 152.

249 A manifold can be defined as: 'A multiplicity in which an identity reveals itself'. Drummond, *Historical Dictionary of Husserl's Philosophy*, p. 127.

250 See Sokolowski, 'Identities in Manifolds', pp. 63–68; Husserl, *Ideas*, p. 84. Some similar ideas are found in al-Māturīdī, *Kitāb al-tawḥīd*, p. 224. See Dorroll, 'The Universe in Flux', pp. 129–32.

251 See Ehring, *Tropes*, pp. 4–5. Note that Ehring does not introduce the terminology of Many Over One in this way at the beginning of his book.

1. One Over Many – Different objects apparently sharing the same property, leading to the questions of property identity and resemblance.
2. Many Over One – Objects having more than one property, leading to the question of object cohesion.
3. One Over Many Times – Objects persisting with the same property, leading to the question of object identity over time.

With respect to One Over Many, the key aspect of tropes is that each property is a particular. This means that, even if I have two apples that are the same shade of green, the greenness (*g*) of apple *A* is a distinct entity from the greenness (*g'*) of apple *B*. On the 'standard model' of trope theory, developed by Keith Campbell, this can be expressed by taking the particular nature of any given trope to be basic and singular.[252] It is thus impossible for the green trope of apple *A* to be shared or duplicated in apple *B*. What must be said is that *g* exactly resembles *g'*. More generally, the notion of green can be understood as the set of all resembling green tropes.[253] I argue that resemblance depends on the interplay of intersubjective human experience with the world, rather than the way things inherently are 'out there'.[254] The membership condition of the set of resembling greenness tropes is thus tied to the intersubjective construction of that particular set, rather than its existence as a Platonic entity in the world. This will prove important presently.

Douglas Ehring attacks the standard model, instead favouring the notion of a natural class trope theory. This position, instead of making the nature of a trope basic, explains it in virtue of the trope's membership in certain natural classes. Thus the resemblance of *g* and *g'* is a function of their co-membership in the class of green tropes.[255] The championing of the unpopular natural class trope theory is one of the

252 Campbell, *Abstract Particulars*, pp. 56–57.

253 Campbell, *Abstract Particulars*, p. 31; Armstrong, *Universals*, pp. 121–22. An objection raised in the literature against this idea is that resemblance itself becomes a universal instantiated within particulars, which leads to a vicious circle when it is, in turn, explained through resemblance. E. J. Lowe shows that, while this may prove a problem for certain types of nominalism, trope theory is able to resist the interpretation of resemblance as anything beyond the nature of particulars. Lowe, *A Survey of Metaphysics*, pp. 363–65.

254 Campbell allows for a 'human contribution' in the classification of properties but thinks that for tropes 'resemblance is an objective primitive'. Campbell, *Abstract Particulars*, p. 31. This accords with his view on compresence. I explain both relations phenomenologically.

255 Ehring, *Tropes*, p. 9. Another option is the resemblance trope theory, which makes the nature of the trope determined by its direct resemblance to other tropes.

distinctive contributions of Ehring's book *Tropes*.[256] A key part of his strategy is to try to undermine the Campbellian model, which he argues is compelling, but flawed.[257] He contends that Campbell claims tropes are simple; yet they seem to need both an intrinsic particularity and a nature, which would make them complex.[258] Ehring elucidates his critique in the following way: if we consider two red tropes, the aspect of each one that grounds its particularity and individuates it from the other one, its 'thisness', is not the same as that which grounds its nature and makes it resemble the other one, its 'redness'.[259]

I am not convinced by Ehring's argument. According to Campbell's theory, each of the two tropes is precisely defined as 'its particular redness' in a way that is prior to either of the quasi-universal constructions of 'thisness' and 'redness'. The resemblance between them is not due to their shared 'red nature', but because they are both property instances of particular redness. Thus, Ehring seems to beg the question by positing his natural classes as more basic than the individual tropes that compose them.

On one level, this is merely a question of which notion to make primitive within any given theory.[260] Nonetheless, it is precisely here that Campbell's view is more intuitive. Arguably, the objects of our experience are individual property instances: when I look at a tomato, I surely see a particular redness, not part of a natural class.[261] Furthermore, there seems something slightly perverse about removing universals from one's ontological universe only to reintroduce natural classes. According to my proposal, the set of all resembling red tropes is nothing more than an ideal grouping of particulars that allows talk about the concept of red. It is certainly not a Platonic entity floating in the aether. Moreover, if we start to see resemblance classes of tropes as inductively constituted from the regularities of experience, we have a good story about how we come to believe in universals to start with.[262]

The case of Many Over One, that objects possess multiple properties, leads immediately to the question of object cohesion, which is central to the articulation of any trope theory. Let us think again about an apple. What is it that makes a single unified apple out of the various identified properties of colour, shape, texture, flavour and so on? If we exclude consideration of universals, two main theories present themselves: trope substrate-attribute theories and trope bundle theories.

256 See Ehring, *Tropes*, pp. 175–201.
257 Ehring, *Tropes*, p. 176, n. 2.
258 Ehring, *Tropes*, p. 176.
259 Ehring, *Tropes*, p. 177. In Māturīdī terms, 'thisness' is the trope's isness, and 'redness' is its whatness. As I have been suggesting, this is a conceptual not ontic distinction.
260 See Miller, 'Are All Primitives Created Equal?', pp. 273–74.
261 See Leftow, 'One Step Toward God', p. 78.
262 Cf. Wolterstorff, *On Universals*, p. 142.

A trope substrate-attribute theory holds that there is some underlying substratum, also called a 'thin particular', to which the various properties attach. The idea is that the properties are possessed by, or attributed to, some other thing within the object, even though it becomes impossible to say anything about what that thing is in itself.[263] In the *kalām* ontologies discussed above, this is the role played by the atom. This position has been heavily criticised on grounds of parsimony and the unsatisfactoriness of positing an unknowable substrate, although defended by some philosophers.[264]

The position that I see as more promising and will develop further is the trope bundle theory. This proposes that a concrete particular is constituted as a bundle of its tropes without any substrate. The notions that require definition are that of bundle and constitution. I argue that a bundle, as an object of knowledge, is conceptualised as the set of tropes constituting a given substance. Thus, for instance, the apple is constituted by the set of its properties. We need to be careful: this does not mean that the apple is identical to its properties taken as a fusion of mereological parts. As discussed in Section II, I take a set to be a categorial intuition of the mind that can verify ontic structures existing in the world. Just as intuitionistic logic allows us to state that the empty set is neither nothing, nor other than it, an apple is neither (merely) its properties taken altogether, nor other than them.

Within this framework, epistemological constitution of the concrete particular as a set of its tropes is something performed by the human mind. We can come at this from two directions. In one sense it is the mind that, upon perceiving various qualia, verifies their constitution as a single object. Yet the world is generally revealed to us as discrete concrete particulars that can conceptually break down into their properties, as in the example of the apple. This takes trope bundle theory in a phenomenological direction, requiring an intimate interplay between the structure of the world and the categories of our minds.[265] Consequently, we can speak about the structure of things using the correspondence theory of truth outlined earlier. We verify the apple when we constitute it as an object of knowledge, which is as a set of its properties. Propositions about these properties are truthbearers, while the tropes to which they correspond are truthmakers: 'the apple is green' (truthbearer) is confirmed as true due to verification

263 This goes back to John Locke who said: 'the substance is supposed always something besides the extension, figure, solidity, motion, thinking, or other observable ideas, though we know not what it is'. Locke, *An Essay Concerning Human Understanding*, p. 137.

264 There are powerful critical arguments in Campbell, *Abstract Particulars*, pp. 7–11. For a defence, see Martin, 'Substance Substantiated', pp. 7–10; Armstrong, *Universals*, pp. 114–16.

265 See Sokolowski, *Introduction to Phenomenology*, pp. 30–31.

of 'the greenness of the apple' (truthmaker).[266] In Husserlian terms, a so-called transcendental object is constituted by the set of its appearances, or 'manifold of noematic profiles'.[267]

This way of looking at trope bundle theory does away with a notion of compresence, which is often posited in the analytic tradition as the irreducible basis of constitution.[268] Instead, compresence is replaced with phenomenological constitution. Ultimately, the substratum in substrate-attribute theories and compresence in bundle theories seem to be alternative ways of tackling the same problem: bridging the gap between a multiplicity of distinct attributes and their logical, or metaphysical, unity within a single concrete particular. The advantage of my solution over the others is that, rather than concretising this gap and generating an unknowable or unanalysable entity to fill it, I suggest that it is inherent in the logical structure of the mind and is constantly transcendentally bridged when approaching the verifiable world.[269]

An argument is sometimes deployed against construing a trope bundle as a set (although it notably also applies to mereological sums and states of affairs), as well as against forming universalised notions with sets of resembling tropes. It makes use of Leibniz's Law, also known as the Indiscernibility of Identicals: if *x* and *y* are the same, then they have exactly the same properties.[270] Thus, any given set must remain unchanging in its members as any change in members amounts to a new set. Applied to trope bundle theory, it would appear to imply that an object has its properties as a matter of logical necessity, which seems untrue of the contingent world. In the case of sets of resembling tropes, the same premise mandates that the resemblance set of a given property, such as greenness, contains every

266 See Mulligan et al., 'Truth-Makers', pp. 295–97. They use the term 'moment', taken from Husserl, to describe an entity that is for all intents and purposes a trope.

267 Laycock, 'Actual and Potential Omniscience', p. 69. Note that this constitution of objects is intersubjective. See page 65.

268 Campbell understands compresence as a bundle of properties coinciding in space-time, although he shows some doubts about tricky cases, such as the possibility of a material object sharing its location with a magnetic field. Campbell, *Abstract Particulars*, pp. 19, 175, n. 5. Ehring bites the bullet on the compresence relation being non-reducible, making it a momentary trope in each bundle. Ehring, *Tropes*, pp. 98, 103. I criticise this idea on page 101.

269 This idea also gets around the problem of what exactly modifying tropes within a bundle theory characterise. The argument is that, because such a theory explains a concrete particular through its bundle of tropes, there is nothing of which the tropes can be properties (except each other). Koons and Pickavance, *The Atlas of Reality*, p. 183. My argument is that the concrete particular, as the intuitionistic set of its properties or Husserlian transcendent object, is precisely the thing that is characterised by its modifying tropes.

270 Sharvy, 'Why a Class Can't Change Its Members', p. 304; Deng, *God and Time*, p. 17.

instance of a green trope, such that more or less instances could not have possibly existed, which also seems erroneous.[271]

Ehring develops a technical solution to this problem involving counterpart theory,[272] but I think the attack can be warded off in phenomenological terms. While a traditional bundle theory is committed to an object as a set of properties and is thereby constrained by the mathematical laws of set composition, I propose that a set is only ever a formal ontological structure by which the mind constitutes its experience of the world.[273] Our enumeration of the set of properties that the apple possesses allows us access to truth insofar as they are verified by the tropes within the apple. The apple *qua* apple is not a set. If it is to change, then no contradiction is raised with the properties of a set, although it would require the object's constitution with a new set of qualities. The source of confusion on this point seems to be, again, the assumption of mathematic realism, in which sets are made a part of material, instead of formal ontology. On the intuitionistic position that I have taken with respect to mathematical entities, sets are no more than ideal mental constructions.[274]

This point helps to clarify considerably the case of One Over Many Times, which refers to the persistence of properties.[275] Ehring is arguably in something of a dilemma here. On the one hand, he wants to use the phenomenon of property persistence as an argument for the utility of positing tropes in the first place, as the endurance of 'this particular greenness' seems to account for what we perceive better than a story involving instantiated universals.[276] On the other hand, his assumption of set realism

271 Loux, *Metaphysics*, p. 79. The difficulties in treating sets as properties are discussed in Wolterstorff, *On Universals*, pp. 173–81.

272 Ehring, *Tropes*, pp. 99–100. Counterpart theory is principally associated with David Lewis. The main idea is that the modal intuition that an object could have had other properties in another possible world is replaced by the object's 'counterpart' having these properties. See Weatherson, 'David Lewis'. The concept of the counterpart is the opposite of Kripke's notion of a 'rigid designator' and he uses it as a prelude to the introduction of his new concept. See Kripke, *Naming and Necessity*, pp. 44–46. A rigid designator is a name that designates the same object in every possible world in which that object exists. Kripke, *Naming and Necessity*, p. 48. In a recent lecture, he adds that it never designates any other object in any world. Saul Kripke, 'Naming and Necessity Revisited' (Lecture, School of Advanced Study, London, 30 May 2019), <https://youtu.be/3zazonG6zBk>, accessed 24 June 2019.

273 See Van Cleve, 'Three Versions of the Bundle Theory', pp. 102–3.

274 See page 84.

275 For an accessible overview of approaches to persistence, see Deng, *God and Time*, pp. 14–16, 18–19.

276 See Ehring, *Tropes*, pp. 50–52. He provides some distinctive arguments for the suitability of tropes in explaining this phenomenon.

in the essential nature of bundle membership means that, as a set, a bundle should not be able to change at all.

Thus, he introduces the idea of four-dimensionalism, in the form of Worm Theory, which analyses objects as four-dimensional space-time worms with related temporal parts, each one existing at its own moment, or Stage Theory, which takes them to be instantaneous stages related through counterpart theory.[277] Both of these theories solve the problem of change, but do not allow a single bundle to stay the same through time. His solution is to argue that at least one trope inside his bundles must be only momentary in duration; this is nothing other than the primitive compresence relation.[278] The picture that Ehring develops is counterintuitive: he would explain a green apple sitting motionless in a fruit bowl as a space-time worm or series of related instantaneous stages, whereby all its tropes persist, except for the one binding them together that continually winks out of existence for an exact duplicate to seamlessly replace it. This position seems to have been reached due to its apparent utility for stitching together various other defensible theories, rather than as part of a coherent description of the world. For the theory that I am articulating, there is no need to posit a compresence relation, let alone a momentary one. With their sets understood as intuitionistic constructions, bundles of tropes persist and change as phenomenologically verified without contradiction.[279]

How do these trope-theoretic insights affect the prior elaboration of al-Māturīdī's ontology? I have argued throughout this chapter that various aspects of his metaphysics can be developed in a Husserlian direction for a contemporary system that is epistemologically and ontologically satisfying. Bearing this in mind, I take his conception of substances and accidents to be translatable into a trope bundle theory. A casualty of the prior *kalām* ontology in my formulation is the successive accidents of endurance that al-Māturīdī seems to have thought were needed to keep things in existence. Although these derive from a theological milieu in which such accidents represent a constant divine imprint on the creation, I do not think that they need to be posited. As I will show in Chapter 6, the endurance of objects can be accounted for by God's action to conserve their existence through intervals of time.[280]

I translate al-Māturīdī's concept of natures (*ṭabāʾiʿ*) as the dispositions of the various tropes within the world to act in regular ways when bundled together as bodies. While I have not attempted to articulate a contemporary

277 For the details, see Ehring, *Tropes*, pp. 100–1.

278 Ehring, *Tropes*, pp. 103–5. This is remarkably similar to the *kalām* idea of an accident of endurance. See page 90.

279 Cf. Pietersma, 'Husserl's Concept of Existence', p. 321.

280 See pages 189–90.

theory of dispositions here, this seems a plausible undertaking. In the case of humanity, the category of the intellect (*ʿaql*), which al-Māturīdī understands as playing a governing role over constituent natures, is extremely important. I defer discussion of the human being in the context of both the Islamic theological tradition and contemporary philosophy to a future volume. The focus here will remain on God.

Even if the ontology developed in this chapter explains the properties within the created order, that does not on its own point to their cause. Arguments of natural theology are required for the inference from the world to its transcendent creator. These will be surveyed in the next chapter.

CHAPTER 3

Natural Theology

Rational arguments for the existence of God have a long history within Judaism, Christianity and Islam, and are an area of study in which the differences between these religious traditions become minimal.[1] They are also often unpopular today. That such arguments are not the main reason for people's faith is no secret. Belief in the existence of God is a subtle matter, usually depending more on personal conviction than the success of an intellectual 'proof'. I have three objectives in devoting a chapter to such arguments. First, I wish to respect their importance in theological and philosophical traditions, and specifically in the system of al-Māturīdī. Second, whether these arguments are successful or not, they often bring to light useful questions, such as those pertaining to possible and necessary

1 Hannah Erlwein has recently argued that, contrary to the common view of scholars, the premodern *kalām* tradition did not present arguments to rationally establish the existence of God. Erlwein, *Arguments for God's Existence in Classical Islamic Thought*, p. 4. Instead, they presupposed the existence of God, and their arguments were made to defend a specific conception of the divine nature (pp. 9–10). This is a bold and innovative claim, though I do not think it is sustainable. It is built on contrasting Muslim *kalām* arguments with 'traditional' Christian arguments for the existence of God in the face of the intertwined history of these very arguments among Jews, Christians and Muslims alike (despite an initial recognition of this point on pp. 2–3). For her study to vindicate this exceptionalism in the Muslim discourse, it would have to show it through sustained comparison with the other traditions. It is also important to consider the polemical context in which Muslim theologians, such as al-Māturīdī, worked and in which they engaged a wide range of philosophies, including those that held the world to be eternal and saw no need for the theistic God. See pages 35, 93. As I show for al-Māturīdī, whom Erlwein also discusses in her book (pp. 61–76), the typical pattern is for the theologian to establish (1) the temporality and non-self generation of the world; (2) that it has a creator; (3) that the Creator is one; (4) that He is not like His creation; and (5) (for Sunnīs) that He possesses substantive attributes. Within this framework, the cosmological and teleological arguments for the existence of God in (2) are just what they appear to be and (3)–(5) provide the proper theistic identification of God, which is not markedly different from contemporary philosophical moves with respect to an argued-for necessary being. See pages 111–12 and 119.

existence. Third, after careful study of their historical and contemporary use, on balance I think that at least some of them remain a credible way to argue rationally in the public square for the existence of a personal creator. No one has the luxury of granting others direct access to their private convictions. Within the domain of theology, the best that theists can do is to attempt to provide a reasoned justification for our belief in God in a logically coherent and consistent way.[2]

Modern discussion of the prevailing arguments for the existence of God begins with Kant's treatment of them in his *Critique of Pure Reason*, which has left an indelible mark on how they are classified and evaluated. He famously puts them into three categories – ontological, cosmological and teleological (which he calls physico-theological)[3] – stating that '[t]here are no more, nor can there be any more such proofs'.[4] His arrangement has proved decisive in contemporary philosophical and theological thought, even though the subsequent literature has provided finer-grained typologies for each category. In this chapter, I will look at the arguments provided by al-Māturīdī in *Kitāb al-tawḥīd* within this framework, as well as discuss natural theology arguments in contemporary philosophy and their significance for the constructive theological project of the present book.

There are various formulations of the ontological argument, but the main idea is that the concept of a necessary being implies its existence. Such a being is inferred, therefore, to be logically necessary without a premise drawn from observation of the world. In the Christian theological tradition, the ontological argument is famously presented by Anselm of Canterbury (d. 502/1109) and thereafter by René Descartes (d. 1060/1650) and Gottfried Wilhelm Leibniz (d. 1128/1716).[5] Many other Christian theologians dismiss it, notably Thomas Aquinas (d. 672/1274).[6]

Al-Māturīdī does not use the ontological argument and, due to its problems, neither shall I. Nonetheless, I will discuss it to present a rounded theological picture and to bring to light some of the philosophical difficulties with speaking about the concept of existence.[7] I will organise my comments around two of Anselm's most famous versions of the argument. Here is the first, found in the second chapter of his *Proslogion*, as reconstructed by David Lewis:[8]

2 See the discussion in Swinburne, 'Philosophical Theism', pp. 3–5.

3 Kant, *Critique of Pure Reason*, pp. 499–524.

4 Kant, *Critique of Pure Reason*, p. 499.

5 Oppy, 'Ontological Arguments'.

6 Aquinas, *The* 'Summa Theologica' *of St. Thomas Aquinas*, vol. 1, pp. 19–22. See Morewedge, 'A Third Version of the Ontological Argument', pp. 192–93.

7 Morewedge, 'A Third Version of the Ontological Argument', p. 214.

8 Lewis, 'Anselm and Actuality', p. 176. See Anselm, *Basic Writings*, pp. 81–82.

P1. Whatever exists in the understanding can be conceived to exist in reality.
P2. Whatever exists in the understanding would be greater if it existed in reality than if it did not.
P3. Something exists in the understanding than which nothing greater can be conceived.
C1. Something exists in reality than which nothing greater can be conceived.

Kant's extremely influential objection to this argument is to deny that existence is a genuine predicate of objects.[9] This amounts to a denial of P1 and P2 above, as he argues that, if 'existence in reality' is predicated of the concept, it would change it such that 'I could not say that the exact object of my concept exists'.[10] To put it another way, positing any predicate presupposes the subject's existence, so it cannot be used to prove it.[11] The obvious question is what to make then of propositions such as 'God exists', which seem coherent. A well-known answer is provided by Gottlob Frege and Bertrand Russell who took existence to be a second-order concept that is able to map a given first-order concept, or in Russell's case a propositional function, to 'true'.[12] This approach has been criticised on account of a problem with such definite descriptions: one is no longer able to state that 'God exists', but only 'a god exists' – that is, an entity matching the concept of God.[13]

I think that a better solution can be found in the stance that Husserl takes towards existential predication, which I discussed in the previous chapter.[14] Husserl's phenomenological verification opposes the shift in intuition from 'existence in understanding' to 'existence in reality' on which the ontological argument depends. He writes:

> [T]he positing of the essence, with the intuitive apprehension that immediately accompanies it, does not imply any positing of individual existence whatsoever; pure essential truths do not make the slightest assertion concerning facts; hence from them alone we are not able to infer even the pettiest truth concerning the fact-world.[15]

9 Kant, *Critique of Pure Reason*, p. 504.

10 Kant, *Critique of Pure Reason*, p. 505.

11 Kant's argument that existence is not a real predicate is inconsistent with his own theory of existential judgements. For Kant, synthetic judgements add a predicate to the concept of a subject; yet he also holds that existential propositions are always synthetic. The result is that 'exists' must be a real predicate. See Bader, 'Real Predicates and Existential Judgements', pp. 1153–54. Thanks to Bruce Reichenbach for pointing this out to me.

12 Nelson, 'Existence'.

13 Mackie, *The Miracle of Theism*, p. 47.

14 See page 79.

15 Husserl, *Ideas*, p. 14.

Charles Hartshorne claims that the weakness of Anselm's second-chapter argument has been used to discredit and ignore the ontological argument, despite the more powerful version that he develops in the third chapter.[16] In summary, this latter argument is as follows:[17]

P1. It is possible to conceive of something in the understanding that necessarily exists in reality.
P2. Something that necessarily exists in reality is greater than something that does not necessarily exist in reality.
P3. Something exists in the understanding, than which nothing greater can be conceived.
C1. If something than which nothing greater can be conceived did not necessarily exist in reality, it would not be something than which nothing greater can be conceived, which is a contradiction. Therefore, something necessarily exists in reality, than which nothing greater can be conceived.

This argument has some remarkable similarities with a version of the ontological argument associated with Ibn Sīnā, although there is considerable debate over his position. In an important article, Toby Mayer shows that, while Ibn Sīnā does engage both ontological and cosmological modes in his complete case for the existence of God, his preferred approach contains an irreducibly ontological aspect. In summary, this occurs in his shift from the concept of a necessary being to its existence in reality, which is supported by his assertion that the conception of such a being as non-existent generates an absurdity.[18] Mayer uses a typology developed by Graham Oppy to classify Ibn Sīnā's ontological argument as modal, due to his focus on the distinction between necessity and possibility, as opposed to Anselm and Descartes who he argues are definitional in approach.[19] I would add that, while Anselm's second-chapter argument is indeed based on definition, the one in his third chapter turns on contrasting modal categories.[20]

In the next chapter, I argue for a conceptualist account of modality based on an intuitionistic stance towards logical and mathematical truths. This view implies that logical necessity applies only to ideal meanings, not ontic realities. The strongest kind of necessity for God or features of the world must therefore be a variety of metaphysical necessity.

16 Hartshorne, *Anselm's Discovery*, pp. 86–90.
17 Hartshorne, *Anselm's Discovery*, p. 96. See Anselm, *Basic Writings*, p. 82.
18 Mayer, 'Ibn Sīnā's "Burhān al-Ṣiddīqīn"', pp. 23–24.
19 Mayer, 'Ibn Sīnā's "Burhān al-Ṣiddīqīn"', pp. 37–38.
20 See Hartshorne, *Anselm's Discovery*, pp. 89–90, 100.

A less technical objection to all forms of the ontological argument is that it does not live up to its own claim to be logically necessary. If it did, it would be an obvious contradiction to deny that a necessary being exists, only possible for Anselm's 'fool'.[21] Yet on the contrary, it has been widely recognised for many centuries that the argument is only convincing to theists, and not even to many of them.[22]

The cosmological argument is more properly a family of arguments that are distinguished by reasoning from an abstract general feature of the world to the existence of a necessary being. Unlike the ontological argument, the being reached through the cosmological argument is metaphysically but not logically necessary. Such necessity is described very well by Bruce Reichenbach:

> A necessary being is one that if it exists, it neither came into existence nor can cease to exist, and correspondingly, if it does not exist, it cannot come into existence. If it exists, it eternally maintains its own existence; it is self-sufficient and self-sustaining. So understood, the cosmological argument does not rely on notions central to the ontological argument.[23]

On this basis, it is possible to dismiss Kant's claim that the cosmological argument collapses into the ontological argument.[24] In contemporary philosophy, the cosmological argument is classified into three types, which can be sketched as follows:[25]

1. The *kalām* cosmological argument (KCA), which argues on the basis that contingent things began to exist.
2. The Leibnizian cosmological argument, which invokes the Principle of Sufficient Reason to argue for the impossibity of contingent things being self-generated.
3. The Thomistic cosmological argument, which relies on the impossibility of an essentially ordered infinite regress.

21 See Anselm, *Basic Writings*, p. 83.

22 See Oppy, 'Ontological Arguments'; Swinburne, *The Christian God*, p. 144. But there have been some recent attempts to revive the argument. Along with the work of Hartshorne, see Plantinga, *The Nature of Necessity*, pp. 196–221; Leftow, 'Individual and Attribute in the Ontological Argument'; Nagasawa, *Maximal God*, pp. 123–24.

23 Reichenbach, 'Cosmological Argument'. Also see Yandell, 'Divine Necessity and Divine Goodness', pp. 321–22. The same point is made in al-Bazdawī, *Uṣūl al-dīn*, p. 27. I distinguish between God's absolute metaphysical necessity and the non-absolute metaphysical necessity of worldly constants that depend on Him. See page 135.

24 Kant, *Critique of Pure Reason*, pp. 509–10.

25 Reichenbach, 'Cosmological Argument'.

It should be noted that, while (1) makes use of both the idea that contingent things need a cause and that the universe began to exist, (2) only makes use of the former proposition. In what follows, I will argue that al-Māturīdī uses a version of (1) and arguably also of (2), although I will focus on the KCA. I will leave aside (3) due to its reliance on an Aristotelian metaphysical framework adopted by neither al-Māturīdī nor the main proponents of contemporary discussions.[26]

Before seeking to establish the existence of the Creator (*muḥdith*), al-Māturīdī takes the preliminary step of showing that the world is not eternal, providing a multitude of arguments to support his case.[27] As I observed in Chapter 1, al-Māturīdī exhibits his non-foundationalist epistemology in the number of arguments he adduces for his core thesis of the temporality of the world. They are meant as dialectical arguments by which he wishes to reveal the premises of his rivals as absurd. In this bout, he produces a flurry of jabs to overwhelm the opponent, rather than relying on the knockout blow of a single demonstrative argument.

When commenting on this topic, Erkan Kurt ignores the complexity of al-Māturīdī's engagement, despite citing his work. He expresses the argument of '*ḥudūth*' (temporality) in a single deductive form and then dismisses it as 'a false syllogism'.[28] Even if his critique of this specific formulation is cogent, it is to defend against such responses that al-Māturīdī produced so many arguments in the first place. Furthermore, one of Kurt's

26 See Copan, 'Introduction', p. 3; Beck, 'A Thomistic Cosmological Argument', pp. 95–101.

27 Al-Māturīdī, *Kitāb al-tawḥīd*, pp. 77–82. These arguments flow into each other, so their exact number depends on how they are counted. They have been studied in detail by Cerić and Rudolph, who both take a cue from al-Māturīdī's reference to his three means of knowledge to classify them. Cerić argues that the first two are based on tradition and a further six are based on the senses. *Roots of Synthetic Theology in Islam*, pp. 111–13. He then turns to other places in al-Māturīdī's book in which he argues rationally against the eternality of the world to extract seven arguments, each based on a distinct premise (pp. 121–37). Rudolph gives a more complete analysis of the section, counting seventeen arguments in total: 1, 2 and 12 rely on authoritative reports; 3 to 7 on sense perception; and 8 to 17 (except 12) on rational enquiry. Rudolph, *Al-Māturīdī and the Development of Sunnī Theology*, pp. 233–37. He also provides a very helpful summary of the core intuitions that underlie each of these sources (p. 238). But he arguably does not sufficiently highlight that an important aim of arguments 11–17 is to refute the counterclaim that al-Māturīdī's belief in perpetual existence in the Hereafter implies the pre-eternity of the world. See al-Māturīdī, *Kitāb al-tawḥīd*, pp. 80–82. This point is both part of the dialectical cut and thrust of al-Māturīdī's approach to theology and his defence of the coherency of combining the doctrines of an eternal afterlife and creation *ex nihilo*. It has also re-emerged as an important theme in contemporary discussions of the KCA (see below). Moreover, his arguments against an infinite regress of accidents are some of the earliest in the *kalām* tradition. See Shihadeh, 'Mereology in *Kalām*', pp. 8–9.

28 Kurt, *Creation*, pp. 58–59.

main criticisms of *kalām* arguments against the pre-eternality of the world is that they undermine perpetual existence in the Hereafter. Here he misses that al-Māturīdī was aware of this aspect of the problem and sought to counter it.[29]

Having established his position that the world had a beginning, al-Māturīdī uses it to outline his clearest version of the KCA as follows:

> The indication that the world has an originator is that its temporality has been proved by what we already clarified and that nothing from it in the manifest realm is found to come together and split apart by itself. It is established that it only occurs on account of something else.[30]

Al-Māturīdī here combines the premise of the temporality of the world, which is his conclusion from the previous series of arguments, with the intuition that effects need a cause. Implicit to the presentation is the premise that there cannot be an infinite regress due to this temporality, so there must be an originator outside the wordly order. This argument does not directly identify the originator with God, or reveal His attributes, which he leaves for later discussion.

Al-Māturīdī also reasons directly from the contingency of the world to the existence of a non-contingent being. I note that in the following formulation of al-Māturīdī, the hidden premise is that accidents are temporally generated:

> Each substance in the world has the capacity to receive power from accidents, yet for the accidents that compose it there is no subsistence and existence other than [that substance]. So, it is established by this that each thing needs another. So, it cannot exist by itself and requires other than it to exist.[31]

If this is read in conjunction with the temporality arguments of the previous section, then it can be taken as additional support for his KCA. If it is read independently of the premise of the world's temporality, then it can be seen as anticipating Ibn Sīnā's version of the so-called Leibnizian argument.[32] For ease of discussion and because the KCA is seen as one of the most important options in contemporary discussion, I will focus on it in this chapter.

29 See page 108, note 27.

30 Al-Māturīdī, *Kitāb al-tawḥīd*, p. 83. See Rudolph, *Al-Māturīdī and the Development of Sunnī Theology*, p. 263; Cerić, *Roots of Synthetic Theology in Islam*, p. 142.

31 Al-Māturīdī, *Kitāb al-tawḥīd*, p. 84. See Cerić, *Roots of Synthetic Theology in Islam*, p. 145.

32 Mayer, 'Ibn Sīnā's "Burhān al-Ṣiddīqīn"', pp. 19–20.

Al-Māturīdī also provides a simple *reductio ad absurdum* to back up his position. He argues: 'Were [the world] to be self-sustaining then it would remain by itself in a singular fashion. As that does not occur, it indicates that it is sustained by other than it'.[33] In effect, he here argues that something non-contingent would stay the same, and thus the flux observed in the world proves its contingency. The contrasting idea of God as timeless and changeless is an important part of the Aristotelian-Neoplatonic rational structure within which al-Māturīdī frames his thought. I will return to the relationship between God and time in Chapter 4.

With a slightly different argument, al-Māturīdī reasons from the inherent logical possibility that the world could have been different, to the existence of a being that particularises it, so that it becomes what it is:[34]

> The world, were it to exist by itself, would have no time more appropriate for it than another, and no state with greater precedence for it than another, and no quality more suitable for it than another. Yet as times, states and qualities differ, it is established that it does not exist by itself. And if it did, then it would be possible that everything would make for itself the best states and qualities, thereby nullifying the evil and bad. Thus, the existence of [such differences] indicates its creation by other than it.[35]

The *kalām* formulation of the argument from particularity, or *takhṣīṣ*, can be traced back to Abū al-Maʿālī al-Juwaynī (d. 478/1085) and prior to him a prominent version can be found in the work of Abū Bakr al-Bāqillānī (d. 403/1013).[36] In this passage, al-Māturīdī therefore takes his place among the early Muslim theologians to make use of the argument. William Lane Craig has sought to prove that, even though the argument from particularity is based on the Principle of Sufficient Reason like the Leibnizian cosmological argument, it is a form of *kalām* cosmological argument. He argues that it uses the premise of the world's temporality to reason that its particular contingent features require a non-worldly being to have selected them.[37] Furthermore, in its move from particularities of the world to a personal agent, this argument may enter the territory of the teleological argument (see below).

33 Al-Māturīdī, *Kitāb al-tawḥīd*, p. 84.

34 Al-Māturīdī's use of the argument of particularity (*takhṣīṣ*) is pointed out by Cerić, but not expanded upon by him. Cerić, *Roots of Synthetic Theology in Islam*, p. 148.

35 Al-Māturīdī, *Kitāb al-tawḥīd*, p. 83.

36 Wolfson, *The Philosophy of the Kalam*, pp. 434–39; Davidson, *Proofs for Eternity, Creation, and the Existence of God*, p. 300.

37 Craig, *The* Kalām *Cosmological Argument*, pp. 10–14.

As his habit dictates, al-Māturīdī supports the argument from particularity with a *reductio ad absurdum*, this time based on the existence of evil. He claims that, if the world existed by itself, it would not make for itself the evil that we witness within it; therefore, this initial premise is false.[38] This argument seems to have some underlying similarity to the Fourth Way of Aquinas in the use of Platonic ideas about the gradation of perfections. The intuition on which it relies is that, if the world existed on its own and independently possessed any kind of perfection – for example, goodness – then it would have it to an unlimited degree. Yet as it is evidently limited due to the existence of evil, its goodness must derive from something else.[39] This line of argument does not, however, appeal to prevailing modern philosophical sensibilities.

The KCA is acknowledged as one of the main rational arguments for the existence of God in contemporary philosophy of religion. Craig is largely responsible for the rehabilitation of its reputation and its contemporary formulation; therefore, a version drawn from his work will form the basis for the following discussion:[40]

P1. Everything that begins to exist has a cause of its existence.[41]
P2. The universe began to exist.
C1. Therefore, the universe has a cause of its existence.
P3. Only a personal agent (not a mechanistic cause) is able to select between possible tensed time effects in causing the universe.
P4. Time is tensed.
C2. Therefore, the cause of the universe is a personal agent.

P1, P2 and C1 comprise the famous form of the argument. The inferred cause transcends time and hence is both eternal and necessary (see Chapter 4). But this does not imply that it is a personal agent who

38 Kholeif comments that al-Māturīdī is the first philosopher or theologian to reason in this unusual way. Kholeif, 'Muqaddima', p. 34. Pessagno adds that no one after him developed it. Pessagno, 'The Uses of Evil in Maturidian Thought', p. 73. Also, see Ibrahim, 'Al-Māturīdī's Arguments for the Existence of God', p. 20.

39 See Feser, *Aquinas*, p. 109.

40 P1, P2 and C1 are set out in these terms in Craig, *The* Kalām *Cosmological Argument*, p. 63. P3 and C2 are implicit in the discussion on pp. 150–51. The addition of 'time is tensed' in P4 is based on Craig's response to the critique of Adolf Grünbaum in Craig, 'Prof. Grünbaum on the "Normalcy of Nothingness"', p. 60.

41 Craig has more recently formulated a restricted version that does the same work, while being easier to defend: if the universe began to exist, the universe has a cause of its beginning. Copan, 'Introduction', p. 4. Al-Māturīdī works with the same kind of specific premises in his dialectics.

chooses to create the universe, one whom theists identify with God.[42] Therefore, P3, P4 and C2 form a supplementary argument for the personal nature of the universe's cause.

These two main elements of the modern KCA can be reconstructed from al-Māturīdī's first two arguments for God in *Kitāb al-tawḥīd* (his KCA and argument from particularity), when read with his prior discussion of the temporality of the world. Although he does not discuss tensed time, it is an assumed premise, because it is merely an affirmation of the common-sense perception of past, present and future. Writing in the early fourth/tenth century, al-Māturīdī deserves more recognition in the historical literature on the Islamic development of the argument than he has hitherto received. Nevertheless, my present focus is on assessing how well the argument fares in contemporary philosophy.

In his classic study of the KCA, Craig does not defend P1 at length, taking it as a self-evident intuition; unlike other aspects of the argument, he has not often returned to it.[43] His most promising justification is based on Kant's idea of the categories, whereby causation is seen as a synthetic *a priori* category by which the mind is able to apprehend the structure of reality. Relying on Stuart Hackett's reformulation of the Kantian insight, he suggests that phenomenal and noumenal realities are to be identified: 'thought and reality are structured homogenously'.[44] I note the similarity of this move to the one that I have made in Chapter 2 with al-Māturīdī and Husserl.[45]

Wes Morriston critiques Craig's use of the intuition that things that begin to exist require a cause, comparing it to the rival intuition that things that begin to exist are made out of something. He shows that, whereas our intuitions of efficient causation may support creation of the world by God, those of material causation oppose its creation *ex nihilo*. Moreover, introducing the supplementary premise that things do not need to be made out of something if they are brought into being by God begs the question at hand. His criticism is not that the intuition Craig introduces is impossible

42 Feser raises a potential weakness in contemporary versions of the KCA, which is that the theist wants to not only establish that a necessary being, God, initially caused the universe to exist, but that He continually conserves it. Feser, *Aquinas*, p. 85. This does not seem to be a fatal objection, as the implication of God's necessary existence for His creative action can be established subsequently. See pages 186–87.

43 Craig, *The* Kalām *Cosmological Argument*, p. 145; Craig, 'The *Kalām* Cosmological Argument', p. 302; Copan, 'Introduction', pp. 4–5.

44 Craig, *The* Kalām *Cosmological Argument*, p. 147.

45 See pages 62 and 64–65. Note that Iqbal is scathing about the idea that the necessity of existence should be proved by the conceptual necessity of causation in this argument. Iqbal, *The Reconstruction of Religious Thought in Islam*, p. 23. But for my approach to modality, all necessity is conceptual in a sense, and I place causation at a level of non-absolute metaphysical necessity that is coherently defined in relation to the absolute metaphysical necessity of God (see pages 135–37).

but rather that, in seeking to vindicate creation *ex nihilo*, he is favourable to the intuition that supports his case.[46] But as shall be discussed in more detail below, if the proponent of the KCA is successful in arguing for the impossibility of an infinite past for the universe, then our intuitions about material causation must be wrong, at least for its beginning. As Craig points out in a reply, despite the baffling nature of creation *ex nihilo*, it is less baffling than spontaneous origination *ex nihilo* would be.[47] In a further rejoinder, Morriston suggests that this is to miss his point, which is to show that such intuitions should not be relied on at all.[48]

Morriston argues that, if efficient causation is a synthetic *a priori* principle, as Craig claims, then it should be inconceivable that, for instance, things pop into existence uncaused. In other words, efficient causation should be logically necessary. Yet following Hume, he suggests that it is possible to imagine uncaused effects (although he provides the caveat that, despite being conceivable, they may be metaphysically impossible).[49] I argue in the next chapter that logical necessity only relates to categorial objects. My counter would be that the causal principle is both synthetic *a priori* and metaphysically (not logically) necessary, because it structures our actual and potential experience of the world. Analogous to the uniformity principle that grounds inductive inference, it is the fact of our intentional constitution of the world through the causal principle that makes imagination of its suspension possible. Although this argument would require more elaboration, I think that on intuitive grounds the causal principle remains in contention as a powerful premise for the KCA.

A notable empirical criticism to P1 has been developed by some philosophers on the basis of the indeterminacy and apparently uncaused effects within quantum phenomena.[50] As Reichenbach points out, this argument's impact depends on one's interpretation of quantum mechanics: 'the more this indeterminacy has ontological significance, the weaker is the Causal Principle. If the indeterminacy has merely epistemic significance, it scarcely affects the Causal Principle'.[51] In Chapter 5, I discuss an argument according to which the claimed indeterminacy of quantum mechanics may never arise from the uncertainty principle, even under the Copenhagen interpretation.[52] More broadly, the Bohrian version of quantum mechanics, which I favour, effectively treats causation as a synthetic *a priori* category that,

46 Morriston, 'Must the Beginning of the Universe Have a Personal Cause?', pp. 155–56.
47 Craig, 'Must the Beginning of the Universe Have a Personal Cause?', p. 97.
48 Morriston, 'Causes and Beginnings in the Kalam Argument', pp. 238–39.
49 Morriston, 'Must the Beginning of the Universe Have a Personal Cause?', p. 157.
50 Reichenbach, 'Cosmological Argument'.
51 Reichenbach, 'Cosmological Argument'.
52 See pages 169–70.

when brought into a given experimental setup, is one of the complementary aspects required to fully describe a quantum event.[53] It thus does not undermine P1.

When introducing his KCA, Craig places the main weight of his argument on P2, which is based on the impossibility of an actually infinite past. His strategy here is interesting. It is clear that he wants to formulate an argument that works for the actual infinities that have taken root in mathematics following Cantor.[54] He even states: 'I have no intention of driving mathematicians from their Cantorian paradise'[55] – a reference to the famous statement of David Hilbert opposing the intuitionism of Brouwer.[56] His principal line of argument is that, despite the dominant mathematical view on infinity, there cannot be an actually infinite series of events or objects in the world.[57] To show the absurdity of this, he references mathematical thought experiments from the early twentieth century: 'Hilbert's Hotel', the infinite hotel that is full, yet can always make room for more guests by shifting them along;[58] and Russell's immortal 'Tristram Shandy', who takes a year to write one day of his autobiography, yet will complete it in an infinite period of time as the two time-periods can be put in a one-to-one correspondence.[59] Joshua Rasmussen compares the KCA to a classic chess opening; in his analogy, these examples have become an important part of the familiar lines studied by experts.[60] In the collected volume *The* Kalām *Cosmological Argument: Philosophical Arguments for the Finitude of the Past*, no less than five chapters are devoted to back-and-forth debate over these two paradoxes.[61] I will not examine these arguments here, but rather will

53 See page 69.

54 Craig, *The* Kalām *Cosmological Argument*, p. 69.

55 Craig, *The* Kalām *Cosmological Argument*, p. 82.

56 Ferreirós, *Labyrinth of Thought*, p. 343.

57 Saeed Foudeh and Bilāl al-Najjār misunderstand Craig's thesis when commenting on their Arabic translation of his online article 'Graham Oppy on the *Kalam* Cosmological Argument'. They show surprise that Craig would think that infinities (*al-lānihāyāt*) can be realised in the world of temporal things (*ʿālam al-ḥawādith*), as this does not help him to establish that the world was originated. In the part that they reference, Craig is actually quoting Oppy who claims that, because Craig accepts Cantorian set theory, he must affirm logically possible worlds (*ʿawālim*) containing actual infinities and therefore cannot argue on *a priori* grounds against their existence. Craig goes on to provide counterarguments against both conclusions. See Foudeh and al-Najjār, *Al-Dalīl al-kawnī ʿalā wujūd Allāh taʿālā*, p. 124, n. 1; Craig, 'Graham Oppy on the *Kalam* Cosmological Argument'.

58 Craig, *The* Kalām *Cosmological Argument*, pp. 84–85.

59 Craig, *The* Kalām *Cosmological Argument*, pp. 97–98.

60 Rasmussen, review of *God and Ultimate Origins: A Novel Cosmological Argument*, by Andrew Ter Ern Loke, p. 189.

61 Chapters 8 and 9 study 'Hilbert's Hotel', while Chapters 12–14 look at 'Tristram Shandy'.

make the point that lively debate four decades after Craig first used these examples points to the inability of either side to score a decisive victory. Behind the thought experiments lies a basic dispute over the intuition of an actual infinity within the world.

An area of weakness for theists, such as Craig and his defenders, is the simultaneous affirmation of a finite past and a potentially infinite eschatological future. Yishai Cohen explores this angle, as encapsulated in the title of his chapter 'Endless Future: A Persistent Thorn in the *Kalām* Cosmological Argument'. This is not at all a new line of attack. Several of al-Māturīdī's arguments for the temporality of the world are concerned with showing that the impossibility of an infinite regress does not rule out an endless future. He states:

> In this manner is the multiplicity of counting, such that when one does not make a beginning point from which to start, the existence of any part of it is not possible. Yet if it has a beginning, it is possible that one persists in it such that it increases, then increases perpetually.[62]

The crux of al-Māturīdī's point can be found in Craig's argument that, while the arrow of time requires a count begun in the past to be finite to reach us in the present, the future can be endlessly extended without becoming actually infinite.[63] Building on the work of Morriston, Cohen posits that, even if such a tensed theory of time is assumed, Craig struggles to find a coherent principle to argue that a past infinite regress of events is an invalid actual infinity, whereas a future infinite progress of events is not.[64] Both of these critics use the argument that God's knowledge of the endless future – for instance, angelic praises – can be plausibly understood as an actual infinity and, for Craig to ward this conclusion off, he has to rely on an unmotivated principle. This is what Cohen calls 'The Actuality-Infinity Principle': in order for x to be actually infinite in quantity, x must be actual.[65] Cohen argues that this is unmotivated because Craig does not provide any compelling reason to suppose that an infinitude of past events would be actual, whereas an infinitude of future events would not.[66] It is at this point that I think Craig's wish to hold on to a Cantorian notion of actual infinity, while denying its actuality-in-the-world, may have come back to bite him. His critics can take his affirmation that an actual infinity is mathematically constructible and wrap it into

62 Al-Māturīdī, *Kitāb al-tawḥīd*, p. 80. See Muhtaroglu, 'Al-Māturīdī's View of Causality', p. 10.

63 Craig, 'The *Kalām* Cosmological Argument', pp. 305–6.

64 Cohen, 'Endless Future', pp. 289–91.

65 Cohen, 'Endless Future', p. 288.

66 Cohen, 'Endless Future', p. 292.

various metaphysical puzzles concerning future events, thereby placing the burden of proof on him to rule them out.

With this logjam in mind, I would like to return to Craig's original discussion and note that, despite his aim to formulate an argument against an actual infinity that works on Cantorian principles, he does point out that intuitionist mathematics immediately blocks the possibility of an infinite past. After all, if an actual infinity cannot be mathematically constructed, how can it be instantiated in the world?[67] As Craig acknowledges, intuitionism has a degree of continuity with the conception of potential infinity that Cantor repudiated, but on which the classical KCA was founded.[68] This gets around the objection by providing a principled reason to rule out a past actual infinity without ruling out a future potential one: intuitionistically any actual infinity is non-constructible and thus incoherent. Due to the arrow of time, though the constructability of a potential infinity applies indefinitely to the future, it can never be applied retrospectively to the past, as pointed out by al-Māturīdī.[69]

Brouwer's principle of the constructible and, therefore, potential nature of infinity is not a return to Aristotle but represents a contemporary perspective opposed to post-Cantorian mathematics. His key innovation is the idea of 'choice sequences', potentially infinite sequences generated by acts of free will. These take two forms: lawlike, because they are generated according to an iterative rule, or lawless, as their next step is determined by an intentional choice.[70] Such a lawless sequence 'is ever unfinished, and the only available information about it at any stage in time is the initial segment of the sequence created thus far'.[71] It is not too difficult to see how the principle of choice sequences could allow the theist to model how the world must have a finite past, yet can have an indefinitely extendable future while avoiding, on defensible mathematical grounds, the counter-arguments of Craig's opponents. In a neat irony, Brouwer's expulsion of mathematicians from their Cantorian paradise may have defended belief in the actual one.

67 Craig, *The* Kalām *Cosmological Argument*, p. 93.

68 Craig, *The* Kalām *Cosmological Argument*, p. 93.

69 In discussing al-Kindī on the temporality of the world, Adamson argues that a potential infinity can be posited in the past, as one would just have to hold that however long ago one proposes the world was originated, the time to it was actually longer than that, yet not actually infinite. Adamson, *Al-Kindī*, p. 96. But I think the direction of the arrow of time is also significant here. It is precisely because the actual past has already been traversed that it is both finite and its point of origin is fixed, unlike the potentially infinite future.

70 Iemhoff, 'Intuitionism in the Philosophy of Mathematics'.

71 Iemhoff, 'Intuitionism in the Philosophy of Mathematics'.

Van Atten points out that similarly, for Husserl, potentially infinite sequences are a type of categorial object constituted by the mind.[72] The actual infinite is uncountable and therefore cannot be intuitively conceived by the phenomenological subject who is limited by the perspective of time-consciousness.[73] Husserl discusses the possibility that one could found mathematical infinities on the presumption of 'higher minds', which equates in the present context to Alvin Plantinga's suggestion that an infinitude of sets requires God's infinite mind to think them up.[74] Husserl rejects this line of reasoning as follows:

> One can entertain the thought that, just as man stands higher intellectually than minerals or [the] jellyfish, there might actually be beings that, compared to man, are more highly developed intellectually, in this sense, that they have fundamentally new ways of knowing at their disposal [. . .] The common talk about possible cognitive natures that are not at all ours and have nothing to do with ours, is pointless, indeed nonsensical: for [then] there is nothing to sustain the unity of the concept of cognition.[75]

Husserl's criticism is not directed at the possibility that a higher mind could have its own higher mathematics, but at the assumption that human beings could reliably access it as a foundation for our own rational world.[76] I take this to be akin to al-Māturīdī's discussion of the principle of *dalālat al-shāhid ʿalā al-ghāʾib*, in which he argues that one must reason from human experience towards God, not the other way around.[77] But whereas Husserl's principle of the unity of knowledge leads him to reject analogy when the idealisation of the human subject falls short,[78] al-Māturīdī thinks that analogy can be used as long as any corresponding howness and whatness are negated. For instance, al-Māturīdī affirms knowledge for God while denying that it is akin to the human equivalent.[79]

I suspect that this apparent divergence between the two thinkers may not be as wide as it first appears. We must remember that, in adopting his methodology of the phenomenological reduction, Husserl is speaking

72 Van Atten, *Essays on Gödel's Reception of Leibniz, Husserl, and Brouwer*, pp. 259–60. See page 82.

73 Van Atten, *Essays on Gödel's Reception of Leibniz, Husserl, and Brouwer*, p. 267.

74 Plantinga, 'Appendix: Two Dozen (or so) Theistic Arguments', p. 212.

75 Van Atten, *Essays on Gödel's Reception of Leibniz, Husserl, and Brouwer*, p. 275.

76 Van Atten, *Essays on Gödel's Reception of Leibniz, Husserl, and Brouwer*, pp. 274–75.

77 See pages 60 and 144.

78 Van Atten, *Essays on Gödel's Reception of Leibniz, Husserl, and Brouwer*, p. 275.

79 See Chapter 5.

as a philosopher and not a theologian. He is keen to restrict his focus, at least at first, to what can be idealised from human conscious experience.[80] From this perspective, Husserl conceives of God as purely transcendent and external to the world and, therefore, bracketed from consideration.[81] Nonetheless, Husserl, a Christian convert from a Jewish family, ponders that, just as it is (human) absolute consciousness that manifests order in the world, there must be a still higher consciousness of the Absolute that provides the rational ground for this.[82] Furthermore, he reflects on how God's consciousness, which is devoid of sensory mediation, differs from its human counterpart, while questioning in the margins of his unpublished manuscript whether this is even thinkable.[83] He highlights that God's consciousness of the world is not bounded within temporality like human experience; yet he acknowledges that such description of God occurs when rational thought attempts to reach past the limits of its own possible experience towards the perfect reality that lies beyond.[84] Husserl's more theological mood, which takes into account the description of God in relevation,[85] is much closer to that of al-Māturīdī and the *kalām* tradition who affirm God's transcendence of the world while accepting that He can be inferred from it.[86]

The KCA, as formulated above, is a deductive argument. If the four premises are true, then its two conclusions are too. The question is, how certain are these premises? Arguably each one rests on a distinct intuition: P1 on the synthetic *a priori* principle of causation; P2 on the impossibility of an actual infinity; P3 on the purposeful choice for a temporal beginning as analogical upon human personhood; and P4 on the direction of the arrow of time. While I have shown that these intuitions are implicit in the arguments of al-Māturīdī, contemporary philosophical theology requires them to be identified and adequately justified. I have indicated that I think there is a good prospect to make that defence from a Husserlian phenomenological stance. P1 and P4 would be defended by placing the human conscious experience of causation and time at the centre of reality (see Chapter 4 for remarks on the Husserlian treatment of time consciousness); P2 is best supported by an intuitionistic perspective on potential infinity, which is most famously associated with Brouwer, but can also be connected to

80 Husserl, *Ideas*, pp. 98–99.
81 Husserl, *Ideas*, p. 113; Bello, *The Divine in Husserl*, p. 28.
82 Husserl, *Ideas*, pp. 98–99; Bello, *The Divine in Husserl*, p. 28.
83 Bello, *The Divine in Husserl*, p. 37.
84 Bello, *The Divine in Husserl*, p. 38.
85 Bello, *The Divine in Husserl*, p. 71.
86 Rudolph, *Al-Māturīdī and the Development of Sunnī Theology*, p. 263. See Mall, 'The God of Phenomenology in Comparative Contrast to that of Philosophy and Theology', pp. 10–12.

Husserl; finally, the discussion above shows that P3 – perhaps the shakiest of the four – can be derived from the analogical move from our conscious personhood to that of God: a teleological argument. In fact, it becomes clear that the classical *kalām* argument rests on an implicit version of the same in its analogy between human and divine conscious choice.

I would argue that a coherent and rational case can be made for the success of the KCA, although it cannot be foundationalist, as the premises are not claimed as indubitable. Returning to al-Māturīdī's reason-tradition dyad and MacIntyre's idea of tradition-constituted enquiry discussed in Chapter 1, it is also useful to reflect on the extent to which the adoption of any set of premises, or indeed their underlying intuitions, rests on one's commitment to a given theological or philosophical intellectual tradition.

Though the KCA may establish that the world came from a necessary being, the theist wishes to show that this was a purposeful creation by God. It has already become apparent that this requires the third of Kant's types of arguments for God, the teleological argument, about which he makes the following comments:

> This proof will always deserve to be treated with respect. It is the proof that is oldest, clearest and most in conformity with human reason. It gives life to the study of nature and derives its own existence from it, and thus constantly acquires new vigour. It reveals ends and intentions where our own observation would not in itself have discovered them, and expands our knowledge of nature by leading us towards that peculiar unity the principle of which is outside nature.[87]

Yet despite giving this argument such a positive reception, Kant does not think that it is sufficient on its own to deliver the mind to certainty about the existence of God.[88] His judgement has largely been accepted in the succeeding literature, and so the argument is typically used today to supplement the KCA by revealing the wisdom underlying the creation of the world in a particular way.[89]

Al-Māturīdī places his teleological arguments after his KCA in such a supplementary order. After presenting the majority of them, he asserts that the 'foundational principle is that one does not become preoccupied with

87 Kant, *Critique of Pure Reason*, p. 520.

88 Kant, *Critique of Pure Reason*, p. 520.

89 Koons, 'A New Look at the Cosmological Argument', pp. 200–1. This is needed because, as Grünbaum argues for a different purpose, God's omnipotent will is not enough to explain the world being as it is: it underdetermines the actual world. Grünbaum, 'A New Critique of Theological Interpretations of Physical Cosmology', p. 33. See pages 172–73.

anything in [the world] except in it there is amazing wisdom and an original indication of those things about which the philosophers cannot grasp the whatness and howness of their emergence into existence'.[90]

The main lines of argument that he develops are as follows:

1. The incapacity of living things to originate themselves and to avoid their corruption and death, which is even more so in the case of the inanimate.[91]
2. The formation of substances from diverse and mutually repelling natures (*ṭabā'i'*),[92] which cannot gather themselves.[93]
3. The need for everything to be sustained by something else, whether by nourishment (in the case of the living) or otherwise. Here he explicitly mentions that this establishes all must come from 'one omniscient, wise (*'alīm ḥakīm*)'.[94]
4. By analogy with human artefacts such as buildings, writings and books, it is known that the world cannot have been self-generated – the classic argument from design.[95]
5. The change and opposition in nature: the living dies, the separated join, the small grows, the putrid becomes clean. This does not occur on its own.[96]

Al-Māturīdī's conclusion is that the world cannot exist except due to another: 'were it possible, then it would be possible for a garment to change colour by itself, not by dye, or a ship to travel along on its own. So, if this cannot be, then there must be an omniscient one to generate it all, omnipotent to do it'.[97] He thus uses teleological arguments to reason from various features of the world to the existence of God, His knowledge, wisdom and power.

In his next section, al-Māturīdī provides arguments to show that there can only be one such creator, not a multiplicity. At the end of his discussion, he usefully provides a summary of the two main types of arguments for this conclusion, which he terms those of *aḥwāl* (states) and *af'āl* (actions). By *aḥwāl* he means the logical conflict that would ensue from multiple gods sharing in the qualities of lordship.[98] This is

90 Al-Māturīdī, *Kitāb al-tawḥīd*, p. 84.
91 Al-Māturīdī, *Kitāb al-tawḥīd*, p. 83; Cerić, *Roots of Synthetic Theology in Islam*, p. 145.
92 See pages 90–93.
93 Al-Māturīdī, *Kitāb al-tawḥīd*, p. 84.
94 Al-Māturīdī, *Kitāb al-tawḥīd*, p. 84.
95 Al-Māturīdī, *Kitāb al-tawḥīd*, p. 84; Cerić, *Roots of Synthetic Theology in Islam*, p. 148.
96 Al-Māturīdī, *Kitāb al-tawḥīd*, p. 84; Rudolph, *Al-Māturīdī and the Development of Sunnī Theology*, p. 263.
97 Al-Māturīdī, *Kitāb al-tawḥīd*, p. 85.
98 Al-Māturīdī, *Kitāb al-tawḥīd*, p. 89. He gives more detailed arguments on pp. 86–87.

the *kalām* argument commonly known as *tamānu*ʿ (mutual nullification), which can be found in the Qur'an.[99] In his more detailed treatment, he cites Q. 17:42: 'Say, "Were there with Him gods as they say, they would have sought a way to possess the throne"'; Q. 21:22, 'If there were in [the heavens and earth] gods beside God, the [heavens and earth] would be corrupted'; and Q. 23:91, 'Nor is there any god beside Him – if there were, each god would have taken his creation aside [and tried to overcome the others]'.[100] The argument of *afʿāl* is an inferential argument that again relies on the conflicting natures within the world that require a single wise power to bring them together.[101]

Like the other arguments for God, different formulations of the teological argument have proliferated in philosophical debate, receiving both supporters and critics. The analogy with human manufacture in (4) above has been criticised since the time of Hume on several grounds. For instance, even if it gives reason to believe that there is an intelligence behind the creation of the universe, this is not necessarily the theistic deity, and it may motivate a regress to the designer of the universe's designer and so on.[102]

A more promising general schema for the teleological argument is as follows:[103]

P1. The universe has feature *R*.
P2. Feature *R* cannot exist except due to an intelligent agent.
C1. The universe cannot exist except due to an intelligent agent.

Given that anything can be identified as *R* in P1, this deductive argument succeeds or fails solely on the plausibility of P2. The difficulty in defending a proposition of this kind is the venerable history of phenomena that at one time seemed the result of intelligence later succumbing to some kind of naturalistic explanation.[104] But if the intuition underlying the argument is credible, I am not sure that this line of reasoning is detrimental to it. Although the individual examples that al-Māturīdī gives may be liable for rejection, it can be supposed that at least one *R* will always remain. The logical result of increasing naturalistic explanation of features of the universe is the so-called Theory of Everything, a single unified theoretical description of all

99 See Gwynne, *Logic, Rhetoric, and Legal Reasoning in the Qur'ān*, p. 176.

100 Al-Māturīdī, *Kitāb al-tawḥīd*, p. 87. Cf. al-Bāqillānī, *Kitāb al-tamhīd*, p. 25. See Cerić, *Roots of Synthetic Theology in Islam*, pp. 169–72; Rudolph, *Al-Māturīdī and the Development of Sunnī Theology*, pp. 268–73.

101 Al-Māturīdī, *Kitāb al-tawḥīd*, p. 89. He gives more detailed arguments on pp. 87–88.

102 Ratzsch and Koperski, 'Teleological Arguments for God's Existence'.

103 Ratzsch and Koperski, 'Teleological Arguments for God's Existence'.

104 Ratzsch and Koperski, 'Teleological Arguments for God's Existence'.

physical reality. Yet it is arguably the best possible candidate for *R*, as only a supremely knowledgeable and wise being could create such an elegant universe. This line of argument fits best in a supporting role to a KCA that establishes that the Creator is a necessary existent and rules out the possibility that the universe is itself the brute ultimate reality.

As the teleological argument relies on the notion that the order witnessed in the world requires an extra-worldly explanation, it has also been criticised on grounds of selection bias. The idea here is that the world could very well have been chaotic, but that human beings could not be in the position to observe it. Contemporary scholars such as Richard Swinburne and Alvin Plantinga have argued persuasively that, just because human observation depends on the ordered nature of the universe, this does not remove the need for this order to be given an adequate explanatory basis. A well-known illustration is the person who survives a firing squad: that they can only observe this fact because they are still alive makes it no less surprising and in need of explanation.[105]

Swinburne has developed a detailed inductive version of the teleological argument, proposing that observational evidence shows the existence of God to be probable.[106] He points out that, while a strict distinction between deductive and inductive argumentative forms is anachronistic to historical theological writing on the existence of God, it is clear that natural theology from the eighteenth century onwards had begun to take the latter approach.[107] I have already observed that some of al-Māturīdī's arguments are not exclusively deductive and that they admit the kind of inferences from observation that fit the inductive model. Revisiting al-Māturīdī's work, and that of the *kalām* tradition, in light of Swinburne's probabilistic analysis would be an interesting project, although it is not part of the present enquiry.

I will, however, give my own brief version of the teological argument in an abductive form. The abductive argument, also known as inference to the best explanation, has the following formal characteristics: a first premise of some surprising observed fact; a second premise that provides an explanation that, were it true, makes the first premise a matter of course; and a conclusion that there is arguably reason to accept the second premise. Abduction frequently occurs in more informal contexts and has been suggested as the

105 Plantinga, *Where the Conflict Really Lies*, p. 203. See Swinburne, *The Existence of God*, pp. 156–57.

106 Swinburne, 'Philosophical Theism', pp. 6–10.

107 Swinburne, 'Philosophical Theism', p. 6. This may be connected to the rise of the intellectual framework that Taylor terms Providential Deism, and an epistemic horizon in which the deployment of arguments for God's existence is dislocated from religious participation within the Christian tradition. See Taylor, *A Secular Age*, pp. 293–95.

unconscious reason that a person's testimony is trusted and even for ascertaining the pragmatic meanings of sentences within conversation.[108] It seems that abductive reasoning can provide valid justification, although arguments making use of it need to be assessed on a case-by-case basis.

The following argument draws on Wheeler's Participative Anthropic Principle (PAP), which I have already discussed in Chapter 2:[109]

P1. Surprising fact *S*: the physical laws of the universe require conscious observers to actualise quantum potentialities.
P2. But if God sets its physical laws, *S* would be a matter of course.
C1. There is reason to suspect God sets its physical laws.

The obvious critical response to this argument is to deny P1, holding that it is a mistaken interpretation of quantum mechanics. Notice that it would not be possible in this formulation of PAP to replace God in P2 with an explanation based on the conjecture of a plurality of multiverses and a selection bias effect. Even if we suppose that there are an indefinite number of universes and we must be observers to witness ours, it does not follow that we must be needed to actualise quantum potentialities. Therefore, if successful, this abductive argument provides justification that the universe's apparent direction towards human consciousness implies the existence of God. Nevertheless, it seems possible to replace P2 with an alternative explanative inference, perhaps based on some form of panpsychism or idealism.[110] These weaknesses mean that, at best, it can only supplement more robust arguments, such as the KCA. I put it forward in the hope that it can be strengthened by others and that it can serve as an illustration of how the present discussion can lead to new arguments of natural theology.

I return to the caveat with which I began this chapter: the hidden movements of the heart are ill-captured by logic. In my view, these arguments serve their purpose if they show that it is rationally defensible to believe in the existence of God. Although the theological discussion in the remainder of this book does not require these arguments to be successful, they may provide scaffolding for themes to come. In particular, the idea of God as an eternal and necessary being may lead us to consider His relationship to the concepts of time and modality, as well as the question of His own nature.

108 Douven, 'Abduction'.
109 See pages 71–72.
110 See Goff et al., 'Panpsychism'; Kastrup, *The Idea of the World*, pp. 94–98.

CHAPTER 4

Divine Nature

We have arrived at God. Revelation is the source of knowledge that sets the guidelines for premodern Islamic discussion of the divine. Universal acceptance of the legitimacy of the Qur'an within the *kalām* tradition means, with the notable exception of a few disputed expressions,[1] that statements of scripture tend to provide the terrain rather than the subject matter of theological engagement. Moreover, it is possible for concepts to be consistent with Qur'anic discourse despite arising from rational sources.[2] My approach in this book is similar insofar as I usually only explicitly reference Qur'anic materials where they are needed to advance the argument or are particularly disputed in the relevant historical debates.

1 The so-called *mutashābih* (ambiguous) attributes are divine properties drawn from primarily the Qur'an, but also the Hadith. Theologians often considered them to conflict with God's transcendence if taken literally. The most famous example of this is the expression '*istawā ʿalā al-ʿarsh* (lit. He ascended the throne)' in Q. 7:54, 10:3, 13:2, 25:59, 32:4 and 57:4. The main interpretive choices available for such expressions were to interpret them figuratively (*taʾwīl*), as adopted by the Muʿtazila and some Ashʿarīs and Māturīdīs, or to consign their meaning to God (*tafwīd*), as generally practised by early figures from the two above-mentioned Sunnī schools and the Ḥanbalīs in whose hands it sometimes spilled over into anthropomorphism. See Gardet, 'Allāh'. The approach towards the *mutashābih* attributes has also often become the site of inter-school identity claims and polemics. See Holtzman, *Anthropomorphism in Islam*, pp. 368–69. Al-Māturīdī has a consistent principle for these scriptural locutions. He argues that, as it is impossible to decisively choose between any of their possible figurative interpretations and as God's transcendence makes a literal reading impossible, one must affirm that they are not similar to the creation and believe in what God intends by them without verifying one meaning over another. Al-Māturīdī, *Kitāb al-tawḥīd*, p. 138. These attributes raise some interesting hermeneutic and theological questions about the purpose and limits of language when applied to God. But the present enquiry is systematic, not exegetical, and so I consider further analysis of them outside its scope.

2 For instance, the concept of God as *qadīm* (eternal). Brodersen, *Der unbekannte* kalām, p. 472; van Ess, *Theology and Society in the Second and Third Centuries of the Hijra, Volume 4*, p. 487.

The theology developed in this chapter centres on the phenomenology of human sense experience and rationality. If the content of our ontology is what can be verified as true,[3] then our speech about God must take the world as a frame of reference. The Islamic tradition has generally affirmed on this basis that scripture uses human language to deliver its audience to realities that transcend it, while differing about if or when it becomes figurative.[4] An illustration of this tendency is that exceptions must be sought in the negative theology sometimes attributed to Jahm b. Ṣafwān or Ismāʿīlī focus on the inner (*bāṭinī*) meanings of scripture, rather than the mainstream *kalām* discourse.[5]

The investigation in this chapter is occupied with two overarching questions: an epistemological enquiry into the limits of language about God and an ontological one into the divine nature itself. I will address them by rereading principles of the Māturīdī approach to the divine in the light of contemporary philosophical theology, especially God's relation to time, necessity and His own nature.

I. Time

One of the most basic aspects of reality that we experience as human beings is the passage of time. Consequently, a perspective towards time must be part of the conceptual apparatus with which we look at the world and think about the divine. The transcendent God discussed in this book exists outside of time, which He has created, but acts immanently within it. This conception of God as *qadīm* (eternal) is a mainstay of the Aristotelian-Neoplatonic background to the early *kalām* enterprise.[6] Time is implicitly defined, following Aristotle, by change in the world.[7] As God does not change, He is not within the temporal order. Only idiosyncratic thinkers, such as Jahm, may have held that God was in time, or was time, notwithstanding a hadith conveying the latter.[8]

3 See page 79.

4 The challenge facing theists on this point is articulated well in MacIntyre, *God, Philosophy, Universities*, p. 7. See the approach taken in al-Māturīdī, *Kitāb al-tawḥīd*, p. 108.

5 See page 145, note 112. Also see De Smet, 'Ismāʿīlī Theology', p. 316.

6 Van Ess, *Theology and Society in the Second and Third Centuries of the Hijra, Volume 3*, pp. 508–9.

7 See Markosian, 'Time'.

8 Van Ess, *Theology and Society in the Second and Third Centuries of the Hijra, Volume 4*, pp. 507–8. This seems a surprising position for Jahm to have held, given his focus on divine transcendence. In a hadith narrated by Abū Hurayra, the Prophet relates the statement of God: 'The son of Adam wrongs Me by cursing time (*al-dahr*) when I am time: in My hand is the command and I rotate day and night'. Al-Bukhārī, *Ṣaḥīḥ*, vol. 3, p. 1515. There exists a claim that this hadith was used by the Ẓāhirīs to consider *al-dahr* (time or fate) one of the divine names. See Goldziher, *The Ẓāhirīs*, pp. 142–44.

The main dispute in theological circles relating to time was over the temporality or eternality of the world, not of God. As summarised by al-Bazdawī, the difference between the generality of Muslims (*ahl al-qibla*) and other theistic traditions (*ahl al-adyān*) on the one hand and many of the *falāsifa* on the other, was that the former distinguished the eternality of God from the creation *ex nihilo* of the world, whereas the latter made the world, or its substance, eternal too.[9] Practitioners of *kalām* were keen to harmonise rationally elaborated concepts of divine transcendence in the Qur'an with what Ian Netton has called the Qur'anic Creator Paradigm. This provided an immanent characterisation of God as creating *ex nihilo*, acting in historical time, guiding His people in such time, and in some way being indirectly knowable by His creation.[10] While the question of creation in the light of God's attributes will appear again in Chapter 6, the central enquiry of the present section is to focus on the relationship between God and time, such that He is neither pulled into the temporal world, nor the things of the world pushed into eternity.[11] To do this, I will review salient features of the Māturīdī tradition's approach to this question, including a conceptual development in the theological articulation of God's eternality and necessity, which paves the way for the subsequent sections. Finally, I will outline my own position.

Al-Māturīdī's stance towards the question of God and time is for the most part implicit within *Kitāb al-tawḥīd*. His methodology of *khilāf* within *dalālat al-shāhid ʿalā al-ghāʾib*, as articulated in Chapter 2, leads him to reason from the changing temporal world to a creator for whom this temporality is negated and who is thus eternal.[12] Al-Māturīdī states that the intellect is only able to verify a conception of God as knowing, powerful, acting and giving eternally; yet the converse is true of temporal things, as 'by His action everything occurs in its own time (*bi-fiʿlihi kullu shayʾin yakūnu fī waqti kawnihi*)'.[13] As he puts it, . . .

> The foundational principle is that God, Most High, when His description is fixed and He is described by action, knowledge, and the like, this description is necessarily in eternity. And if created things that are known, powered and willed are mentioned with Him under His description, the times of these things are mentioned too, as their

9 Al-Bazdawī, *Uṣūl al-dīn*, p. 27.

10 Netton, *Allāh Transcendent*, p. 22.

11 See Deng, *God and Time*, p. 22.

12 See page 76. Rudolph, *Al-Māturīdī and the Development of Sunnī Theology*, p. 268.

13 Al-Māturīdī, *Kitāb al-tawḥīd*, p. 98. See al-Samarqandī, *Jumal min uṣūl al-dīn wa-yalīhu sharḥuhu*, p. 21. Cf. Madelung, 'Abu l-Muʿīn al-Nasafī and Ashʿarī Theology', pp. 328–29.

eternality cannot be conceived (*li-alā yutawahhama qidamu tilka al-ashyā'*).[14]

I suggest that it is no accident of expression that al-Māturīdī frames the question of temporality and eternality by what the mind can conceptualise, but that this fits with his epistemological stance towards the rationality of reality.[15] An insight on which I will build is that, if the times for the creation of things are not mentioned, this either implies that these things are atemporal or that God did not know them other than in their times, both of which are absurd.[16]

This opposition between the eternality of God and the temporality of the world was continued by many of the theologians that followed in the Māturīdī tradition. Al-Sālimī seems to be the first who begins to look in more detail at the specific characteristics of created things in order to show their difference from the eternal.[17] He draws five distinctions that distinguish God from creation:[18]

1. God is neither the first nor the last, but the first with no beginning and the last with no ending.
2. God has no *jins* (genus) or *naw'* (species).
3. God has no change of state (*ḥāl*) or description according to state.
4. God has no spatial location.
5. God has no temporal location.

Al-Sālimī's idea of God's timelessness is an important point, and I will return to it in discussing contemporary approaches. A more rigorous argument is also presented from the time of al-Sālimī onwards, providing a *reductio ad absurdum* if the Creator is assumed to be temporal: such an imagined being would need a further creator, and this leads to an infinite regress. Therefore, the Creator must be eternal.[19]

14 Al-Māturīdī, *Kitāb al-tawḥīd*, p. 111. In his *Ta'wīlāt al-qur'ān* he applies this principle exegetically to Q. 41:10, which reads in the context of God's creation of the earth, 'He measured out its varied provisions for those who seek them – all in four Days'. He stresses that, when this period is mentioned, it applies to created things and effects whose eternality cannot be conceived, not to God's creative action itself. Al-Māturīdī, *Ta'wīlāt al-qur'ān*, vol. 13, pp. 111–12. The language of the two passages is very close, so it seems possible that the discussion in *Kitāb al-tawḥīd*, which lacks a Qur'anic reference, builds on the exegetical problem in *Ta'wīlāt al-qur'ān*.

15 See page 62.

16 Al-Māturīdī, *Kitāb al-tawḥīd*, p. 111.

17 Brodersen, *Der unbekannte* kalām, p. 472.

18 Al-Sālimī, *Al-Tamhīd fī bayan al-tawḥīd*, p. 100.

19 Al-Sālimī, *Al-Tamhīd fī bayan al-tawḥīd*, p. 99; al-Nasafī, *Tabṣirat al-adilla*, vol. 1, p. 261; al-Lāmishī, *Kitab al-tamhīd li-qawā'id al-tawḥīd*, p. 49. See Brodersen, *Der unbekannte* kalam, p. 470.

At the end of the fifth/eleventh and beginning of the sixth/twelfth centuries, there is a shift in Māturīdī texts to incorporate discussion of God's necessity alongside His eternality. This concept had been present in Transoxianan *kalām* discourse since the turn of the fifth/eleventh century and was picked up by Ibn Sīnā who developed and popularised it.[20] Al-Bazdawī argues that the eternal necessarily exists (*wājib al-wujūd*), as it is not possible to conceive of it not existing at a time. More specifically, its timeless nature means that, if it exists, it can never have come to exist in the past nor cease to exist in the future and is thus absolutely metaphysically necessary.[21] This is also the position earlier held by al-Kindī.[22] While necessity is therefore a corollary of eternality, the converse is also true, as mentioned in the previous chapter and shown by al-Ṣābūnī: if an absolutely metaphysically necessary being exists, it has always existed and always will.[23] This is not the stance of Ibn Sīnā who claims that God's existence is logically necessary.[24] The difference between the two conceptions returns to the distinction between cosmological and ontological arguments. Those who advocate the cosmological argument hold that through *a posteriori* reasoning one argues from the temporality and contingency of the world to the existence of an eternal and necessary being. Proponents of the ontological argument see the eternal necessary existence of this being as an *a priori* truth. I will return to the concept of necessity and its application to God in the next section.

In contemporary discussions of time and God, the main debates are on the theorisation of time in the world, the nature of God's eternality, and the relationship between the two. In the case of time, an important distinction has been maintained since the work of J. M. E. McTaggart at the beginning of the twentieth century:[25]

1. Tensed time (A-theory) – past, present and future times are aspects of reality.
2. Untensed time (B-theory) – only earlier or later times are aspects of reality.

One way to look at this distinction is that A-theorists argue that there is a special 'metaphysical privilege' held by the present as time flows, while B-theorists deny this, treating time more like space.[26] Given that

20 Wisnovsky, *Avicenna's Metaphysics in Context*, pp. 239–43.
21 Al-Bazdawī, *Uṣūl al-dīn*, p. 27; Leftow, *Time and Eternity*, pp. 65–66.
22 Adamson, *Al-Kindī*, p. 99.
23 Al-Ṣābūnī, *Al-Bidāya fī uṣūl al-dīn*, p. 21. See page 107.
24 Morewedge, 'A Third Version of the Ontological Argument', p. 193. See Leftow, *Time and Eternity*, p. 66.
25 Markosian, 'Time'.
26 Deng, *God and Time*, pp. 6–7.

the existence of tense is an apparently basic aspect of human experience, a common conclusion to draw from the debate is that for A-theorists the passage of time is part of the world, while for B-theorists it is an aspect of human perception.[27] I suggest that this dichotomy, which has become central to discussions of God's relationship to time, can be bridged with Husserlian phenomenology. Husserl had a sustained interest in the question of time consciousness, returning to it at multiple occasions in his life.[28] For the present purpose, the interesting aspect of his approach is the combination of a successive, untensed 'objective time' with flowing, tensed time, as experienced in perception. Whereas most A-theorists have developed a realist theory of tensed time, Husserl's view is that the experience of tense structures the unfolding phenomena of objective time.[29] He writes: 'Time is fixed, and yet time flows. In the flow of time, in the continuous sinking down into the past, a nonflowing, absolutely fixed, identical, objective time becomes constituted'.[30] From this stance, objects are phenomenologically constituted in time, just as they are in space,[31] a point that should not be surprising given the similarities of the concepts Many Over One and One Over Many Times discussed in Chapter 2.[32]

Before making use of these ideas about time, I shall review contemporary philosophical debate on how to construe its relationship to God. The classical theistic view, as discussed above, is timelessness, such that God exists outside of time and experiences no temporal succession.[33] But more recently a number of so-called temporal views have become popular, including forms of omnitemporality, such that God exists at every time, or even if God is said to exist in His own divine time, that He experiences temporal succession.[34]

The combination familiar from the *kalām* tradition and used within the classical KCA, that time is tensed yet God timeless, has come under especial criticism. The tenor of the objection is that, while it seems unproblematic for a timeless God to know the untensed sequencing of all events, it is harder to say how He would know tensed facts, such as 'I am reading now', as this nowness is tied to one's temporal perspective.[35] Richard Sorabji points out

27 Leftow, *Time and Eternity*, p. 18.
28 Kortooms, *Phenomenology of Time*, p. xiii.
29 Roth, 'Experiencing Real Time', p. 100.
30 Husserl, *On the Phenomenology of the Consciousness of Internal Time*, p. 67.
31 See Husserl, *On the Phenomenology of the Consciousness of Internal Time*, pp. 68–69.
32 See pages 100–1.
33 Sorabji, *Time, Creation and the Continuum*, p. 254.
34 Deng, *God and Time*, pp. 38–39.
35 Sorabji, *Time, Creation and the Continuum*, pp. 258–59. See Pike, *God and Timelessness*, pp. 88–89.

that the same objection was made by Ibn Sīnā when arguing that God could not know particulars: whereas He could know about eclipses in general, He could not know about an individual eclipse, as that would require change from thinking it is present to thinking it is past.[36]

Brian Leftow provides a way for understanding the idea of eternity to overcome this objection. He treats eternity as a 'null time' – that is, although it is outside the temporal sequence of the universe, it can be logically treated as timelike for discussing God's relationship to the creation.[37] Leftow argues that 'God's seeings of temporal events all occur at once and involve direct realist perception'.[38] This models God's knowledge of the creation on human realist perception and is therefore causal between eternal and temporal events. It also invokes the 'specious present', a concept of the present moment.[39] Leftow seeks to solve some of the problems raised by this position by supplementing it with the Anselmian idea that '*what God sees* is all temporal events occurring at once', which leads him to argue that temporal events occur both in time and eternity.[40] This idea of occurrence proves very significant for Leftow's model of the relationship between God and time, as it lets him define 'now' and 'occurring now' as 'primitive terms univocally applicable to temporal and eternal or timeless things'.[41]

At this juncture, it is useful to signal my divergences from Leftow's position. While I agree with formulating eternity as a null time, I take a position closer to one that he considers and rejects, which is to construe '*God's seeings* of temporal events all occur at once' as a theistic version of phenomenalism.[42] As mentioned above, I do not hold a realist view of tense, but see it as the basis on which the human mind constitutes the objective reality of time. Therefore, God timelessly knows and creates the human consciousness that ideally constitutes tensed reality. In my model, time cannot escape its ideal verification by the human mind. If it is said that tensed time is a product of our consciousness and untensed time a feature of the world, my response, based on universal experienceability, is that its untensed nature can only be understood as – in principle – a phenomenologically verified reality.[43] Human ideal consciousness is at the centre of the story of time, just as it is with space and indeed causation. One result of this

36 Sorabji, *Time, Creation and the Continuum*, p. 260.

37 Leftow, *Time and Eternity*, p. 51.

38 Leftow, *Time and Eternity*, p. 220.

39 Leftow, *Time and Eternity*, p. 221. For discussion of the 'specious present', see Le Poidevin, 'The Experience and Perception of Time'.

40 Leftow, *Time and Eternity*, pp. 218–19, 221.

41 Leftow, *Time and Eternity*, p. 239.

42 Leftow, *Time and Eternity*, pp. 218–19.

43 See page 64.

is that it becomes a kind of metric for time. This means consciousness can be used to peg the beginning of time to a finite period before the present instant. Thus, one cannot argue that time is eternal on the basis that there is no time before time itself.[44]

Given the above, I define 'now' and 'occurring now' as the constitution of phenomena in time. From the divine perspective, God does not just see phenomena but transcendently creates their possible or actual constitution in consciousness. The significance of this view is that temporal things would not have to occur in eternity in order for them to occur 'now' from the timeless perspective of their creator, even though that 'now' must sit within their time sequence, or *fī waqti kawnihi* in the language of al-Māturīdī.

I propose to use some of Leftow's technical terminology to advance this line of argument. He defines some terms that relate to the A-theory and B-theory of time as follows:[45]

1. A-occurs – an Event *E* A-occurs iff *E* occurs now.
2. B-occurs – an Event *E* B-occurs iff *E*'s location in a B-series of earlier and later events is *t*, and it is now *t*.

According to this formulation, though everything that B-occurs happens now, or A-occurs, events in the B-series that are not at *t* do not happen now, as they are located in the temporal past or future. Furthermore, A-occurring events not in the B-series at all – in other words, the actions of God – do not B-occur, as they are not in the temporal timeline.

Leftow goes on to connect the eternal and temporal timeframes by defining what he calls A- and B-simultaneity, which leads him to hold that temporal things occur also in the eternal now.[46] I argue that my alternative definition of time results in a more promising conclusion. I propose that, more simply, . . .

3. From an eternal reference frame, all B-series events A-occur.
4. From a temporal reference frame, all B-series events B-occur.

Bearing in mind the difference in occurrence that I defined from the perspective of God and the human being, (3) means that all temporal things are created at once by Him in their places within the B-series. For the human being, (4) means that each event in the B-series is constituted in the sequential present. I think this formulation obviates the

44 Cf. Swinburne, *The Christian God*, p. 94.
45 Leftow, *Time and Eternity*, p. 239.
46 See Leftow, *Time and Eternity*, pp. 239–41.

conclusion that temporal events exist in eternity. Although from the perspective of God they are all created in the timeless moment in which His actions occur, as created entities they are constituted within the B-series of events in time. This amounts to a contemporary elaboration of al-Māturīdī's position. Moreover, while for human beings only a single moment at a time is metaphysically privileged in its constitution, for God all moments are attended to equally, whether constituted by an actual temporal consciousness or not.

Returning to the objection that, if God is timeless, He cannot know tensed time expressions, such as 'now', I think that it arises from a realism about time that I reject. The position I have taken is that phenomenal reality is pegged to its potential verification in human consciousness. Any 'now' that we can imagine within the B-series would be the 'now' constituted by a consciousness posited at that time. In this picture, it seems unreasonable to respond that God cannot know that 'now', given that He creates each event in the B-series and each potential or actual constituting consciousness of B-occurrence. Furthermore, because of (3), His knowledge does not change due to the flow of time experienced by human beings.[47]

II. Modality

In the previous chapter, I used the concept of necessity to describe God as the necessary being. I will now delve further into how I understand modality in relation to things in the world and divinity. A useful starting point is to consider the idea's background in the *kalām* tradition. Among Māturīdī theologians, early discussion of the concept of necessity emerges from the implications of God's eternality and thus means absolute metaphysical necessity. The existence of God is proved based on an inference made from the world, as in the cosmological argument, and then it may be concluded that this existence is necessary. This is the type of necessity that I will defend for God in my constructive discussion below. But I will briefly pick up the earlier thread of logical necessity in the ontological argument to consider the reception of Ibn Sīnā's ideas by the Māturīdī tradition.

There is little doubt that the Avicennan corpus was a significant factor for the entry of the language of necessity and specifically the term *wājib al-wujūd* into Māturīdī *kalām* texts of the fifth/eleventh and sixth/twelfth centuries, such as those of al-Bazdawī and al-Ṣābūnī.[48] Yet a strict definition of necessity seems only to emerge from certain scholars who adopted

47 See page 167.

48 Al-Bazdawī, *Uṣūl al-dīn*, p. 27; al-Ṣābūnī, *Al-Bidāya fī uṣūl al-dīn*, p. 21; al-Ṣābūnī, *Al-Kifāya fī al-hidāya*, p. 60. See Wisnovsky, 'One Aspect of the Avicennian Turn in Sunnī Theology', pp. 94–95.

an explicitly Avicennan philosophical methodology in their books. As far as I can tell, the earliest Ḥanafī figure to do so was Shams al-Dīn al-Samarqandī in his *Al-Ṣaḥāʾif al-ilāhiyya*, even though, as I have already pointed out, he cannot properly be considered a Māturīdī.[49] For the present discussion, the pertinent point is not whether such individuals used an Avicennan-inspired concept of necessity, but to what extent they followed Ibn Sīnā's idea of God as logically, rather than metaphysically, necessary. Al-Samarqandī provides six formulations of Ibn Sīnā's 'Leibnizian' cosmological argument, arguing from the contingency of things in the world to a metaphysically necessary creator, but he provides no hint of a truly ontological argument to establish a logically necessary one.[50] The same is true of another proponent of this philosophical mode of *kalām*, Ṣadr al-Sharīʿa al-Maḥbūbī, in his *Taʿdīl al-ʿulūm*.[51]

For my own theological use of the concept of necessity, I will look at the question of definition, before examining the relationship between necessity and human minds, then necessity and God. Plantinga, who draws from the Latin Christian tradition, compares the concept of necessity *de re*, the property of something being necessary, with necessity *de dicto*, the necessary truth of a proposition. He shows that there is an equivalency between the two types, such that . . .

> An object *x* has a property *P* essentially just in case it is not possible that *x* should have lacked *P*; a proposition *p* is necessarily true just in case it is not possible that *p* should have lacked the property of being true.[52]

Take the proposition 'a triangle has three sides' as a paradigm case of a necessary truth. That any triangle necessarily, or essentially, has three sides makes the proposition necessarily true and *vice versa*.[53] Of course, necessity has its counterpart in contingency, such that an object has a property contingently, or accidentally, if it could have lacked it. Therefore, a contingent proposition can be defined as one that could have lacked the property of being true.[54]

49 See al-Samarqandī, *Al-Ṣaḥāʾif al-ilāhiyya*, pp. 126–28. See page 42.

50 Al-Samarqandī, *Al-Ṣaḥāʾif al-ilāhiyya*, pp. 306–9. The position that God is known in the world via inference, but not necessary knowledge, is also held by most of the Muʿtazila (except for a group known as *aṣḥāb al-maʿārif*). See Pines, 'A Study of the Impact of Indian, mainly Buddhist, Thought on Some Aspects of Kalām Doctrines', pp. 7–10.

51 Al-Maḥbūbī, 'Taʿdīl al-ʿulūm', MS Cod. Arab. 43, fol. 48v; al-Maḥbūbī, 'Taʿdīl al-ʿulūm', MS Landberg 394, fol. 102v. MS Landberg 394 is a student's commentary that contains the entire text. See Dallal, *An Islamic Response to Greek Astronomy*, pp. 4–5.

52 Plantinga, *The Nature of Necessity*, p. 28.

53 See Plantinga, *The Nature of Necessity*, p. 42.

54 Plantinga, 'Two Concepts of Modality', p. 190. See Husserl, *Ideas*, p. 13.

Mehmet Reçber comments that, whereas the necessary-contingent dichotomy refers to metaphysical modality, it has respective epistemological and semantic counterparts in the *a priori-a posteriori* and analytic-synthetic distinctions.[55] But a degree of caution is needed when deliminating these concepts, as it is not always the case that the necessary is analytic and known *a priori* (like the sides of a triangle), while the contingent is synthetic and known *a posteriori* (like the colour of an apple).[56] For example, I have already commented favourably on Kant's notion of synthetic *a priori* categories and the *a posteriori*-necessary cosmological argument while rejecting its *a priori*-necessary ontological counterpart.

One way to express the difference between necessary and contingent propositions and properties is through possible world semantics. By possible world, I do not mean an ontic reality that exists like the actual world, as held by David Lewis.[57] I take the concept as a way of expressing the modal intuition that some things can be conceived as being other than they are, while others cannot. Combining this insight with the distinction between *de dicto* and *de re* necessity, Plantinga gives the example that, if *de dicto* possibly something is red, then the proposition 'something is red' is true in at least one possible world. Therefore, *de re* something is possibly red, or red in at least one possible world.[58] Anything that is logically necessary exists in every possible world, meaning that it is impossible to conceive of a world without it. Candidates for this type of necessity include mathematical truths, such as a triangle having three sides; logical truths, such as the laws of Non-contradiction and Identity; what Leftow refers to as necessary truths about creatures, such as water is H_2O;[59] and the existence of God, according to the ontological argument.

I will mention four main types of propositions that will give an even finer-grained typology of the way in which I distinguish between modalities.[60]

55 Reçber, *Necessity, Logic and God*, p. 15.

56 See Plantinga, *The Nature of Necessity*, pp. 6–8; Kripke, *Naming and Necessity*, pp. 34–39.

57 Menzel, 'Possible Worlds'.

58 Plantinga, *The Nature of Necessity*, p. 57.

59 Leftow, *God and Necessity*, p. 209.

60 In what follows, logical and metaphysical necessity (and their contraries) correspond closely to what Leftow calls narrow and broad-logical necessity. Leftow, 'Necessity', p. 21. See Hanna's distinction between 'the kind of necessity that flows from the nature of concepts' and 'the kind of necessity that flows from the immanent structures of things in the manifestly real world'. Hanna, *Cognition, Content, and the A Priori*, p. 159. Swinburne uses various terminologies in his works. Compare Swinburne, *The Coherence of Theism*, revised edn, p. 19, with Swinburne, *The Coherence of Theism*, 2nd edn, pp. 47–53. The treatment that fits best with the present book is found in his *The Christian God*. Here Swinburne argues that logical necessity only relates to human concepts, while the ultimate forms of necessity (in summary) are ontological necessity, which reports an everlasting

1. Logically necessary propositions are ideally verifiable as true in all possible worlds and their falsity is a self-contradiction.[61] For instance, 'triangles have three sides'.
2. Metaphysically necessary propositions are ideally verifiable as false in some possible worlds, but true in the actual world. There are three kinds:
   (a) absolute metaphysical necessities always obtain in the actual world and are not due to anything else. For example, 'God exists'.
   (b) metaphysical necessities always obtain in the actual world and are due to absolute metaphysical necessities, that is, God and His attributes. For example, 'everything that begins to exist has a cause of its existence'.
   (c) actual necessities are merely possible in themselves but necessary for as long as they exist on account of the absolute metaphysical necessities that determine their existence.[62] Every proposition about a possible thing that exists for any period of time in the actual world is of this type. For instance, 'there is an apple in the fruit bowl now' (when there is).[63]
3. Metaphysically impossible propositions are ideally verifiable as true in some possible worlds, but false in the actual world. They are the converse of the three kinds of metaphysical necessities:
   (a) absolute metaphysical impossibilities never obtain in the actual world due to a contrary absolute metaphysical necessity. For instance, 'God does not exist'.
   (b) metaphysical impossibilities never obtain in the actual world due to a contrary metaphysical necessity. For example, 'something can begin to exist without a cause of its existence'.
   (c) actual impossibilities are merely possible in themselves but become impossible for as long as they are not realised due to not being determined by absolute metaphysical necessities. Every proposition about an unrealised possible thing is of this type. For example, 'there is not an apple in the fruit bowl now' (when there is).

event without a cause, and metaphysical necessity, which reports an everlasting event with an ontologically necessary cause. See Swinburne, *The Christian God*, pp. 96–97, 118. I too take logical necessity as 'not a very deep feature of the world' and distinguish between the ontological necessity of God and the metaphysical necessity of features of the world due to God. But to avoid confusion with the ontological argument, I prefer to speak of absolute metaphysical necessity with respect to God and His eternal attributes, and (non-absolute) metaphysical necessity for that which always obtains in the actual world.

61 See Swinburne, *The Coherence of Theism*, revised edn, pp. 16–20.

62 See Fackenheim, 'The Possibility of the Universe in al-Farabi, Ibn Sina and Maimonides', pp. 304–5, n. 4.

63 The assimilation of the logically possible but actual to category 2 (c) and the logically possible but non-actual to category 3 (c) has important implications for thinking about divine creative action and the world. See page 187.

4. Logically impossible propositions are ideally verifiable as false in all possible worlds and their truth is a contradiction. For instance, 'triangles have two sides'.

While the above types of propositions take a value of either true or false, which is in principle knowable, even if only by God (see Chapter 5), some propositions may be neither true nor false (due to dropping LEM and bivalence). These can be thought of as propositions with meanings that cannot fully capture the nature of the object receiving verification. In general, we can say that, for any object *O* and property *p*: if it is neither true nor false that '*O* is identical to *p*', then *O* is neither *p*, nor other than *p*. (Note that I exclude propositions that are both true and false due to the argument that the Law of Non-contradiction is presupposed in rational activity).[64]

Applying this idea to the above typology, we arrive at two additional cases:

5. Logically indeterminate propositions are verified as neither true nor false in all possible worlds. For instance, 'a singleton is its member'.[65]
6. Metaphysically indeterminate propositions are always verified as neither true nor false in the actual world. They are also of three kinds:
   (a) absolute metaphysically indeterminate. For example, 'God is His attributes'.
   (b) metaphysically indeterminate. For example, 'every object is its constituent tropes'.[66]
   (c) actual indeterminate. For example, 'this apple is its greenness, shape, taste . . .'; 'this heap of wheat minus one grain is still a heap'.[67]

At this point, a theological problem may be raised. If I reject logical necessity for God, how can I affirm it for logical and mathematical truths? Does this make God less necessary than these abstract objects? My response draws from my conception of possible worlds. By stating that possible

64 See page 83.

65 The Goldbach conjecture that 'every even integer (greater than 2) is the sum of two prime numbers' and other unsolved or unsolvable mathematical problems seem candidates for this category. See pages 81–84.

66 See page 98.

67 This is a premise of the Sorites paradox. If it is true, then a heap of wheat can never disappear, even if reduced by every grain. If it is false, then removing a single grain prevents if from being a heap. Both alternatives seem false, which has led some philosophers to propose three-valued logics with an indeterminate value as a potential solution (among others). See Hyde and Raffman, 'Sorites Paradox'.

worlds are what it is conceivable that there could be, I borrow from Husserl in holding modal properties to be intentional constructions of the mind.[68] Logical necessity is thus used for the verification of a class of propositions that relate to categorial entities presupposed in rational activity. In other words, though the logically necessary refers to what there rationally must be, it does not represent a greater level of actuality than absolute metaphysical necessity. I suggest that this latter class is the coherent form for statements about God.[69]

In my reading, the *a priori* necessity of things, whether analytic (such as logical laws) or synthetic (such as causation), is presupposed by the categories of human thought.[70] By defining existence in every possible world as a property indexed to the intentionality of the human mind, denying logical necessity for God while affirming it for mathematical and logical truths is not a theological problem. From this constructivist position, logical necessity refers only to those objects that the mind cannot conceive of as non-existent and those propositions that it cannot conceive of as untrue without self-contradiction. But, to reject the ontological argument is precisely to accept that the mind can conceive of God as non-existent, however repugnant this may be to the committed theist. Hence, my stance on possible worlds raises no additional theological problems to my rejection of the ontological argument – and I have already argued that point.

Reçber points out the close connection between such conceptualism of modal properties and intuitionism;[71] yet he is critical of this approach because of the restrictions that it sets on the assertability of necessity due to the epistemic limits of human minds.[72] He objects to the idea that what is knowable to human beings should exhaust what is in principle knowable, claiming, like Badiou, that constructability is an unfounded restriction.[73] His main argument, based on the possibility of higher minds, is reminiscent of the position critiqued by Husserl, which attempts to establish infinities on the same basis.[74]

My response is that the assertability of reality is grounded in our phenomenological experience. The default for modal categories, like mathematical truths, is that they are intuitions of the mind. They are encountered in consciousness, so the burden of proof should be on those who argue

68 Smith and McIntyre, *Husserl and Intentionality*, pp. 297–300.

69 See Swinburne, *The Coherence of Theism*, revised edn, p. 22.

70 Cf. Reçber, *Necessity, Logic and God*, pp. 11–13. Note that my rejection of the necessity of LEM returns to its non-constructibility. See pages 81–82.

71 Reçber, *Necessity, Logic and God*, p. 116.

72 Reçber, *Necessity, Logic and God*, pp. 118–19.

73 Reçber, *Necessity, Logic and God*, p. 119.

74 Reçber, *Necessity, Logic and God*, pp. 118–19. See page 117.

for a realist foundation for them outside of it.[75] From this perspective, the introduction of the idea of higher minds, whether non-human or God, has no bearing on necessity, which is a concept that we can only use with the propositions that we can consciously formulate. In other words, necessary logical and mathematical truths are only so because they are necessarily verified as true constructions by the mind. Epistemically, we have no basis to apply modal concepts of necessity and possibility outside of their potential use in our consciousness.

So, what is the relationship of necessity to God? First comes the question of God's existence and nature. I have already given my support to a theological conception of God that is absolutely metaphysically, but not logically, necessary.[76] This means that, although He does not exist in every world possibly conceivable to human minds, if He exists, He exists eternally without beginning or due to anything else. There is a strand of theological thinking that finds an affirmation of this kind of necessity for God deeply unsatisfying. A modern expression of this position is given by David Bentley Hart:

> So a god conceived as necessary in only this sense would not provide any ultimate solution to the question of existence but would himself be just another existential mystery added to all the others. The regress of ontological causes would still not have reached back to its first term.[77]

The reasoning underlying this theological move is that the existence of God has meaning only when it is understood as logically necessary. The explanation for why He exists is solved by it being inconceivable that He does not. Yet as I have already pointed out in the context of the ontological argument, human beings prove capable of conceiving that God does not exist. But, even if the premise is granted and it is assumed that non-believers are deluded in the face of the logical inescapability of divine existence, where does this leave us? I argue that logical conceivability reflects certain necessities about the categories with which human minds operate, and these in turn are grounded in the way things necessarily are. From this constructivist perspective, there is nothing wrong with God being the ultimate existential mystery upon which all others depend – to think otherwise would be to make the abstract terms of logic more ultimate than Him.

Nevertheless, conceiving logically necessary truths as ideal constructions of the human mind does not negate their correspondence to reality.

75 Cf. Kastrup, *The Idea of the World*, pp. 31–32.
76 Cf. Hanafi, *Taʾwīl al-ẓāhiriyyāt*, p. 397.
77 Hart, *The Experience of God*, p. 115.

This is because God's wisdom ensures the world is indexed to the consciousnesses that presuppose them. For example, God eternally verifies the proposition 'triangles have three sides' because it is His wise nature to create a world in which consciousnesses are unable to conceive of its falsity. Another way to put this point is that God's absolute metaphysical necessity grounds the logical necessities that appear to the mind. This point can be compared to Hassan Hanafi who, when adapting a passage from Husserl's *Formal and Transcendental Logic* to his theistic paradigm, comments: 'God is the measure of necessary knowledge and the guarantor of the truths of the mathematical sciences and objectivity – necessary knowledge is transformed into a creation'.[78] In this picture, one is in danger of self-contradiction in attempting to imagine that God could have made a different set of logically necessary truths. Such constructions are presupposed in our thinking and are part of the rational framework that allows discourse about the nature of God, making Him an intentional object of thought.[79] Moreover, as these truths are based on the absolute metaphysical necessity of divine wisdom, they could not, in fact, be other than they are. As I will discuss in Chapter 5 when I return to these questions, grounding logic in God's wisdom allows it to be securely used to reason about His nature without raising the ultimacy concern that He is bound by it.

What, then, can be said about so-called 'secular' necessary truths, such as 'water is H_2O'? Again, I hold that the modal work happens within the construction of the *de dicto* propositions themselves. So, to say that, necessarily, water is H_2O is just to say that the mind cannot conceive of being unable to verify this identity once it is known.[80]

Leftow seeks to show that, if God's nature – which he calls His deity – determines the nature of water, then a theological problem is generated in the hypothetical case that the contingent molecular facts had been different.[81] Specifically, he argues that, had there been no such thing as H_2O, then the nature of God would fail to have one of its necessary attributes (the one that determines the 'water is H_2O' identity relation) and therefore

78 Hanafi, *Taʾwīl al-ẓāhiriyyāt*, p. 397.

79 Hanafi, *Taʾwīl al-ẓāhiriyyāt*, pp. 392–93; Husserl, *Ideas*, p. 161.

80 Compare with Swinburne who argues that a proposition is metaphysically necessary if it contains a rigid designator that can only be determined by investigation in the world. For example, 'water is H_2O' only becomes necessary once the molecular composition of water is known. Swinburne calls the word water an example of an 'uniformative designator', as opposed to H_2O, which is an 'informative designator', as it specifies necessary and sufficient conditions for its object to be what it is. He then argues that there are no metaphysical necessities other than ones that can be reduced to logical necessities by substituting informative designators for uninformative ones. Swinburne, *The Coherence of Theism*, 2nd edn, pp. 47–53.

81 Leftow, *God and Necessity*, p. 210.

would not exist. Furthermore, this implies that God would not exist due to lacking a necessary attribute merely because of alternate contingent facts about water, which is counterintuitive.[82] Leftow thus concludes that God does not have a nature.

The crux of Leftow's contention is that, seemingly, contingent aspects of the world give rise to necessary truths about them, and we want to hold that God is the ultimate ground for these necessities, yet also that He could have changed any contingency. I suggest that placing logical necessities into the realm of mentally indexed constructions solves the problem because, as Hanafi argues, they are transformed into part of the creation. Unlike a possible world without the Law of Non-contradiction, a world in which God does not create H_2O is coherently imaginable and would mean a different set of secular necessary truths to be verified by human minds. Though such an alternative is actually impossible due to God's wisdom, this fact has no counterintuitive consequences for His nature.

My constructivist position also solves some of the strange consequences of theistic realism about abstract objects. Plantinga states: 'Sequences of natural numbers, for example, are necessary beings and have been created neither by God nor by anyone else. Still, each such sequence is such that it is part of God's nature to affirm its existence'.[83] A Platonic realm of uncreated necessary objects that God must affirm as existent is an anathema to Māturīdī theology. Morris and Menzel take a different path, affirming both the Platonic existence of abstract objects and their creation by God. This, however, leads them to the bizarre position that God's properties are self-created.[84] My account of abstract objects puts necessary truths into the created order via the human minds that would construct them.

It may be contended that this perspective limits God's knowledge of necessity by defining it with respect to the consciousness of contingent beings. Yet I am really arguing for the converse: it is our modal intuitions of possibility and necessity that are epistemically bounded by the divinely determined categories of our thinking. Consider this point in the context of my theological project. I frame theological activity as a pushing outward of the human mind to what can be said about a world with consciousness at its heart, and about God as transcendent to it. Anything that can be expressed theologically will emerge from that conscious experience and, like verbal revelation, face the constraints inherent in human thought and language. This includes the question of God's nature, although, as I shall presently argue, it does not prevent the affirmation of a concrete ontology for it.

82 Leftow, *God and Necessity*, pp. 210–11.
83 Plantinga, *Does God Have a Nature?*, p. 143.
84 Morris and Menzel, 'Absolute Creation', pp. 358–59.

III. Nature

My discussion so far has circled around the nature of God and His attributes, and it is now time to approach the question head on. First, I will examine the framework utilised by the *kalām* tradition, which adapted the language of Aristotelian-Neoplatonic thinking for its own theological ends. Contextualising the contribution of al-Māturīdī and his early school in this conversation, I will show that it differs in crucial ways from the classical tradition bearing his name, which was influenced by developments in Ashʿarism. Then, I will recast his position as part of my contemporary theological project.

Al-Māturīdī sits in the camp of Sunnī theologians, like those from the Ashʿarī and Ḥanbalī traditions, who apply language drawn from analysis of the world to discuss God through substantive properties. This is opposed to the position taken by Muʿtazilī, Ibāḍī and classical Shīʿī theologians who use a variety of strategies to avoid this imputation and to establish a doctrine of divine simplicity. One may say that the Sunnīs think that a principle of analogy can establish a theory of individuated divine attributes to match the outward language of scripture and the others believe that God's transcendence negates this idea.

A comparable, yet distinct, debate is found in medieval Christian theology, although it is one in which the dominant position is divine simplicity. Whereas all major proponents accept the idea of simplicity, it becomes severely attenuated in the work of Duns Scotus (d. 708/1308). By simplicity, he means that God is affirmed as transcendent in having no spatial or temporal parts, composition in form and matter, or accidental change, but He is not identical with His attributes, nor are they identical with each other.[85] Thus, Scotus develops a position of substantive, or formally distinct, attributes that are possessed by God's essence, which is parallel to the classical Ashʿarī-Māturīdī position (see below). This is to be contrasted with Aquinas for whom simplicity additionally means that all of God's attributes are identical to each other, His essence and existence.[86]

One must be careful in mapping debates over the nature of God and the language used to refer to Him in the Christian tradition onto Islamic thought. While Scotus holds a univocal theory of reference in which a term is used for both creation and God in the same sense, Aquinas, a prominent defender of conventional divine simplicity, affirms an analogical theory in which a term is used in different senses that are related in appropriate ways.[87] According to Richard Cross, univocity entails weak simplicity (possessing

85 Cross, *Duns Scotus*, p. 29.
86 See Cross, *Duns Scotus*, pp. 43–45.
87 See Rolnick, 'Realist Reference to God', pp. 212–14.

distinct attributes) and strong simplicity entails rejecting univocity, which explains the positions held by Scotus and Aquinas, respectively.[88] But this does not mean that analogy entails strong simplicity, nor that weak simplicity entails rejecting analogy. In the present study I argue that al-Māturīdī consistently adopts an analogical theory of reference and a theory of distinct attributes, although these concepts must be understood within his own intellectual milieu.[89]

A key term for the present discussion is the Arabic word *dhāt*, which is commonly translated in *kalām* discussions as essence and is often understood as an ontic substratum that possesses qualities.[90] Van Ess suggests that this word emerged in the *kalām* tradition from rendering Aristotle's term *καθ' αὑτό*, meaning 'in its own nature',[91] as *bi-dhātihi*.[92] I propose that al-Māturīdī's use of *bi-dhātihi* for God's nature, and his use of *al-dhāt* for Him as a complete 'subject' who possesses attributes, reflects this early terminology rather than the later concept of a divine essence with attributes additional to it. Moreover, he should be construed as affirming only a conceptual distinction between God's existence and His nature. See, for instance, his statement '[God's] existence in His nature in eternity (*bi-mawjūdin bi-dhātihi fī al-azal*)'.[93] A passage supporting this interpretation is found in al-Māturīdī's above-mentioned defence of applying the language of 'thing' to God.[94] He argues that, whereas something not being a thing would negate its reality, calling God a thing acts as 'an affirmation of the subject and magnification of Him (*ithbāti al-dhāti wa-ta ʿẓīmihi*)'.[95] This is contrasted with the position that God has a body, which does not establish either 'praise or magnification of His existence (*yuḥmadu*

88 Cross, *Duns Scotus*, pp. 44–45.

89 Considering al-Māturīdī's position according to the categorisation scheme provided by Alston, he embraces three of the five features pertaining to 'otherness': God's incorporeality, infinity and timelessness (A–C), while rejecting the features of absolute simplicity and not considering Him a being (D–E). Al-Māturīdī's analogical approach to reference is in fourth place on Alston's scale between straight univocity (1) and symbolic expression (6). This is a useful gauge of the emphasis on pure transcendence within his system. See Alston, *Divine Nature and Human Language*, pp. 64–65.

90 Frank translates *dhāt* as 'essence' or 'thing-itself'. See Frank, *Beings and Their Attributes*, p. 53. Dhanani understands it as 'object', or, more precisely, 'a distinct entity having particular differentiating attributes'. Dhanani, *The Physical Theory of Kalām*, pp. 29. See also Rahman, 'D͟hāt'.

91 Aristotle, *Metaphysics, Volume I: Books 1–9*, trans. Hugh Tredennick, pp. 146–47.

92 Van Ess, *Theology and Society in the Second and Third Centuries of the Hijra, Volume 4*, p. 491. The translation of *dhāt* as the nature of a thing is also attested in the Arabic lexicographical tradition. Lane, *Lexicon*, vol. 1, p. 985.

93 Al-Māturīdī, *Kitāb al-tawḥīd*, p. 104. See page 76.

94 See pages 74–75.

95 Al-Māturīdī, *Kitāb al-tawḥīd*, p. 106.

wujūduhu aw yuʿaẓẓamu)'.[96] Note the parallel between the subject (God) and His existence (*wujūd*).

The inapplicability of 'body' to God turns on the question of the whatness of the subject (*māʾiyyat al-dhāt*):

> In the visible world, from a man's statement 'thing', the whatness of the subject (*māʾiyyat al-dhāt*) is not known, and neither is it [known] from the statement 'knowing and powerful'. From the first, only existence and isness is understood. From the second, it is described [with the quality (*al-ṣifa*)],[97] not an elaboration of the whatness of the subject. This is unlike a man's statement 'body', which mentions the whatness by which it is the possessor of parts, sides, the possibility of annihilation, or the acceptance of accidents (*al-aʿrāḍ*). The same is true of 'the human being' and the rest of substances.[98]

Al-Māturīdī's employment of the concept *māʾiyyat al-dhāt* in this passage is revealing for his understanding of *dhāt*. He does not use the term for a substance stripped of its properties, but for one comprised of them. When he writes about *māʾiyyat al-dhāt* for the body as its possession of accidental qualities, he is not thinking in terms of a substratum but applying the idea of whatness to its properties taken together as a single nature.

One who is familiar with the discussions of classical *kalām* on the concept of *dhāt* may find al-Māturīdī's usage of the term disorienting. He consistently refuses to reify it as a substratum, or essence, of which God's attributes are predicated. Instead, he uses it to refer to God's existent nature, which, unlike the creation, is not grounded on anything else and never changes. For al-Māturīdī, God's nature is comprised of the attributes that are eternally predicated of Him and are hence essential attributes: literally attributes of the subject (*ṣifāt al-dhāt*). He states, 'they are essential attributes, and He is eternally attributed with them (*hiya ṣifāt al-dhāt wa-huwa lam yazal bi-hā mawṣūfan*)'.[99] Moreover, the effect of each attribute in the world allows an inference to its subject, God.[100] Following the Ḥanafī position, al-Māturīdī argues that all of God's actions, or active attributes (*ṣifāt al-fiʿl*), are *ṣifāt al-dhāt*.[101] He therefore writes of God acting by Himself (*bi-nafsihi yafʿalu*), just as He knows and has power

96 Al-Māturīdī, *Kitāb al-tawḥīd*, p. 106.
97 The word *al-ṣifa* has been added here on the margin of the manuscript. Al-Māturīdī, 'Kitāb al-tawḥīd', fol. 20v.
98 Al-Māturīdī, *Kitāb al-tawḥīd*, p. 106.
99 Al-Māturīdī, *Kitāb al-tawḥīd*, p. 119.
100 Al-Māturīdī, *Kitāb al-tawḥīd*, p. 198. See page 63.
101 Al-Māturīdī, *Kitāb al-tawḥīd*, p. 115.

in His nature (*bi-dhātihi*),[102] and of creating due to creative action being of His nature.[103] Al-Māturīdī understands God's existence as eternal in contrast to the temporal world and, as expressed in His nature, with the set of attributes predicated of Him. In other words, verification of God's eternal existence is affirmation of His eternal nature and *vice versa.*

In theology, the question, 'What is God?', implies its correlative, 'With what language can we speak of God?'[104] This latter query cuts to the metaphysical heart of any endeavour to construct a theological system. The problem is how to present a coherent account of the properties possessed by material world, transcendent God, and the language of scripture that links them. From the principle of *khilāf*, al-Māturīdī argues that it is impossible for there to be a likeness (*shibh*) between God and the creation in any aspect.[105] As discussed previously, al-Māturīdī understands likeness to be explained by body and accident,[106] the whatnesses of temporal things. Yet his insistence on negating likeness is a way to clear the ground for his process of *mithl*, which allows speech about God and necessarily makes use of analogical inference from the world:

> There is no way to know the veiled reality except by indication from the manifest one. Therefore, when one wants the description of the High and Majestic, that is the path of knowledge in the manifest world and [it provides] the possibility of speech. [This is] because we lack the capacity for cognising with names other than that which we have witnessed, and there is no pointing to what we have not taken in with the senses and realised through perception. Were that a capacity we possibly possessed, we would have said so. But [we desired] to remove any anthropomorphism from our statement 'knowing not like the knowers (*ʿālimun lā ka-l-ʿulamāʾ*)', and this is the type [of approach] in all by which we name and describe Him.[107]

For al-Māturīdī, discussion of God's attributes is only possible with analogical language derived from an extension of worldly experience. This kind

102 Al-Māturīdī, *Kitāb al-tawḥīd*, p. 112.

103 Al-Māturīdī, *Kitāb al-tawḥīd*, p. 164. Compare with Cerić and Rudolph who presuppose the classical concept of a substratum-essence to which God's attributes are superadded. See Cerić, *Roots of Synthetic Theology in Islam*, p. 180; Rudolph, *Al-Māturīdī and the Development of Sunnī Theology*, p. 282.

104 Janet Soskice further divides the enquiry into the positive epistemological question 'What can we know about God?' and the deeper mystery of negative theology, 'How can *anything* be said of God?' See Soskice, 'Naming God', p. 254.

105 Al-Māturīdī, *Kitāb al-tawḥīd*, p. 91.

106 This is stated explicitly in al-Māturīdī, *Kitāb al-tawḥīd*, p. 89. See page 74.

107 Al-Māturīdī, *Kitāb al-tawḥīd*, p. 91.

of reasoning works from the bottom up to infer what can be known about God.[108] There is an ontology to the divine nature, which according to Sunnī theologians like al-Māturīdī is not metaphysically simple; hence the recurring talk of distinct, or substantive, divine attributes. Also, description of divine attributes does not operate independently of the revealed language of scripture, because it has to tap into a source of knowledge separate from reason in order to connect the world analogically to God.[109] Al-Māturīdī's follower in the early Samarqandī tradition, Abū Salama al-Samarqandī, comments that it is necessary to verify God's substantive attributes such as knowledge, power and action, because each one is a derived noun (*ism mushtaqq*) from the established meaning of God knowing, possessing power and acting.[110]

As I show in greater detail in Chapter 7 in the context of al-Māturīdī's debate with Muʿtazilism over the divine attribute of speech, he argues that an account of divine attributes cannot be developed except via the properties of things in the world.[111] He contends that the Muʿtazila, who combine substantive properties for objects in the world with merely nominal attributes for the divine, lapse into inconsistency in their process of analogy between the manifest and veiled realms. His quarrel with the Muʿtazila is that in the fear of *tashbīh*, clothing God in the temporality of worldly qualities, they fall into *taʿṭīl*, denuding Him of His rightful attributes. The broader accusation against divine simplicity is that it dashes any hope of a consistent scheme of predication between the level of human and divine, leaving no basis by which to speak about God. Thus, the Muʿtazilī position collapses into that of Jahm.[112] Al-Māturīdī holds that it is untenable to see God as simple or to judge His different attributes as mere mental individuations based on the naming of His actions within creation. Rather, despite possessing distinct attributes, God remains 'one not by the aspect of number (*wāḥidun lā min jihati al-ʿadad*)'.[113]

108 Cf. Soskice, *Metaphor and Religious Language*, p. 65.

109 Hall, *Knowledge, Belief, and Transcendence*, pp. 119–20. Compare with Aquinas' theory of analogy, in which God's action in the world has a 'proportional similarity' with the objects of experience. This means that He can be named with genuine properties while preserving the intelligibility of theological language (as opposed to equivocal reference) and transcendence (as opposed to univocal reference). See Ross, 'Analogy as a Rule of Meaning for Religious Language', pp. 132–33.

110 Al-Samarqandī, *Jumal min uṣūl al-dīn wa-yalīhu sharḥuhu*, pp. 20–21.

111 See pages 197–99.

112 Al-Māturīdī states: 'the basic [position] against the denier of the attributes [. . .] is that what Jahm says becomes necessary with respect to the nullification of [God's] names, attributes, and their temporal generation, so He would be unknowing and without power, then knowing. God is majestic and exalted over that.' Al-Māturīdī, *Kitāb al-tawḥīd*, p. 130.

113 Al-Samarqandī, *Jumal min uṣūl al-dīn wa-yalīhu sharḥuhu*, pp. 18–19. The discussion draws on al-Māturīdī, *Kitāb al-tawḥīd*, p. 85.

By tracing the history of the Samarqandī Ḥanafī and Māturīdī tradition, it is possible to see the stages of development that opened a gap between al-Māturīdī's thought and that of the classical school. His immediate successors seem to have followed him in affirming the eternality of God's attributes without relating them to a substratum. This is the apparent position of Abū Bakr al-ʿIyāḍī in *Al-Masāʾil al-ʿashar al-ʿIyāḍiyya*.[114] Abū Salama al-Samarqandī, in his *Jumal min uṣūl al-dīn*, paraphrases al-Māturīdī in writing that '[God] is eternally attributed with everything attributed to Him [. . .] He does not resemble the attributes of created things just as in respect of His nature He does not resemble the nature of created things'.[115]

One of the more explicit expressions of this position is found in *Sharḥ al-fiqh al-akbar*, which may be from the second half of the fifth/eleventh century.[116] Here we find the doctrine that there is no difference between God's *dhāt* and His *ṣifāt*. This is said to be opposed by the Ashʿarīs and Muʿtazila in their treatment of the *ṣifāt al-fiʿl* as temporal, which opens up a distinction between the two.[117] The criticism of the other groups only makes sense if God's *dhāt* is His nature, which comprises all of His attributes, including for Māturīdīs His actions, rather than a substratum. This also bears some similarity to the position ascribed to Aḥmad b. Ḥanbal (d. 241/855), in which he declares that it is 'not permitted to single out [God] from His attributes (*lā yajūzu an yanfarida al-ḥaqqu ʿan ṣifātihi*)'.[118] The first in the Māturīdī school to shift from this approach is al-Sālimī who declares that '[God's] attributes are established in His essence (*ṣifātuhu taqūmu bi-dhātihi*)', an understanding that he takes from a development within Ashʿarī discourse.[119] As Angelika Brodersen points out, al-Sālimī is one of the first figures in the emerging Māturīdī tradition to discuss Ashʿarī views and, while often in polemical opposition, does adopt some of them, such as atomism.[120]

The earliest Ashʿarīs do not seem to have understood God's *dhāt* as a substratum. Abū al-Ḥasan al-Ashʿarī writes, similarly to al-Māturīdī,

114 Özen, 'IV. (X.) Yüzyılda Māverāünnehir'de Ehl-i Sünnet-Muʿtezile Mücadelesi ve Bir Ehl-i Sūnnet Beyannamesi', p. 84.

115 Al-Samarqandī, *Jumal min uṣūl al-dīn wa-yalīhu sharḥuhu*, p. 19. An incorrect *wāw* has been inserted before the second mention of *dhāt* that is not present in the earlier edition. See al-Samarqandī, 'Jumal uṣūl al-dīn', p. 15.

116 See the discussion on page 32, note 114.

117 Al-Samarqandī, 'Sharḥ al-fiqh al-absaṭ', pp. 140–41.

118 Al-Tamīmī, *Iʿtiqād al-imām al-munabbal*, p. 53. ʿAbbād b. Sulaymān, a contemporary of Ibn Ḥanbal, refused to use the terms *dhāt* or *nafs* with respect to God due to a similar concern. See Frank, '"*Lam yazal*" as a Formal Term in Muslim Theological Discourse', p. 267, n. 34.

119 Al-Sālimī, *Al-Tamhīd fī bayan al-tawḥīd*, p. 119; al-Sālimī, 'Al-Tamhīd fī bayan al-tawḥīd', p. 115.

120 Brodersen, *Zwischen Māturīdīya und Ashʿarīya*, pp. 6–7.

that the *ṣifāt al-dhāt* are all to be affirmed of God's nature (*li-dhātihi*).[121] His student at one remove, Abū Isḥāq al-Isfarāyīnī, merely states that they eternally describe Him and are neither Him, nor other than Him (but see below).[122] The crucial turning point seems to be al-Isfarāyīnī's student, ʿAbd al-Qāhir al-Baghdādī (d. 429/1037). When discussing al-Bāqillānī's rejection of the attribute of *baqāʾ* (permanence) as one of the *ṣifāt al-dhāt*, he states that he refused it as 'an additional attribute over the existence of the essence of the Eternal (*maʿnan zāʾidan ʿalā wujūdi dhāti al-bāqī*)'.[123] The emergence of this idea in the *kalām* tradition seems to have occurred at a similar time to Ibn Sīnā's ideas with respect to the essence-existence distinction and the conceptualisation of necessity.[124] The position is consolidated by al-Juwaynī who defines the substantive attributes (which he calls *ṣifāt al-maʿnā*) as 'every description [such that] it indicates a meaning additional to the essence (*maʿnin zāʾidin ʿalā al-dhāt*)'.[125] Al-Juwaynī attributes this formulation to al-Ustādh [Abū Isḥāq al-Isfarāyīnī], which, if correct, would place it a generation earlier than I have suggested. In any case, the explicit doctrine of God's attributes as additional to His essence is certainly not introduced by al-Rāzī, as claimed by the contemporary theologian Muḥammad Ṣāliḥ al-Ghursī.[126]

At the beginning of the classical period of Māturīdī *kalām*, the different strands of thought on the status of divine attributes are documented by al-Bazdawī. He points out two rival positions using the standard example of God's knowledge:[127]

1. God is knowing with knowledge (*ʿālimun bi-l-ʿilm*).
2. God is knowing and has knowledge (*ʿālimun wa-lahu ʿilm*).

Proponents of the second formulation felt that the first one implied that God only became knowing with His knowledge. The first group responded that, so long as God is affirmed as eternally knowing, there is no problem. Al-Bazdawī then quotes al-Māturīdī, a member of the first group, as follows: 'the attribute is ascribed to God, Most High, not God, Most High, to the attribute. It is not said, "knowing by His knowledge (*ʿālimun bi-ʿilmihi*)", rather, "knowing with knowledge (*ʿālimun bi-l-ʿilm*)". When it is said, "With whose knowledge?", it is said, "With His

121 Al-Ashʿarī, *Kitāb al-lumaʿ*, p. 31. Also see Frank, 'The Ashʿarite Ontology', p. 174.
122 Frank, 'Al-Ustādh Abū Isḥāḳ', p. 134.
123 Al-Baghdādī, *Kitāb uṣūl al-dīn*, p. 90.
124 See pages 77–78 and 132–33.
125 Al-Juwaynī, *Al-Shāmil fī uṣūl al-dīn*, p. 308.
126 Al-Ghursī, *Taḥqīq masāʾil muhimmāt min ʿilm al-tawḥīd wa-l-ṣifāt*, pp. 180–81.
127 The following discussion is in al-Bazdawī, *Uṣūl al-dīn*, p. 45.

knowledge"'.[128] It seems that, despite his reservations, al-Māturīdī was willing to accept the less favourable formula for the sake of clarifying that the knowledge in question was God's unique attribute.[129]

Al-Bazdawī discusses a group from the *ahl al-sunna wa-l-jamāʿa* who argue that, while God's attributes are substantive entities, they are also not different from each other – just as they are neither the same nor other than God's *dhāt* – a position that can be traced to al-Sālimī.[130] A related question concerns the number of God's attributes. The logic of al-Sālimī's position is that God's attributes cannot be given a number, although he acknowledges other approaches in the broader tradition, including one that treats each attribute as distinct (as followed by al-Māturīdī and the early school).[131] Later figures, such as al-Ṣābūnī, argue that there is no contradiction in God having an unlimited number of attributes, even if they lie beyond our knowledge unless informed by revelation.[132]

There is also the problem of how to conceive of the eternality of God and His attributes. Al-Bazdawī highlights that some had begun to say that 'God's attributes are eternal, but with an eternality established in the essence and not in them (*bi-qidamin qāʾiman bi-l-dhāt wa-lā bihā*)'.[133] This position, which I have already pointed out from al-Sālimī, is an instance of the substratum reading of *dhāt* that was to become dominant in the classical tradition. Al-Ṣaffār mentions the opinion of those who said that God was eternal with eternality (*qadīmun bi-qidam*) like He was knowing with knowledge (*ʿālimun bi-ʿilm*). Nevertheless, he avers, Abū al-ʿAbbās al-Qalānisī (a theologian of the late third/ninth century who is recognised as a precursor to al-Ashʿarī)[134] criticises this for meta-qualification of attributes (*waṣf al-ṣifa*),

128 Al-Bazdawī, 'Al-Muyassir fī al-kalām [Uṣūl al-dīn]', fol. 20v. The printed edition by Hans Peter Linss cites al-Māturīdī incompletely and inaccurately. See al-Bazdawī, *Uṣūl al-dīn*, p. 45. I am grateful to Ayedh Aldosari for sharing a copy of the manuscript with the correct reading.

129 An argument attributed to the Muʿtazila is that knowledge is general such that, were it to be affirmed of God, He would have to partake in it alongside others, leading to a similarity with the creation. Al-Ṣaffār, *Talkhīṣ al-adilla*, vol. 1, p. 92. See the discussion on pages 117–18.

130 Al-Bazdawī, *Uṣūl al-dīn*, pp. 45–46; al-Sālimī, *Al-Tamhīd fī bayan al-tawḥīd*, p. 138.

131 Al-Sālimī, *Al-Tamhīd fī bayan al-tawḥīd*, p. 138. There is an interesting resonance with al-Sālimī's thought in the positions taken many centuries later by Abū Naṣr al-Qūrṣāwī (d. 1227/1812) against the late classical Sunnī theological consensus. Al-Qūrṣāwī contested several doctrines professed by al-Taftāzānī, who represented the mainstream view. Significantly in the present context, these include that God's attributes possess differentiation (*mughāyara*) and multiplicity (*taʿaddud*). See Spannaus, *Preserving Islamic Tradition*, pp. 153–60.

132 See al-Ṣābūnī, *Al-Kifāya fī al-hidāya*, p. 100.

133 Al-Bazdawī, *Uṣūl al-dīn*, p. 45.

134 See Bin Ramli, 'The Predecessors of Ashʿarism', pp. 221–23.

as it implies that His attributes need a further attribute of eternality, which would be incoherent.[135] Again, al-Māturīdī's expression is praised as best: 'God is eternal with His attributes (*inna allāha qadīmun bi-ṣifātihi*)'.[136]

These positions relate to debates on substantive divine attributes traced by Wisnovsky in the *kalām* tradition from at least the time of ʿAbd Allāh b. Kullāb (d. *ca* 240/854–55). There is a striking parallel to al-Māturīdī's formulation in the version earlier used by Ibn Kullāb: 'He is eternal, never-ending with His names and attributes (*innahu qadīmun lam yazal bi-asmāʾihi wa-ṣifātihi*)'.[137] Wisnovsky suggests that, as Ibn Kullāb evidently saw the divine attributes as eternal, this formulation amounts to both a predication of eternality to God and a meta-qualification of eternality to His attributes.[138] As Wisnovsky implicitly acknowledges, this is not actually to be found in Ibn Kullāb's words, which are open to interpretation, but in the inferences derived by those theologians who followed him, of which he focuses on the Ashʿarī tradition.[139] Wisnovsky provides two options:[140]

1. God is eternal through an eternality (*qadīm bi-qidam*).
2. God is eternal in Himself (*qadīm bi-nafsihi*).

He reasons that, if (1) is correct, then God's attributes themselves have a meta-attribute of eternality, which leads to meta-qualification and an infinite regress. But if (2) is correct, then God's attributes either cannot truly be termed eternal or may seem to be eternal in a problematically independent way.[141]

What does my analysis of the Māturīdī tradition add to this discussion? The meta-qualification of attributes involved in (1) has many problems and should be dismissed. This leaves (2) and the need for an articulation that maintains the eternal status of attributes without making them separate entities. To do this, I think it is useful to return to al-Māturīdī's conception of God's eternality and to provide another option. It should be recalled that al-Māturīdī's principle of *khilāf* does not establish God's eternality in positive terms, but by negating from him the contingency of created things. This leads to the following:

3. God is eternal as temporality is negated from Him.

135 Al-Ṣaffār, *Talkhīṣ al-adilla*, vol. 1, p. 208.
136 Al-Ṣaffār, *Talkhīṣ al-adilla*, vol. 1, p. 209.
137 Al-Ashʿarī, *Maqālāt*, vol. 1, p. 229; Wisnovsky, *Avicenna's Metaphysics in Context*, p. 230. Frank shows that Ibn Ḥanbal held the same position. See Frank, '"*Lam yazal*" as a Formal Term in Muslim Theological Discourse', pp. 250–51.
138 Wisnovsky, *Avicenna's Metaphysics in Context*, pp. 230–31.
139 Wisnovsky, *Avicenna's Metaphysics in Context*, pp. 231–33.
140 Wisnovsky, *Avicenna's Metaphysics in Context*, p. 231.
141 Wisnovsky, *Avicenna's Metaphysics in Context*, pp. 231–32.

The eternal status of God's attributes still requires comment. In my reading of al-Māturīdī's theology, God's attributes are not understood as additional to His nature (*dhāt*) or self (*nafs*). While God is neither His attributes nor other than them, His *dhāt* comprises these attributes. This 'comprising without a substratum' is what is captured by the particle *bi* in the expressions *bi-ṣifātihi* and *bi-dhātihi*. Within such a conception, to negate temporality from God is to negate it from His nature and the attributes comprised thereby, which remain eternal and yet also integral to Him.[142]

Theological nuances premised on a non-substratum conception of the *dhāt* have proved hard to spot, because the substratum became central to classical articulations of *kalām* and has since been presupposed when reading figures from before the shift.[143] This can already be seen in the difficulty that Abū al-Muʿīn al-Nasafī has with the statement of al-Māturīdī that 'God is knowing in His nature (*bi-dhātihi*), living in His nature and powerful in His nature', which he declares cannot mean a denial of substantive attributes.[144] This problem only arises when *dhāt* is taken to mean a substrate-like essence to which attributes are additional (*zāʾid*), as expressed by ʿAlāʾ al-Dīn al-Usmandī (d. 552/1157) and al-Ṣābūnī in their use of variations on the phrase *warāʾa al-dhāt* (additional to the essence).[145]

Taking a step back, the theological development is as follows. For al-Māturīdī, God is a concrete particular (*ʿayn*) with an eternal nature (*dhāt*), which is comprised of the attributes (*ṣifāt*) predicated of Him. By the classical period, however, God is analysed as an eternal essence (*dhāt*) of which His attributes are predicated. The difference, in short, is from a bundle theory to a substrate-attribute theory. A famous illustration of this point is found in the phrasing of the formula for speaking about God's attributes as neither Him, nor other than Him (*lā huwa wa-lā ghayra huwa*). This was adopted by al-Māturīdī, again in common with al-Ashʿarī, from the ideas of early theologians such as the Imāmī Hishām b. al-Ḥakam,

142 Compare with Ross, *Philosophical Theology*, pp. 56–57.

143 There are striking resemblances to Kuhn on paradigm shift in science: 'Since new paradigms are born from old ones, they ordinarily incorporate much of the vocabulary and apparatus, both conceptual and manipulative, that the traditional paradigm had previously employed. But they seldom employ these borrowed elements in quite the traditional way. Within the new paradigm, old terms, concepts, and experiments fall into new relationships one with the other. The inevitable result is what we must call, though the term is not quite right, a misunderstanding between the two competing schools'. Kuhn, *The Structure of Scientific Revolutions*, p. 149.

144 Al-Nasafī, *Tabṣirat al-adilla*, vol. 1, p. 433.

145 Al-Usmandī, *Lubāb al-kalām*, p. 82; al-Ṣābūnī, *Al-Kifāya fī al-hidāya*, p. 86. See the general discussion in al-Ghursī, *Taḥqīq masāʾil muhimmāt min ʿilm al-tawḥīd wa-l-ṣifāt*, pp. 180–81.

the Zaydī Sulaymān b. Jarīr and, most famously, the proto-Sunnī Ibn Kullāb.[146] This version remained standard into the classical period as preserved within *Al-ʿAqida al-Nasafiyya* and other Māturīdī texts,[147] although it was transmitted by figures such as al-Sālimī in a version that replaced Him (*huwa*) with His essence (*dhātuhu*).[148] Later in the classical tradition, the commonly accepted interpretation of this doctrine switches, as attested in *Lubāb al-kalām* of al-Usmandī[149] and in the commentary of Ḥuṣam al-Dīn al-Sighnāqī (d. 714/1314) on the *Tamhīd* of Abū Muʿīn al-Nasafī: 'the attributes of God are not the same as the essence, and not other than the essence (*ṣifāta allāhi lā ʿayna dhātihi wa-lā ghayra dhātihi*)'.[150] In this formulation, God has been definitively substituted with His substratum essence, to which the attributes are related.

A second question concerns the logic by which the so-called Kullābī formula operates. Within classical logic, anything that is not-*x* must be other-than-*x* due to LEM, which makes the formula an apparently contradictory notion. This point was exploited by opponents of this approach to the divine attributes, such as the Muʿtazilī al-Kaʿbī who is quoted as drawing this implication.[151] The response of the classical Māturīdī al-Ṣaffār was to declare that a different logical scheme applies to God than to things within the world, effectively suspending LEM for Him alone.[152]

I think such an answer risks arbitrariness and incoherence. Even if we want to declare that God cannot be trapped within the logic that applies to the created world, we have no other language available to us. Moreover, from the perspective of al-Māturīdī, we must reason from the indications of the world towards God, as it is the rationality of reality that allows us to speak about the divine. It would therefore seem more promising to utilise a system of intuitionistic logic that can consistently speak about both the

146 Al-Māturīdī, *Kitāb al-tawḥīd*, p. 118. See al-Ashʿarī, *Kitāb al-lumaʿ*, p. 43. This can be found for Hishām, Sulaymān, and inferred for Ibn Kullāb and his followers in al-Ashʿarī, *Maqālāt*, vol. 1, pp. 107–8, vol. 1, p. 138, and vol. 1, p. 232, respectively. In all cases the formula mentions either God or a referring pronoun and not the word *dhāt*. Madelung's translation of Hishām's definition of the divine attributes as 'being neither identical with nor other than their substratum' seems to be an interpolation of the later *kalām* conception. Madelung, 'The Shiite and Khārijite Contribution to Pre-Ashʿarite *Kalām*', p. 126.

147 Al-Nasafī, *Al-Tamhīd fī uṣūl al-dīn*, p. 42; al-Nasafī, 'Matn al-ʿaqīda al-Nasafiyya', p. 52; al-Lāmishī, *Kitab al-tamhīd li-qawāʿid al-tawḥīd*, p. 67.

148 Al-Sālimī, *Al-Tamhīd fī bayan al-tawḥīd*, p. 120.

149 Al-Usmandī, *Lubāb al-kalām*, p. 82.

150 Al-Sighnāqī, 'Al-Tasdīd fī sharḥ al-tamhīd', pp. 177–78. The same point is better known from the subsequent discussion in al-Taftāzānī, *Sharḥ al-ʿaqīda al-Nasafiyya*, pp. 44–45. He glosses *ghayr* as 'separable from' to preserve LEM.

151 Al-Ṣaffār, *Talkhīṣ al-adilla*, vol. 1, p. 95.

152 Al-Ṣaffār, *Talkhīṣ al-adilla*, vol. 1, p. 97.

world and God, as introduced in Chapter 2. From a historical angle, it seems plausible to explain the existence of the Kullābī formula as evidence for a different approach to logic in early *kalām*. One possibility that I have already mentioned is the use of Stoic logic. Interestingly, Abū ʿUthmān al-Jāḥiẓ (d. 255/869) is cited as adopting, like some Stoics, a logic containing logical gaps by which some statements may be neither true nor false.[153] The proposition *lā huwa wa-lā ghayra huwa* also fits the form used in Stoic logical statements that were able to deal with two or more conjuncts,[154] and placed negations at the front of each assertible.[155]

Assuming that the formula was first proposed within an intellectual framework lacking LEM (possibly influenced by Stoic logic) makes better sense of it, preserving a logical gap by which God's attributes are neither affirmed as Him, nor other than Him, within human knowledge.[156] An illustrative example of this procedure in the thought of al-Māturīdī is his suspension (*waqf*) of the identity of God's speech in the following terms: 'It is said it is not God, nor other than Him, so it is a suspension on account of knowledge and it is the truth based on what has been established for the [attributes] of knowledge and power'.[157]

I will now seek to provide a more rigorous contemporary account of the relationship between God's nature and His attributes by utilising the resources of possible world semantics. Plantinga introduces two key definitions:

1. *E* is an essence if and only if there is a world *W* in which there exists an object *x* that (1) has *E* essentially, and (2) is such that there is no world *W** in which there exists an object distinct from *x* that has *E*.[158]
2. *S* is an essence if and only if *S* is a complete and consistent set of world-indexed properties.[159]

I suggest that essence here can be read as that which I have been referring to as a nature (*dhāt*). From definition (1), an object with such a nature has it necessarily and uniquely. From (2), a nature must be a complete and consistent set of properties possessed or not possessed (hence world indexed) within world *W*.

By substituting the revised definition (2) into (1), we get:

153 Van Ess, 'The Logical Structure of Islamic Theology', p. 31. See page 37.
154 Barnes, 'Introduction', p. 102.
155 Barnes, 'Introduction', p. 114.
156 See the related discussion in Wisnovsky, 'Essence and Existence in the Eleventh- and Twelfth-Century', pp. 35–40.
157 Al-Māturīdī, *Kitāb al-tawḥīd*, p. 122. The attribute of speech according to al-Māturīdī is discussed on pages 196–202, and his understanding of *waqf* on page 202.
158 Plantinga, *The Nature of Necessity*, p. 72.
159 Plantinga, *The Nature of Necessity*, p. 77.

3. A complete and consistent set of world-indexed properties is a nature if and only if there is a world *W* in which there exists an object *x* that (1) has this complete and consistent set of world-indexed properties essentially, and (2) is such that there is no world *W** in which there exists an object distinct from *x* that has this complete and consistent set of world-indexed properties.

Applying this to God, we get:

4. A complete and consistent set of world-indexed properties is a divine nature if and only if there is a world *W* in which there exists an object (God) that (1) has this complete and consistent set of world-indexed properties essentially, and (2) is such that there is no world *W** in which there exists an object distinct from *x* that has this complete and consistent set of world-indexed properties.

World *W* is a possible world, a logically conceivable reality.[160] As mentioned in Section II of this chapter, I argue that *W*, the possible world that includes the transcendent existence of God with His nature, is the actual world as a matter of absolute metaphysical necessity. Furthermore, because of (4), God's nature is fixed. So, God is an object, or concrete particular (*ʿayn*), and His divine nature (*dhāt*) is a complete and consistent set of properties (*ṣifāt*) that He has essentially and that no other object may possess. I will therefore build on the position that I took in Chapter 2, where I suggested that an ontology can be formulated with an intuitionistic set theory corresponding to tropes as its truthmakers. In this system, we know every concrete particular by the phenomenological verification of its set of tropes. We can think of God's attributes as divine tropes and state $\{a, b, c \dots\} \in G$, meaning that God possesses divine tropes $\{a, b, c \dots\}$ as His nature; or that, as a concrete particular, He is neither the same as, nor other than, divine tropes $\{a, b, c \dots\}$. Another way to write this would be $G\,\{a, b, c \dots\}$ where *a*, *b*, and *c* are an infinitude of His divine tropes, including His actions.[161]

To clarify what is at stake in a theory of divine tropes, it is useful to compare it to some of Leftow's ideas. He makes a similar move in suggesting that

160 This must be distinguished from the world in the sense of everything except God. See page 2, note 7 and page 134.

161 There seems good reason to argue that those of God's actions having effect within created existence are potentially infinite to avoid paradox. See pages 115–16. But this does not necessarily rule out a transcendent actual infinite with respect to His attributes and actions in themselves. See page 117. A comparison can be made here with the views of Spinoza and Descartes. See Melamed, 'Hasdai Crescas and Spinoza on Actual Infinity and the Infinity of God's Attributes', pp. 211–14.

God's powers, His willing, knowing and so on, can be wrapped into a master property using a 'double-aspect' theory. If God is divine, then His divinity or His deity – that is, His nature – is a quality with descriptive content identical to its dispositional powers.[162] He then follows Aquinas in arguing that, in fact, there is no property of deity distinct from God Himself.[163] The end result is akin to a classical Muʿtazilī approach: God has powers without substantive properties or a complex nature.[164] There is, however, a curious tension in Leftow's case. Two chapters prior to his argument that the concept of deity can swallow distinct attributes and then in turn be eliminated entirely, he states that a 'thin partial deity theory' will be unavoidable. He qualifies this with the proviso that, once he introduces it, he will continue to speak of his position as a non-deity theory, as it does not harm his wider project of explaining secular necessary truths.[165] Leaving the peculiarity of this stance aside for now,[166] I do not accept the adoption of Aquinas' formulation as, unlike Leftow, I am not committed to divine simplicity. Despite this difference in positioning, Leftow provides a very useful analysis of the various possibilities for theories of properties that could be applied to God.

Leftow dismisses realism, including Platonism, on the basis that any ontological work done by universals can be replaced by constructions involving God. Moreover, universals can be possessed by more than one entity, whereas the properties of God are unique, or haecceities in the language of Duns Scotus.[167] This leaves various types of nominalism, which Leftow classifies as follows:

1. Natural class nominalism – properties are defined by membership of natural classes. This is summarily dismissed as false.[168]
2. Concept nominalism – properties are defined by coming under concepts. This is false, and even if conceivable, is inapplicable to God's properties on the basis that they should be more substantive than merely falling under a concept.[169]

162 Leftow, *God and Necessity*, p. 304.
163 Leftow, *God and Necessity*, p. 307.
164 A similar position is reached in Ross, *Philosophical Theology*, p. 62.
165 Leftow, *God and Necessity*, p. 247. For an example of why he feels compelled to keep a notion of deity to explain necessary truths such as 'whatever is divine is personal', see pp. 254–55.
166 See the comments on page 155, note 172.
167 Leftow, *God and Necessity*, pp. 305. See also pp. 246–47.
168 Leftow, *God and Necessity*, p. 305. See also pp. 231–32, 244–45. He gives a fuller treatment in Leftow, 'One Step Toward God', pp. 75–87. Also see my comments on page 97.
169 Leftow, *God and Necessity*, p. 305. See also pp. 230–31, 243–44. See page 199.

3. Ostrich nominalism – properties are defined via direct reference to concrete particulars. This is inapplicable to God, because it avoids talk of attributes.[170]
4. Resemblance nominalism – properties are defined through the resemblance of particulars. This is inapplicable, because describing attributes in this way fails on uniqueness grounds when applied to God.[171]
5. Mereological nominalism – properties are defined as the aggregates of all things possessing them. This is inapplicable, since, if God's attributes are unique, then his attributes are just Himself.[172]
6. Trope theoretic nominalism – properties are defined as tropes. This is applicable as long as in the case of God the tropes are non-free-floating (meaning that they cannot exist without a concrete particular 'bearing' them) and non-resembling.[173]

Thus, Leftow's analysis, which is an example of the procedure known in the Islamic intellectual tradition as *al-sabr wa-l-taqsīm* (examination and classification),[174] results in a clear advantage to a certain type of trope theory

170 Leftow, *God and Necessity*, p. 305. See also p. 231. See Koons and Pickavance, *The Atlas of Reality*, p. 139.

171 Leftow, *God and Necessity*, p. 305. See also pp. 232, 245. Rodriguez-Pereyra, 'Nominalism in Metaphysics'.

172 Leftow, *God and Necessity*, p. 305. Rodriguez-Pereyra, 'Nominalism in Metaphysics'. But note that, despite rejecting this as an appropriate property theory of deity, it is precisely the position that Leftow argues himself to in stating that 'God is the whole ontology for *God is divine*'. Leftow, *God and Necessity*, p. 307. It remains unclear to me which theory of deity is to ground his thin partial deity theory. I suspect that, as he ultimately falls back on saying that the truthmaker for truths like 'whatever is divine is personal' is God Himself, it is a form of ostrich nominalism.

173 Leftow, *God and Necessity*, p. 305. See also pp. 232–33. Leftow does, however, immediately provide a brief argument against tropes. He suggests that they 'mirror' universals in the sense that where a realist would posit a universal, a trope theorist is committed to a sum of resembling tropes. As Leftow argues that theists can replace universals with ideas in the mind of God, or the like, so they should do the same for tropes. Leftow, *God and Necessity*, p. 305. The mirroring argument strikes me as a sleight of hand: as I argued in Chapter 2, while exactly resembling tropes can stand in for universal concepts in our theories, they are never possessed by more than one thing in reality, unlike universals. Also, divine tropes are unique, so there is no possible resemblance. Thus, the transformation is not perfect and arguments against realism cannot go through. The move to shift the work of property instances into the divine mind also worries me, as it seems tantamount to saying not just that a given temporal instance of redness is known and created by God, but that it indwells.

174 It would be the type *al-sabr wa-l-taqsīm al-muntashir* (open examination and classification), in which the subject is split into more than two categories, but the resultant knowledge is non-definitive, as opposed to the definitive *al-munḥaṣir* (closed) with two disjunctive categories. See al-Raysūnī, *Al-Tajdīd al-uṣūlī*, p. 402. Note also that this latter kind relies on LEM.

for the divine nature and attributes. This is encouraging since I have identified trope theory as both my preferred philosophical account of properties and as suitable for application to God's attributes.

I have discussed the way in which I use trope theory as ontology in both the previous and present chapter. Here I want to clarify some of the particularities of how it can be applied to God before arguing against Leftow's rejection of it as a theoretical option, despite his obvious sympathy towards it. I have proposed a phenomenological trope theory, which takes a Husserlian spirit towards the verification of entities in knowledge while avoiding some of Husserl's complexities.[175] When applying this to God, we must recall that He has a unique kind of transcendence that cannot be expressed through the essences, or whatnesses, of contingent things.[176]

In Chapter 2, I used the categories of One Over Many, Many Over One and One Over Many Times to look at property identity, object cohesion and object identity over time, respectively. As God's tropes are unique, there is no question of them identically resembling those held by other concrete particulars, so we may safely ignore One Over Many. Likewise, because His tropes are eternal and unchanging, we may discard One Over Many Times. Returning to the *kalām* methodology of this book, I note that these two categories are otiose due to the principle of *khilāf*. Just as al-Māturīdī observed, their case is clearer than Many Over One, which makes use of the principle of *mithl*.[177] What remains is to explain how it is possible for God to be ontologically non-simple without this challenging His unicity – which, it turns out, is Leftow's main objection. An important aspect of a trope-theoretic approach to the divine ontology is to insist that God's tropes must be non-free-floating. As Leftow argues, . . .

> So even if we let tropes float in general, we could not let deity-tropes float, else we would be creating a class of entities such that God requires one of them to exist, but these do not require God to exist – 'constructing' God from entities more ultimate in reality than He. Ultimacy considerations rule this out.[178]

I concur that tropes are also non-free-floating in the case of worldly concrete particulars.[179] The difference is that non-divine tropes are accidental:

175 See page 95.

176 See Husserl, *Ideas*, p. 99; Morujão, 'Is There a Place for God after the Phenomenological Reduction?', pp. 447–48; Sokolowski, *The God of Faith and Reason*, pp. 47–48. See page 76.

177 See page 60.

178 Leftow, *God and Necessity*, p. 233.

179 Compare with the argument of al-Māturīdī, which concludes that 'it is established the attributes are integral to the particulars'. See page 198.

they contingently and temporally characterise their objects. As defined above, God's properties form a complete and consistent set: they cannot be removed or altered. By conceiving of God as possessing a set of divinity tropes as His nature, I reach towards a contemporary Kullābī formula that God is established in our knowledge as neither this set of divine tropes, nor other than them. This is a phenomenological statement made within intuitionistic logic, which preserves God's transcendence over our created minds by stating that the set-theoretical structure is merely a categorial construction corresponding to His real ontology. The tropes that we posit are the truthmakers for our statements about God's actions and attributes. This way of speaking allows an indefinite number of actions and attributes to be discussed, and for there to be ones that we do not know about.[180]

The fundamental challenge that Leftow sets for a trope theory of deity is what 'ontological work it can do which God or constructions involving God cannot do at least as well'.[181] My answer is one that would not be out of place coming from al-Māturīdī against the Muʿtazila: it allows a credible account of God's distinct attributes, which is desirable on scriptural and rational grounds. It should also be recalled that Leftow himself is not able to eliminate a concept of God's nature.

The key question remains whether the conception of a non-simple God violates divine unicity. From the perspective of the *kalām* tradition, this way of discussing attributes and actions does not seem to be any more problematic than the Māturīdī (and more broadly Sunnī) approach to the subject. The broad consensus of Sunnī theologians was that the support of scriptural language and rational coherency gained by affirming substantive divine attributes was worth drawing the Muʿtazilī accusation that this position is incompatible with *tawḥīd*. With respect to the concerns of contemporary philosophical theology, I argue that the ultimacy considerations Leftow brings up can be dealt with by properly specifying the essential nature of divine tropes. Here one might also raise the concern that this theory makes the trope as a category in some sense prior or foundational to God. But it should be recalled that one of the attractions of trope theory is the lack of an ontic universal of trope, or property. All that exists are unique particulars possessed by concrete objects.

I argue that this approach tackles a perennial theological problem in contemporary terms while remaining recognisably within the contours of the Māturīdī *kalām* tradition. Moreover, one of the distinctive advantages garnered by the adoption of a trope theory for properties

180 See page 148.

181 Leftow, *God and Necessity*, p. 305.

is that it establishes a point of contact between the divine and human levels. Tropes are causally active and thus it becomes possible to state how God's attributes each relate to the creation. The remaining chapters of this book look at specific cases of such activity: God's omniscience and wisdom, creative action, and speech.

CHAPTER 5

Omniscience and Wisdom

One of the most important divine attributes in the theology of theistic traditions is God's knowledge, or omniscience (*ʿilm*). It has already come up several times in this book as a standard example, and it is attested extensively in the Qur'an,[1] as well as demonstrated rationally via the teleological argument. The early Māturīdī tradition is interesting for highlighting the significance of God's wisdom (*ḥikma*) as a distinct attribute to be affirmed alongside His knowledge. As I discussed in *The Qur'an and the Just Society*, this position was notably abandoned by later Māturīdīs in favour of assimilating it to His attribute of *takwīn*, while Ashʿarīs explained God's wisdom either through His knowledge or as something imputed to Him due to the nature of His creation.[2] In exploring al-Māturīdī's position in conversation with contemporary philosophical theology, I will suggest that wisdom may play a complementary role as a non-propositional ground for propositionally conceived omniscience, and underpin God's 'moral' nature and action in the world. I will not, however, engage with the question of reconciling divine foreknowledge with human free will, nor explore the meta-ethical uses of wisdom, as I judge that these are topics better tackled within the broader frame of theological anthropology and ethics.[3]

Al-Māturīdī's affirmation of both knowledge and wisdom may have a Qur'anic origin: the pairing of the intensive active participles *ʿalīm* (omniscient) and *ḥakīm* (wise) occurs thirty-five times in the Qur'an in a variety of

1 Though God's omniscience is frequently mentioned in the Qur'an and Muslim theologians agree on it (although not necessarily its interpretation), verses used by Māturīdī theologians because they seem to underscore God's substantive attribute of knowledge, include Q. 4:166 and 11:14. See al-Ṣaffār, *Talkhīṣ al-adilla*, vol. 1, p. 96.

2 Harvey, *The Qur'an and the Just Society*, pp. 29–30.

3 This also follows the structure of premodern *kalām* texts. As al-Māturīdī's *Kitāb al-tawḥīd* is my most significant model in this regard, it is notable that he treats fate after prophecy, but before sin and faith. See the contents page in al-Māturīdī, *Kitāb al-tawḥ īd*, p. 538.

formulations.[4] Notwithstanding that *ḥakīm* in the Qur'an cannot be assumed to only denote God's wisdom but could also refer to His knowledge, perfect action, or even justice,[5] this collocation seems significant.

God's knowledge is one of the first questions discussed in the section on divine attributes in *Kitāb al-tawḥīd*, although the treatment is not extensive. Al-Māturīdī starts from the previously argued point that God is fundamentally different from the creation and that His action, which is able to create from nothing, arises from choice (*ikhtiyār*), not natural disposition (*ṭibāʿ*).[6] Such action is based on knowing the things acted upon, their particular howness, needs and what allows them to live.[7] Furthermore, he succintly redeploys his teleological argument: the temporal world could only have emerged into existence due to God's knowledge in His creation of it.[8]

The Māturīdī tradition develops this idea slightly, though most theologians are more concerned with affirming that God's knowledge is one of His substantive attributes than with developing a detailed theory about it. An interesting development, which takes place in contestation with certain Muʿtazilī ideas, is that, according to al-Sālimī, God knows what is non-existent (*maʿdūm*),[9] or in the slightly later and more technical formulation of Abū al-Muʿīn al-Nasafī, His knowledge has a connection (*taʿalluq*) with the non-existent.[10] It is possible that the Māturīdī position derives, on the one hand, from rejecting the common Muʿtazilī doctrine that the non-existent is a thing (*al-maʿdūm shayʾ*) and, on the other hand, from denying that the non-existent is not known (*al-maʿdūm ghayr maʿlūm*), which was attributed to the early Muʿtazilī Hishām b. ʿAmr (d. 226/840–41).[11]

The Māturīdīs, situating themselves between these two extremes, reason that, as God creates from absolutely nothing, there is no shadowy list

4 The phrase *al-ʿalīm al-ḥakīm* occurs in Q. 2:32, 66:2, 12:83, 12:100; *ʿalīm ḥakīm* in Q. 4:26, 8:71, 9:15, 9:28, 9:60, 9:97, 9:106, 12:6, 22:52, 24:18, 24:58, 24:59 49:8, 60:10; *ʿalīman ḥakīman* in Q. 4:11, 4:17, 4:24, 4:92, 4:104, 4:111, 4:170, 33:1, 48:4, 76:30; *al-ḥakīm al-ʿalīm* in Q. 43:84, 51:30; and *ḥakīm ʿalīm* in Q. 6:83, 6:128, 6:139, 15:25, 27:6. Al-Sighnāqī tries to explain the *taqdīm* (prepositioning) and *taʾkhīr* (postpositioning) of the two words based on the context of the verses in question, though only for four cases: Q. 2:32, 8:71, 12:6 and 51:30. Al-Sighnāqī, 'Al-Tasdīd fī sharḥ al-tamhīd', pp. 218–19.

5 See Abdel Haleem, 'The Role of Context in Interpreting and Translating the Qur'an', pp. 49–50; Harvey, *The Qur'an and the Just Society*, pp. 9, 24. With respect to these three linguistic possibilities for *ḥakīm*, see al-Rāzī, *Mukhtār al-ṣiḥāḥ*, p. 62.

6 Al-Māturīdī, *Kitāb al-tawḥīd*, p. 108.

7 Al-Māturīdī, *Kitāb al-tawḥīd*, p. 109.

8 Al-Māturīdī, *Kitāb al-tawḥīd*, p. 109. Cf. al-Nasafī, *Tabṣirat al-adilla*, vol. 1, p. 364. See pages 119–20.

9 Al-Sālimī, *Al-Tamhīd fī bayan al-tawḥīd*, p. 127.

10 Al-Nasafī, *Tabṣirat al-adilla*, vol. 1, pp. 362–63.

11 Al-Nasafī, *Tabṣirat al-adilla*, vol. 1, p. 128. See pages 76–77.

of non-existent things waiting for Him to add the extra ingredient of existence. Yet God also knows precisely what will arise from non-existence. Thus, in classical-era works written by al-Ṣaffār, and those after him, there is the idea that God's knowledge has a connection with all that is knowable (*ma ʿlūm*), whether existent or not.[12] In the late classical period, a figure such as Mullā ʿAlī al-Qārī (d. 1014/1606) is able to expand on this by stating that God's knowledge encompasses 'particulars, universals, existents, non-existents, possibilities and impossibilities (*al-juz ʾiyyāt wa-l-kulliyāt wa-l-mawjūdāt wa-l-ma ʿdūmat wa-l-mumkināt wa-l-mustaḥīlāt*)'.[13]

My constructive treatment of God's knowledge in this chapter builds on this tradition. I will use the discussions in Chapter 4 about God's relationship to time, which includes the existent and non-existent, as well as His relationship to modality, which deals with the possible and impossible.[14] First, however, I will turn to the *kalām* treatment of the concept of divine wisdom, which unlike knowledge does not put Māturīdīs in large-scale agreement with Ashʿarīs. In fact, it is an aspect greatly emphasised in the writings of al-Māturīdī and the earliest tradition and thereafter neglected, without ever entirely disappearing.

Al-Māturīdī discusses the divine attribute of wisdom most directly in a section of *Kitāb al-tawḥīd* in which he writes: 'People differ in response to the questioner's query: "Why did God create the creation?"'[15] This section opens with the second *basmala* in the book, and the second of four invocations of praise for God using a phrase with the word *al-ḥamd*.[16] Rudolph suggests that this unusual feature reflects a process of composition on the part of al-Māturīdī who brought together sections written at different times to make up the work as a whole.[17] It is therefore plausible that there is a distinct treatise between the second and third *ḥamd*s, the shortest in *Kitāb al-tawḥīd*, which takes divine wisdom as its major theme, a further indication of the significance he accords to his deliberations on the topic.[18]

12 Al-Ṣaffār, *Talkhīṣ al-adilla*, vol. 1, p. 94; al-Taftāzānī, *Sharḥ al-ʿaqīda al-Nasafiyya*, p. 47.
13 Al-Qārī, *Sharḥ kitāb al-fiqh al-akbar*, p. 15.
14 The trope theory that I adopt only recognises particulars as an ontic category. This means that propositional reference to universals is explained as to sets of resembling tropes. See pages 96–97. Likewise, God's knowledge of apparent universals can be explained by reference to particulars. In one sense, this is an inversion of Ibn Sīnā's famous position that God only knows universals.
15 Kholeif uses this entire sentence for his section heading, while Topaloğlu and Aruçi truncate it to 'Why did God create the creation?' Al-Māturīdī, *Kitāb al-tawḥīd*, p. 163; al-Māturīdī, *Kitāb al-tawḥīd*, ed. Fathalla Kholeif, p. 96.
16 See al-Māturīdī, *Kitāb al-tawḥīd*, pp. 65, 163, 177, and 301.
17 Rudolph, *Al-Māturīdī and the Development of Sunnī Theology*, pp. 215–16.
18 See al-Māturīdī, *Kitāb al-tawḥīd*, pp. 163–76.

Al-Māturīdī gives no fewer than eight different answers to the question, of which the first is most closely connected to his theological ideas of divine wisdom.[19] He starts by remarking that some people say that this question is itself corrupt and that God cannot be asked it. He is eternally wise, omniscient and self-sustaining, so it is impossible that He is ever ignorant of how to realise His wise intent or has a need that would lead Him to depart from it in order to secure a certain benefit. Al-Māturīdī also cites Q. 21:16–23, 'We did not create the heaven and the earth and what is between them in play [. . .] He will not be asked about what He does, yet they will be asked', as scriptural evidence for this view.[20]

I submit that al-Māturīdī adopts this first position as his own. He commences with it without presenting a rebuttal, then later recalls it,[21] and it is consistent with the rest of his theology. Moreover, it becomes apparent that, while God's knowledge is an important attribute that acts in harmony with, or allows Him to express, His wisdom, it is not to be identified with it. God's wisdom encompasses His deepest intent in creating the world, which for al-Māturīdī is not the same as His knowledge of it. Meanwhile, His will (*irāda*) is not mentioned at all in this context, despite its prominence elsewhere alongside His knowledge, power and creative action when presenting the 'mechanics' of creation.[22] Within al-Māturīdī's system, wisdom is the ultimate ground of God's action and is unable to be further analysed or to act in accord with a higher, master attribute.[23] As he goes on to say, it can only be given a *ta'wīl*, or parabolic illustration, as *iṣāba* (hitting the mark), which is 'putting everything in its place', and thus also justice.[24] But such an explanation, if taken charitably, can only be an illustrative picture; if taken uncharitably, it is circular, as the 'place' of everything can, for al-Māturīdī, only be explicable with reference to God's wisdom. This attribute, therefore, remains brute. He comments: 'intellects are limited from attaining the essential being (*kunh*) of the wisdom of lordship, based on the preceding position that obligates wisdom for everything in the manner in which God created it – even if one does not know its whatness'.[25]

19 Al-Māturīdī, *Kitāb al-tawḥīd*, pp. 163–66.

20 Al-Māturīdī, *Kitāb al-tawḥīd*, p. 163.

21 See the quotation that ends this paragraph, which comes from a later subsection on the wisdom of the creation of harmful things.

22 Al-Māturīdī, *Kitāb al-tawḥīd*, pp. 98, 109, 110–11. See Chapter 6.

23 See Rudolph, 'Al-Māturīdī's Concept of God's Wisdom', p. 51.

24 Al-Māturīdī, *Kitāb al-tawḥīd*, p. 164. See p. 193; al-Māturīdī, *Ta'wīlāt al-qur'ān*, vol. 5, p. 107. This perhaps reflects Aristotle's discussion in 'Alpha 2' of the *Metaphysics*, in which he speaks of wisdom as 'that which discerns for what end each thing must be done'. Aristotle, *Metaphysics*, trans. Hugh Lawson-Tancred, p. 8.

25 Al-Māturīdī, *Kitāb al-tawḥīd*, p. 175. See pp. 180–81.

Franz Rosenthal argues that, while there was a well-established distinction between wisdom and knowledge in the Late Antique world, one in which at times wisdom held a superior rank, the Qur'anic prominence of knowledge precluded this from becoming dominant within Islamic thought.[26] This argument is sound in its generality but finds an exception in the thought of al-Māturīdī, as I have illustrated. It is also notable that the early fourth/tenth-century debate in Rayy between the philosopher Abū Bakr al-Rāzī and Abū Ḥātim al-Rāzī on prophecy uses the phrase 'the wisdom of the Wise (*ḥikmat al-ḥakīm*)'.[27] There is little doubt that al-Māturīdī's emphasis on wisdom is linked to the currents of thought prevalent in his milieu, but the precise genealogy is difficult to determine. Based on his discussion in the present section of *Kitāb al-tawḥīd*, it is possible to highlight his reception of two sources, the Baghdadī Muʿtazila, to whom he is opposed, and al-Ḥusayn al-Najjār, to whom he is favourable.[28]

Al-Māturīdī discusses a second answer to the question of why God created the creation, which he attributes to a group of the Muʿtazila. They claim that God's creation of the world is explained by Him doing what is most beneficial (*al-aṣlaḥ*).[29] Even though he does not name this group, the fact that this is a known Baghdadī Muʿtazilī position,[30] combined with his concern to refute the teachings of al-Kaʿbī, leaves little doubt about its identity. His response is that what must be meant by most beneficial is wisdom, in which case they agree with him. He argues that, if they do not share his idea of wisdom, but instead stipulate *al-aṣlaḥ* as meaning that God must do what is most beneficial for others, this will inevitably lead to incoherence. Whereas some people may experience a benefit, others will experience corruption. It is here that he contrasts this idea with a higher wisdom that puts everything in its right place.[31]

The view of al-Najjār is quoted by al-Māturīdī as the final of the eight answers that he gives to the question under consideration. It consists of a qualified list of manifestations of divine wisdom, such that the world can be said to have been created as 'an indication (*dalāla*) and proof (*ḥujja*); then a sign (*ʿibra*) and admonition (*ʿiẓa*); then a blessing (*niʿma*) and mercy (*raḥma*); then nourishment (*ghidhāʾ*) and sustenance (*qiwām*); and disposal of needs (*al-mutaṣarraf fī al-ḥawāʾij*)'.[32] Moreover, al-Māturīdī finds

26 Rosenthal, *Knowledge Triumphant*, pp. 35–37.

27 Al-Rāzī, *Rasāʾil falsafiyya*, p. 295.

28 For background information on these traditions as sources for al-Māturīdī's theology, see page 30.

29 Al-Māturīdī, *Kitāb al-tawḥīd*, p. 163.

30 Frank, '*Kalām* and Philosophy', p. 93.

31 Al-Māturīdī, *Kitāb al-tawḥīd*, p. 164.

32 Al-Māturīdī, *Kitāb al-tawḥīd*, pp. 165–66.

implicit agreement from al-Najjār for his position that what can be a blessing for one person may be a tribulation for another and that the changes and variations observed in the world show that it cannot have been created for benefit and utility alone.[33] In the next section, in which al-Māturīdī discusses the wisdom of God's command and prohibition, he goes so far as to say 'the words of al-Ḥusayn, already mentioned, suffice . . .', though he does, in fact, elaborate further.[34]

The immediate transmitters of al-Māturīdī's teachings retained some of his focus on God's wisdom, as shown by al-Rustughfanī in his extant responsa[35] and by Abū Salama al-Samarqandī who puts wisdom next to knowledge in his list of divine attributes.[36] In a later section focused on refuting the doctrine of *al-aṣlaḥ*, al-Samarqandī mentions that God is *ḥakīm ʿalīm* – foregrounding wisdom – and declares, following al-Māturīdī, that it is forbidden for His action to depart from His wisdom. He argues that, while injustice and folly are rationally abhorrent in general, within different contexts a single thing could be variously just or unjust, and it is thereby impossible to apply a human measuring scale to the moral action of God.[37] This is a restatement of al-Māturīdī's critique that the Muʿtazilī idea of *al-aṣlaḥ* makes a category mistake with its invalid stipulation to the basic property of God's wisdom. I propose that this early Māturīdī move to affirm a distinctive divine attribute of *ḥikma* can ground notions of God's mercy, justice and goodness, supporting a theodicy and ethical project. But these applications are not the focus of the present book, although Chapter 7 includes some relevant discussion relating to divine speech.[38]

Māturīdī theologians from the fifth/eleventh century onwards consistently reduce the centrality of wisdom as a divine attribute in favour of knowledge or creative action, without rejecting it outright. An early example is al-Sālimī. He does not give *ḥikma* the prominence afforded to it by al-Māturīdī and al-Samarqandī but does mention it in a section on God's favour and justice (*al-faḍl wa-l-ʿadl*).[39] He engages with the question of how

33 Al-Māturīdī, *Kitāb al-tawḥīd*, p. 166.

34 Al-Māturīdī, *Kitāb al-tawḥīd*, p. 166.

35 Al-Rustughfanī argues that a jinn cannot possess a body, as it would oppose God's wisdom to enter an already occupied space. See al-Rustughfanī, 'Bāb al-mutafarriqāt min fawāʾid', MS Yeni Cami 547, fol. 291v; al-Rustughfanī, 'Bāb al-mutafarriqāt min fawāʾid', MS Veliyüddin Efendi 1545, fol. 283v.

36 Al-Samarqandī, *Jumal min uṣūl al-dīn wa-yalīhu sharḥuhu*, p. 19. But note that Ibn Yaḥyā al-Bashāgharī omits it when citing Abū Salama's text in his commentary (p. 85).

37 Al-Samarqandī, *Jumal min uṣūl al-dīn wa-yalīhu sharḥuhu*, p. 24.

38 See pages 216–18. See also the discussion in Harvey, *The Qur'an and the Just Society*, pp. 27–42; Harvey, 'Whose Justice? When Māturīdī Meets MacIntyre' (forthcoming).

39 This terminology reflects al-Māturīdī's treatment. See al-Māturīdī, *Kitāb al-tawḥīd*, p. 193.

to reconcile God's wisdom with His willing of disbelief (*kufr*), the association of partners (*shirk*), blasphemy (*sabb*) and other foul things. Al-Sālimī's answer is that it is the same as His creation of a soul that He knows will disbelieve and so on: He wills His creation of it with His knowledge of it.[40] It seems that this is the beginning of accommodation to the Ashʿarī position, which does not recognise a place for wisdom within the divine attributes distinct from God's knowledge. Al-Bazdawī represents the other direction in which the notion of wisdom was shifted: divine action. He includes in his book a brief section titled 'Why did God create the world?' This section indicates direct influence from al-Māturīdī's discussion; yet he states that God's will is behind the creation of the world, associating *ḥikma* with Muʿtazilism and the idea of *al-aṣlaḥ*. While he does argue that God is *ḥakīm*, he interprets this as His perfect action, which sets the stage for later articulations of it as *takwīn*.[41]

Subsequent Māturīdī theologians go in two directions. Some figures, such as Abū Ḥafṣ al-Nasafī, Abū Thanāʾ al-Lāmishī (d. after 539/1144) and al-Ṣābūnī ignore wisdom in their treatment of the divine attributes, although the latter two use it when accounting for God's sending of messengers, divine justice (*taʿdīl*) and injustice (*tajwīr*), as well as related questions.[42] Here an expression emerges, which is attributed to al-Māturīdī: 'wisdom is that which has a praiseworthy result (*al-ḥikmatu mā lahu ʿāqibatun ḥamīdatun*)'.[43] This is drawn from al-Māturīdī's comment in his *Taʾwīlāt al-qurʾān*, in the context of his argument about the world sustaining, that an action lacking a praiseworthy result is futile and thereby leaves wisdom.[44] Whereas al-Māturīdī used the divine attribute of wisdom to ground what is praiseworthy, these later members of his school had begun to define wisdom in terms of it. Other Māturīdīs – such as Abū al-Muʿīn al-Nasafī, Abū al-Barakāt al-Nasafī (d. 710/1310) and ʿAbd al-Raḥmān Shaykhzāde (d. 944/1537) – equate wisdom to knowledge or divine creative action (*takwīn*), both of which are eternally ascribed to God.[45] An interesting position combining both knowledge and action in the definition of wisdom can be found

40 Al-Sālimī, *Al-Tamhīd fī bayan al-tawḥīd*, p. 136.

41 Al-Bazdawī, *Kitāb uṣūl al-dīn*, p. 163.

42 See al-Nasafī, 'Matn al-ʿaqīda al-Nasafiyya', pp. 52–53; al-Lāmishī, *Kitab al-tamhīd li-qawāʾid al-tawḥīd*, pp. 86–87, 102; al-Ṣābūnī, *Al-Bidāya fī uṣūl al-dīn*, pp. 46, 61.

43 Al-Ṣābūnī, *Al-Bidāya fī uṣūl al-dīn*, p. 61.

44 Al-Māturīdī, *Taʾwīlāt al-qurʾān*, vol. 8, p. 109. The word praiseworthy is only found in one of the manuscripts used for the edition. For discussion of this argument as found in *Kitāb al-tawḥīd*, see pages 70–71.

45 Al-Nasafī, *Al-Tamhīd fī uṣūl al-dīn*, p. 62; al-Sighnāqī, 'Al-Tasdīd fī sharḥ al-tamhīd', p. 219; al-Nasafī, *Tabṣirat al-adilla*, vol. 1, p. 587; al-Nasafī, *Sharḥ al-ʿumda*, p. 212; Shaykhzāde, *Kitāb naẓm al-farāʾid*, p. 28. See Harvey, *The Qur'an and the Just Society*, p. 30. For further discussion of *takwīn*, see Chapter 6.

in the work of al-Ṣaffār, even though he does not elaborate the divine attribute with it: 'wisdom is an expression for a specific knowledge; it is knowledge by which its holder adheres to justice in the utmost of perfection (*al-ḥikma ʿibāratun ʿan ʿilmin makhṣūṣin wa-huwa al-ʿilmu alladhī yulāzimu al-ʿālimu bihi al-ʿadla fī ghāyat al-iḥkām*)'.[46]

Turning to my own constructive discussion of divine omniscience and wisdom, it is useful to draw together the ideas that I have developed over the course of the preceding chapters. I have already taken the definition of knowledge attributed to al-Māturīdī as the property of an individual that corresponds to given things and have recast it as the verification of propositions that correspond to objects in the world. Here a proposition is an ideal meaning, or content of intentional experience, directed at a given object. This can be either a categorial structure, such as a number, or an ontic structure in the world, in which objects are bundles of property instances, or tropes.[47]

So much for human knowledge. According to the theological method adopted in this study, such knowledge must be in some respects the model that allows us to speak about divine omniscience, despite there being a significant gulf by which the latter transcends it. Some recent debates in philosophical theology have discussed whether God's knowledge should be construed as propositional, or if there is a non-propositional formulation that could make greater sense of it.[48] My framework of enquiry leads me to propose that every possible object of knowledge is verifiable by a proposition in consciousness. It thus seems plausible to state: God knows for every proposition *p* whether it is true, false, or neither true nor false.

This is a version of the formulation proposed by Linda Zagzebski,[49] modified to take account of my doubts about the principle of bivalence. Zagzebski raises two potential problems with the kind of principle she presents: first, that propositional knowledge, even of everything, can seem indirect and removed from direct experience of the world; and second, that such a list of propositions fragments God's knowledge of the world into discrete units.[50]

A response to the first point should take account of my proposed model's interplay between consciousness and the world. Within this system, God's knowledge is not just an abstract enumeration of true propositions, but His verification of each proposition about its object. There is no need to make this

46 Al-Ṣaffār, *Talkhīṣ al-adilla*, vol. 1, p. 39.
47 See pages 80–82, 87, 98–99.
48 Wierenga, 'Omniscience', p. 133.
49 See Zagzebski, 'Omniscience', p. 262.
50 Zagzebski, 'Omniscience', p. 263.

conditional on any particular means, notwithstanding that in the Qur'an and the Islamic theological tradition God is repeatedly described as All-Hearing and All-Seeing. He directly and intuitively verifies each proposition via His intimate acquaintance with its object of knowledge, its lack thereof, or its indeterminacy.[51] Also, if God is to know impossibilities, it is difficult to think what this could mean other than a second-order verification of the relevant propositions – it cannot refer to anything existing within the world.[52]

The second point also benefits from reflection on the phenomenological nature of my system. That God's knowledge can be explicated with reference to discrete propositions is arguably only problematic if what is knowable within the world is not so divided. Yet I have consistently argued that the whole of creation can be measured, even if only ideally, by the intentionality of human consciousness. That the proposition is the increment of such measuring is then a consequence of the nature of the world to which knowledge – even that of God – pertains. In a move that will re-occur for God's creative action and speech, I propose to understand God's attribute of knowledge as a shorthand for an indefinite number of divine acts that verify propositional meanings. Nevertheless, the whatness of God's knowledge is not the same as for other consciousnesses. God does not accidentally possess knowledge of a limited set of propositions, but essentially knows all propositions that are knowable.

Moreover, as a timeless being, all of God's knowledge is occurrent, forever known and never changing.[53] According to my formulation 'from an eternal reference frame, all B-series events A-occur',[54] God's knowledge of all propositions includes those that are possible from the perspective of any temporally (or spatially) indexed consciousness within the world. This position can be developed to solve the kind of problems connected to God's knowledge of temporally indexed events that are frequently cited in the literature.[55] Thus, for instance, God can verify the truth of 'I am reading now', by His direct eternal knowledge of this proposition as indexed to my particular consciousness at this time.[56]

Not only can the idea of omniscience be put into productive conversation with that of divine timelessness, but it also benefits from engagement with modality. Drawing on my discussion of modality in Chapter 4,

51 See Alston, 'Does God Have Beliefs', pp. 294–95. See also Morris, *Our Idea of God*, pp. 86–87.

52 See Laycock, 'Actual and Potential Omniscience', p. 72. Also see the discussion on page 79.

53 Wierenga, 'Omniscience', p. 131.

54 See page 131.

55 See Grim, 'The Being that Knew Too Much', pp. 141–42.

56 For a more detailed formulation of omniscience according to this idea, see Wierenga, 'Timelessness out of Mind', p. 155.

I propose that God's omniscience consists of His verification of each proposition of the six kinds that I discussed.[57] God verifies the logical necessities and impossibilities ideally held by human minds, the various grades of metaphysical necessities and their contraries (including actualised and non-actualised possibilities), as well as indeterminacies of various kinds. His omniscience thus extends to the propositions describing all possible worlds that can be considered objects of knowledge, though He verifies all those that do not pertain to the actual world as false (and necessarily so). Plantinga explains this idea by imagining a book of maximal possible propositions for each possible world. It is only in the actual world that the book contains only true propositions.[58] Plantinga states: 'the set of books (the library, as we might call it) remains the same from world to world; what varies is the answer to the question which book contains only true propositions'.[59] I would add that, if certain propositions take the value of neither true nor false, then God verifies them too.[60]

The question of divine omniscience has been much discussed and often challenged within recent philosophical literature. By articulating how my position could respond to arguments from a range of traditions, I aim to demonstrate its versatility and to further refine its meaning. I will discuss four critiques of omniscience drawn from analytic philosophy, physical science, phenomenology and Reformed theology.

Patrick Grim has repeatedly criticised the idea of God's omniscience on logical grounds, often seeking to entrap the idea of this divine attribute within well-known philosophical paradoxes. A good example of this is what he calls 'The Divine Liar', based on the Liar's Paradox:

1. *X* does not believe that (1) is true.

The idea here is to substitute God for *X*. If (1) is true, then God does not believe a truth, so is not omniscient. If (1) is false, then it is false that God does not believe (1) is true, meaning He believes it. This, however, entails that He believes something that is false, so He is not omniscient.[61] Grim also develops a Cantorian argument against omniscience. In this case, he considers any set of truths *T* and observes that for each element of its power set (the set of all subsets) there will be a unique truth – for instance, the truth of whether that element contains a particular truth. By Cantor's Theorem, a power set must contain more members than its set. This means

57 See pages 135–36.
58 Plantinga, *The Nature of Necessity*, p. 46.
59 Plantinga, *The Nature of Necessity*, p. 47.
60 See pages 80 and 136.
61 Grim, 'Problems with Omniscience', p. 2.

that it must contain more truths than were contained in *T*, which, as *T* is any set of truths, means that there cannot be a set of all truths. If omniscience is to have knowledge of the set of all truths, then it is unattainable.[62]

I will not attempt to reply to these arguments but to sidestep them. As Grim himself points out, an approach to logic that rejects LEM is able to affirm a category of indeterminate propositions that are neither true nor false and can avoid the inference of arguments such as the Liar's Paradox.[63] In the case of the Cantorian argument, my related embrace of intuitionism explicitly denies use of the power set or actual infinities more generally. Laura Crosilla comments: 'there seems to be no way of giving constructive sense to the set of all subsets of an infinite set'.[64] This means that, from an intuitionistic point of view, we would want to hold that the set of all truths that God knows is a potential not actual infinity and as such cannot be transcended by use of a power set operation. As I pointed out when discussing the KCA, this position allows a formulation of God's omniscience with respect to the creation, as a believer in creation *ex nihilo* wants to avoid the emergence of actual infinities. For his part, Grim seems to accept that a thoroughgoing mathematical constructivism rules out his argument, even though he apparently assumes that this would be too much of an unpalatable option for his interlocutors.[65]

A second possible critique of divine omniscience is based on the idea of quantum indeterminacy, as deferred from Chapter 2.[66] The Copenhagen interpretation is often understood to lead to a fundamental indeterminacy when a measurement is taken. For instance, if the momentum of a particle is measured precisely, then due to the Heisenberg uncertainty principle it does not have a determinate position. The inference is then made that its position is indeterminate. David Glick argues that this simply does not follow. Instead, it lacks both the determinable of position and the corresponding determinate.[67] In other words, for such a particle, it is not that its position just cannot be known by us (on an epistemological reading), or that its position is indeterminate (on an ontological reading), but that it does not have a position at all. He generalises this idea and defends it as the sparse view of the Copenhagen interpretation of quantum mechanics.[68] This position seems to reflect Bohr's idea of complementarity particularly

62 Grim, 'The Being that Knew Too Much', pp. 147.
63 Grim, 'Problems with Omniscience', p. 11.
64 Crosilla, 'Set Theory'.
65 Grim, 'On Sets and Worlds', pp. 188–89.
66 See page 70.
67 Glick, 'Against Quantum Indeterminacy', p. 3.
68 See Glick, 'Against Quantum Indeterminacy', pp. 3–8.

well.[69] Following Glick, the simplest solution may be to deny that quantum phenomena throw up any indeterminate propositions.

Yet even if the Copenhagen interpretation is taken to imply ontological indeterminacy about certain measured particles, the resultant propositions about them can be placed under category 6 mentioned in Chapter 4 (metaphysically indeterminate propositions).[70] The famous two-slit experiment may illustrate the point. In this experiment, single particles are fired at two narrow slits. When which slit a given particle *p* goes through is measured, then it is found that it only goes through either slit 1 or slit 2. But if it is not measured, the interference effect is as if the particle goes through both (like a wave). Take the following propositions: 'when not measured, particle *p* goes through just one slit', or 'when not measured, *p* is a single particle'. Both propositions are verified as neither true (because of the interference effect), nor false (because a single particle was fired). One might suggest that such a lack of measurement applies only to human beings and not to God. My reply is that intersubjective human knowledge is implicated in the constitution of reality and therefore also in the propositions that theologically link it to God's omniscience. More broadly, if knowledge is propositional, then indeterminacies within propositions of all kinds, not just ones generated by quantum mechanics, will be reflected therein.

A third angle from which to critique the idea of divine omniscience is represented by Steven Laycock who explicates a Husserlian argument based on the constitution of objects. For Husserl, an object is given as the transcendent set of its every possible appearance.[71] This means that, if God was 'the subject of every possible adequate perception', He would arguably not be in a position to understand this transcendence: '"Perfect knowledge" would be *perfect ignorance* of transcendence and intentionality'.[72] This is similar to the above-mentioned contention about God's knowledge of temporal events. Laycock expresses some doubt on this point, as it certainly seems that, 'even were an infinite mind simultaneously to apprehend the object through *every possible* profile, every element, that is, within the infinite manifold-set, the transcendent object itself could not simply be "absorbed" into immanence'.[73] Nevertheless, he goes on to argue that, as on Husserlian grounds the object cannot be identical to the set of its every perception, it leaves a gap between the transcendent object and its subjective appearances. He claims that the only way to close this gap is to acknowledge that the transcendent object becomes a thing that

69 See page 69.
70 See page 136.
71 See page 95.
72 Laycock, 'Actual and Potential Omniscience', p. 69. See Husserl, *Ideas*, p. 81.
73 Laycock, 'Actual and Potential Omniscience', p. 70.

God cannot know once every perception is achieved.[74] Thus, according to Laycock, God is potentially omniscient: He can always increase in knowledge without ever reaching a point of perfect knowledge.[75] This is reminiscent of Hartshorne's process theology, which he termed neo-classical theism, and his idea of God perpetually surpassing His own greatness, rather than the static perfection of scholastic theology and *kalām*.[76]

I have argued in this book that the gap identified by Laycock is basic to the logical distinction between a set and its elements as intuitionistically constructed categorial objects. This means that I have proposed several indeterminate modal categories – logical and metaphysical – for the verification of propositional knowledge. The upshot is that, if God knows every appearance associated with a given object, or in my terms, each of its phenomenological tropes, He affirms that the object is neither these tropes, nor other than them. God's verification of indeterminacy solves the problem of knowing the transcendental constitution of objects while retaining perfect omniscience.[77] Moreover, affirmation of a 'determinable indeterminacy' is exactly the place to which Husserl's own reflections on his contentions lead.[78]

A final question about God's omniscience is raised by Nathan Shannon when commenting that all we can say about God's propositional knowledge is formulated within the limits of rational thought. If our reasoning is based on human concepts of logic – as he says, 'our modal categories are *our* model categories' – do we then end up constructing God's knowledge of the world's possibilities based on our experience of its contingent actuality? And are we then committed to God's nature as somehow correlated to the world?[79] Shannon takes this in the direction of seeing God as radically incomprehensible to our concepts and thus requiring scripture to affirm the logic of His triune nature.[80]

While I agree that God cannot be bound by the logical ideas that He has created within us,[81] this does not prevent us from speaking about God's knowledge or force us to leave rationality at the door when approaching revelation. When we theologise, we build a model to speak about the divine with the tools of thought and language. Yet for the theist, God has granted these as means to turn towards Him. The conceptual move from

74 Laycock, 'Actual and Potential Omniscience', pp. 71–72.
75 Laycock, 'Actual and Potential Omniscience', p. 76.
76 See Hartshorne, *Omnipotence and Other Theological Mistakes*, pp. 8–10.
77 See pages 98–99.
78 See Husserl, *Ideas*, pp. 82–83.
79 Shannon, 'The Epistemology of Divine Conceptualism', p. 3.
80 Shannon, 'The Epistemology of Divine Conceptualism', p. 7. There are some similarities with the approach taken by Ibn Taymiyya. See page 61, note 25.
81 See Shannon, 'The Epistemology of Divine Conceptualism', pp. 3–4.

human knowledge to God's omniscience is analogical and no worse off for being so. The best that we can do in articulating that omniscience is to speak of eternal divine meanings that verify our conceptual modalities. But we can also begin to touch something deeper. There must be some aspect of the divine nature that determines metaphysical necessities within the world and the validity of the logical concepts through which we express truth about God. Here we can return to al-Māturīdī's idea of eternal divine wisdom as an ultimate non-propositional ground for the nature of the world.[82]

Zagzebski has commented on the significance of God's wisdom, distinct from His omniscience, as connected to both intellectual and moral perfection, as well as on the rarity of its discussion by contemporary philosophers.[83] It makes sense that a brute attribute would not be easily amenable to analysis. Nevertheless, I will present what I think can be said about it from a contemporary Māturīdī perspective. Though we cannot directly say of what God's wisdom consists, we can look at how it affects His action through the modal categories of knowledge discussed in Chapter 4. I suggest that God's wisdom, which is absolutely metaphysically necessary, is both the basis for the categories by which the human mind constitutes the phenomenal world and for the modal status of the propositions that it verifies. From all possible propositions, it is divine wisdom that determines which ones are metaphysically necessary and impossible, actually necessary and impossible, and so on. This makes non-propositional wisdom the ground for the modal status of the propositions within omniscience.

To hold that the above is the case and to attempt to identify examples relies, as pointed out by J. Meric Pessagno about al-Māturīdī, on the principle that 'reality is rational and therefore subject to reasonable analysis'.[84] Yet the possibility that human beings are sometimes able to correctly identify propositions that are metaphysically necessary due to God's wisdom is not to make that wisdom entirely comprehensible. With respect to Māturīdī thought, I can illustrate this point by considering a class of 'moral' propositions relating to God's commands. In particular, I shall look at how al-Māturīdī distinguishes his position from that of the Muʿtazilī al-Kaʿbī on the question of *taklīf mā lā yuṭāq* (burdening beyond capacity).[85] Al-Māturīdī remarks that, whereas al-Kaʿbī claims that, in general, for God to burden an individual beyond their

82 This idea has some similarity to the distinction in Reformed Scholasticism between ineffable archetypal divine self-knowledge and ectypal 'theology' – that is, knowledge communicable to human beings and able to accommodate propositions. See Sutanto, 'Two Theological Accounts of Logic', pp. 4–6, 9–10.

83 Zagzebski, 'Omniscience', p. 269.

84 Pessagno, 'The Uses of Evil in Maturidian Thought', p. 63.

85 On this concept, see Harvey, *The Qur'an and the Just Society*, p. 33.

capacity is *a priori* rationally repugnant (*qabīḥ fī al-ʿaql bi-l-badīha*), this is, in fact, only the case for outward capacity (*al-quwwa al-ẓāhira*) or wellness (*ṣiḥḥa*).[86] Abū al-Muʿīn al-Nasafī gives in this context the worldly example of a master commanding his lame slave to run or his blind slave to see, which he says would contravene wisdom.[87] Al-Māturīdī's position is that God can only burden an individual beyond their capacity when it is not rationally known. He provides a Qur'anic example, as follows: 'Then Moses' companion [al-Khaḍir] is favourably approved while knowing that [Moses] would lack capacity [to have patience with him] (*thumma ṣāḥibu mūsā bi-mā yaʿlamu annahu lā yastaṭīʿu qubila*)'.[88] Al-Māturīdī draws the analogy that, just as al-Khaḍir is favoured by God when requiring Moses to be silent about the things he sees, despite knowing his incapacity to do so, it is not rationally repugnant for God to burden those He knows will fail. He classes this as a case of someone failing to act on their power, as opposed to being prevented from having capacity in the first place.[89]

In the present context, my objective is not to reach a conclusion on this specific question but to show that God's wisdom delineates the class of metaphysically necessary propositions (here of obligations imposed on the human being). This argument indicates how an elucidation of the attribute of wisdom can act as a foundation for meta-ethics. Thinking of God's wisdom as a non-propositional complement to His knowledge also has relevance in the theological articulation of His speech (*kalām*), which is the focus of Chapter 7. I will argue that His wisdom both provides the basis for Him to enter the normative relations necessary for speech and determines the specific meanings underlying His revealed communication.

But a Māturīdī conception of divine wisdom also holds the prospect of resolving another perennial theological problem: the conflict felt between the apparently impersonal natural laws by which the world operates and the personal action of God as its *ex nihilo* creator and responsive Lord.[90]

86 Al-Māturīdī, *Kitāb al-tawḥīd*, pp. 351–52.

87 Al-Nasafī, *Tabṣirat al-adilla*, vol. 2, pp. 786–87.

88 This reading is exactly according to the wording in the manuscript. See al-Māturīdī, 'Kitāb al-tawḥīd', fol. 139r. Topaloğlu and Aruçi follow Kholeif in deleting two words (*thumma* and *qubila*) to render the sentence as God having burdened *ṣāḥib mūsā* with something of which He knows he is incapable. See al-Māturīdī, *Kitāb al-tawḥīd*, p. 352; al-Māturīdī, *Kitāb al-tawḥīd*, ed. Kholeif, p. 266. They take it to be a reference to God's knowledge of Pharaoh's inner barriers to faith (p. 352, n. 3). But the words allude to al-Khaḍir's statement in Q. 18:67: 'You will not be able to bear with me patiently (*innaka lan tastaṭīʿa maʿiya ṣabran*)'. An additional support for this interpretation is that al-Māturīdī refers to al-Khaḍir as *ṣāḥib mūsā* several times in his *tafsīr*. See al-Māturīdī, *Taʾwīlāt al-qurʾān*, vol. 9, pp. 85, 96.

89 Al-Māturīdī, *Kitāb al-tawḥīd*, p. 352.

90 See Taylor, *A Secular Age*, pp. 362–63.

God's wisdom grounds both cosmic metaphysical necessities that are perceived as regularities and particular divine acts that are never arbitrary or capricious. This role will remain in the frame during the next chapter, in which I discuss God's creative action or – in distinctively Māturīdī terms – the attribute of *takwīn*.

CHAPTER 6

Creative Action

God's creation of the world is central to theism. Like many Jewish and Christian theologians and unlike the majority of the *falāsifa*, Muslims working in the *kalām* tradition agree that, whereas God is eternal, the world is not.[1] This engenders the tricky problem of how to conceive of the relationship between the two. On this question, Māturīdīs affirm divine creative action (*takwīn*) as an eternal attribute, one of the *ṣifāt al-dhāt*. This is the classical school's most distinctive doctrine and the key position setting it apart from its closest rival, Ashʿarism.[2] At the level of theological intuition, Māturīdīs reason that, if God is eternal yet creates a temporal world, then the act of creating must take place with God in eternity, even if its effects are time-bound. In fact, Māturīdīs hold that *takwīn* is only one especially notable example of God's actions, which are eternal without exception.

This position was common among Ḥanafīs in al-Māturīdī's era, such as Abū Muṭīʿ Makḥūl al-Nasafī (d. 318/930) and al-Ḥakīm al-Samarqandī in his own region, as well as Abū Jaʿfar al-Ṭaḥāwī (d. 321/933) in Egypt.[3] It seems to go back to the early Ḥanafism of the second/eighth and third/ninth centuries,

1 A notable exception on the side of the theologians is Ibn Taymiyya, who argues that the series of objects created by God has no beginning in time. See Hoover, 'Perpetual Creativity in the Perfection of God', pp. 289–90. An exception among the *falāsifa* is al-Kindī, who follows the Christian John Philoponus (d. 570 CE) in arguing that the world had a temporal beginning. Adamson, *Al-Kindī*, pp. 74–75.

2 Madelung, 'Abu l-Muʿīn al-Nasafī and Ashʿarī Theology', p. 324; Kholeif, *A Study on Fakhr al-Dīn al-Rāzī*, pp. 89–90. The question of *takwīn* is the first one discussed by the Ottoman theologian Ibn Kamāl Bāshā in his prominent text comparing the differences between the two schools. Foudeh, *Masāʾil al-ikhtilāf bayna al-Ashāʿira wa-l-Māturīdiyya*, p. 19.

3 See al-Nasafī, *Kitāb al-radd ʿalā ahl al-bidaʿ wa-l-ahwāʾ*, p. 106; al-Wafī, *Salām al-aḥkam ʿalā sawād al-aʿẓam*, p. 60; al-Ṭaḥāwī, *Matn al-ʿaqīdat al-Ṭaḥāwiyya*, pp. 9–10. See Madelung, 'Abu l-Muʿīn al-Nasafī and Ashʿarī Theology', p. 326.

perhaps Abū Ḥanīfa himself,[4] as a doctrine in common with Sunnī traditionalists.[5] The historical significance of al-Māturīdī's discussion of *takwīn* in *Kitāb al-tawḥīd* is that he provides the earliest sustained *kalām* treatment of the position.[6] The tenor of his disquisition is defence of an established creedal point – the eternality of God's creative action – that has come under attack, most likely from the Muʿtazila. He does not mention the name of this group when writing about *takwīn*, even though he first rebuts the prominent figure al-Kaʿbī in the subsequent section on the eternality of God's actions, which is at the theological heart of the dispute.[7] But al-Māturīdī provides an implicit critique of the Muʿtazilī position with his argument that, if God's action was nothing other than His creation, then He should be directly attributed with harm and evil. When *takwīn* is instead taken as an eternal attribute, bad things can be termed the effects of God's action and ascribed to the creation.[8]

Ibn Yaḥyā al-Bashāgharī contextualises al-Māturīdī's position, placing it between the Muʿtazila who make *takwīn* into the *mukawwan* (created thing) and the *mujbira* (determinists) who deny the action of human

4 While the theological principle of the eternality of God's actions is not directly mentioned in *Al-Fiqh al-absaṭ*, there is an affirmation of God's pleasure (*riḍā*) and anger (*ghaḍab*), and to 'describe Him as He describes Himself'. Abū Ḥanīfa, *Al-ʿĀlim wa-l-mutaʿallim*, ed. Muḥammad Zāhid al-Kawtharī, p. 56. There is explicit mention of the eternality of the *ṣifāt al-fiʿl* in *Al-Fiqh al-akbar II* (al-Qārī, *Sharḥ kitāb al-fiqh al-akbar*, p. 184), but I argue that this is a later text. See page 32.

5 Al-Bazdawī, *Uṣūl al-dīn*, p. 77; Kholeif, *A Study on Fakhr al-Dīn al-Rāzī*, p. 90. See *Kitāb al-tawḥīd* by Ibn Khuzayma (d. 311/923–24), in which he argues that, as God's speech 'Be! (*kun*)' creates the creation (*yukawwinu al-khalq*), this demonstrates the distinction between His speech and the created thing (*mukawwan*). Ibn Khuzayma, *Kitāb al-tawḥ īd wa-ithbāt ṣifāt al-rabb ʿazza wa-jalla*, p. 391. Although technically this is an argument for the eternality of God's speech, it draws the key distinction between God's eternal creative action and the temporal created world. A-Bazdawī argues that Māturīdīs can accept that God's speech creates the world, so long as this distinction is maintained. See page 181. Al-Ashʿarī does not name *takwīn* in his description of the doctrine of Ibn Kullāb but shows that he held all of God's actions to be eternal, including His mercy. Al-Ashʿarī, *Maqālāt*, vol. 1, p. 229.

6 Although acknowledging al-Māturīdī's original theological elaboration of the Qur'an, Daccache suggests a significant influence from the Neoplatonic doctrine of the Qarmatians, an Ismāʿīlī movement that emerged in the third/ninth century. Daccache, *Le Problème de la Création du Monde*, pp. 328–29, also see pp. 294–95. This explanation is undermined by the foundation of al-Māturīdī's notion of *takwīn* in an earlier common Ḥanafī approach towards divine action and that Neoplatonism was introduced into Qarmatian thought by the contemporaneous Muḥammad b. Aḥmad al-Nasafī (d. 331/942). See Daftary, 'Carmatians'; van Ess, review of *Kitāb al-tawḥīd*, by Abū Manṣūr al-Māturīdī, ed. Fathalla Kholeif, p. 559.

7 See al-Māturīdī, *Kitāb al-tawḥīd*, p. 113.

8 Al-Māturīdī, *Kitāb al-tawḥīd*, p. 110. Compare with the early Ibāḍī al-Fazārī in al-Salimi and Madelung, *Early Ibāḍī Theology*, p. 29.

beings, attaching it to the *mukawwin* (creator).[9] Only the *ahl al-sunna wa-l-jamāʿa*, a term that al-Māturīdī does not use himself, preferring *ahl al-ḥaqq* (people of truth),[10] give both human action as *mukawwan* and God's *takwīn* their due.[11]

In a manner that should now be familiar, al-Māturīdī utilises his theological methodology of *mithl* to draw an analogy between the action of a person in the world and God. Just as a person with the power to do things does not manifest their power without a corresponding action, God's power is verified through His action.[12] In fact, he even argues that it is better to affirm that the creation proceeds by natures (*ṭabāʾiʿ*) and nutriment (*aghdhiya*), albeit with more to be said along with them, than that God created it with no attribute other than the creation itself. At least these natural processes have some degree of verification, unlike the latter position.[13] While he writes of *takwīn* as such an attribute, it is fairly obvious from his treatment that he accepts that this term comprises a multitude of creative actions.

For al-Māturīdī, the corollary of God's eternality is that all of His attributes are eternal, including His actions, such as creating.[14] Al-Māturīdī offers a *reductio ad absurdum* against the opponent's proposition that God does not create from eternity. If this proposition is true, then it must have been initially (*fī al-aṣl*) impossible for a given action to arise from Him, then it became possible. But either (1) God makes it possible on

9 Al-Samarqandī, *Jumal min uṣūl al-dīn wa-yalīhu sharḥuhu*, pp. 92–93.

10 See al-Māturīdī, *Kitāb al-tawḥīd*, pp. 270, 438. Al-Ḥakīm al-Samarqandī prominently discusses the importance of following the generality of Muslims (*jamāʿat al-muslimīn*) linking it to the perfection of the Prophet's practices (*sunan*). He also uses the term *ahl al-ʿadl* (people of justice). Al-Wafī, *Salām al-aḥkam ʿalā sawād al-aʿẓam*, pp. 18, 147. This reflects the terminology of Abū Ḥanīfa in his letter to ʿUthmān al-Battī. See Abū Ḥanīfa, *Al-ʿĀlim wa-l-mutaʿallim*, ed. Muḥammad Zāhid al-Kawtharī, p. 38. Abū Muṭīʿ al-Balkhī, the Transoxianan student of Abū Ḥanīfa, uses the term *ahl al-sunna wa-l-jamāʿa* in his *Al-Fiqh al-absaṭ*. Abū Ḥanīfa, *Al-ʿĀlim wa-l-mutaʿallim*, ed. Muḥammad Zāhid al-Kawtharī, p. 56. The term *ahl al-sunna wa-l-jamāʿa* does not seem to have been adopted in the works of the Samarqandī Ḥanafī *kalām* tradition until the generation after al-Māturīdī; for instance, by his student al-Rustughfanī. See al-Rustughfanī, 'Bāb al-mutafarriqāt min fawāʾid', MS Yeni Cami 547, fol. 297v; al-Rustughfanī, 'Bāb al-mutafarriqāt min fawāʾid', MS Veliyüddin Efendi 1545, fol. 290v. This usage is continued by Ibn Yaḥyā al-Bashāgharī in the latter half of the fourth/tenth century. See al-Samarqandī, *Jumal min uṣūl al-dīn wa-yalīhu sharḥuhu*, pp. 210, 217, 219, 231. This also seems to be around the same time that it was used by Abū al-Layth al-Samarqandī. See Rudolph, *Al-Māturīdī and the Development of Sunnī Theology*, p. 61.

11 Al-Samarqandī, *Jumal min uṣūl al-dīn wa-yalīhu sharḥuhu*, p. 93.

12 Al-Māturīdī, *Kitāb al-tawḥīd*, p. 110.

13 Al-Māturīdī, *Kitāb al-tawḥīd*, p. 110.

14 Al-Māturīdī, *Kitāb al-tawḥīd*, p. 111. See Rudolph, *Al-Māturīdī and the Development of Sunnī Theology*, p. 287.

account of Himself, but then it can never become possible (as God does not change) or (2) He makes it possible due to other than Himself, but this begs the question (of creation). Therefore, the initial proposition is false.[15]

Having argued for the cogency of his concept of *takwīn*, al-Māturīdī defends it from two main lines of attack: (1) that the eternality of *takwīn* implies an eternal *mukawwan*, and (2) that for God to create from eternity though the creation appears within time amounts to incapacity (*ʿajz*).

In discussing the first problem, he draws an analogy with God's power, will and knowledge, which are eternal divine attributes that take temporal objects. The foundational principle is that, whereas God creates in eternity, the times of the things that He creates are mentioned with them, just as He knows, wills and has power over them.[16] Were the things that God creates not pegged from eternity to the time of their occurrence, then either they would have an atemporal index, or God would be ignorant of them when they are not happening. Both, he avers, are impossible.[17] This is one of al-Māturīdī's most significant theological moves in relation to *takwīn* and was continued by much of the school tradition that followed him. Ibn Yaḥyā al-Bashāgharī expands the point by pointing out that, if things did not happen in their allotted times, then God would be ignorant and incapable, and He would change His mind (*badāʾ*), which is a sign of both these debilitations.[18]

Al-Māturīdī's defence with respect to the second question is that God would only be incapable if He created from eternity, but the created effect did not occur in its allotted time. He again draws the analogy with His eternal willing and knowing of created things, which by the same logic should be construed as compulsion and ignorance with respect to their objects.[19] Here, al-Māturīdī offers an opposing principle: it is actually the one who cannot transcend the occurrence of their action at its time who is incapable.[20] God remains free and fully capable, while it is the human being who is confined by temporal means and stuck in occupation with their action.[21]

15 Al-Māturīdī, *Kitāb al-tawḥīd*, p. 110.

16 Al-Māturīdī, *Kitāb al-tawḥīd*, pp. 110–11.

17 Al-Māturīdī, *Kitāb al-tawḥīd*, p. 110. See the discussion on pages 126–27.

18 Al-Samarqandī, *Jumal min uṣūl al-dīn wa-yalīhu sharḥuhu*, p. 93. For comments on *badāʾ* in al-Māturīdī's thought, see Harvey, 'Al-Māturīdī on the Abrogation of the Sharīʿa in the Qur'an and Previous Scriptures', pp. 515–16.

19 Al-Māturīdī, *Kitāb al-tawḥīd*, p. 111.

20 Al-Māturīdī, *Kitāb al-tawḥīd*, pp. 111–12. This possibly reflects the Aristotelian idea that time 'belongs to the order of passivity and not of activity: it causes aging, consumes, leads to oblivion'. Cassin, *Dictionary of Untranslatables*, p. 25.

21 Al-Māturīdī, *Kitāb al-tawḥīd*, p. 112.

The final arguments given by al-Māturīdī for *takwīn* concern revelation. He points out that everyone treats God's injunctions and prohibitions as applying to their own time despite knowing that they were revealed to the Prophet Muḥammad. Thus, the reality of God's actions of commanding and prohibiting must be within an eternal 'time', with their effects applying to diverse times.[22] Al-Māturīdī also argues that his stance towards *takwīn* provides the easiest interpretation of the Qur'anic statement 'Be! (*kun*)', which became a *locus classicus* of discussions about *takwīn*, although in *Kitāb al-tawḥīd* he does not tie it down to a specific verse.[23] In his *Taʾwīlāt al-qurʾān*, he first discusses this topic under Q. 2:117: 'He is the Originator of the heavens and the earth, and when He decrees something, He says only, "Be!" and it is (*fa-innamā yaqūlu lahu kun fa-yakūn*)'. He argues that this does not reflect a literal word with the letters *kāf* and *nūn* spoken by God, but is used because it is the shortest way in Arabic to express a complete, understood meaning.[24] Under Q. 36:82, he expands on this to explain that *kun* reflects the speed of God's command and His ease of creation.[25] He also derives from the expression that, if *kun* represents *takwīn* and *fa-yakūn* the *mukawwan*, then the two cannot refer to the same thing.[26]

The next major theological treatment of *takwīn* is found in al-Sālimī's *Al-Tamhīd*. While his discussion begins from a critique of the position that *takwīn* and the *mukawwan* are the same, by his time the principal opponents have changed to al-Ashʿarī and the Karrāmiyya.[27] Al-Sālimī provides a more eloquent technical formulation that he argues should be understood as the correct relationship between the concepts: creative action is the act of the Creator, and the created thing is the effect of the creative action (*al-takwīnu fiʿlu al-mukawwini wa-l-mukawwanu taʾthīru al-takwīn*).[28] He also astutely identifies the question as subsidiary to that of the status of God's attributes and whether any of them are temporal.[29] Al-Sālimī argues that, if *takwīn* and *mukawwan* are conflated, then God's creative action is something that issues (*yabdaʾu*) out from Him and dwells in the created thing. With this picture in place, he seeks to place his opponents on the horns of a dilemma: either *takwīn-mukawwan* is temporal,

22 Al-Māturīdī, *Kitāb al-tawḥīd*, p. 112. See page 130.

23 Al-Māturīdī, *Kitāb al-tawḥīd*, p. 113.

24 Al-Māturīdī, *Taʾwīlāt al-qurʾān*, vol. 1, p. 220. But certain Arabic verbs become a single letter in the imperative. For instance, *waqā* (to protect) becomes *qi* (protect!) Thanks to Devin Stewart for raising this point.

25 Al-Māturīdī, *Taʾwīlāt al-qurʾān*, vol. 12, p. 115.

26 Al-Māturīdī, *Taʾwīlāt al-qurʾān*, vol. 1, p. 220, vol. 8, pp. 111–12.

27 Al-Sālimī, *Al-Tamhīd fī bayan al-tawḥīd*, p. 136; Brodersen, *Zwischen Māturīdīya und Ashʿarīya*, pp. 91–92.

28 Al-Sālimī, *Al-Tamhīd fī bayan al-tawḥīd*, p. 136.

29 Al-Sālimī, *Al-Tamhīd fī bayan al-tawḥīd*, p. 137.

so that God becomes the site for temporal things[30] or it is not, so that time becomes eternal.[31]

More fine-grained distinctions are found in *Uṣul al-dīn* of al-Bazdawī, including differentiation between the individual positions of named Muʿtazilī theologians. This detail allows him to provide a satisfying breakdown of the differences between the major interlocutors on the *takwīn-mukawwan* debate. Whereas the Ashʿarīs and some of the Muʿtazila see no difference between the two concepts, other Muʿtazilīs treat them as distinct but equally temporal. This second position is the same as the Karrāmiyya (contra al-Sālimī), except the latter argue that the accidents of *takwīn* are housed in God.[32] Al-Bazdawī also mentions an unnamed Ashʿarī who said that the position of the *ahl al-sunna wa-l-jamāʿa* (by al-Bazdawī's reckoning) was a recent innovation and amounted to the eternality of the world. He responds to this figure by citing al-Māturīdī's work and claiming that the idea predates al-Ashʿarī and even Abū Ḥanīfa.[33]

Al-Bazdawī's writing bears the imprint of al-Māturīdī's theological system. He follows the earlier scholar's arguments closely when warding off the claim that an eternal *takwīn* would imply either an eternal world or the separation of God's creative act from its created effect.[34] He develops the tradition further in his counter to the argument that the action (*fiʿl*) of a human being is identical to their action's effect (*mafʿūl*), so the same should be the case for God. Al-Bazdawī responds by proposing that an action is established in its actor (*fāʿil*) and that therefore in the case of God it must be eternal because He is so. The connection between God and the world is that the actions of humans are the effects of the actions of God.[35] While he mentions the case of human action because of its theological prominence, the same applies to all creation and can be schematised as follows:

God: actor (eternal); action (eternal); effect (created)

=

World: actor (created); action (created); effect (created)

30 This seems especially directed at the Karrāmiyya. Al-Sālimī travelled to Būzjān, 743 km from Samarqand, to debate them. See Brodersen, *Zwischen Māturīdīya und Ashʿarīya*, p. 93.

31 Al-Sālimī, *Al-Tamhīd fī bayan al-tawḥīd*, p. 137. Cf. al-Samarqandī, *Jumal min uṣūl al-dīn wa-yalīhu sharḥuhu*, p. 93.

32 Al-Bazdawī, *Uṣūl al-dīn*, p. 76.

33 Al-Bazdawī, *Uṣūl al-dīn*, p. 76. See Madelung, 'Abu l-Muʿīn al-Nasafī and Ashʿarī Theology', pp. 324–25.

34 Al-Bazdawī, *Uṣūl al-dīn*, p. 80.

35 Al-Bazdawī, *Uṣūl al-dīn*, pp. 79–80.

Al-Bazdawī also continues al-Māturīdī's polemics over the Qur'anic phrase *kun fa-yakūn*. He is willing to concede that God creates via His speech, as implied by the outward meaning of the verses featuring the phrase, so long as his opponents accept the distinction between *takwīn* and *mukawwan*. In the case of the Ashʿarīs, he is able to point out that, as they already accept that God's attribute of speech is eternal, the implication of God creating via speech is that His creating is eternal too.[36] If, however, they take the phrase as expressing God's swiftness in creation, this is fine, as long as they say that, like His speech, His act of creation is not a created thing.[37] The strategy of using the Ashʿarīs' position on God's eternal speech to force them to agree with the Māturīdīs on *takwīn* builds on a latent possibility in al-Māturīdī's discussion and it is effective because there does not seem to be a good reason why God's speech is not itself an action (see Chapter 7).

The same approach emerges in al-Bazdawī's response to an objection that will prove central to theological assessment of the debate: making *takwīn* eternal nullifies God's attribute of power (*qudra*).[38] The opponent's contention is that creating possible things should fall within the domain of God's omnipotence; yet the Māturīdīs, by giving this function to *takwīn*, have excluded it. Here, al-Bazdawī once more suggests that God's power is necessary for His *takwīn*, just as it is for His speaking, seeing and hearing.[39] A generation later, Abū al-Muʿīn al-Nasafī adds another distinction to this position, arguing that affirming God's power over the world does not necessitate the realisation of what He has power over, which requires a separate attribute.[40]

The treatment of *takwīn* by Abū al-Muʿīn al-Nasafī takes up the largest space of any single theological topic in his major work, *Tabṣirat al-adilla*,[41] and it garners a more succinct treatment in his *Al-Tamhīd*.[42] As with many other topics, al-Nasafī consolidates the previous tradition, preserving the main doctrine while adding new responses to the critiques developed by opponents up until his time, especially the Ashʿarīs.[43] He also lists new adversaries in the dispute – namely, the Najjārīs and, joining the Ashʿarīs

36 Al-Bazdawī, *Uṣūl al-dīn*, pp. 78–79.
37 Al-Bazdawī, *Uṣūl al-dīn*, p. 79.
38 Al-Bazdawī, *Uṣūl al-dīn*, p. 80.
39 Al-Bazdawī, *Uṣūl al-dīn*, p. 81.
40 Al-Nasafī, *Al-Tamhīd fī uṣūl al-dīn*, p. 53.
41 Al-Nasafī, *Tabṣirat al-adilla*, vol. 1, pp. 491–572. See Madelung, 'Abu l-Muʿīn al-Nasafī and Ashʿarī Theology', p. 324.
42 Al-Nasafī, *Al-Tamhīd fī uṣūl al-dīn*, pp. 50–58.
43 See al-Nasafī, *Tabṣirat al-adilla*, vol. 1, pp. 499–539.

as 'the theologians of *ahl al-ḥadīth*', the Kullābīs and Qalānisīs.[44] Yet as much as al-Nasafī multiplies the arguments, the analytical framework inherited from the earlier tradition remains static. A good indication of this can be drawn from Brodersen's study of theologians after al-Māturīdī, in which she identifies six distinct arguments for the proposition of the eternality of God's creative action and eleven arguments for the non-identity of *takwīn* and *mukawwan*. She lists Abū al-Muʿīn al-Nasafī as the earliest to use four of the six arguments in the former case[45] and four of the eleven in the latter case.[46]

As Kholeif points out, cutting through this array of arguments gets to the core of the debate between the Māturīdīs and Ashʿarīs over *takwīn*.[47] The relevant Qur'anic verses can be understood in ways that support both positions,[48] so only a close look at the meaning of God's creative action within the theological systems of the two schools will settle the question. Kholeif argues with considerable subtlety that the crux of the difference over *takwīn* is the status of God's attributes of action and the interplay with God's omnipotence, which each school affirms but construes in its own way. For the Ashʿarīs, God's power is what provides the capacity both to bring things into existence and to realise their creation.[49] God's *takwīn* is therefore, like all *ṣifāt al-fiʿl*, merely a conceptual relationship that the mind forms between Him and the object of His power.[50] The Māturīdīs conceive of omnipotence solely as a capacity that connects to the potential existence of things, but not to the realisation of their creation.[51] It is only the presence of a substantive, eternal attribute of *takwīn* that can bridge this gap between potentiality and actuality.

How significant is this dispute between the two positions? Kholeif suggests that it is not merely verbal and comes down in favour of the Ashʿarī conceptualisation. He argues that the usual understanding of God's power

44 Al-Nasafī, *Tabṣirat al-adilla*, vol. 1, p. 492. It seems that the latter two figures had an independent following from al-Ashʿarī, at least for a period. See Bin Ramli, 'The Predecessors of Ashʿarism', p. 215.

45 The fifth argument, that the attribute 'creator' is one of praise and should not therefore be gained from making the creation, is anticipated by the Ḥanafī Sufi Abū Bakr al-Kalabadhī (d. 385/995) from Balkh. See al-Kalabadhī, *Kitāb al-taʿarruf li-madhhab ahl al-taṣawwuf*, pp. 16–17. The other two are from al-Sālimī. Brodersen, *Der unbekannte* kalam, pp. 552–53.

46 Of the remaining arguments, two are from al-Samarqandī, one from al-Sālimī, and four from al-Bazdawī. Brodersen, *Der unbekannte* kalam, pp. 554–56.

47 See Kholeif, *A Study on Fakhr al-Dīn al-Rāzī*, pp. 90, 104.

48 Kholeif, *A Study on Fakhr al-Dīn al-Rāzī*, pp. 103–4; Madelung, 'Abu l-Muʿīn al-Nasafī and Ashʿarī Theology', pp. 327–28.

49 See Kholeif, *A Study on Fakhr al-Dīn al-Rāzī*, pp. 92–95.

50 Kholeif, *A Study on Fakhr al-Dīn al-Rāzī*, pp. 90–91.

51 Kholeif, *A Study on Fakhr al-Dīn al-Rāzī*, p. 92. A similar argument is made in al-Ghursī, *Taḥqīq masāʾil muhimmāt min ʿilm al-tawḥīd wa-l-ṣifāt*, p. 201.

is to include both capacity and realisation, and the Māturīdīs, in effect, take a natural aspect away from power and give it to *takwīn*.[52] Saeed Foudeh, a prominent contemporary Muslim theologian, argues that the difference between the two schools is not foundational (*aṣlī*), as neither side nullifies God's omnipotence. He reasons that, though they differ on whether the relationships (*taʿalluqāt*) of eternal capacity and temporal realisation relate back to one eternal attribute, *qudra*, in the case of the Ashʿarīs, or two, *qudra* and *takwīn*, in the case of the Māturīdīs, the foundational matter is that both relationships are affirmed. Moreover, he suggests that God's omnipotence cannot be negated by affirming an additional attribute of perfection.[53] This second-order collapse of difference between the two positions in the interest of pan-Sunnī harmony is reminiscent of earlier Ottoman-era efforts to analyse the two schools.[54] But it would seem that, while Foudeh skillfully frames his *aṣl* through the affirmation of God's attribute of power – the doctrine in common – he neglects to deal with the Māturīdīs' position that any rejection of the eternality of God's creative action, or other actions, is a negation of His essential attributes.

To differing extents, both Kholeif and Foudeh are attracted to the idea that divine creative action can be expressed as a function of omnipotence. This pull towards theological consolidation is strong, yet it is not the only relevant consideration in play. The Māturīdī case has its own claim to theological elegance. Instead of affirming for God a set number of eternal attributes, with others given a merely conceptual status, it proposes that He has an infinitude of eternal attributes and actions of the same class.[55] This reduces an entire category, which has its own parsimonious appeal.[56] Furthermore, Ashʿarīs accept God's hearing and seeing as essential attributes despite the possibility of putting their functions under God's knowledge (as some Muʿtazila did).[57] Their independent status reflects their scriptural prominence, something that the Māturīdīs were keen to argue in the case of God's creative action. This shows that there can be no resolution to the debate over *takwīn* without one over the conceptualisation of divine action more generally.

52 Kholeif, *A Study on Fakhr al-Dīn al-Rāzī*, pp. 94–95.

53 Foudeh, *Masāʾil al-ikhtilāf bayna al-Ashāʿira wa-l-Māturīdiyya*, pp. 24–25.

54 See al-Izmīrī, 'Sharḥ masāʾil al-khilāfiyyāt fī mā bayna al-Ashʿariyya wa-l-Māturīdiyya', fol. 124v.

55 Al-Ṣaffār points out that, when Māturīdīs use the term attribute of action (*ṣifat al-fiʿl*), they mean an attribute that is an action. Al-Ṣaffār, *Talkhīṣ al-adilla*, vol. 1, pp. 461–62.

56 Cowling, 'Ideological Parsimony', p. 3890.

57 El Omari, *The Theology of Abū l-Qāsim al-Balkhī/al-Kaʿbī (d. 319/931)*, p. 38.

In my view, the Ashʿarī stance that makes divine actions relational and therefore not within the class of eternal attributes is consistently undermined by their own commitment to the eternality of God's speech, hearing and seeing. These were all considered eternal actions by al-Māturīdī and his earlier followers, only entering the standard lists of essential attributes in the classical period.[58] Seen historically, every such move to accommodate the Ashʿarī position and to match their seven essential attributes acted to weaken the polemical force of the Māturīdī stance towards eternal divine action and to isolate *takwīn* as the single exception, eventually becoming the subject of harmonisation manoeuvres.

Behind this debate in Sunnī *kalām* lies the vexed question of the connection between creator and creation. The Māturīdīs bite the bullet on God's action 'at a distance'. God is eternal and acts in eternity, yet the effects of His action occur within time in the world. Ash'arīs place the connection on the other side of the transcendent divide: things appear in the world, and human beings impute them to God as His action. For the Māturīdīs, if that is the case, then there can be no verified link between God and the actualities that obtain in the world.[59] If it is argued that God's power is sufficient to supply this link, the logic of the Māturīdī position is to ask why the same would not be true for God's revealed communication.[60] So, while Kholeif is right that many of the Ashʿarī and Māturīdī arguments speak past each other due to their differences in parsing God's power and creative action,[61] the Ashʿarīs do seem to have a problem maintaining consistency between their position on divine creative action and the other attributes that they wish to claim as eternal. Such is the tension of combining an *ahl al-ḥadīth* notion of eternal speech with an essentially Muʿtazilī theology of creation.

As I am also seeking to intervene in the question of God's creation of the universe within contemporary philosophical theology, it is useful to step back from the specificities of classical Ashʿarī-Māturīdī polemics to reframe what is at stake in the debate. Kathryn Tanner makes the following pivotal point:

> In the cosmologies of the Hellenistic era, which were formed through the confluence of Platonic and Aristotelian categories, the transcendence and direct involvement of God with the non-divine appear to

58 For instance, al-Bazdawī treats God's speech, hearing and seeing separately as kinds of divine action. See al-Bazdawī, *Uṣūl al-dīn*, p. 43–44, 62–75. For the Ashʿarī list of seven essential attributes, see al-Baghdādī, *Kitāb uṣūl al-dīn*, p. 90. Māturīdīs adopt the format in the late sixth/twelfth century. See al-Usmandī, *Lubāb al-kalām*, p. 82; al-Ṣābūnī, *Al-Bidāya fī uṣūl al-dīn*, p. 26.

59 Al-Māturīdī, *Kitāb al-tawḥīd*, p. 110; al-Nasafī, *Al-Tamhīd fī uṣūl al-dīn*, p. 52.

60 Al-Nasafī, *Al-Tamhīd fī uṣūl al-dīn*, p. 53.

61 Kholeif, *A Study on Fakhr al-Dīn al-Rāzī*, p. 104.

> be mutually exclusive, to vary inversely in degree. The more transcendent God is the less God is directly involved with the world; and vice versa.[62]

My project, like many theologies that take seriously a rational articulation of God's transcendence, has a background in Aristotelian-Neoplatonic concepts and is thus liable to this critique. It is yet another way of restating a continual question underlying the present study: how is God to be affirmed as transcending the world and personally acting in it in ways both acceptable to reason and to the language of scripture? The way to do this, Tanner suggests, is to resist 'simple univocal attribution of predicates to God and the world and a simple contrast of divine and non-divine predicates'.[63] God cannot be just one more thing in the order of creation if He is going to be its cause and explanation; yet equally He cannot be spoken about in entirely contrastive terms if He is going to be directly active in it (rather than via a series of intermediates, as in Neoplatonic emanationist schemas). Translating this into the Māturīdī language that I have been using, we arrive at the idea of verification, or *taḥqīq*, which sits between the extremes of *tashbīh* and *taʿṭīl*.

The key features of al-Māturīdī's approach to divine creation that I want to retain are as follows. First, God's creative action to realise the actual world is distinct from His omnipotence as the potentiality to realise any possible world. Second, God's creative action is a substantive eternal attribute. Third, the effect of this creative action (or, more precisely, these actions) is the creation, each part of which occurs in its appropriate time, as the time sequence itself is part of the created order. I will develop a position on creation along each of these three lines. In doing so, I will stick to the level of theological principle and will avoid tackling the applied questions of human action and free will. These are important topics and ones that I think can be dealt with coherently according to the framework that I am developing, but they deserve a fuller treatment in a theological anthropology.

The cogency of a distinction between God's omnipotence and His creative action has been pointed out by more than one contemporary Christian theologian. Rowan Williams observes that power is exercised upon something, and this is not the case for the act of creation. Instead, 'creation presupposes a divine potentiality, or resourcefulness, or abundance of active life; and "power" can sometimes be used in those senses'.[64] Leftow, after assessing a number of classical and contemporary approaches to omnipotence, develops a complex definition of range, strength, lack of defect and

62 Tanner, *God and Creation in Christian Theology*, pp. 38–39.

63 Tanner, *God and Creation in Christian Theology*, p. 47.

64 Williams, *On Christian Theology*, p. 68.

not bringing about the impossible due to God's own nature or action. He does not, however, include the actual realisation of creation in his definition, as his discussion is exclusively focused on the power to do so.[65] The figure who has devoted the most sustained attention to divine creation in terms that are helpful to my project is James F. Ross. He argues that God's omnipotence ranges over all possible states of affairs and allows Him the choice to bring the actual world into being.[66] Moreover, he is at pains to point out that the actual world does not follow a state of mere possibility but occurs instead of its mere possibility.[67] Ross holds that omnipotence does not realise the existence of the world. Instead, 'creation is a universal transcosmic force, constant, invariant, whose entire *effect* is the *being* of everything and every other force that there is, and whose entire effect *might* have been the being of whatever else is merely possible'.[68] Furthermore, he suggests that the universe is dependent on God as an effect without in any sense inhering in Him.[69]

Though I agree with Ross when he singles out the creative force that gives existence to the universe, I disagree with his conclusion, following Aquinas' position of divine simplicity, that this force is God Himself as pure being.[70] My theological framework dictates that God only has effects via His attributes - causally active as divine tropes - so bringing into existence must be the role of an attribute, namely *takwīn*, which has precisely this meaning. (I here follow the construal of *takwīn* as a convenient shorthand for all of God's creative actions).

An illustrative picture, albeit one facing the limitations of any such analogy, may help to clarify how I conceptualise the role of the various divine attributes in the manifestation of creation. Consider a person with a gun at a firing range. Various possible targets are known and are within the power of the weapon to reach; one is chosen; the trigger is pulled; the gun fires and hits the target. For the purpose of the example, the possible targets and weapon are the possible worlds God knows via His omniscience and has the power to create via His omnipotence; choosing the target is determined by His wisdom; the trigger is His will; the gun firing is His creative action and hitting the target is its effect in creating the actual world.

An important theological question should be raised at this juncture. As I treat *takwīn* as an eternal attribute, does that mean that God's creation of the world is necessary? This can only be answered by clarifying in what

65 Leftow, 'Omnipotence', pp. 190–91.
66 Ross, 'Creation', p. 614.
67 Ross, 'Creation', p. 621. Cf. al-Māturīdī, *Kitāb al-tawḥīd*, p. 371.
68 Ross, 'Creation II', p. 118.
69 Ross, 'Creation II', p. 124.
70 Ross, 'Creation II', pp. 125–26.

sense necessity is meant. I have distinguished in Chapter 4 between logical necessity, absolute metaphysical necessity, metaphysical necessity and actual necessity,[71] stating that God's creation of the actual world is necessary in only this final sense. I will now recap these distinctions and proceed to argue that this is not a defect in God. Recall that logical necessity refers to something that we cannot conceive to be other than the case. Yet it seems that we can conceive of God not creating the universe. Absolute metaphysical necessity refers to eternal entities that lack any cause, and this is the level at which the Māturīdī theologian may place both creative action and wisdom. Non-absolute metaphysical necessity is any aspect of the created order that always holds in the actual world, whereas actual necessity is the existence of any aspect of the world, rather than its mere possibility to exist differently or not to exist at all. If God does not change and possesses eternal attributes of creative action and wisdom, then despite what can be logically conceded as alternative possibilities, the actual world is necessary in the sense of depending on these absolute necessities and fitting within certain necessary limits that they determine. Or, to look at it in another way, it is of the divine nature to wisely create from eternity. This provides a neat point of return to al-Māturīdī's answer to the question 'Why did God create the creation?'

It is productive to put this position into conversation with the parallel ideas of Aquinas and Ibn Sīnā. On two important questions, the hypothethical possibility of not creating the world and its creation *ex nihilo*, al-Māturīdī sides with the Christian theologian ahead of the Muslim philosopher. While Aquinas and Ibn Sīnā both also hold the world to be necessary, the former understands this to be a 'hypothetical necessity', meaning that intrinsically the world is merely possible with the immutable and eternal will of God bringing it into existence.[72] This is broadly equivalent to what I have discussed above with respect to actual necessity. The world could logically be different. Other potential creations, or none, are known to God just as they can be imagined by us, and He does not lack the power to have realised them. Nevertheless, God's eternal wisdom has guided His creative action that these possible worlds are not actual.[73] As would require further elaboration, I think

71 See pages 135–36.

72 Acar, *Talking about God and Talking about Creation*, pp. 163–64.

73 Cf. Alston, *Divine Nature and Human Language*, p. 123. Alston lists nine divine attributes according to the 'classical' position of Aquinas and the 'neo-classical' one of Hartshorne. He splits them into two groups and argues that the four attributes of the first group (absoluteness, pure actuality, total necessity and absolute simplicity) can be abandoned for their neo-classical alternatives while retaining the classical view on the second group. My position is to affirm three of Alston's four adjustments in some form. Thus, I agree that God is internally related to creatures via attributes such as His knowledge and

that this position does not eliminate free will. God's wisdom, which is not within the temporal series, determines that actions are performed freely.[74] Ibn Sīnā makes use of the similar distinction of 'necessity on account of another',[75] yet differs from the two theologians in understanding God and His nature to be logically necessary. As such, it is not logically possible for the universe to have not existed or to be different than it is.[76] Furthermore, this kind of necessity makes the creation appear to be an impersonal or natural effect of God's being instead of a personal effect of His attributes.

Second, as a corollary to the above position, al-Māturīdī and Aquinas agree, contra Ibn Sīnā, that God creates a temporal world, not an eternal one. As discussed in Chapter 3, the personal nature of God makes it conceivable that He chooses specific times of creation.[77] In other words, since the actual world is purposively created instead of its possible alternatives, it can exist at a given time. I have supplemented this proposition with an additional element, the idea that human consciousness acts as the metric for time and consequently that time is not to be thought of as eternal due to the supposed incoherence of its beginning.[78] To practically illustrate this point, consider that current cosmology tells us the universe is 13.8 billion years old and that the measurement is taken from our present place on the timeline. It is not logically impossible that its age could have been 20 billion years or that it could have been destroyed one billion years previously. Moreover, we can understand this latter case as a logical possibility, even though it would have meant that no human would have ever measured its age. This is an application of the universal experienceability implied by a Husserlian position on the constitution of the universe.[79]

Comparison with Aquinas shows that the actual necessity of the world is not dependent on the eternality of *takwīn* but is a common feature of retaining the Aristotelian-Neoplatonic understanding of God as eternal and changeless. Within the classical *kalām* schools, an Ashʿarī or Muʿtazilī position must, I argue, arrive at the same doctrine, or introduce change into God. If it is a metaphysical, rather than merely logical, possibility for God to create a different world, or none, then it must be conceded that God knowing the actual world is not necessary. Yet then God is no longer absolutely

actions (p. 127), that He does not actualise every (logical) possibility for Him and that He is non-simple, possessing substantive attributes. But I retain the classical position that every truth about God is necessarily true. This includes God's knowledge of the things made actually necessary instead of their mere possibility.

74 See Ross, *Philosophical Theology*, p. xxi.

75 See Campanini, *An Introduction to Islamic Philosophy*, pp. 84–85.

76 See Acar, *Talking about God and Talking about Creation*, p. 167.

77 See pages 110–11.

78 See pages 130–31.

79 See Husserl, *Ideas*, pp. 92–93.

metaphysically necessary, which leads to the collapse of the classical *kalām* framework.[80] I use 'knowing' because it is agreed upon among the schools of *kalām* (despite differences over its construal). In discussion with Ashʿarīs, the same argument could be formulated using the eternal will or speech.

When putting theistic creation into a contemporary philosophical framework, one also comes to the question of how to simultaneously conceive of God's creation *ex nihilo* and His conservation of creation through time. As I have mentioned in Chapter 2, al-Māturīdī seems to have held that God perpetuates objects through time by forming their constituent accidents into bodies and sustaining them with a specific accident of endurance.[81] Additionally, I presented my own ontological position in which tropes can be formed into phenomenologically verified bundles and persist over time.[82] How should this view be married to divine creative acts that occur in eternity and have their effects at different times?

I propose to draw on William Lane Craig's argument that the difference between God's initial creation *ex nihilo* and the conservation of an object is not to be parsed in the action but in its object.[83] Craig provides three significant definitions:[84]

E1: *e* comes into being at *t* iff (i) *e* exists at *t*, (ii) *t* is the first time at which e exists, and (iii) *e*'s existing at *t* is a tensed fact.
E2: God creates *e* at *t* iff God brings it about that *e* comes into being at *t*.[85]
E3: God conserves *e* iff God acts upon *e* to bring about *e*'s existing from *t* until some $t^* > t$ through every sub-interval of the interval $t \rightarrow t^*$.[86]

80 See Alston, *Divine Nature and Human Language*, pp. 126–28.
81 See page 90.
82 See page 101.
83 Compare al-Māturīdī's approach on page 127, note 14.
84 Craig, 'Creation and Divine Action', pp. 318–19.
85 This is equivalent to Quinn's formulation: 'At *t* God introduces *x* into existence = df At *t* God creates *x*, and there is no *t'* such that *t'* is before *t* and *x* exists at *t'*.' Quinn, 'Divine Conservation, Continuous Creation, and Human Action', p. 71.
86 This is similar to Quinn's formulation: 'At *t* God preserves *x* = df At *t* God conserves *x*, and there is a *t'* such that *t'* is before *t* and *x* exists at *t'*.' Quinn, 'Divine Conservation, Continuous Creation, and Human Action', p. 71. But, as he points out, it does not preclude the conserving of things that exist only intermittently (p. 74). He suggests that this view allows for the resurrection of human beings, though I am not sure that it can coherently do so, or that it is even a consistent formulation of conservation. Surely something that is brought back into existence after not existing has, in fact, been recreated. On the topic of resurrection, I would think that, as long as the soul is continually conserved, as it would be in Craig's definition, then it would be no problem to hold that the body is resurrected in a fresh creation.

Thinking about these definitions according to the ideas of time that I discuss in Chapter 4,[87] creation *ex nihilo* is the name for God's creative action when He creates something at its first time in the B-series, whereas conservation is His bringing it to exist from one point in the B-series to another. While this distinction is meaningful from a creaturely perspective, for the divine these events all instantaneously A-occur. In the words of Ross, 'it was never nondenominatively true of God that He had not created anything "yet". That is because there can be no basis in God's reality for a "not yet", which requires the beginning to be and ceasing to be of the being of things, either accidental or substantial'.[88]

Al-Māturīdī ends his section on *takwīn* in *Kitāb al-tawḥīd* with an acknowledgement of the difficulty for the created being to fathom the ceaseless creative ability that has brought it into existence. Thus, he says in conclusion:

> This is a chapter that were one to try to reach the furthest extent in it, one would be diverted from reaching the end [and] the objective. Yet we hope that there is sufficiency in that to which we have alluded for the one possessing intellect and understanding.[89]

I feel a similar impoverishment in attempting to elaborate an adequate contemporary formulation of a Māturīdī theology of creation but will nevertheless attempt to summarise my position, as follows: God's creation of the world is a non-absolute metaphysical necessity that occurs by virtue of His wisdom. He creates the actual world by His eternal creative action instead of any of the possible worlds that He has the power to create. Furthermore, while from the divine perspective of timelessness everything is created instantaneously *ex nihilo*, from the temporal perspective objects are conserved through time.

Of such objects, the status of none with respect to creation is more controversial than the Qur'an. It is this scripture, and more generally what it means for God to speak, that will comprise the final investigation of this book.

87 See pages 130–32.

88 Ross, 'Creation', p. 622.

89 Al-Māturīdī, *Kitāb al-tawḥīd*, p. 113. See Kholeif, *A Study on Fakhr al-Dīn al-Rāzī*, p. 104.

CHAPTER 7

Divine Speech and the Qur'an

A defining fact about Islam is the centrality of the Qur'an, which is understood as both revelation and divine speech. Yet how to unite the immanence of an Arabic scripture that can be recited, heard, written and read with the transcendence appropriate to God is one of the oldest problems in Islamic theology. In the contemporary academic literature, Islamic articulations are often located by the monotheistic traditions that precede them. Whereas some argue that in Islam the 'inlibration' of the Qur'an plays a conceptually analogous role to the incarnation of Jesus as *logos* in the Christian tradition,[1] others draw a parallel between the recited and written *muṣḥaf* (codex) and Moses hearing God in the burning bush in Exodus 3:4, as well as receiving divinely inscribed tablets at Sinai in Exodus 31:18 and 34:1.[2] In fact, one locus of Muslim discussions on this question concerns the modality of Q. 4:164: 'God spoke directly to Moses (*wa-kallama allāhu mūsā taklīman*)'. The tablets (*al-alwāḥ*), which are mentioned in the Qur'an in Q. 7:145, 7:150 and 7:154, do not receive significant attention in the *kalām* tradition because they present a less direct parallel to God's speech.

1 See Wensinck, *The Muslim Creed*, p. 150; Wolfson, *The Philosophy of the Kalam*, p. 246; Arkoun, *The Unthought in Contemporary Islamic Thought*, p. 74; Burrell, *Towards a Jewish-Christian-Muslim Theology*, p. 172. Nasr Abu Zayd uses the comparison to severely criticise the dominant Sunnī theological position on the eternality of God's speech. He argues that, while Muslims rightly understood Jesus to have an entirely human nature and saw the idea of incarnated divinity as delusion (*tawahhum*), with the exception of the Muʿtazila they adopted this very same position for the Qur'an. Abu Zayd, *Naqd al-khiṭāb al-dīnī*, pp. 204–5. There is a good discussion of the comparison in Neuwirth, *The Qur'an and Late Antiquity*, pp. 92–95. She is critical of the analogy if understood as a book taking the place of incarnation. Drawing on the work of Daniel Madigan, she suggests that God's word, or *logos*, is embodied by 'a sensorily perceptible acoustic-linguistic manifestation' (p. 95).

2 See van Ess, *Theology and Society in the Second and Third Centuries of the Hijra, Volume 1*, p. 39; Smith, 'Scripture as Form and Concept', p. 42; Neuwirth, *The Qur'an and Late Antiquity*, p. 91.

The controversy of the *miḥna* (trial) in the third/ninth century, by which the Caliph al-Maʾmūn (r. 198–218/813–33) placed the Muʿtazilī formulation of the Qur'an's createdness at the centre of Abbasid political life, highlights the historical significance of this theological question and ensures its continued resonance in Muslim thought. In the twentieth century, the respective emigrations of the scholar Fazlur Rahman from Pakistan in 1968 and Nasr Abu Zayd from Egypt in 1995 were due, in part, to persecution connected to their rethinking of the link between divine speech and its worldly manifestation.

This chapter examines the Māturīdī theological discourse on the divine attribute of speech and its connection to the recited and written Arabic Qur'an (as well as other revealed scriptures addressed by the tradition). Taking a cue from the coverage of this topic within *kalām* manuals, I do not attempt to examine the doctrine of divine revelation (*waḥy*) as it relates to the Prophet Muḥammad but will defer that to a future treatment of prophecy. The discussion will begin with the topic's roots in the contested legacy of Abū Ḥanīfa, then its articulation in the work of al-Māturīdī, followed by the Māturīdī school. Finally, my own constructive theological approach will engage with contemporary philosophical theology and Islamic thought to present a fresh perspective on this perennially thorny topic.

It is fitting to start with the ideas of Abū Ḥanīfa, as he is not only a central figure in the genealogy of the Māturīdī tradition, but one of the earliest individuals to be associated with the doctrine of the 'creation of the Qur'an (*khalq al-qurʾān*)', rivalled in notoriety only by Jahm b. Ṣafwān.[3] Multiple disputed reports, including those of his students and even his grandson Ismāʿīl b. Ḥammād, assert that he held the Qur'an to be created, that he was forced to repent to the rival jurist and qadi of Kufa, Ibn Abī Laylā (d. 148/765), and, in some, that he admitted his repentance was not genuine.[4] Perhaps these could be dismissed as hearsay if Abū Ḥanīfa's writings and early documented teachings put forward a different position, but the evidence is inconclusive. Recall that I have argued in Chapter 1 for the later provenance of the two main texts ascribed to him that explicitly discuss divine speech, *Al-Fiqh al-akbar II* and *Kitāb al-waṣiyya*.[5] In *Kitāb al-ʿālim wa-l-mutaʿallim* he does mention that God chose Moses for His

3 Some reports cite an even earlier proponent of this view in al-Jaʿd b. Dirham, said to be the teacher of Jahm. See Watt, 'Early Discussions about the Qur'ān', p. 28.

4 See al-Khaṭīb al-Baghdādī, *Tārīkh madīnat al-salām*, vol. 15, pp. 518–27; al-Ashʿarī, *Al-Ibāna ʿan uṣūl al-diyāna*, p. 29. A summary is given in van Ess, *Theology and Society in the Second and Third Centuries of the Hijra, Volume 1*, p. 220.

5 See pages 31–32. A rejection of the above reports based on the authenticity of these texts is precisely the strategy used by Iblāgh. See Iblāgh, *Al-Imām al-aʿzam Abū Ḥanīfa al-mutakallim*, pp. 172–73.

messengership and 'favoured him with His speech to him, such that He did not make between Him and Moses a messenger'.[6] But this, of course, does not settle the key theological questions. Although elements of the early Ḥanafī tradition have sought to disavow Abū Ḥanīfa's connection to what became considered a heretical doctrine by emphasising a traditionalist position of uncreation (*ghayr makhlūq*), or the more cautious suspension of judgement (*waqf*),[7] it seems, as Madelung has argued, that there must be something underlying the accusations levelled at him.[8] The key point of enquiry is then to determine what an accusation of *khalq al-qur'ān* may have meant theologically within his milieu and not necessarily to read later Muʿtazilī connotations into it.

It is always hard to disentangle historical events from layers of polemic within the early *kalām* tradition. Nonetheless, it seems that theological discourses rejecting anthropomorphic accounts of the divine and stressing God's transcendence emerged in the first half of the second/eighth century with the contentions of Jahm acting as a convenient marker.[9] Given this premise, two things become clear: first, it is not surprising that the question of God's speech through the Qur'an would be one of the earliest addressed;[10] second, it seems that the pejorative name Jahmī was applied by traditionalists to anyone holding a theology of rational transcendence and does not denote a single cohesive group.[11] Thus, the Ḥanafī Bishr al-Marīsī (d. 218/833) was termed a Jahmī at least in part because he adopted the

6 Abū Ḥanīfa, *Al-ʿĀlim wa-l-mutaʿallim*, ed. Muḥammad Zāhid al-Kawtharī, p. 28.

7 Ibn Shujāʿ al-Thaljī reports in his *Kitāb al-ḥikāyāt* from al-Ḥasan b. Ziyād that Abū Ḥanīfa, Abū Yūsuf and Zufar all said that the Qur'an was the speech of God and did not go further. Al-Nāṭifī, *Al-Ajnās fī furūʿ al-fiqh al-Ḥanafī*, vol. 1, p. 443. Thanks to Salman Younas for the reference. Abū ʿAlāʾ al-Ustawāʾī (d. 432/1040–41) reports Abū Yūsuf saying that he debated with Abū Ḥanīfa about the Qur'an for a month, whereupon they agreed it was uncreated. Al-Ustawāʾī, *Kitāb al-iʿtiqād*, p. 173. Also see Dorroll, 'The Doctrine of the Nature of the Qur'ān in the Māturīdī Tradition', pp. 127–28.

8 Madelung, 'The Origins of the Controversy Concerning the Creation of the Koran', p. 510. Abdur-Rahman Momin has implausibly argued that nothing but jealousy and malice on the part of his rivals caused these ideas to be attributed to him. See Momin, 'Imām Abū Hanīfa and the Doctrine of Khalq al-Qur'ān', pp. 43–47.

9 Van Ess, *Theology and Society in the Second and Third Centuries of the Hijra, Volume 4*, p. 492. This point relates to discursive theology and does not imply that transcendent beliefs did not exist prior to this.

10 Madelung follows Abū Hilāl al-ʿAskarī (d. after 395/1004) in arguing that Abū Ḥanīfa's stance emerges from his legal position that swearing by the Qur'an is invalid as it is in the world and thus other than God, rather than from a theological principle. Madelung, 'The Origins of the Controversy Concerning the Creation of the Koran', pp. 508–11. I see no reason why such a position could not reflect a shared programme of legal and theological thought. If anything, the stated derivation of this legal rule seems to flow from theological considerations, not *vice versa*.

11 Watt, *The Formative Period of Islamic Thought*, p. 147.

doctrine of *khalq al-qur'ān*.[12] In *Al-Radd 'alā al-zanādiqa wa-l-jahmiyya*, a text attributed to Aḥmad b. Ḥanbal,[13] it is reported about the Jahmiyya that they said with respect to God's speech to Moses: 'He created something that expressed God (*innamā kawwana shay'an fa-'abbara 'an allāh*)'.[14] This formulation is important for the tenor of later rational solutions.

For the negative theology of Jahm, like the Mu'tazila who were still to come, the created status of the Qur'an reflects a stance that not only rejects the potentially anthropomorphic doctrine of God literally speaking in Arabic, but any substantive divine attributes. Abū Ḥanīfa's position is distinct from that of Jahm on this latter point: in *Al-Fiqh al-absaṭ*, even though he is reported as saying that God is not described with the attributes of created things, he goes on to discuss a number of substantive attributes and actions that must be affirmed of Him.[15] Did he also think that God has a substantive and transcendent attribute of speech? One is not mentioned in the text, though such a position would not immediately conflict with an affirmation of the created status of the Arabic Qur'an and is exactly the doctrine ascribed to him via the later *Kitāb al-waṣiyya* and *Al-Fiqh al-akbar II*.[16]

I propose that some suggestive inferences can be drawn in relation to another discourse that goes back to the juristic legacy of Abū Ḥanīfa. He held the rare position that it is permissible to recite the Qur'an in Persian translation within ritual prayer even if one knows Arabic. In this he was opposed and his view downplayed by his main successors Abū Yūsuf (d. 182/798) and Muḥammad b. al-Ḥasan al-Shaybānī (d. 189/805).[17] An obvious implication – inferred by al-Sarakhsī (d. 483/1090) a few centuries later – is that Abū Ḥanīfa held that God's speech as His attribute is the meaning behind its formulation within any particular created language.[18] Such a position appears

12 See al-Khaṭīb al-Baghdādī, *Tārīkh madīnat al-salām*, vol. 7, pp. 532, 534–35; van Ess, *Theology and Society in the Second and Third Centuries of the Hijra, Volume 3*, pp. 189–91.

13 This has been disputed, see al-Najjār, *Tabri'at al-imām Aḥmad bin Ḥanbal min kitāb al-radd 'alā al-zanādiqa wa-l-jahmiyya*, pp. 25–31. Yet the book's theme is not anachronistic, as the similarly named works of other third/ninth-century traditionalists make clear. See Brown, *The Canonization of al-Bukhārī and Muslim*, p. 77.

14 Ibn Ḥanbal, *Al-Radd 'alā al-zanādiqa wa-l-jahmiyya*, p. 265. Madelung cites the same report as 'Himself' (*'an nafsihi*). Madelung, 'The Origins of the Controversy Concerning the Creation of the Koran', p. 506.

15 Abū Ḥanīfa, *Al-'Ālim wa-l-muta'allim*, ed. Muḥammad Zāhid al-Kawtharī, pp. 56–57.

16 Abū Ḥanīfa, *Waṣiyya*, pp. 40–42; al-Qārī, *Sharḥ kitāb al-fiqh al-akbar*, pp. 184–85.

17 Al-Shaybānī, *Al-Aṣl*, vol. 1, pp. 16, 219; Zadeh, *The Vernacular Qur'an*, p. 55. There is a precedent for this view in a statement attributed to Mujāhid b. Jabr (d. 103/721–22). He suggests that the presence of non-Arabic words in the Qur'an attested by early figures is evidence that altering language does not invalidate prayer when the meaning is kept the same, as what is permissible in part of speech is permissible in all of it. Al-Qudūrī, *Al-Tajrīd*, vol. 2, p. 514.

18 Al-Sarakhsī, *Al-Mabsūṭ*, vol. 1, p. 37. See page 205.

on the one hand to increase revelation in universality, while on the other to diminish the unique significance of Arabic.

A related view ascribed to Abū Ḥanīfa by the Ḥanafī jurist al-Kāsānī (d. 587/1191) is that previous divine revelations – the Torah, Evangel and Psalms – can be recited in prayer so long as one is satisfied that the specific passages have not been corrupted.[19] The idea animating al-Kāsānī's discussion, shared with other Transoxianan Māturīdī theologians of his era, is that, despite reciting in a different language, one connects to the meanings of God's unitary speech beyond the world. Admittedly there is some doubt about the provenance of this legal rule, let alone its theological resonances in the second/eighth century. As Gabriel Reynolds points out, there seems to be no direct early record of it in the Ḥanafī tradition.[20] I would suggest, however, that there is a clue in the construction of the relevant section in *Al-Aṣl*, an extensive juristic compendium ascribed to al-Shaybānī. First the passage states Abū Ḥanīfa's opinion on the acceptability of recitation in Persian (and in some manuscripts adds the opposition of his two students). Then there is an abrupt transition to the rejection of reciting prior scriptures in prayer by Abū Yūsuf and al-Shaybānī but no mention of the view of Abū Ḥanīfa.[21] In other words, there is a plausible lacuna in the text for Abū Ḥanīfa's positive stance on this question, as mentioned by al-Kāsānī, before its presumable suppression in the prevalent written documentation of the school.[22]

Devotional engagement with the Torah is not entirely unknown among early Muslims. For example, the first/seventh-century figure Abū al-Jald al-Jawnī in Basra alternated every week between reading the Qur'an and the written Torah. People would gather when he completed the latter, and he used to say that mercy descended at that time.[23] Just as the allowance to recite in translation seems predicated on opening up a deeper appreciation of God's message for those of Persian backgrounds, retention of pre-Qur'anic scripture within the ritual prayer may have been a facilitation for Jewish and Christian converts. Weighing the evidence, it seems more likely that al-Kāsānī is providing a theological explanation for an obscure early practice than innovating from scratch.

Interesting too, given Abū Ḥanīfa's view on the Persian language, is an interpretation of the notion that the Qur'an was revealed in *sabʿat aḥruf* (seven, or multiple, lections) indicated in the Hadith literature. This

19 Al-Kāsānī, *Badāʾiʿ al-ṣanāʾiʿ fī tartīb al-sharāʾiʿ*, vol. 1, p. 531.

20 Reynolds, 'God has Spoken Before', pp. 281–86.

21 Al-Shaybānī, *Al-Aṣl*, vol. 1, p. 219.

22 See Zadeh, *The Vernacular Qur'an*, pp. 55–56.

23 Ibn Saʿd, *Kitāb al-ṭabaqāt al-kabīr*, vol. 9, p. 221; Abbott, *Studies in Arabic Literary Papyri: Volume 2, Qurʾānic Commentary and Tradition*, p. 9.

much-disputed phrase relates to the multiplicity of differences observed in the Qur'an's recitation. One opinion, expressed by hadiths ascribed to the Prophet and also to the prominent companion ʿAbd Allāh b. Masʿūd, is that *sabʿat aḥruf* refers to the permissibility of reciting words and phrases of equivalent meaning.[24] Notably, a number of the readings ascribed to Ibn Masʿūd are of this type[25] and possibly represent what Benjamin Sommer has referred to in the Jewish context as a participative rather than stenographic mode of revelation.[26] Ibn Masʿūd is a key figure in the scholarly ancestry of the Ḥanafī school, and his Qur'anic readings became part of its juristic heritage and were praised by al-Māturīdī.[27] Another early Ḥanafī scholar, al-Ṭaḥāwī, formulated an explicit theory that reciting according to meaning (*qirāʾa bi-l-maʿnā*) was permitted on the basis of ease, although its unrestricted practice had been discussed in some form in scholarly circles from at least the time of Muḥammad b. Sīrīn (d. 110/729) and Muḥammad b. Shihāb al-Zuhrī (d. 124/741–42).[28]

To sum up, Abū Ḥanīfa's contribution to the theological discussion of the Qur'an is more nuanced than assimilating him to the traditionalist uncreation or suspension of judgement positions adopted by his early followers, a Muʿtazilī notion of God's created speech, or the developed theological articulations found in *Kitāb al-waṣiyya* and *Al-Fiqh al-akbar II*. Instead, his views seem to be part of the pre-history of the solution often credited to Ibn Kullāb and thereafter taken on by the Ashʿarīs and Māturīdīs, in which God's speech must be understood on two levels: one of meaning as the eternal attribute, and another of created form, which is realised within particular expressions (*ʿibārāt*), languages and revealed dispensations.[29] In my reading, however, there is a second aspect of his legacy, which emerges fully only within the Māturīdī tradition: an appreciation of the multiplicity of translations by which the eternal speech can be expressed.

Al-Māturīdī takes up the Ḥanafī position on divine speech with a delicate theological goal. His principal opponents are not traditionalists who

24 See al-Dānī, *Al-Aḥruf al-sabʿa li-l-qurʾān*, pp. 21–22; al-Shaybānī, *Kitāb al-āthār*, vol. 1, pp. 280–81; Zadeh, *The Vernacular Qur'an*, p. 98.

25 See ʿAbd al-Jalīl, 'Ẓāhirat al-ibdāl fī qirāʾāt ʿAbd Allāh b. Masʿūd wa-qīmatuhā al-tafsīriyya', p. 211.

26 Sommer, *Revelation and Authority*, pp. 43–44.

27 Al-Māturīdī, *Taʾwīlāt al-qurʾān*, vol. 15, p. 236. See Harvey, 'The Legal Epistemology of Qur'anic Variants', pp. 78–79.

28 Al-Ṭaḥāwī, *Sharḥ mushkil al-āthār*, vol. 8, p. 124; Abū ʿUbayd, *Faḍāʾil al-qurʾān*, p. 347; Muslim, *Ṣaḥīḥ*, vol. 1, pp. 321–22. See Zadeh, *The Vernacular Qur'an*, p. 95.

29 See van Ess, *Theology and Society in the Second and Third Centuries of the Hijra, Volume 4*, pp. 206–7. Ibn Kullāb's reasoning for the eternality of God's speech seems to be its creative function, which is like the position of Ibn Khuzayma. See page 176, note 5.

would see his view as too transcendent towards the Qur'an. Instead, he is worried about the Mu'tazila, again likely represented by al-Kaʿbī, who argue against the eternality of God's speech. Al-Māturīdī's dialectical theological approach to the question is complex and made harder by his difficult style of writing. Instead of giving a step-by-step commentary, I will reconstruct and analyse the main elements of his argument in a deductive form, showing how he defends each disputed premise and attacks the view of his opponent. Note that this has required a rearrangement of the order of some of his arguments in *Kitāb al-tawḥīd*, as well as a critical selection of the parts that I deem essential to his theological case.

P1. Speaking is an action.
P2. All of God's actions are eternally attributed of His nature.
C1. If God speaks, it is an eternal action.
P3. Only a deficiency makes a being silent or incapable of speaking.
P4. God is not deficient.
C2. God speaks eternally and is never silent.

The first premise is granted in principle by both parties. Al-Māturīdī argues that God's speech is one of His attributes of action; as he puts it, 'attribute of speech and action (*ṣifat al-kalām wa-l-fiʿl*)' or 'reality of action and speech (*ḥaqīqat al-fiʿl wa-l-kalām*)'.[30] While this may seem an unsurprising assumption, it singles him out from both the Muʿtazila and al-Ashʿarī when combined with P2, which is the same doctrine that undergirds his position on *takwīn*. As I discussed in the previous chapter, the Muʿtazila understood God's actions as temporally generated creations. Al-Māturīdī characterises his opponent as arguing for the temporality of God's speech by means of expressions in the Qur'an that refer to the revelation arriving.[31] In contrast, he establishes from the outset that God's speech, like His other actions, is not characterised by either change or cessation.

According to al-Māturīdī, the opponent also attempts to negate P2 by arguing that God's actions are things that God first creates and then attributes to Himself. This example is illustrative of what is at stake between himself and presumably al-Kaʿbī with respect to the theory of properties underlying God's attributes:

> [Al-Kaʿbī] claims: 'Merciful (*raḥīm*) is an attribute, unlike mercy (*raḥma*). [This is because] everyone who performs the attribute of a thing, he is described by it; just as the one who reviles another or glorifies him is his reviler or glorifier. In the same manner, He created

30 Al-Māturīdī, *Kitāb al-tawḥīd*, p. 116–17.
31 Al-Māturīdī, *Kitāb al-tawḥīd*, p. 116.

> mercy and it is not permissible that He be attributed with it when He created it until He says, "I am merciful." So, by that we know that the attribute is His statement that He is merciful'.[32]
>
> Abū Manṣūr, may God have mercy on him, says: how unaware he is of this confusion about the attributes so that he begins such in the explanation of the attributes of God; glorified is God above the like of this imagination, and He is transcendent. Were the attribute in reality [merely] the attribution of the attributor (*waṣf al-wāṣif*), it renders futile speech of the creation, because the creation is [made up of] substances (*aʿyān*) and attributes (*ṣifāt*). And it renders futile his [own] speech about joining together, splitting apart, movement and rest, which particulars are not free from in the affirmation of their temporality, though they are free from the attribution of the attributor for them. So, it is established that the attributes are integral to the particulars, not as he mentions.[33]

Al-Kaʿbī is here classified by al-Māturīdī as subscribing to a type of concept nominalism, the metaphysical position that a given property only exists when it comes under a certain concept.[34] This position, adopted also by al-Jubbāʾī, was attractive to the Muʿtazila as a nostrum that allowed them to account for apparent substantive attributes mentioned in scripture without violating divine simplicity.[35] In the example that al-Māturīdī provides, al-Kaʿbī views God's mercy as His creation, whereas the attribute of His being merciful is a concept that only applies to Him after His statement to that effect.[36]

Al-Māturīdī's response is that al-Kaʿbī's top-down approach to attribution is confused. The only correct way to reason must be one that can take

32 Both printed editions of *Kitāb al-tawḥīd* render this phrase as 'His statement, "Indeed He is merciful (*qawluhu innahu raḥīm*)"'. See al-Māturīdī, *Kitāb al-tawḥīd*, p. 119; al-Māturīdī, *Kitāb al-tawḥīd*, ed. Kholeif, p. 56. That would imply a direct Qur'anic quotation, such as Q. 5:39: 'Indeed God is forgiving, merciful (*inna allāha ghafūrun raḥīm*)'. As there is no such phrase in the canonical text of the Qur'an, it may be better to read al-Māturīdī as using indirect speech, as follows: 'His statement that He is merciful (*qawluhu annahu raḥīm*)'. The manuscript allows for this possibility because it leaves the *alif* in the relevant word unvocalised. See al-Māturīdī, 'Kitāb al-tawḥīd', fol. 27r.

33 Al-Māturīdī, *Kitāb al-tawḥīd*, p. 119.

34 This is formally stated in al-Māturīdī, *Kitāb al-tawḥīd*, pp. 113–14. He critiques the idea with respect to God being the creator on p. 164. See also al-Kaʿbī, *ʿUyūn al-masāʾil wa-l-jawābāt*, pp. 101–2; El Omari, *The Theology of Abū l-Qāsim al-Balkhī/al-Kaʿbī (d. 319/931)*, p. 107; Rodriguez-Pereyra, 'Nominalism in Metaphysics'.

35 See Frank, *Beings and Their Attributes*, pp. 18–19.

36 For further discussion of Muslim theological positions regarding mercy, see Harvey, 'The Revelation of Mercy in the Light of Islamic Theology', pp. 53–54.

account of predication in the visible world and then apply it to what is veiled from us. In the world, it is obvious that concrete particulars have attributes irrespective of whether we hold concepts about them. For instance, a red garment is not understood as only red when described by the concept of redness, but as having a red nature.[37] As I argued in Chapter 2, al-Māturīdī affirms a kind of trope theory in place of his opponent's concept nominalism. He critiques his opponent in the passage above for falling into inconsistency with his own beliefs about temporal particulars to which he would want to apply a more common-sense regime of predication.[38] The result for al-Māturīdī is that God does not merely possess the quality of mercifulness as a self-given epithet after creating mercy, but due to the action of mercy being integral to His nature. The same is true for His speech.

Although al-Māturīdī was not aware of the ideas of his geographically distant contemporary al-Ashʿarī, it is possible to use the above argument to critique his position. Like the Muʿtazila, al-Ashʿarī held that God's actions are created things, yet he also took God's speech to be an eternal attribute.[39] From al-Māturīdī's theological perspective, there is no consistent basis on which to argue that mercy is one of God's actions, but that speech is not. So, it seems that he would put al-Ashʿarī under pressure to either adopt the Muʿtazilī position on God's speech as created like other attributes of action or to accept the Māturīdī position that all actions are eternal. Yet again, it may be observed that the polemics as they played out in history were different and that the tendency of classical Māturīdism was to gradually shift the classification of God's speech from an attribute of action to an essential attribute to conform with the Ashʿarī position.[40] Thus, this point is neither usually identified in the classical *ikhtilāf* literature, nor in contemporary research, as a significant difference between the two Sunnī schools.[41] Notably, within recent *kalām* discussions, Abu Zayd draws on the Muʿtazilī tradition to assert that, as God's speech requires a worldly correlate to address, it is an attribute of action and part of the created order.[42] As I have shown, this argument might be effective against an Ashʿarī perspective that distinguishes between the *ṣifāt al-dhāt* and *ṣifāt*

37 Al-Māturīdī, *Kitāb al-tawḥīd*, p. 119.

38 The opponent's response, which al-Māturīdī records, is that ordinary speech about the properties of objects is a convenient metaphor for the reality, which is their divine concept nominalism.

39 Al-Ashʿarī, *Al-Ibāna ʿan uṣūl al-diyāna*, p. 23.

40 See page 184.

41 Haidar, *The Debates between Ash'arism and Māturīdism in Ottoman Religious Scholarship*, p. 85; Cerić, *Roots of Synthetic Theology in Islam*, pp. 184–87; Spevack, 'The Qur'an and God's Speech According to the Later Ashʿarī-Māturīdī Verifiers', pp. 56–57.

42 Abu Zayd, *Al-Naṣṣ al-sulṭa al-ḥaqīqa*, pp. 68–69.

al-fiʿl in the same way as the Muʿtazila, yet wants to include speech in the former category. It would not work against the early Māturīdī position in which this distinction is not made.

Notice that, whereas C1 of al-Māturīdī's argument above shows that, if posited, God's speech must be eternal like His other actions, it does not prove that God in fact speaks. This is shown via P3 and P4. Al-Māturīdī reports his opponent as attacking P3 in the following way: the implication of the argument (of *ahl al-sunna*)[43] is that, in the world, anyone who can possibly speak can (through choice) be silent or (unwillingly) be mute. But then, by analogy with persons in the world, God too is possibly silent or mute, so why presume that He speaks at all? Furthermore, a young child is not mute, yet cannot speak, so the analogy is false.[44]

Al-Māturīdī responds by clarifying that the correct definition is that it is possible for a person in the world to be silent or incapable of speech.[45] But the opponent is confused, as not speaking in the world is caused by a deficiency that leads to silence or incapacity, and this must be negated for God.[46] The case of a young child (who is incapable of speech) is included under the definition. Moreover, the opponent is degraded in trying to make this kind of example about God.[47] It can be seen that P4, God's lack of deficiency, is another mutually agreed premise, although the implications that al-Māturīdī draws from it are different from his opponent.[48]

As this argument against the Muʿtazila shows, al-Māturīdī holds that one cannot escape inferring from the world, specifically from the speaking human being, to affirm God's action of speech.[49] Yet in what should have become a familiar move to the reader over the course of this book, al-Māturīdī immediately blocks similarity between the creation and God's speech by alluding to several verses of the Qur'an: Q. 42:11: 'There is nothing like Him'; Q. 13:16: 'Do they make for God partners, who create a creation like His, so it is indistinguishable from His?'; and Q. 17:88: 'Say, "Even if all mankind and jinn came together to produce something like this Qur'an, they could not produce anything like it, however much they helped each other."'[50] Al-Māturīdī comments:

> So affirmed for Him is dissimilarity from the speech of all creation according to what is established for His nature (*dhāt*). This means

43 This is an interlinear addition in the manuscript. Al-Māturīdī, 'Kitāb al-tawḥīd', fol. 26r.
44 Al-Māturīdī, *Kitāb al-tawḥīd*, pp. 117–18.
45 Al-Māturīdī, *Kitāb al-tawḥīd*, p. 118.
46 Al-Māturīdī, *Kitāb al-tawḥīd*, pp. 118, 120–21.
47 Al-Māturīdī, *Kitāb al-tawḥīd*, p. 118.
48 Al-Māturīdī, *Kitāb al-tawḥīd*, pp. 118, 120.
49 Al-Māturīdī, *Kitāb al-tawḥīd*, p. 121.
50 Al-Māturīdī, *Kitāb al-tawḥīd*, p. 121.

> that all the speech of the creation was never tried with reaching the limits of its meanings (*maʿānīhi*). He has mentioned the speech of the ant, the hoopoe, the glorification of the mountains and other [things] from which nothing is understood via alphabetical letters or human language.[51]

His argument is that, even though God must be understood as speaking, His speech cannot be like human speech. It is different in its fundamental ontology, which is not accidental, nor involves separation, joining, limits, increase or decrease,[52] and that means it cannot be exhausted by temporal forms. The reference to the 'speech' of other non-human entities mentioned in the Qur'an is to defend the validity of the revealed manifestation of God's speech indicating underlying meanings that transcend human language. The point of contact between the two levels for al-Māturīdī is expressed by the term concordance (*muwāfaqa*). He writes, 'what is attributed to God from speech between [Him and] the creation is metaphorical upon concordance with what is known to be the speech that is His attribute (*mā yuḍāfu ilā allāhi min al-kalāmi bayna al-khalqi fa-huwa majāzun ʿalā al-muwāfaqati bimā yuʿrafu bihi al-kalāmu alladhī huwa ṣifatuhu*)'.[53] He also remarks, 'what is heard from the creation [that is, the recited Qur'an] is the speech of God due to its concordance, just as it is said in letters, lyrical poems and speeches'.[54]

Here he compares the role of writing in allowing us to hear or read the words of another who is distant in time or place with the facility of revealed language to convey the transcendent speech of God. Al-Māturīdī's formulation of the relationship between the two levels of speech, then, does not privilege the Arabic language, nor a specific ordered composition, in uniquely capturing divine discourse. In fact, he merely observes it is conceivable that God allows us to hear His speech through what is not His speech, without specifying further conditions.[55] But with respect to God's miraculous speech to Moses, the limiting case of what is possible for human beings in the world, al-Māturīdī rules out hearing Him directly.[56]

In al-Māturīdī's commentary in *Taʾwīlāt al-qurʾān* on Q. 41:44: 'If we had made it a foreign recital (*wa-law jaʿalnāhu qurʾānan aʿjamiyyan*) . . .', he remarks that this turn of phrase indicates that, had it been revealed in a

51 Al-Māturīdī, *Kitāb al-tawḥīd*, p. 121.

52 Al-Māturīdī, *Kitāb al-tawḥīd*, p. 121.

53 Al-Māturīdī, *Kitāb al-tawḥīd*, p. 117.

54 Al-Māturīdī, *Kitāb al-tawḥīd*, pp. 121–22. See al-Māturīdī, *Taʾwīlāt al-qurʾān*, vol. 8, p. 351.

55 Al-Māturīdī, *Kitāb al-tawḥīd*, p. 122.

56 Al-Māturīdī, *Kitāb al-tawḥīd*, p. 122. This is considered a subsidiary point of difference with the Ashʿarīs. See Shaykhzāde, *Kitāb naẓm al-farāʾid*, pp. 15–17.

foreign language, it would still be a recital (or: Qur'an) and that differing its language does not change or alter it from being so.[57] This goes beyond his statements in *Kitāb al-tawḥīd* to make the explicit claim that what is essential to the Qur'an is not its outward linguistic form but its meaning that can be conveyed in any language. He then states that this is evidence for Abū Ḥanīfa's position on the permissibility of reciting in Persian during prayer.[58] His comments may have inspired the developed remarks of al-Sarakhsī.

At the very end of his treatment, al-Māturīdī responds to the position of *waqf*, adopted by some of his forerunners in the Ḥanafī school. He explains that *waqf* can be taken as a suspension of knowledge with respect to God's speech in more than one sense, providing a master class in disambiguation:[59]

1. Suspending knowledge on whether God's speech is Him or other than Him – this is the correct way to affirm God's speech and other attributes as essential.
2. Suspending knowledge on whether God's speech is a creation or not – this is rejected as both tradition and rationality demonstrate that His speech must be an essential attribute (including actions) or a temporal creation.
3. Suspending knowledge on whether God speaks essentially or not – this is just ignorance and requires instruction (as provided by al-Māturīdī's prior arguments).
4. Suspending knowledge on the intent of the questioner until it becomes clear: 'Is what he means by the speech of God and the Qur'an a divisible, multi-part entity or what cannot be attributed with anything from that?' – this is entirely proper.

Al-Māturīdī's position is that *waqf* is appropriate in accepting some ambiguity between God and His own eternal attributes (1), as well as in making sure that what the interlocutor means by the Qur'an is understood (4). This is an important consideration given how easy it was for protagonists of this theological debate to understand the referent of the term Qur'an in vastly different ways.[60] Al-Māturīdī rejects suspending knowledge on whether God's speech is a creation (2) or whether it is eternal (3), which amounts to the same thing conversely formulated.[61]

57 Al-Māturīdī, *Taʾwīlāt al-qurʾān*, vol. 13, p. 145.

58 Al-Māturīdī, *Taʾwīlāt al-qurʾān*, vol. 13, p. 145.

59 Al-Māturīdī, *Kitāb al-tawḥīd*, pp. 122–23.

60 See van Ess, 'Ibn Kullāb et la *Miḥna*', p. 1469; Spevack, 'The Qur'an and God's Speech According to the Later Ashʿarī-Māturīdī Verifiers', pp. 85–87.

61 Ibn Ḥanbal is reported by his student Ḥarb b. Ismāʿīl al-Kirmānī (d. 280/893) as rejecting the position of *waqf* as disbelief along with that of *khalq al-qurʾān* and the Kullābī formula. See al-Kirmānī, *Kitāb al-sunna*, pp. 52–53. Thanks to Salman Younas for the reference.

The Samarqandī Ḥanafis in the generations following al-Māturīdī kept to the essentials of his view in affirming the following: the eternality of God's attribute of speech; the temporality of the created Arabic form through which it is expressed; and the link between the two in its meaning. For, example, Abū Salama al-Samarqandī states that it is permissible to call what is in the codices and memorised in the hearts the Qur'an and God's speech 'based on what is understood from its meaning (*ʿalā al-mafhūmi min al-maʿnā*)'.[62]

Further evidence for the early development of Māturīdī thinking on how human language is understood to carry divine meanings can be found in the surviving responsa of al-Māturīdī's student al-Rustughfanī. There is an interesting discussion of *kalām allāh* buried in his defence of the reality of the Beautific Vision (*ruʾya*) against the Muʿtazila. He reports that the Muʿtazila argue that the word 'never (*lan*)' in God's statement to Moses in Q. 7:143, 'You will never see me (*lan tarānī*)' is used for eternity (*taʾbīd*) in Arabic, so He will not be seen in the Hereafter. Al-Rustughfanī's response is that, when a person swears to never speak to someone, he means the worldly life not the Hereafter. He considers the Muʿtazilī rejoinder that this word is the speech of God, and so it applies to both realms, but he has an answer ready: 'we understand from the speech of God what we understand from the speech of human beings, because the Qur'an was revealed in their language, and the word *lan* in the Arabic language is without doubt for the world'.[63]

Al-Rustughfanī provides more insight into his position in a response dedicated to the Qur'an. He provides Qur'anic evidence for five ways in which the Qur'an interacts with the created order: it is revealed (*munazzal*) to the Prophet, recited (*maqrūʾ*) by the tongues, heard (*masmūʿ*) by the ears, memorised (*maḥfūẓ*) by the hearts and written (*maktūb*) in the codices. He then attributes to a figure named Abū ʿAbd Allāh Muḥammad b. Aslam the following formula: 'the Qur'an by my utterance is uncreated, yet my utterance of the Qur'an is created (*al-qurʾānu bi-lafẓī ghayru makhlūqin wa-lafẓī bi-l-qurʾāni makhlūqun*)'.[64] At the end of his response, he affirms a further nuanced expression: 'The Qur'an is the speech of God, and God, Most High,

62 Al-Samarqandī, 'Jumal uṣūl al-dīn', p. 19.

63 Al-Rustughfanī, 'Bāb al-mutafarriqāt min fawāʾid', MS Yeni Cami 547, fol. 293v; al-Rustughfanī, 'Bāb al-mutafarriqāt min fawāʾid', MS Veliyüddin Efendi 1545, fols 286r–286v.

64 Al-Rustughfanī, 'Bāb al-mutafarriqāt min fawāʾid', MS Yeni Cami 547, fol. 300v; al-Rustughfanī, 'Bāb al-mutafarriqāt min fawāʾid', MS Veliyüddin Efendi 1545, fol. 294r. The verses he cites for the five respectively are as follows: Q. 4:105, 73:20, 9:6, 29:49 and 3:79. There are remarkable similarities between this answer and the treatment of the subject in *Al-Fiqh al-akbar II*, which gives four of the five words (except *masmūʿ*) and uses the expression 'our utterance of the Qur'an is created, our writing of the Qur'an is created, and our recitation of the Qur'an is created, but the Qur'an is not created (*lafẓunā bi-l-qurʾāni makhlūqun wa-kitābatunā lahu makhlūqatun wa-qirāʾatunā lahu makhlūqatun*

with His attributes is eternal, not generated (*bi-ṣifātihi qadīmun ghayru muḥdathin*)'.[65] On the one hand, this recalls the language of al-Māturīdī in the description of the eternality of God's attributes.[66] Yet on the other, it is close to a formula that is first attested in Abū Bakr al-Iyāḍī's *Al-Masāʾil al-ʿashar al-ʿIyāḍiyya*: 'the Qur'an is the speech of God and the speech of God is not created'.[67] The version of al-Rustughfanī, who likely died before Abū Bakr al-Iyāḍī,[68] thus appears to be an intermediate stage between that of al-Māturīdī and later Samarqandī Ḥanafīs.

As pointed out by Dorroll, this precise mode of expression was used by Samarqandī scholars who wanted to affirm the Qur'an as God's speech but were uncomfortable with the overt traditionalist Ḥanafī position that it was His uncreated speech (as held, for example, by al-Ḥakīm al-Samarqandī).[69] Ibn Yaḥyā al-Bashāgharī elaborates that the purpose of this expression was to avoid giving the mistaken impression that the outward form of the Qur'an, the letters and syllables that compose it, was the uncreated speech of God. Instead, *kalām allāh* is what is understood from it.[70] The continuity with al-Māturīdī's fourth type of *waqf* above should be clear.

Ibn Yaḥyā also raises an interesting argument that links the question of the Qur'an's status to the discourse surrounding its inimitability, a connection that remained important in the centuries that followed. He argues that, if the Qur'an was entirely created, then nothing would remain of its inimitability (*iʿjāz*) except the Arabic composition (*naẓm*), and that is not something that orators and litterateurs are unable to match.[71] In his view, then, the Qur'an's inimitability comes from its meaning, which is eternal divine speech. The premise that the eloquence of the Arabic compositional

wa-l-qurʾānu ghayru makhlūqin)'. Al-Qārī, *Sharḥ al-fiqh al-akbar*, p. 184. There is also a resemblance to expressions in *al-Waṣiyya* and the book of the late-fourth/tenth-century al-Kalabadhī. See Abū Ḥanīfa, *Waṣiyya*, p. 41; al-Kalabadhī, *Kitāb al-taʿarruf li-madhhab ahl al-taṣawwuf*, p. 18. Given prior discussion on the dating of *Al-Fiqh al-akbar II*, the use of Qur'anic evidence to establish the five kinds of interactions and al-Rustughfanī's citation of a more obscure authority than Abū Ḥanīfa, it appears his text is the earliest known origin for the more famous creedal formulations.

65 Al-Rustughfanī, 'Bāb al-mutafarriqāt min fawāʾid', MS Veliyüddin Efendi 1545, fol. 294r.

66 See page 149.

67 Özen, 'IV. (X.) Yüzyılda Māverāünnehirʾde Ehl-i Sünnet-Muʿtezile Mücadelesi ve Bir Ehl-i Sūnnet Beyannamesi', p. 84. See Dorroll, 'The Doctrine of Nature of the Qur'ān in the Māturīdī Tradition', p. 132.

68 Özen, 'IV. (X.) Yüzyılda Māverāünnehirʾde Ehl-i Sünnet-Muʿtezile Mücadelesi ve Bir Ehl-i Sūnnet Beyannamesi', p. 69.

69 Al-Wafī, *Salām al-aḥkam ʿalā sawād al-aʿẓam*, p. 136. See Dorroll, 'The Doctrine of Nature of the Qur'ān in the Māturīdī Tradition', pp. 132–33.

70 Al-Samarqandī, *Jumal min uṣūl al-dīn wa-yalīhu sharḥuhu*, p. 99. See Dorroll, 'The Doctrine of Nature of the Qur'ān in the Māturīdī Tradition', pp. 136–37.

71 Al-Samarqandī, *Jumal min uṣūl al-dīn wa-yalīhu sharḥuhu*, pp. 100–1.

form of the Qur'an was in principle achievable by humans and jinn was not new; it had been central to al-Naẓẓām's doctrine of *ṣarfa* (prevention), God's direct intervention to prevent the challenge being met.[72] Yet the significance of Ibn Yaḥyā's treatment is that, by stripping the fatalistic notion of *ṣarfa* from the argument, he turns al-Naẓẓām's concept against the Muʿtazilī doctrine of God's created speech – it is only its eternal meaning that prevents the Qur'an being matched. Here, he draws from the orientation of al-Māturīdī, and before him Abū Ḥanīfa, towards the pre-eminence of the Qur'an's meaning ahead of its form, to advance a new theological argument in the light of prevailing debates over literary theory and *iʿjāz*.

This idea is developed further by al-Sarakhsī a century later in the context of his defence of Abū Ḥanīfa's position that the Qur'an could be recited in Persian translation during prayer. He reasons as follows:

> The obligation is to recite that which is inimitable (*muʿjiz*) and inimitability is in meaning, as the Qur'an is a proof for all people; the incapacity of Persians in matching it is only manifest in their own tongue (*al-wājibu ʿalayhi qirāʾatu al-muʿjizi wa-l-iʿjāzu fī al-maʿnā fa-inna al-qurʾāna ḥujjatun ʿalā al-nāsi kāffatan wa-ʿajzu al-fursi ʿan al-ityāni bi-mithlihi innamā yaẓharu bi-lisānihim*)'.[73]

This argument is based on al-Sarakhsī's acceptance of the early Samarqandī Ḥanafī understanding of *iʿjāz* solely as meaning, which he attributes to Abū Ḥanīfa in contrast to his two students.[74] More broadly, as Travis Zadeh catalogues in considerable detail, even though the Ḥanafīs were not the only group to think that the Qur'an could and should be translated into other languages, they stand out as the standard bearers of this view due to the distinctive jurisprudential and theological tendencies bequeathed by the early tradition in Kufa and their integrative approach towards adapting Islam to a Persianate environment.[75]

72 Van Ess, *Theology and Society in the Second and Third Centuries of the Hijra, Volume 3*, pp. 446–47.

73 Al-Sarakhsī, *Al-Mabsūṭ*, vol. 1, p. 37. See Zadeh, *The Vernacular Qur'an*, p. 113. I think this is a better reading than Reynolds', 'if Persians are unable to perform this [in Arabic] they should bring [it] forth in their own tongue'. Reynolds, 'God has Spoken Before', p. 586. Compare with al-Bāqillānī's argument that non-Arabic speakers should rely on the inability of the Arabians in the Prophet's time to match the Qur'an despite their acknowledged eloquence. Al-Bāqillānī, *Kitāb al-tamhīd*, p. 154. For further discussion of this 'circumstantial' approach, see Vasalou, *The Miraculous Eloquence of the Qur'an*, p. 33.

74 Al-Sarakhsī, *Al-Mabsūṭ*, vol. 1, p. 37. Note that Zadeh incorrectly associates al-Sarakhsī with the understanding of *iʿjāz* as both *naẓm* and *maʿnā*. See Zadeh, *The Vernacular Qur'an*, p. 114.

75 See Zadeh, *The Vernacular Qur'an*, pp. 105–26.

Sharḥ al-fiqh al-akbar, another text from near the beginning of the classical Māturīdī tradition, is one of the first works to contrast the Samarqandī formulation for the Qur'an, discussed above, with the position of the Ashʿarīs. The author points out that, whereas the Samarqandī Ḥanafīs call the Qur'an *kalām allāh*, though clarifying that no aspect of temporal creation is thereby meant, the Ashʿarīs state that what is written in the *muṣḥaf* is not God's speech but an *ʿibāra* (expression) and imitation (*ḥikāya*) of it.[76] This is mainly a debate over a preferred theological formula. Some of the Samarqandī Ḥanafīs felt that their careful choice of words was the correct way to emphatically affirm that the Qur'an was God's speech without negating divine transcendence and were suspicious of terminology that did not make the identification explicit. There may have also been some reservation about the origin of the technical terms in the *kalām* to the west. Ibn Kullāb had treated the terms *ʿibāra* and *ḥikāya* as interchangeable,[77] the Muʿtazilīs Abū Hudhayl and Jaʿfar b. Mubashshir (d. 234/849) had made use of *ḥikāya*,[78] while al-Bāqillānī and Ibn Fūrak wrote of *ʿibāra* with the latter openly repudiating *ḥikāya*.[79]

Nevertheless, elements of this terminology had started to gain ground among Māturīdīs from the fifth/eleventh century onwards. Al-Sālimī describes the created manifestation of the Qur'an, from its recitation to its suras and verses, as a *ḥikāya* and a disclosure (*bayān*) of the meaning of the speech of God. But he still insists that the Qur'an is the speech of God without *ḥikāya*.[80] The problem with this latter statement, and indeed all univocal identification of the Qur'an with God's attribute of speech, is that it arguably puts into question the status of prior divine scriptures that would also need affirmation as *kalām allāh*.

This question begins to receive some resolution in the theology of al-Bazdawī. Once more, he builds his analysis on a close appreciation of the approach of al-Māturīdī, showing a sophisticated ability to dialectically deploy the idea of metaphor. On the question of the eternality of God's speech, he highlights its incompatibility with silence and muteness, arguing that, if it is possible to affirm it as a reality, it cannot be taken as a metaphor in the way that the Muʿtazila claim.[81] Yet he proposes that the Arabic Qur'an is to be understood as a composition (*manẓūm*) that acts

76 Al-Samarqandī, 'Sharḥ al-fiqh al-absaṭ', pp. 154–55.

77 Van Ess, 'Verbal Inspiration?', p. 1763.

78 Van Ess, *Theology and Society in the Second and Third Centuries of the Hijra, Volume 3*, pp. 306–7.

79 Al-Bāqillānī, *Kitāb al-tamhīd*, p. 251; Ibn Fūrak, *Maqālāt al-shaykh Abī al-Ḥasan al-Ashʿarī*, p. 60.

80 Al-Sālimī, *Al-Tamhīd fī bayan al-tawḥīd*, p. 192. See Dorroll, 'The Doctrine of Nature of the Qur'ān in the Māturīdī Tradition', pp. 139–40.

81 Al-Bazdawī, *Uṣūl al-dīn*, p. 67.

through metaphor as an indication (*dāll*) to God's speech.[82] He illustrates this idea with a written couplet by the pre-Islamic poet Imruʾ al-Qays, which he points out is merely an indication to his actual speech. Echoing al-Māturīdī, he argues that the same is true for every message and oration. God can create such a composition in the Heavenly Tablet (*al-lawḥ*) or in an angel, and it is called the Book of God or the Qur'an, because it indicates His eternal speech.[83] With his original terminology, al-Bazdawī prefers a transcendent theology to the traditionalist Ḥanafī approach that affirms the Arabic Qur'an as uncreated and betrays little sign of influence from the Ashʿarī discourse, despite his similar doctrinal position.

Al-Bazdawī also adds a point of considerable interest in stating that God's speech is not qualified by any language and hence that the Arabic and Hebrew of scriptures revealed in these languages are part of their created compositions. This means that the Qur'an can be defined as the Arabic composition that is an indication to God's speech, and the Torah is its Hebrew equivalent.[84] This is consistent with al-Māturīdī's approach to the question, although it goes beyond him in illustrating how the forms of revealed dispensations in different languages are rooted in the meanings of transcendent divine speech. Yet in a brief discussion of *iʿjāz* in a separate section, al-Bazdawī follows the opinion that it consists of both *naẓm* and *maʿnā*, which seems at odds with his wider theological inclinations.[85]

Once more, the main elements of Abū al-Muʿīn al-Nasafī's treatment of God's speech are familiar from the preceding tradition, although his elaboration and refutation of various views, especially those of the Muʿtazila, are exhaustive. He seems to be one of the first Māturīdī theologians to use the Ashʿarī term *ʿibāra* to mean an indication (*dāll*) to God's speech, replacing al-Bazdawī's term *manẓūm*.[86] Zadeh cites a text in which al-Nasafī argues for the validity of the term *ḥikāya*, based on the previous Māturīdī tradition and against Ashʿarīs who felt that it led to the Muʿtazilī inference that the imitated thing, God's speech, is also created.[87] As I have shown, this usage is not common within the main extant Māturīdī texts, only appearing within al-Sālimī's *Al-Tamhīd*. Moreover, I do not think much of importance turns on the debate concerning the acceptability of this technical term; more significant are the underlying theological and linguistic frameworks adopted by the two rival schools.

82 Al-Bazdawī, *Uṣūl al-dīn*, p. 68.
83 Al-Bazdawī, *Uṣūl al-dīn*, p. 68.
84 Al-Bazdawī, *Uṣūl al-dīn*, p. 70.
85 Al-Bazdawī, *Uṣūl al-dīn*, p. 227.
86 Al-Nasafī, *Al-Tamhīd fī uṣūl al-dīn*, p. 44; al-Nasafī, *Tabṣirat al-adilla*, vol. 1, p. 435.
87 Zadeh, *The Vernacular Qur'an*, pp. 291–92; al-Nasafī, *Tabṣirat al-adilla*, vol. 1, pp. 485–86.

Abū al-Muʿīn al-Nasafī adds to al-Bazdawī's comments on the relationship between divine speech in different languages and scriptures that God's speech in Syriac is the Evangel. He compares it to the different languages in which God is named and even the different words used to express one meaning in the same language.[88] In this vein, his successor, al-Ṣābūnī, provides the example that a single meaning, the instruction to stand, can be given from master to slave via speech, writing, or gesture.[89] As Zadeh demonstrates at greater length for Abū al-Muʿīn and his student Abū Ḥafṣ al-Nasafī, author of an early Persian translation of the Qur'an, the tradition continued to articulate a linguistic theory whereby temporal expressions are always fluid and translatable – fixity is only to be sought in eternal divine meanings.[90]

This approach to language is not found in Abū al-Muʿīn al-Nasafī's stance on the Qur'an's *iʿjāz*, which like al-Bazdawī he describes as both *naẓm* and *maʿnā*.[91] It seems that this position, which became dominant within Māturīdī thought, results from a separation of the question of *iʿjāz* from the linguistic debates involved in the theological articulation of divine speech. Rejecting the emphasis on meaning alone as the basis for Qur'anic inimitability, which was ascribed to Abū Ḥanīfa and continued by Abū Salama al-Samarqandī and al-Sarakhsī, such figures adopt a presumably more effective polemical strategy inspired by their Ashʿarī counterparts. Here, al-Nasafī's debt to al-Bāqillānī's idea of the Qur'an as *sui generis*, neither poetry nor prose, is especially apparent.[92]

The dominant classical theory expressing Qur'anic inimitability in both form and meaning was formulated a generation before al-Nasafī by the Ashʿarī linguist ʿAbd al-Qāhir al-Jurjānī (d. 471/1078) in his *Dalāʾil al-iʿjāz*. He fervently argued that meanings are ordered by their corresponding arrangement of wordings.[93] This not only meant framing the inimitability of the Qur'an as its eloquence manifested within a specific compositional form, but implied that this form was uniquely tied to the eternal divine speech in a manner impossible for a translation.[94] By adopting this model, classical Māturīdism again sacrificed theological consistency to match an influential Ashʿarī doctrine.

The debate over the outward expression of the Qur'anic text is paralleled by one over how to analyse the inward meaning(s), as recorded by

88 Al-Nasafī, *Tabṣirat al-adilla*, vol. 1, p. 435.
89 Al-Ṣābūnī, *Al-Kifāya fī al-hidāya*, pp. 117–18.
90 Zadeh, *The Vernacular Qur'an*, pp. 290, 292–93.
91 Al-Nasafī, *Baḥr al-kalām*, p. 203; al-Nasafī, *Tabṣirat al-adilla*, vol. 2, pp. 741–52.
92 Al-Nasafī, *Tabṣirat al-adilla*, vol. 2, p. 741; al-Bāqillānī, *Iʿjāz al-qurʾān*, pp. 30–32.
93 Al-Jurjānī, *Dalāʾil al-iʿjāz*, p. 64. See Larkin, *The Theology of Meaning*, pp. 54–55.
94 For al-Jurjānī's merging of the linguistic and theological understanding of *maʿnā*, see Larkin, *The Theology of Meaning*, pp. 67–69.

the Ottoman scholar Shaykhzāde in his *Naẓm al-farāʾid*, which details differences between the Māturīdīs and Ashʿarīs. He cites the main view of the Māturīdī tradition, through figures such as al-Rustughfanī and Abū al-Muʿīn al-Nasafī, as holding that outward Qur'anic expressions refer to 'linguistic meanings, specific individuals and their states (*al-maʿānī al-lughawiyyati wa-l-ashkhāṣi wa-aḥwālihā*)'.[95] He compares this to what he characterises as the dominant Ashʿarī view that such expressions refer to a single matter, although dividing over whether this is a singular individuality (*waḥda shakhṣiyya*) or a singular type (*waḥda nawʿiyya*), such as the informative utterance (*khabar*).[96]

It may be possible to relate this difference back to the basic theological conception of divine speech according to al-Māturīdī and al-Ashʿarī. For al-Māturīdī, though God's speech has no aspect of temporality, nothing rules out plurality in its meanings as His action. In fact, he explicitly affirms the transcendence of His speech in terms of these multiple meanings being infinitely beyond the reach of created beings. Ḥanafīs were keen to quote verses in support of this idea, such as Q. 18:109: 'Say, "If the whole ocean were ink for writing the words of my Lord, it would run dry before those words were exhausted" – even if We were to add another ocean to it'.[97] The clearest expressions from al-Ashʿarī's own extant works on this point stick to the traditionalist understanding of the Qur'an as God's eternal speech.[98] But Ibn Fūrak records that he adopted a nuanced distinction between outward articulation and inward meaning similar to Ibn Kullāb, leading to the further elaboration of the doctrine of *kalām nafsī* (internal speech) by his successors.[99]

According to Ibn Fūrak, al-Ashʿarī analyses God's speech as consisting of four kinds: command (*amr*), prohibition (*nahy*), report (*khabar*) and address (*khiṭāb*).[100] He also says that God's speech is 'understood by the one who understands it and cognises its meanings (*mafhūmun li-man fahimahu wa-ʿarafa maʿānīhi*)'.[101] The critical point is whether these types of meanings are aspects of the eternal attribute or are understood from it. This latter interpretation seems vindicated by his emphatic statement that,

95 Shaykhzāde, *Kitāb naẓm al-farāʾid*, p. 12.
96 Shaykhzāde, *Kitāb naẓm al-farāʾid*, p. 12.
97 Shaykhzāde, *Kitāb naẓm al-farāʾid*, p. 12.
98 See al-Ashʿarī, *Al-Ibāna ʿan uṣūl al-diyāna*, pp. 24–26.
99 Ibn Fūrak, *Maqālāt al-shaykh Abī al-Ḥasan al-Ashʿarī*, pp. 59–69, 192 and 198. Daniel Gimaret argues that this reflects al-Ashʿarī's own position. Gimaret, *La Doctrine d'al-Ashʿarī*, pp. 201–6. See also Frank, 'Elements in the Development of the Teaching of al-Ashʿarī', pp. 169–70; Allard, *Le Problème des Attributs Divins*, pp. 413–16. Thanks to David Vishanoff for his comments on this point.
100 Ibn Fūrak, *Maqālāt al-shaykh Abī al-Ḥasan al-Ashʿarī*, p. 65.
101 Ibn Fūrak, *Maqālāt al-shaykh Abī al-Ḥasan al-Ashʿarī*, p. 59.

while it encompasses limitless meanings, it remains an undifferentiated singularity.[102]

The view that differentiation in God's speech is only applied within the created sphere goes back to the formulation of Ibn Kullāb.[103] Such a position raises the obvious problem of grounding the different judgements within the normative content of divine speech. For some Ashʿarīs, such as al-Bāqillānī and al-Juwaynī, the single eternal attribute of speech was therefore understood as consisting of its particular commands and assertions.[104] Furthermore, as Omar Farahat implicitly points out, the logic of this move was to define 'divine speech as meanings that constitute attributes of God'.[105] Yet if divine speech is not truly a single attribute, but in effect a multiplicity of eternal speech acts, it would seem that the magical aura around the seven essential attributes has been dispelled and the Māturīdī position that God's actions are eternal all but conceded.

So far in this chapter, I have tried to shed new light on the theology of divine speech within the Ḥanafī-Māturīdī school. While the transcendence and eternality of God's speech is strenuously upheld, there is a sustained focus on its multiplicity – the translatability of its outward expressions matched by the plurality of its inward meanings. I will now turn to how such insights may be brought to bear on an extension of this tradition.

Contemporary theistic philosophy of religion usually ties the question of God's speech to that of revelation. George Mavrodes introduces three models of revelation, of which one, the 'communication model', reflects the idea of revelation as the self-disclosure of God conceived as personal and speaking.[106] He also points out that conceiving of revelation in this way raises the question of whether the concept of revelation should include not just assertions – the most obvious kind of communication – but also commands and questions.[107] His conclusion is that this is mainly a terminological quibble, and although he is not inclined to include them, he sees no problem in stretching the idea of revelation in this way.[108] A second question in Jewish

102 Ibn Fūrak, *Maqālāt al-shaykh Abī al-Ḥasan al-Ashʿarī*, pp. 66. He is, however, ascribed the position that God's speech in its eternality is nothing but *khabar* in al-Bayāḍī, *Ishārāt al-marām*, p. 179. Cf. Vishanoff, *The Formation of Islamic Hermeneutics*, pp. 156–57, n. 22.

103 Vishanoff, *The Formation of Islamic Hermeneutics*, p. 153.

104 Vishanoff, *The Formation of Islamic Hermeneutics*, p. 179; Farahat, *The Foundation of Norms in Islamic Jurisprudence and Theology*, pp. 111–12.

105 Farahat, *The Foundation of Norms in Islamic Jurisprudence and Theology*, p. 114.

106 Mavrodes, *Revelation in Religious Belief*, pp. 111–12.

107 Mavrodes, *Revelation in Religious Belief*, p. 119.

108 Mavrodes, *Revelation in Religious Belief*, p. 122. Nicholas Wolterstorff is more assertive on this point, seeking to argue that, though normative elements are part of speech, they are not the media of revelation, but merely occur as part of its content. Wolterstorff, *Divine Discourse*, p. 35. I will not attempt to analyse Wolterstorff's distinction, as it is not relevant to my concerns in this chapter.

and Christian theology is how to deal with the many Biblical texts in which divine communication seems to manifest through the telling of history by (inspired) human authors, rather than God's direct speech.[109]

Some of these questions do not really arise in Islamic thought. For the Qur'an, there is a complete, unambiguous match between revelation and divine speech, such that it is explicitly understood to be God's spoken revelation to the Prophet Muḥammad, in which He informs, commands, prohibits and questions.[110] Moreover, Q. 96:1, traditionally considered the first revelation, commands the Prophet: 'Speak in the name of your Lord who created (*iqraʾ bi-ismi rabbika alladhī khalaq*)'.[111] At the same time, the Qur'an shows God speaking without obvious revelation – for example, to His angels and to the people of Paradise and Hell[112] – and there are arguably modes of revelation, or inspiration, that do not require divine speech, such as the prophetic Sunna.

It is useful at this juncture to introduce a four-stage model developed by Mohammed Arkoun. He describes how the Word of God is received through a process of Qur'anic Discourse, thereby making its way into the Official Closed Corpus in the form of the *muṣḥaf*, and then finally engaged through the discourses of an Interpretive Community.[113] Mapping three of the four stages of this model onto my discussion so far will help to set the scope for the remainder of this chapter:

1. Word of God – the nature of God's attribute of speech.
2. Official Closed Corpus – the expressions of the Arabic Qur'an in the canonical *muṣḥaf* and *qirāʾāt* (oral readings).
3. Interpretive Community – the theological articulations of the Māturīdī tradition and its interlocutors.

109 Wolterstorff, *Divine Discourse*, p. 30.

110 The divine voice is maintained despite the Qur'an frequently quoting various figures including prophets, angels and the Devil. A few verses, such as Q. 19:64 and Q. 37:164–66, appear to be implicitly in the voice of angels, although this proves no great problem for the scripture's framing. Richard Bell's claim that the first-person plural of majesty, which is frequently used in the Qur'an, can often be read as angels instead of God seems a great exaggeration. See Bell, *Introduction to the Qur'ān*, pp. 61–62.

111 Michael Levine points to the 'first page of the Koran' as an example of implicit deputisation in the context of speech-act theory. Levine, 'God Speak', p. 9. But it is unclear whether he means Q. 96:1 or more likely the *basmala*, 'In the name of God . . .' Whereas Q. 96:1 provides an explicit instruction for the Prophet to recite in God's name, the *basmala* is usually read as an invocation for performing an action seeking God's blessing, as used by Noah when disembarking from the Ark in Q. 11:41 and Solomon in his letter to the Queen of Sheba in Q. 27:30. I thank Sohaib Saeed for his reflections on this question.

112 For example, see Q. 2:32, 43:68–70 and 23:108, respectively.

113 Arkoun, *The Unthought in Contemporary Islamic Thought*, p. 99. A broadly similar model is found in Saeed, *Interpreting the Qur'an*, pp. 39–41.

The missing stage is what Arkoun terms Qur'anic Discourse, by which he means the process of revelation, particularities of individual discourses revealed at different times and in dialectical tension with opponents, and the Qur'an's metaphorical, semiotic and intertextual structure, before it was transformed into a canonical scripture.[114] Although I do not necessarily endorse Arkoun's specific understanding of these elements, I fully agree with the significance of this stage of analysis. Several modern Muslim thinkers have shown an interest in rethinking the process of revelation and the role of the Prophet Muḥammad within it. Prominent names in this regard include Arkoun himself, Nasr Abu Zayd, Abdolkarim Soroush and Fazlur Rahman.[115] Recent non-Muslim scholars have generally been more reluctant to address this question, likely due to its polemical connotations, with Watt a notable exception.[116] There have also been a plurality of figures, with both confessional and non-confessional perspectives, who have argued for the significance of examining the process of Qur'anic formulation into canon, as well as the structure and dynamics of Qur'anic discourses in their canonical order.[117]

Despite the inherent interest of studying Qur'anic Discourse in Arkoun's sense, I think that it is neither within the scope of my current project, nor necessary for it. The first proposition is easy to defend: the structure of the *kalām* manuals on which I am building, my avowed intention to deal with questions of prophecy and revelation at a later time, as well as the dictates of space, make more than brief comments on the question untenable. The second proposition may be more contentious. One may feel that, in order to theologically connect the locutions in the *muṣḥaf* to the attribute of divine speech (however conceived), one must have a fully realised account of the 'process' by which the Qur'an as an 'event', in the words of Anthony Johns, emerged from it.[118] I do not think that this is the case. Again, it is of course very desirable to be able to account in theological terms for the historical processes that led to the Qur'an as a canonical text. Yet when one holds the *muṣḥaf* in one's hands, or recites a verse from it, there are pertinent theological questions that are of a more universal quality: in what sense does

114 See Arkoun, *The Unthought in Contemporary Islamic Thought*, pp. 80–83.

115 See Arkoun, *The Unthought in Contemporary Islamic Thought*, pp. 72–74; Abu Zayd, *Naqd al-khiṭāb al-dīnī*, p. 126; Soroush, *The Expansion of Prophetic Experience*, pp. 17–18; Rahman, *Islam*, p. 33. The same figures, except for Arkoun and the addition of Muhammad Shabestari, are studied in Akbar, *Contemporary Perspectives on Revelation and Qur'anic Hermeneutics*.

116 See Watt, *Islamic Revelation in the Modern World*, pp. 108–13.

117 For example, see the work of Mohammed Arkoun, Nasr Abu Zayd, Angelika Neuwirth, M. A. S. Abdel Haleem, Aziz Al-Azmeh, Nicolai Sinai, Anthony Johns, Michel Cuypers, Salwa El-Awa and many others.

118 Johns, 'A Humanistic Approach to *iʿjāz* in the Qur'an', p. 80.

God speak? And how do expressions that one can read or recite relate to that speech?

As premodern Muslim theologians understood, these two questions are not dependent on analysis of the particularities of revelation to the Prophet Muḥammad and the canonisation activities of the early community. The first one concerns the rational possibility and nature of divine speech, while the second one examines the connection of speech in principle between human and divine levels. As we have seen, the answer to these questions could be applied to the Torah as much as to the Qur'an. Using technical language adopted by Wolterstorff from John Austin, the scope of this chapter includes the illocutionary level of divine speech, God's commands, assertions and so on, as well as the locutionary level of human language in Qur'anic expressions, but not the perlocutionary level of its reception by the Prophet and those after him until today.[119]

In what follows, I aim to show that Wolterstorff's construal of speech act theory for divine speech can be combined effectively with the theological position that I have been developing. For a start, Wolterstorff acknowledges that individual instances of speech acts are tropes, which fits the position that I have adopted.[120] More importantly, Wolterstorff presents a careful account of what speech involves, which underpins his later discussion of how it can be said that God speaks. Before turning to that pragmatic level of analysis, I will consider again what it means to attribute the property of speech to God in ontological and epistemological terms.

Merold Westphal points out that some picture of predication, which Wolterstorff does not supply in his book, is needed for the claim that God literally speaks, a position on which they both agree.[121] Westphal's suggestion, following Aquinas, is that God's speech must be understood as literal but analogical:

> It is analogical because divine discourse is both like and unlike human discourse; but this is not metaphor, because the performance of illocutionary acts belongs properly and primarily to God and only derivatively and by participation to human creatures.[122]

In its general analogical movement and assertion of the real primacy of the divine over the worldly level, this description is akin to that of

119 Wolterstorff, *Divine Discourse*, pp. 32–33. For discussion of some of the problems associated with revelation via intermediaries, see Mavrodes, *Revelation in Religious Belief*, pp. 145–47.

120 Wolterstorff, *Divine Discourse*, p. 77.

121 Westphal, 'On Reading God the Author', pp. 273–74.

122 Westphal, 'On Reading God the Author', p. 273.

al-Māturīdī,[123] while in the specific disavowal of metaphor it is similar to the position adopted by al-Bazdawī.[124] In his response to Westphal, Wolterstorff points out that the context of Aquinas' introduction of the category literal but analogical is the doctrine of divine simplicity. The predication of anything to God must be an analogy because God is simple, and so predicates cannot apply univocally between the human and the divine.[125] Wolterstorff seems unwilling to concede that the predication of speech to God should be taken as analogical, preferring instead to state that it is a borderline case, an example of language that does not fit very well.[126] It is possible that he avoids affirming analogy from an understanding that it entails divine simplicity and is thereby problematic for the predication of distinct qualities to God.[127]

But whereas simplicity arguably requires analogical predication, I have already proposed that the converse is not true.[128] The Māturīdī position towards divine attributes that I have been exploring is to affirm them as both substantive and analogical with created properties. This means that they can be distinguished from God and each other but lack the whatnesses of their worldly counterparts. So, for example, God's speech is not the same as His power, and the diverse functions of speech and power as humanly possessed properties act as useful analogies to this truth. At the same time, there is a very real difference in the eternal nature of God's speech and power to anything that can be exercised by contingent creatures. In the language that I have been using, divine tropes never exactly resemble created ones.

Returning to Wolterstorff's account of the features that characterise speech, he highlights a crucial distinction between illocutionary speech acts as normative activity and the locutionary utterance of certain words or other indications used to convey them. At the social level of discourse, a speaker makes assertions and commands, for instance, not just by the appropriate vocalisations or gestures, but because their speech acts put them into a certain normative standing of 'having asserted . . .' or 'having commanded . . .'[129] This forms one half of an ordered pair, the other being an action in a certain manner and circumstance for a person at a time, such that performing it would count as performing the speech act.[130]

123 See page 60.
124 See page 206.
125 Wolterstorff, 'Response to Helm, Quinn, and Westphal', p. 299.
126 Wolterstorff, 'Response to Helm, Quinn, and Westphal', p. 300.
127 See Wolterstorff, 'Divine Simplicity', pp. 534–35, 551.
128 See pages 141–42.
129 Wolterstorff, *Divine Discourse*, p. 85.
130 Wolterstorff, *Divine Discourse*, pp. 89–90.

He points out that this is all embedded in a system of language and sets of arrangements for speaking: individual stipulations or conventions, which are socially grounded.[131] In a powerful passage, Wolterstorff remarks:

> The myth dies hard that to read a text for authorial discourse is to enter the dark world of the author's psyche. It's nothing of the sort. It is to read to discover what assertings, what promisings, what requestings, what commandings, are rightly to be ascribed to the author on the ground of her having set down the words that she did in the situation in which she set them down.[132]

Wolterstorff hits on a dual insight with implications for the way in which divine speech can be conceptualised and justified (it also has hermeneutic applications, but I will not engage them here). On the one hand, language is intersubjective. We inhabit a shared world of discourse, and the propositions that we can form about it, if asserted, only make sense within this context. Moreover, our knowledge of the world operates within the conventions of social language. This means that, when God speaks to us, He speaks to us in a way that we can understand within the conventions by which language is expressed.[133] On the other hand, if speech is inherently normative, as this theory demands, then in order to understand how God can speak, one must show how He can enter into normative relations with human beings.[134]

Wolterstorff thus goes looking for a theory through which God can be situated within the frame of moral rights and duties that he makes central to speech. It is obvious that God commands and obligates human beings, but the above account requires more than that; it needs Him to be obliged in some sense too. If speech is normative in the way that Wolterstorff claims, then God does not only obligate Himself through explicit promises, important though these may be, but even through the merest assertion. Why? Because when entering the normative standing of 'having asserted', one takes on all the obligations associated with that act – for instance, the obligation not to assert what is inconsistent.

The theory that Wolterstorff reaches for is a version of divine command theory. A standard account of this theory, and one influential at the time

131 Wolterstorff, *Divine Discourse*, p. 91. There are significant parallels with ideas developed by Adolf Reinach, a student of Husserl, in the early twentieth century. See MacIntyre, *Edith Stein*, pp. 55–57.

132 Wolterstorff, *Divine Discourse*, p. 93.

133 This point could be used to justify al-Māturīdī's position that even Moses required a created language as a medium for his reception of divine speech. See page 201.

134 Wolterstorff, *Divine Discourse*, p. 95.

he was writing, claims that God cannot be obliged, and so he makes it his main objective to rebut this position.[135] In a critical response to his work, Philip Quinn points out that God may not be subject to obligations, yet still have other normative conditions attach to His speech.[136] For instance, even if He is not obliged to be consistent in His assertions, it may be good for Him to be so. In responding to this point, Wolterstorff argues that such an idea of God's goodness as the ultimate ground of obligation is precisely what is at stake between a standard divine command theory and his view. As he describes the standard theory, it claims that an act is obligatory if it is required on pain of disobeying the command of God. This makes God's commands the basic ground of morality and cannot apply to God Himself. Wolterstorff's preferred understanding of the theory is that an act is obligatory if it is required on pain of moral impairment. This means that God can be obliged by His own assertions due to his moral perfection.[137] The upshot of this is that Wolterstorff responds to Quinn's contention by clarifying that he sees the concept of obligation ultimately subservient to God's goodness.

Translating this discussion into the field of Islamic theology, I wish to return to a theme that I have already touched on in Chapter 5 of the present book and addressed more fully in Chapter 2 of *The Qur'an and the Just Society*: grounding a natural law theory on the Māturīdī concept of God's wisdom.[138] In the present context, I understand my formulation of divine wisdom as able to avoid the argument within divine command theory over God's ability to take on obligations. I see God's eternal attribute of wisdom as the ground for His own promises, the commands given to humanity, and any other obligations or normative standings taken on as part of speech. Wisdom thus fills a role akin to God's goodness within much of Christian thought. This is significant when comparing it to the best known Islamic divine command theory, which was developed within Ashʿarism and still has defenders today.[139]

In order to move the debate forward from my previous articulations, I will respond to a thoughtful review of *The Qur'an and the Just Society* by Edward Moad who raises the question of whether my account of wisdom really provides the foundation for human ethical activity that I think it does.[140] I appreciate his detailed engagement and constructive critique of

135 Quinn, 'Can God Speak? Does God Speak?', p. 260.
136 Quinn, 'Can God Speak? Does God Speak?', pp. 260–61.
137 Wolterstorff, 'Response to Helm, Quinn, and Westphal', p. 297.
138 See Harvey, *The Qur'an and the Just* Society, pp. 41–42; Harvey, 'Whose Justice? When Māturīdī Meets MacIntyre' (forthcoming).
139 See Farahat, *The Foundation of Norms in Islamic Jurisprudence and Theology*, pp. 223–25.
140 The following discussion is with reference to Moad, review of *The Qur'an and the Just Society*, by Ramon Harvey, p. 3.

my work, although I do not agree with his analysis of the Māturīdī position. Hopefully, in true MacIntyrean fashion his objections will allow me to better formulate my case, while at the same time allowing me to show how this encounter advances the present argument about God's speech.

The background to Moad's contention is the debate between the Muʿtazila, moral realists, and the Ashʿarīs, moral anti-realists. I broadly agree with his characterisation of their positions as the two horns of a Euthyphro dilemma: either morality is set externally, in which case it is restrictive to God's freedom, or internally by God's fiat, in which case it appears arbitrary. In the present context, the claim that God is morally arbitrary entails Wolterstorff's point that He cannot take on obligations inherent to speech, for example, to promise. Moad acknowledges that I introduce the Māturīdī attribute of eternal divine wisdom to try to find a resolution to this problem, but he thinks that I am unsuccessful. His argument is that, because Māturīdīs hold that wisdom cannot be independent of God, it falls under the same charge of anti-realism, and therefore arbitrariness, as the Ashʿarī system. In other words, he contends that there is no difference between grounding moral value in God's willed commands and in His wisdom, as neither one allows a realism that underwrites the possibility of natural moral knowledge.[141]

I think Moad here misses a crucial distinction between the schools in the Māturīdīs' construal of wisdom. While basing moral value on God's wisdom means that it is not independent of Him like the Muʿtazila claim, it is also not a position of anti-realism like the Ashʿarīs. For the Ashʿarīs, it is only contingently true that our ideas of what is right and wrong may match that which God commands. There is no reason why the command that is received today must match the one that was received under a previous dispensation. Moreover, there is no attribute to determine the consistency of the eternal will with the order of creation and no basis for human knowledge to be able to link the two.[142] Hence, Omar Farahat argues that the claim that the Ashʿarī conception of God is arbitrary is inaccurate; it is rather that we have no epistemic basis to know what design there may be in His actions.[143] But this means that, if Wolterstorff is right, the Ashʿarī picture provides us with no guarantee that God is bound by the normative

141 For a related discussion, see Hare, *God's Command*, p. 220.

142 Kurt argues that the Ashʿarīs did uphold the principle of divine wisdom and that their stance was an unintentional consequence of their reaction to the Muʿtazila. Kurt, *Creation*, pp. 45–46. I would answer that the reality of a theological position is precisely revealed in its response to challenges, and the Ashʿarī counter to Muʿtazilism reveals a system in which divine wisdom can only be conceived on the basis of the untrammelled divine will.

143 Farahat, *The Foundation of Norms in Islamic Jurisprudence and Theology*, p. 98.

obligations of speech acts and will not lie or fail to keep His promises. The use of scriptural descriptions to ground this belief would be circular.

This is not at all the same as the Māturīdī position, in which divine wisdom acts as a ground for morality, the nature of the world and knowledge about it. To put it another way, our natural knowledge reflects what God has – through His wisdom – determined to be the good.[144] Yet as a matter of absolute metaphysical necessity, God is bound to act according to His own wisdom. This ensures the required consistency for moral knowledge, as it is known by human actors that for God to act against what He has determined to be the good would be rationally abhorrent. For the purpose of the present chapter, this ensures that God can enter normative standings in His speech with humanity.

The arguably problematic nature of the Ashʿarī system is implicitly identified by Abu Zayd in his book *Naqd al-khiṭāb al-dīnī* in the course of arguing that all texts emerge from a created linguistic system.[145] He proposes that, if the Qur'an is not understood in this way, but is treated differently due to its divine origin, then it becomes unapproachable to human beings.[146] While he denies that he adopts the theology of the Muʿtazila, but instead wants to show that their position illustrates a way forward, his comments strikingly parallel the critique made by the Muʿtazilī ʿAbd al-Jabbār al-Hamadhānī (d. 415/1025) towards al-Bāqillānī.[147] David Vishanoff demonstrates the extent to which al-Bāqillānī's hermeneutic treats divine speech as inherently ambiguous due to its restriction to Arabic expressions without ordinary non-linguistic cues.[148] Whereas al-Bāqillānī regards the need to suspend judgement barring definitive evidence 'a corollary of his Ashʿarī theory of God's eternal speech',[149] based on the above discussion I would argue that this relative inaccessibility is not due to the speech's eternality, but the anti-realism of the Ashʿarī approach to it.[150] The Māturīdī system, as I have been interpreting it, uses the notion of eternal divine wisdom to both preserve a shared regime of meaning between God and humanity, and to maintain theological transcendence. This normative

144 In al-Māturīdī's picture, God sets the bounds of how much of His wisdom and moral value can be naturally known, which is limited. Harvey, *The Qur'an and the Just Society*, p. 37. See pages 172–73. The important point is that this theological position justifies a core of rational inferences about God's actions that securely grounds the 'moral' relationship between human and divine.

145 Abu Zayd, *Naqd al-khiṭāb al-dīnī*, p. 203.

146 Abu Zayd, *Naqd al-khiṭāb al-dīnī*, p. 206.

147 Vishanoff, *The Formation of Islamic Hermeneutics*, pp. 146–47.

148 Vishanoff, *The Formation of Islamic Hermeneutics*, pp. 181–84.

149 Vishanoff, *The Formation of Islamic Hermeneutics*, p. 182.

150 On this point, see Farahat, *The Foundation of Norms in Islamic Jurisprudence and Theology*, pp. 97–98.

link is also expressed by the Māturīdī emphasis on the translatability of the meanings of God's speech, demonstrating confidence that ambiguities within the Arabic text of the Qur'an do not threaten its communicative function.

In these features, my development of the Māturīdī tradition has both similarities with, and important differences to, the theory of speech acts that Vishanoff extracts from the work of the Ḥanbalī Abū Yaʿlā (d. 458/1065–66). Like Abū Yaʿlā, I understand speech as acts that take their meaning through address within certain sets of circumstances.[151] Yet unlike him, I neither accept a divine command theory, nor that the Arabic words of the Qur'an are eternal. I contend that, in the way in which I have framed the discussion, it is possible to avoid the paradox that Vishanoff identifies in Abū Yaʿlā's claim that God's speech is an eternal act.[152]

If I have shown how to understand the claim that God speaks, what then does it mean for the Qur'an to be divine speech? (Deferring discussion of the revelation question means that I am, for the present study, taking the divine origin of the Qur'an as a premise). I should mention from the outset that I am not merely looking here for a formulation of words to preserve the doctrine that the Qur'an is eternal but want to get to the substance of the relationship between the temporal Arabic expressions of the Qur'an and the eternal meanings of God's speech.[153]

I have already constructively argued that God's action of speaking is not metaphorical but analogous to human speech. Looking at the Māturīdī tradition, the most significant strand of theology independent of the Ashʿarī system is that traced from al-Māturīdī to al-Bazdawī. I have already noted the consistency and development between their positions. In summary,

151 Vishanoff, *The Formation of Islamic Hermeneutics*, pp. 244, 247–48.

152 See Vishanoff, *The Formation of Islamic Hermeneutics*, pp. 248–49.

153 A proposal somewhere between a new theological position and a reformulation of terms is made in an unpublished text by al-Ghursī, as described by Aaron Spevack. He draws on later Ashʿarī-Māturīdīs to provide a new category in between *kalām nafsī* and *kalām lisānī*, which he terms *kalām-maʿnawī-nafsī*. This is an aspect of the eternal divine attribute of speech in an Arabic language form of the Qur'an, which retains the sequencing of letters but lacks temporal succession or instantiation in any written or oral creation. Spevack, 'The Qur'an and God's Speech According to the Later Ashʿarī-Māturīdī Verifiers', pp. 73–76. This idea is interesting but certainly problematic from the Māturīdī standpoint, as it is unclear that Arabic, or any language, can exist without temporality. The features al-Ghursī describes for *kalām-maʿnawī-nafsī* seem to have a whatness that is drawn from creation, and as such do not meet the Māturīdī condition for the avoidance of *tashbīh*. Spevack rightly points out that these qualities represent a step towards a Ḥanbali position (pp. 72–73). But it is notable that the Ḥanbalī theologian Abū Yaʿlā was against a concept of sequence within divine speech. See Vishanoff, *The Formation of Islamic Hermeneutics*, p. 249, n. 428.

both adopted three strategies for relating God's action of speaking to the Qur'an (or a prior revealed scripture):

1. The Qur'an acts as an indication (*dāll*) or concordance (*muwāfaqa*) to the meanings of God's speech.
2. It is metaphorically, not literally, God's speech.
3. It is analogous to sending a message or writing down a poem.

As I have shown in the preceding discussion, one must not get stuck on the specific terminology introduced to indicate the relationship between temporal human language and eternal divine meanings at the expense of clarifying its nature. Whether one uses *dāll*, *muwāfaqa*, *ʿibāra* or *ḥikāya*, the real question is how to adequately explain what kind of process these terms stand in for. The invocation of metaphor is of a different order and the motivation for it is obvious enough – both were concerned that to say the Qur'an was literally God's speech would lead to the traditionalist position that its Arabic form is eternal. Yet the reason for the reticience of other Māturīdīs on this point is that they worried that, if the Qur'an was only metaphorically God's speech, it was not actually so at all. I consider this a misstep by the two thinkers, because it leads to an unnecessary problem avoided by the third strategy, which invokes an apt analogy between the Qur'an and the familiar messages sent by human beings.[154] Not only does this cohere with the analogical move at the heart of *kalām* reasoning about divine attributes, but it also fits with the Qur'an's self-proclaimed status as a message and provides a direct point of entry to Wolterstorff's use of speech act theory. Wolterstorff points out that, when a prophet speaks on behalf of God, the illocutionary speech of the divine is expressed via locutions in human language.[155]

Taking this model in specifically Islamic terms, I propose that the Arabic expressions of the Qur'an are literally God's locutionary speech conveyed through a created medium, while the eternal meanings thereby expressed are His illocutionary speech. Instead of leaving the connection between created expression and divine meaning a mystery papered over with a technical term, it is possible to provide a credible theory. The eternal, normative illocutionary aspects of God's speech, grounded in wisdom, correspond to their created indications in the context of generated arrangements and the language conventions by which these are known. When God speaks through the Qur'an, He is ultimately generating Arabic locutions (with His *takwīn*) that work to perform the required illocutionary speech act within

154 See Soskice, *Metaphor and Religious Language*, p. 64.
155 Wolterstorff, *Divine Discourse*, pp. 47–48.

the context of the revealed utterance and subsequently in its recording and transmission. This theory is extremely powerful: it can deal with the possibility of recitation according to meaning within the early community, the translation of the Qur'an and the revelation of previous scriptures in other languages.

The only way in which I think one can make sense of the range of manifested divine speech is by construing it as eternal action, specifically an illocutionary plurality of divine speech acts with corresponding created locutions. Just as in the previous chapter I argued that *takwīn* must be considered a shorthand for the totality of God's eternal actions, so too must *kalām* be considered the name for a plurality of God's speech acts.[156] This is not a case of composition within a single attribute, but a multiplicity of eternal divine tropes that comprise God's nature. Based on the principles that I have outlined in Chapter 4, I think that this position can be coherently held without violating divine transcendence or unicity.[157] If one is willing to admit that God is non-simple and has substantive eternal attributes, then possession of an infinite or indefinite number of them is no less defensible than a finite, or small, number such as seven. In fact, I think it is a less arbitrary and more coherent proposition.

As this discussion illustrates, the present chapter on God's speech and the possibility of divine communication within creation is the culmination of the book. Only through reasoning analogically from the world to God against the backdrop of revealed scripture and then developing a systematic theory of the divine nature with deeper investigation into key attributes is it possible to rationally account for the Qur'an as *kalām allāh*. If this is the apex of the current theological enquiry, it is now incumbent on me to look back at what I have discovered and ahead to what may come from it.

156 If God's *takwīn* can be subsumed within His *kalām* – which I have indicated is a direction envisaged by Māturīdī theologians (see page 181) – then this position may be comparable to the Breath of the All-Merciful (*nafas al-raḥmān*), as expressed by Muḥyī al-Dīn Ibn al-ʿArabī (d. 638/1240). See Chittick, *The Sufi Path of Knowledge*, p. 19. A contemporary version of this idea is found in Kurt, *Creation*, pp. 65–71. The current enquiry shows that such a view of divine creative speech can coherently fit within a Māturīdī approach to transcendence and action.

157 See pages 156–57.

Conclusion

From the first pages of this book, I have set out to tackle the theological problem of finite human reasoning about God, eternal and transcendent. The mode of thought that I have pursued is couched within a specific, venerable intellectual tradition, the Māturīdī school of Islamic *kalām*. Although I frame my project within the field of contemporary philosophical theology, it is this *kalām* tradition in which it is rooted, from which it draws vitality and, I hope, for which it grows seeds for future renewal.

In this conclusion, I organise summative remarks on the three major themes that comprise my approach to working from a theological tradition, each drawing on material from various chapters. This will allow me to trace connections between the different parts of my enquiry in a way that was not always possible within the foregoing text. These themes are as follows: (1) the system of al-Māturīdī; (2) the development of the Māturīdī tradition subsequent to al-Māturīdī, including debate with the Ashʿarī school; and (3) my constructive solutions to contemporary theological and philosophical problems.

My reading of al-Māturīdī's theological system is at the heart of the intellectual contribution of this book. Along with my main intention to use his positions – sometimes surprising by the orthodoxies of later Sunnī *kalām* – as a springboard for my own thought, in select areas I have advanced new interpretations of his ideas. Rudolph's magisterial work in tracing al-Māturīdī's predecessors and examining important elements of his system has made my job considerably easier, and I have sought to verify, refine and build upon his findings.

A significant contention within this project is that al-Māturīdī, although deeply concerned with providing an epistemic justification for belief in God and the truth of Islam, is not a foundationalist. In contrast to a commonly held interpretation of his admittedly opaque text, I argue that his position is closer to what Wykstra terms 'sensible evidentialism'. He accepts the possibility of providing secure rational justification for theological beliefs while admitting their social embedding within given traditions. To understand his epistemic approach requires appreciation of the delicate interplay that he articulates between human reason and tradition. The three ways to gain truth – the senses, reports and enquiry – are not treated as indubitable foundations, but means available for proper public justification of belief. Of these, I propose a revised interpretation of his theory of *tawātur*, arguing for a naturalistic reading that founds its certainty on a socially grounded, rational process of investigation.

For al-Māturīdī's ontology, I vindicate Rudolph's case that he is not an atomist, but rather that he holds a variety of bundle theory, against recent alternative interpretations. Yet I bring additional evidence to demonstrate that his conception of *ṭabāʾiʿ*, accident-like natures that form into bodies, should not be identified with the ancient doctrine of four primary qualities or elements. Discussions drawn from his *Taʾwīlāt al-qurʾān* show that, while he was aware of several such definitions of *ṭabāʾiʿ* within his milieu, his own use of the term is closer to the philosophical notion of dispositions.

Al-Māturīdī's theological method draws from a varied heritage with a genealogy indebted to Transoxianan Ḥanafism, Baghdadī Muʿtazilism, the thought of figures such as al-Ḥusayn al-Najjār, al-Kindī's reception of the Aristotelian-Neoplatonic tradition, hints of Stoic ideas and more. A point I highlight as integral to his system is that human reason is placed at the centre of the world and acts as the basic metric by which reality is to be measured and the nature of God articulated. He adopts a procedure that he calls *taḥqīq*, or verification, which allows for both *mithl*, analogical inference of God based on aspects of the world, and *khilāf*, God's transcendent difference from it. When applying *mithl*, al-Māturīdī is consistently careful to note that, whereas analogy verifies God's *hastiyya*, or isness, it does not indicate that God's *māʾiyya*, or whatness, is like that of created things. In the case studies of Chapters 5 to 7, this means that, while God has knowledge, wisdom, creative action and speech by analogy with a person, His possession of these attributes is not within time and space, nor subject to the contingencies of His creation. One of the significant consequences of *mithl* is that it provides a kind of 'bottom-up' predication system, an inference that just as properties are integral to their objects in the world, God possesses substantive attributes as His divine nature. Moreover, unlike the classical Māturīdī tradition, this nature, or *dhāt*, is neither a reified substratum, nor different from the set of His attributes. At the same time, al-Māturīdī avoids any possibility of anthropomorphism, or *tashbīh*.

The method of *khilāf* is 'clearer' as al-Māturīdī himself puts it and, as well as restricting the extent of *mithl*, leads to more succinct treatments of God's eternality and lack of change. It also lets him develop a version of the *kalām* cosmological argument based on the impossibility of a pre-eternally existing world. Yet it is *mithl* that suggests that God acts as a personal agent instead of a 'natural' cause in determining the state of the actual world. This is one of the early examples of the argument of *takhṣīṣ* within the *kalām* tradition.

In my investigation of al-Māturīdī's theology of the divine nature and attributes, I have confirmed Rudolph's finding that he does not build on a sophisticated existing Ḥanafī tradition in this area, as could be claimed if *Al-Fiqh al-akbar II* was understood as available in his milieu. Instead, while there are certain continuities with prior Ḥanafī thought, he does break fresh theological ground. Nowhere is his voice more distinctive in the *kalām* tradition than when he discusses God's wisdom, or *ḥikma*. In his treatment, he defends an eternal attribute of wisdom that is the ultimate explanation for God's creation of the world, the ground for His actions and the possibility of their rational appreciation by human beings. Though traces of his understanding remain in the tradition that took his name, it never again was so central to a Sunnī theological system.

A second divine attribute to which al-Māturīdī contributed a decisive intervention is that of creative action, or *takwīn*. Whereas the idea that God's actions are eternal already existed within the Ḥanafī tradition, al-Māturīdī seems to have been the first figure to provide a systematic rational defence of the doctrine in the face of Muʿtazilī critique. His contribution provides the major lines of enquiry that the Māturīdī tradition developed to greater heights of sophistication: he argues that it is not a sign of God's incapacity for His actions to be eternal, but their effects temporal; that likewise this position does not necessitate the eternality of the world; and that it can coherently interpret the Qur'anic phrase '"Be!" and it is (*kun fa-yakūn*)'.

The final attribute that I have discussed is divine speech, which is integrally connected to the Qur'an. I have suggested that al-Māturīdī's position may have built on certain elements of Abū Ḥanīfa's contested legacy by treating the Arabic form of the Qur'an as a created entity and, in consonance with this, not limiting the expression of divine speech to any single language. He expends considerable effort to defend against Muʿtazilī attack the proposition that God really speaks and does so eternally. The core principle, once again, is that divine speech must be understood as literal yet analogous to human speech. This means that, for al-Māturīdī, God's speech is an eternal action and all elements of contingency within the world are to be negated from it. When discussing the Qur'an, the manifestation of divine speech in the world, al-Māturīdī reaches for several techniques to reinforce God's transcendence. He uses the term concordance (*muwāfaqa*), metaphor (*majāz*), and – in my view most coherently – the analogy of a message or other kind of recorded speech. He also highlights that no created form can exhaust the multiplicity of divine meanings and that God can express His speech via something else without restriction. Finally, he precisely delineates the questions upon which one may suspend judgement (*waqf*) with respect to God's speech.

Before widening the scope from al-Māturīdī's own contributions, I am now in the position to make a brief general observation about the relationship between his two surviving texts, *Kitāb al-tawḥīd* and *Ta'wīlāt al-qur'ān*. The typical pattern in the *Ta'wīlāt*, which may well have been compiled from his lectures, is to introduce technical theological problems related to Qur'anic verses after his initial consideration of various interpretations of their basic import. His solutions appear to utilise summaries of positions that are articulated with more complexity within the dialectical structure of *Kitāb al-tawḥīd*. In his theological treatise, although he regularly cites Qur'anic verses in the context of substantiating his arguments, he rarely provides detailed exegetical elaboration. Nonetheless, I have found occasions in which a position that may have been derived in connection to an exegetical problem is introduced within *Kitāb al-tawḥīd*, without reference to specific verses.[1] This all points to a complex interdependence between al-Māturīdī the theologian and al-Māturīdī the theologically minded exegete. A study that attempts to unravel the methodological and thematic connections between these two modes of his intellectual life would be of great value.

Al-Māturīdī's specific achievements combined with his relatively unexceptional status within the formative period of the tradition suggest that his reputation and authority increased after sustained reflection upon the power and originality of his theological arguments. The Māturīdī school developed by filtering his articulations through both internal debate and external polemics with other traditions. I identified four periods within this process. When the earliest stage, up until the end of the fifth/eleventh century, draws from the teaching of al-Māturīdī, it does so as just one among several significant fourth/tenth-century Samarqandī theologians. During this time, al-Māturīdī was not necessarily considered more notable than his contemporary al-Ḥakīm al-Samarqandī or his student al-Rustughfanī. The foregrounding of al-Māturīdī as the most important single figure in the tradition is a marker of the onset of the classical period and appears to be provoked by the entry of Ashʿarism as a defined body of thought into Transoxiana. This competition may account for the shift towards formulations sharing a common language and theological structure, even though key doctrinal differences remained. Several centuries later, it is again an Ashʿarī, Fakhr al-Dīn al-Rāzī, who is the decisive figure in influencing the classical Māturīdī school to adopt a philosophical idiom derived from the internalisation of Avicennan themes. Despite the claims to demonstration (*burhān*), this seems a second-order move of dialectic (*jadal*). In the late classical period, there is an increasing syncretism

1 See page 127, note 14.

between Ashʿarīs and Māturīdīs, and their differences become both formalised and harmonised in *ikhtilāf* literature. The common practice of commenting on Ḥanafī and Māturīdī creedal texts – principally *Al-ʿAqīda al-Nasafiyya*, *Al-Fiqh al-akbar II* and *Al-ʿAqīda al-Ṭaḥāwiyya* – allows core doctrines from the formative and classical periods to coexist with late classical philosophical elaboration. Finally, the *kalām jadīd* of the modern period has three main objectives: to popularise a streamlined theology, to address new questions raised by changed intellectual conditions and to seek engagement and critical synthesis with Western thought.[2] In placing this book within the *kalām jadīd* approach, I am primarily interested in the second and third elements.

In his entry in the first edition of the *Encyclopaedia of Islam*, Duncan MacDonald points to a decisive influence of Māturīdī ideas relating to morality on Ashʿarī thinking until the modern period.[3] The present study has not covered themes relevant to examining this claim, but it has shown that, at least in the fundamental questions of theological method and divine attributes, the two major shifts by which the early Samarqandī tradition became the classical Māturīdī school and then joined the Ashʿarī-Māturīdī pairing were provoked and shaped by Ashʿarī thought. The extent of influence in the other direction is open to further investigation.

Whereas al-Māturīdī upholds God's eternality as part of His transcendent difference from the contingent world, subsequent members of the tradition develop this idea in certain respects. Al-Sālimī explicitly states that God does not have a temporal location; al-Bazdawī shows that eternality implies metaphysical necessity; and al-Ṣābūnī shows the converse is also true. Although Ibn Sīnā's idea of logical necessity became influential within some discourses, especially as transmitted through the work of al-Rāzī, metaphysical necessity, and the cosmological argument that supports it, remained dominant within Māturīdī *kalām*. But a topic in which the Māturīdī tradition increasingly diverged from the position of al-Māturīdī and the early Samarqandī school is the conception of God's *dhāt* as a substratum in which His attributes are established, rather than as a nature comprising His attributes. As far as I have been able to determine, this development is first introduced into Māturīdī *kalām* by al-Sālimī and continues alongside the earlier reading, eventually displacing it. The source is a prior Ashʿarī articulation of the concept, which seems to have emerged from the same milieu as Avicennan ideas that give an ontic primacy to God's *dhāt*. This appears to have opened the space for it to be conceived as

2 See Wielandt, 'Main Trends', p. 749.
3 MacDonald, 'Māturīdī'.

a substratum to which substantive attributes were additional (*zāʾid*). Further research is required to isolate the precise origin of this doctrine.

The influence of Ashʿarism is also prominent in Māturīdī theological developments with respect to individual divine attributes. While there was always a lot in common between the two traditions in their treatment of omniscience, the case is different for the notion of God's wisdom. From the classical era onwards, the early Māturīdī emphasis on this attribute as the basis for an ethical account of divine action was downplayed in favour of an Ashʿarī strategy to understand it as God's knowledge or His perfect action. This meant that it diminished as a distinction between the schools in their conceptions of God, instead often flowing into the debate over creative action, or *takwīn*. As my own constructive arguments show, especially in Chapter 7, the negation of God's wisdom as a substantive eternal attribute does considerable damage to the coherence and versatility of the Māturīdī theological project.

Though the classical Māturīdī tradition's defence of *takwīn* is significant, I have indicated the extent to which it merely works out of the implications of the main theses articulated by al-Māturīdī, expanding the number of arguments for them and responding to objections, instead of developing its core theological conceptions. The main fronts are over whether the category of *ṣifāt al-fiʿl* is eternal and whether there truly is a distinction between *takwīn* and *mukawwan*, as the Māturīdīs in both cases claim and the Ashʿarīs reject. I have also highlighted that notable contemporary commentators on this debate, including Kholeif and Foudeh, have recognised that the attribute of *takwīn* must be construed in relation to the function of God's power, or *qudra*. Kholeif favours the Ashʿarī stance that God's power does not merely define the potential range of God's creative action, but His actual realisation of it. Foudeh, meanwhile, attempts a late classical harmonisation manoeuvre, arguing that each of the two schools affirms what is most important: God's capacity and His realisation of creation within time. I have argued that this approach does not do justice to the particularities of each school's system. As I have suggested, the Māturīdī stance, which treats all of God's acts as eternal, is able to reveal an inconsistency between the Ashʿarī position on divine creative action and speech, hearing and seeing. These latter three properties were treated as actions by the early Māturīdī school before they were systematically brought into line with the dominant Ashʿarī picture of seven essential attributes.

The Māturīdī tradition's stance on the question of divine speech does not undergo a single, linear development, but consists of several interacting strands sharing the core principles of its eternality and transcendence over the contingency of creation. From the early Samarqandī school onwards, there are two main tracks, one which veers closer to al-Māturīdī's position by focusing on the eternality of the Qur'an through its meaning, and another which prefers a cautious, semi-traditionalist formulation that identifies the Qur'an with the speech of God while affirming that His speech is not created. Whereas al-Māturīdī's approach is most closely adhered to by al-Bazdawī, who explicitly accounts for the translatability of the meaning of divine speech into various languages of scripture, the traditionalist track, as represented by the author of *Sharḥ al-fiqh al-akbar*, maintains the earlier Samarqandī position and criticises the Ashʿarī use of the language of *ʿibāra*, or expression, to refer to the created Arabic form. The prevailing classical synthesis is forged by Abū Muʿīn al-Nasafī who takes the concepts of al-Bazdawī and articulates them in the Ashʿarī idiom.

Yet I have argued that focusing on terminology can do injustice to the underlying conceptual positions. When the relevant linguistic discussions relating to the inimitability (*iʿjāz*) of the Qur'an are taken into account, it becomes apparent that the Ḥanafī-Māturīdī approach is defined by a concept of divine speech in which a given meaning can be expressed in any number of linguistic forms, while the dominant Ashʿarī theory holds that each meaning is associated with a single one. Moreover, this debate over outward diversity is matched by another on the inward dimensions of God's speech. The Māturīdīs embrace a multiplicity of meanings within divine speech, a position that I argue is based on the adoption of God's speech acts as varieties of eternal action. The Ashʿarīs have two main positions, with al-Ashʿarī following Ibn Kullāb in understanding divine speech as comprised of a single meaning, with its differentiation occurring within creation, and later prominent figures taking it to contain many meanings. I have highlighted that this latter position amounts to the affirmation of a plurality of speech acts, which indicates from another angle an inconsistency in classical Ashʿarī treatment of the divine attributes.

My own constructive theological efforts are likely to be held up to distinct criteria by the various audiences to which this book is addressed. For those coming to it as a work of *kalām jadīd*, there may be an interest in how well I remain within acceptable canons of Islamic doctrine while articulating positions that are credible in contemporary thought. Philosophers of religion may be more interested in the attempts that I have made to solve problems that cut across theistic and philosophical divides.

In setting out the extent of my engagement with key modern philosophical figures in Chapter 1, I highlighted two as especially significant. MacIntyre's meta-theory of tradition-constituted enquiry justifies situating my thought within the Māturīdī tradition. But I acknowledge that MacIntyre is a moral philosopher and that this project is engaged theologically with questions that do not always overlap with his main concerns.[4] When dealing with specific

4 For an attempt to engage much more substantively with MacIntyre's work, see Harvey, 'Whose Justice? When Māturīdī Meets MacIntyre' (forthcoming).

themes, I have found that putting the ideas of al-Māturīdī and his school in conversation with Husserl has been especially fruitful. It should be clear from my treatment that I am not claiming to be a Husserlian *per se*, nor to have solved every problem raised by introducing Husserl's complex and difficult system to a *kalām* school with a different intellectual trajectory. Instead, I suggest that some of Husserl's concepts, especially his resolution of the realism-idealism dichotomy and the centrality of intentional consciousness for any account of the world, are suitable for rearticulating a core orientation in al-Māturīdī's thought.

The animating idea of a transcendent God who is theologically known through a rational world, which provides the title for the present monograph, is central to al-Māturīdī's contribution to *kalām*, even if it is a more peripheral aspect of Husserl's philosophy. I have argued that, when consciousness is placed at the centre of the world in principle, it leads in a teleological direction towards the transcendent divine. This insight enables important forays in epistemology, ontology and rational arguments for God's existence, as well as proving useful for theology. Seen from a wider historical frame, phenomenology constitutes a rejection of the mechanistic world assumed by modernity's dominant materialism. Husserl's ideas make it possible to recapture elements of the Aristotelian heritage that mesh well with theism, such as teleological thinking, without some of the attendant ontological baggage. As an aside, I have also attempted to show how this post-Kantian philosophical position can be harmonised with Bohr's Copenhagen interpretation of quantum mechanics, although I have been careful not to overstate the case.

Epistemologically, I reject more than a conceptual distinction between existence and essence, taking existence as the verification of a certain nature in an intentional object. I focus on intersubjective propositions that correspond to constructible categorial objects, concrete particulars within the world, or God who is transcendent to both. In all cases, objects of knowledge must be subject to verification by consciousness in principle. This position leads to an intuitionism in mathematics and a logic that drops both bivalence and LEM as found in Brouwer and (I argue following van Atten) Husserl. It is then possible to ground an intuitionistic set theory, such that in discussion of ontological properties, whether of things in the created order, or God, the abstract objects involved in structure are ideal. The deeper implication of this position is to reject the typical philosophical assumption of the post-Cantorian approach to infinity and to contrast a finitude of human concepts with the transcendent infinitude of the divine. This move is directly opposed to Badiou who argues that only a radically Platonic set theory can offer a final break from God by grounding ontology in the void.

My approach to ontology interprets al-Māturīdī's implicit bundle theory as tropes. Although I adopt several features of the so-called Campbellian standard model of tropes – particulars that form concrete objects as bundles without substrates – I replace the compresence relation that accounts for the bundle possessing its tropes with phenomenological constitution. If things in the world are intentional objects that must be, in principle, constituted by consciousness, likewise their tropes are intentional property instances that are verified as possessed by their objects. A Husserlian understanding of intentional constitution takes the place of the relationship between an object and its tropes explained by a primitive compresence relation or substrate. Another way to put this is that an object is verified as a set of its tropes, in which the ontology of the set is understood intuitionistically, such that the object is neither 'just' its tropes, nor other than them. The apparent existence of universals in the world is explained by resemblance between tropes, so that these universals exist only conceptually. My phenomenological approach also solves a problem often identified in the literature: that if a given bundle is conceived as a set, it cannot undergo change while remaining the same set.

Although I see these proposals as coherent and able to eloquently engage some of the main debates in contemporary ontology, I recognise that they would have to be considerably developed to take their place within that particular philosophical subdiscipline. I argue that they are, however, adequate as a basis for developing my account of divine properties, which is my main objective. I have also highlighted that it may be a fruitful project to use these ideas to reconceive al-Māturīdī's idea of natures (*ṭabāʾiʿ*) as a trope-theoretic account of dispositions and to discuss the human being, especially in terms of the mind or the soul.

Looking towards the divine, I have built on my assessment of al-Māturīdī's rational arguments for God to make some relevant interventions in contemporary debates, albeit acknowledging their limitations given my scope. While I point out that Hartshorne's reading of Anselm's third ontological argument is akin to one interpretation of Ibn Sīnā's version, I reject this category of argument on several grounds. I discuss the *kalām* cosmological argument, as revived by Craig, in more detail. My major contribution to natural theology is through my phenomenological and intuitionistic mathematical position, which allows a coherent defence of Craig's version of the KCA from some of the most important criticisms that it has faced. Yet I accept that the KCA is only as strong as its various premises and that the version I have defended may not be intuitively plausible to everyone. The teleological argument, as I have discussed it, supports the KCA by providing a supplementary reason to think that the world exists due to God's wisdom. As a new idea on this topic, I can offer my adaption of Wheeler's PAP thesis as an abductive argument for a divine presence behind the universe. If the Copenhagen interpretation of quantum mechanics legitimately reveals that the universe is directed towards human consciousness, then arguably this provides a suggestive inference towards a wise creator.

On the nature of God, I propose a phenomenological account of time constitution that bridges the gap between prevailing A and B accounts. Critically adapting Leftow's ideas, I argue that God is timeless and knows tensed particulars constituted by potential or actual human consciousness without drawing objects into eternity. I contend that this provides a contemporary formulation of al-Māturīdī's position. My approach to modal concepts is based on my prior intuitionism. This means that logical necessity and impossibility refer only to what can be conceived, while the strongest ontological categories are what I term absolute metaphysical necessity and impossibility, which are grounded in God's nature. This level, at which I place God's wisdom, determines two weaker senses of necessity: metaphysical necessity and impossibility in the sense of that which always obtains in the world; and realised and unrealised possibilities, which I call actual necessities and impossibilities. Finally, I accept indeterminate categories for these levels, based on my rejection of bivalence. I conclude that parsing necessity in this way can solve the problem of how it is that mathematical facts and propositions about so-called secular necessities can be logically necessary, though God's existence is not. More generally, my position establishes God's priority over abstract objects without invoking bizarre ideas like the self-creation of His attributes.

On the question of which property theory to use in my theology, I build on al-Māturīdī's position whereby the divine nature is comprised of God's attributes by adapting definitions proposed by Plantinga. I take God's nature to be a set of properties, interpreted in intuitionistic terms as an ideal structure that corresponds to the real ontology of the divine. This preserves the indeterminacy of the so-called Kullābī formula that God's attributes are neither Him, nor other than Him. I engage again with the work of Leftow to elaborate God's eternal attributes through a theory of divine tropes, which are eternal, unchanging and non-free-floating. I argue that this kind of trope theory can preserve a simultaneous account of God's substantive attributes and His unicity, or *tawḥīd*, amounting to both a new Māturīdī position within contemporary *kalām* and a fresh perspective in the field of philosophical theology.

I discuss specific divine attributes to apply my theological method and to extend the enquiry to aspects of God's nature and action that directly impinge on the created order. I account for God's omniscience of the world through propositional categories. The principle of the rationality of reality is what makes it possible for such categories to be the basis of divine knowledge and solves two potential problems identified by Zagzebski. This knowledge is not indirect, as God is able to directly verify every such proposition. Meanwhile, its apparent fragmentation is a function of human consciousness as the increment by which the world is measured.

A Māturīdī theology should articulate a concept of divine wisdom. I propose that it is a kind of higher-order non-propositional knowledge that represents God's deepest intent in creating the world. Despite acknowledging the difficulty of explaining such a brute wisdom, I argue that it can be understood by the human mind to some extent because non-absolute metaphysical necessities and impossibilities depend on it. I give the example of the well-known Māturīdī discussion of burdening beyond capacity (*taklīf mā lā yuṭāq*), although the applications of this theological move are not restricted to it alone. As I have suggested, such a conception of divine wisdom has profound implications for grounding Islamic ethics.

Looking at the question of divine creative action through a contemporary lens, I use an insight from Tanner to press for both affirming God's transcendence over what He creates and the personal nature of His action. In Māturīdī terms, this amounts to verification, or *taḥqīq*. I develop this position along three lines: first, omnipotence, as God's potential to create, is distinguished from His realised creative action; second, God's creative action is eternal and the attribute of *takwīn* is treated as a mere shorthand for an unlimited number of eternal acts; and third, the effects of this action are solely within time with the distinction between creation *ex nihilo* and conservation defined at the level of effect, not attribute. I also argue that, if God's nature is necessary, then due to His eternal wisdom the existence of the actual world must be necessary instead of its logical possibility to not have existed. Conversely, the existence of other worlds must be impossible instead of their logical possibility to have existed.

The final constructive theological treatment in this book is on divine speech and the Qur'an, in which I engage extensively with the ideas of Wolterstorff. I argue for the coherence of leaving the question of revelatory process aside for the purpose of enquiry and limiting my scope to the illocutionary level of divine speech and the locutionary level of the Qur'anic text and recitation. I also pick up on a point made by Quinn: that a literal, yet analogical, construal of divine attributes is required to underpin Wolterstorff's pragmatics. I recognise that, following Aquinas, analogical as opposed to univocal reference is usually associated with divine simplicity. But drawing on earlier discussion in the book, I argue that use of analogy does not imply simplicity and, if there is an entailment, it is in the other direction.

With discussion of predication out of the way, I propose that Wolterstorff's use of speech act theory fits very well with my own systematic concerns. Individual speech acts can be understood as tropes, and the two levels of the illocutionary and locutionary can correspond effectively to the existing Māturīdī conception of divine meaning and created form. I thus adopt the main elements of Wolterstorff's account of the normative relations underpinning illocutionary speech and their relationship to specific language contexts without adjustment. Where I differ is on how to ground the concept of divine normativity. Instead of the divine command theory that he uses, I articulate a Māturīdī normative basis for the truthfulness and consistency of divine speech based on God's wisdom. Here I build on previous work in *The Qur'an and the Just Society* by engaging with a review of that book by Moad and comparing a Māturīdī approach with an Ashʿarī divine command theory. I conclude that, without a notion of eternal wisdom like the Māturīdī system or divine goodness as Wolterstorff acknowledges for Christian theology, the Ashʿarī proponent would struggle to ground divine speech in normative terms for the human actors engaging with it.

Turning to the Qur'an, I do not focus on terminology and verbal formulas; rather, I revisit the message analogy used by al-Māturīdī and al-Bazdawī to apply Wolterstorff's theory. Only a theological approach amenable to multiple speech acts, in the sense of illocutionary meanings, can adequately account for the diversity within the content of God's eternal speech. The Māturīdī commitment to the eternality of divine action, combined with the notion of eternal wisdom as a kind of moral guarantor, allows a contemporary articulation of God's speech from eternity to an audience that can have confidence in His message. Although the Ashʿarī theory of divine speech is superficially similar to its Māturīdī equivalent, it fails on two counts: it lacks an eternal 'moral' attribute and, if adopting multiple speech acts, is once more inconsistent with the school's approach to divine action. More generally, my discussion shows that Wolterstorff's theology of divine speech can be effectively applied beyond the specificities of Christian thought. It may even be more natural within Islamic theology due to the uniformity of the Qur'an as direct divine speech, compared to the more diffuse Biblical picture. I also show that a different normative theory, a wisdom-based natural law approach, may be used with Wolterstorff's ideas, instead of the arguably problematic divine command theory.

Founding my project explicitly in the Māturīdī school has furnished me with specific insights into the trajectory of the tradition and what may become of it. I have persistently noted the extent to which the major shifts in Māturīdī theological formulations have adapted to the language and structure of Ashʿarism and, at least on the territory of the divine attributes, progressively moved towards its system. Late classical harmonisation and syncretism have tended to mask a number of profound differences between the two schools and the fact that, in bringing them closer together, ground has been given on the Māturīdī side, sometimes at the expense of the internal logic of al-Māturīdī's original system.

Yet I have also suggested that a deep reading of Māturīdism points to a weakness in Ashʿarism on certain divine attributes. I have shown that the Ashʿarī adoption of the Muʿtazilī position on the creation of divine actions arguably conflicts with their stance on God's eternal speech. If

God's actions are just His creations, why are His speech acts not created, as the Muʿtazila maintain? But if God's speech acts are granted a special eternal status, why not do the same for the acts of creation? A second problem emerges even if divine speech can be construed as a single eternal attribute: what aspect of the divine nature accounts for the consistency required for engagement within the world of human discourse? On all these counts, I have argued that the Māturīdī position of eternal divine actions, whether speech or creation, as well as wisdom, allows for a coherent, systematic response. These are not merely verbal differences but cut to the heart of the viability of the respective traditions to stand up to contemporary theological scrutiny and, crucially, to act as the ethical foundation needed in the world today. My intention here is not the refutation of a rival school for its own sake, but to draw attention to these potentially problematic aspects of Ashʿarism and to rigorously challenge its proponents in the best way.

From these observations, I suggest that Māturīdism should uncouple from the late classical Ashʿarī-Māturīdī pairing and re-establish the structure of its own thought, as I have attempted to do in this book. It is only through continual self-refinement that a theological tradition can remain supple and vibrant: a tree without new green shoots is dead or dying. Furthermore, this should be a sincere intellectual endeavour – a quest to ascend the theological mountain. It must not become solely a performative assertion of Ḥanafī-Māturīdī identity or a nationalist project, as is sometimes associated with the otherwise vibrant scholarship occurring today in Turkey. The vision of *kalām jadīd* that I present in this book concerns how we can best use the faculties of reason gifted to us by God to know Him. I have argued that such an activity must happen within the contingent traditions into which we are born or which we have chosen to join. In turn, it is inevitable that any successful theological formulation will affect identity. But, to make the expression of an identity the purpose of one's enquiry is surely to co-opt its integrity.

So too would an insularity that prevents active engagement with the representatives of other traditions, religions and philosophies. The format of this work, an academic monograph, announces my conviction that Islamic theology can fit within a contemporary intellectual landscape dominated by Christian philosophical theology. I have not only taken representatives of the fields of philosophy and theology as interlocutors for my own ideas but have actively sought to build on what I judge to be the best, or at least most useful, concepts and arguments. I hope that, as academic Islamic philosophical theology continues to develop as a discipline, work such as the present book will aid other scholars to engage these fields. Beyond their role as voices from an underrepresented theistic tradition, new works can contribute to the intellectual resources of all. I also suggest that there should be at least some inherent interest in systematic approaches to familiar questions that draw on an unfamiliar, yet related, theistic tradition. In topics such as the divine nature, wisdom, creation and speech, the distinctively Māturīdī position that all of God's attributes and actions are eternal leads to original, contemporary theological articulations, even if one may not agree with them.

What next? In the introduction and at several points in the text, I have mentioned that this book does not deal comprehensively with all the main themes covered in a *kalām* manual, such as al-Māturīdī's *Kitāb al-tawḥīd*. I intend to write a follow-up volume that will build on the present enquiry to examine a gamut of anthrocentric questions, including the nature of the human being, prophecy, fate and human freedom, faith, sin, moral responsibility and the Hereafter. In fact, these questions, and others that are of an even more applied tenor, are often publicly deemed more important than the metaphysical and theocentric ones engaged here. But if what I have written holds muster, at least in its essential outline, then it should serve as a secure basis to discuss them. In so doing, I will be resuming my conversation with the Sign of Guidance (*ʿalam al-hudā*), Abū Manṣūr Muḥammad b. Muḥammad b. Maḥmūd al-Māturīdī al-Samarqandī, the tradition that takes his name and the contemporary world.

Glossary of Arabic Terminology

Note: *kalām* terms mainly reflect usage within the Māturīdī tradition. For words open to significant dispute in their theological interpretation, I have placed my preferred constructive reading first.

al-ʿālam al-ṣaghīr	the microcosm
ʿaraḍ (pl. *aʿrāḍ*)	accident
al-aṣlaḥ	the most beneficial (a Baghdadī Muʿtazilī doctrine of divine action)
ʿaql	reason, intellect, mind
ʿaṣl	foundational principle
ʿayn	concrete particular, substance
badāha	necessary knowledge
burhān	demonstration, proof
dalālat al-shāhid ʿalā al-ghāʾib	the manifest indicates the veiled
dāll	indication (of divine speech by human language)
dhāt	nature; subject; essence
falāsifa	philosophers
falsafa	philosophy
ghāʾib	veiled realm
ḥāshiya (pl. *ḥawāshī*)	super-commentary
hastiyya	isness
hayūlā	prime matter
ḥikāya	imitation (of divine speech by human language)
ḥikma	wisdom; divine attribute of wisdom
ḥudūth	temporality
ḥukamāʾ (sing. *ḥakīm*)	philosophers
ʿibāra	expression (of divine speech by human language)
ijmāʿ	consensus
ijtihād	exhaustive legal enquiry
ilhām	spiritual insight
ʿilm	knowledge; divine attribute of omniscience
irāda	will; divine attribute of will
ithbāt	affirmation (of God's attributes)
ʿiyān	perception

iʿjāz	inimitability (of the Qur'an)
jadal	dialectic
jawhar (pl. *jawāhir*)	substance; atom
jism (pl. *ajsām*)	body
al-juzʾ alladhī lā yatajazzaʾ	atom
kalām allāh	divine action, or attribute, of speech
(*ʿilm al-*)*kalām*	rational, dialectical or philosophical theology
kalām jadīd	renewed theology
kalām nafsī	internal speech
kayfiyya	howness; modality
khabar (pl. *akhbār*)	report; informative utterance
khilāf	transcendence
luṭf	kindness or grace (from God)
maʿdūm	non-existent
al-maʿdūm shayʾ	the non-existent is a thing (a Muʿtazilī doctrine)
māʾiyya (also: *māhiyya*)	whatness; essence
majāz	metaphor
manẓūm	composition (of human language to indicate divine speech)
mithl	analogy
muṣḥaf	codex (of the Qur'an)
mutawātir	continuous mass-transmitted (report)
muwāfaqa	concordance (of human language with divine meanings)
naẓar	enquiry
qadīm	eternal, timeless
qiyās al-ghāʾib ʿalā al-shāhid	the veiled is analogous to the manifest
qudra	power; divine attribute of omnipotence
samʿ	tradition
shāhid	manifest realm
shayʾ (pl. *ashyāʾ*)	thing
shayʾiyya	thingness; essence
ṣifa (pl. *ṣifāt*)	divine attribute; quality, accident
ṣifāt al-dhāt	essential attributes
ṣifāt al-fiʿl	active attributes
ṭabāʾiʿ (sing. *ṭabīʿa*)	natures; dispositions; elements
taḥqīq	verification (of God's attributes)
takwīn	divine creative action
tashbīh	anthropomorphism
taʿṭīl	nullification of attributes
tawātur	continuous mass transmission
tawḥīd	unicity, oneness
ṭīna	prime matter, raw material
waqf	suspending judgement
wujūd	existence
zāʾid	additional (of attributes to God's essence)

Bibliography

I. Arabic Manuscript Sources

Al-Andukānī, Kamāl al-Dīn, 'Sidq al-kalām fī 'ilm al-kalām', MS Muṣṭafā Darwīsh 265.

Al-Bazdawi, Abū al-Yusr, 'Al-Muyassir fī al-kalām [Uṣūl al-dīn]', Raza Library, Rampur, MS 1536.

Al-Izmīrī, Muḥammad b. Walī, 'Sharḥ masā'il al-khilāfiyyāt fī mā bayna al-Ash'ariyya wa-l-Māturīdiyya', Körprülü Library, Istanbul, MS Muḥammad 'Āṣim 254.

Al-Maḥbūbī, Ṣadr al-Sharī'a, 'Ta'dīl al-'ulūm', Universitätsbibliothek Leipzig, MS Cod. Arab. 43.

Al-Maḥbūbī, Ṣadr al-Sharī'a, 'Ta'dīl al-'ulūm', Staatsbibliothek Berlin, MS Landberg 394.

Al-Māturīdī, Abū Manṣūr, 'Kitāb al-tawḥīd', Cambridge University Library, Cambridge, MS Add.3651.

Al-Māturīdī, Abū Manṣūr (pseudo), 'Kitāb al-uṣūl'/'Uṣūl al-dīn', Bodleian Library, Oxford, MS Marsh 629, fols 1v–15r.

Al-Rustughfanī, Abū al-Ḥasan, 'Al-As'ila wa-l-ajwiba', Süleymaniye Library, Istanbul, MS Murad Mulla 1829, fol. 154v.

Al-Rustughfanī, Abū al-Ḥasan, 'Bāb al-mutafarriqāt min fawā'id al-shaykh al-imām al-ajall Abī al-Ḥasan 'Alī b. Sa'īd al-Rustughfanī raḥimahu Allāh', in Aḥmad b. Mūsā al-Kashshī, 'Majmū' al-ḥawādith wa-l-nawāzil', Beyazit Library, Istanbul, MS Veliyüddin Efendi 1545, fols 276v–302v.

Al-Rustughfanī, Abū al-Ḥasan, 'Bāb al-mutafarriqāt min fawā'id al-shaykh al-imām al-ajall Abī al-Ḥasan 'Alī b. Sa'īd al-Rustughfanī raḥimahu Allāh', in Aḥmad b. Mūsā al-Kashshī, 'Majmū' al-ḥawādith wa-l-nawāzil', Süleymaniye Library, Istanbul, MS Yeni Cami 547, fols 285v–307v.

II. Arabic Printed Primary Sources

'Abduh, Muḥammad, *Risālat al-tawḥīd*, ed. Muḥammad 'Amāra (Cairo: Dār al-Shurūq, 1994).

Abū Ḥanīfa, al-Nu'mān b. Thābit, *Al-'Ālim wa-l-muta'allim riwāyat Abī Muqātil 'an Abī Ḥanīfa raḍiya Allāhu 'anhumā wa-yalīhi risālat Abī Ḥanīfa ilā 'Uthmān al-Battī thumma al-fiqh al-absaṭ riwāyat Abī Muṭīʿ ʿan Abī Ḥanīfa raḥimahum Allāh*, ed. Muḥammad Zāhid al-Kawtharī (Cairo: Maṭbaʿat al-Anwār, 1949).

Abū Hanīfa, al-Nuʿmān b. Thābit, *Waṣiyya*, ed. Abū Muʿādh Muḥammad b. ʿAbd al-Ḥayy ʿAwayna (Beirut: Dār Ibn Ḥazm, 1997).

Abū ʿUbayd b. Sallām, *Faḍāʾil al-qurʾān*, ed. Marwān al-ʿAṭiyya, Muḥsin Kharāba and Wafāʾ Taqī al-Dīn (Damascus: Dār Ibn Kathīr, 1995).

Al-Ashʿarī, Abū al-Ḥasan, *Maqālāt al-islāmiyyīn wa-ikhtilāf al-muṣallīn*, ed. Muḥ ammad Muḥyī al-Dīn ʿAbd al-Ḥamīd, 2 vols (Cairo: Maktabat al-Nahda al-Miṣriyya, 1950).

Al-Ashʿarī, Abū al-Ḥasan, *Kitāb al-lumaʿ fī al-radd ʿalā ahl al-zaygh wa-l-bidaʿ*, ed. Ḥammūda Ghurāba (Cairo: Maṭbaʿa Miṣr, 1955).

Al-Ashʿarī, Abū al-Ḥasan, *Al-Ibāna ʿan uṣūl al-diyāna* (Beirut: Dār Ibn Zaydūn, n. d.).

Al-Azharī, Abū Manṣūr, *Muʿjam tahdhīb al-lugha*, ed. Riyāḍ Zakī Qāsim, 4 vols (Beirut: Dār al-Maʿrifa, 2001).

Al-Baghdādī, ʿAbd al-Qāhir, *Kitāb uṣūl al-dīn* (Istanbul: Maṭbaʿat al-Dawla, 1928).

Al-Bāqillānī, Abū Bakr, *Kitāb al-tamhīd*, ed. Richard J. McCarthy (Beirut: Al-Maktaba al-Sharqiyya, 1957).

Al-Bāqillānī, Abū Bakr, *Iʿjāz al-qurʾān*, ed. Ṣalāḥ b. Muḥammad b. ʿAwīḍah (Beirut: Dār al-Kutub al-ʿIlmiyya, 2001).

Bāshā, Ibn Kamāl, *Al-Munīra fī al-mawāʿiẓ wa-l-ʿaqāʾid* (Istanbul: Dār al-Lubāb, 2018).

Al-Bayāḍī, Kamāl al-Dīn, *Ishārāt al-marām min ʿibārāt al-imām Abī Ḥanīfa al-Nuʿmān fī uṣūl al-dīn*, ed. Muḥammad ʿAbd al-Raḥmān al-Shāghūl (Cairo: Al-Maktabat al-Azhariyya li-l-Turāth, 2008).

Al-Bazdawī, Abū al-Yusr, *Uṣūl al-dīn*, ed. Hans Peter Linss (Cairo: Al-Maktaba al-Azhariyya li-l-Turāth, 2003).

Al-Bazdawī, Abū al-Yusr, *Maʿrifat al-hujaj al-sharʿiyya*, ed. ʿAbd al-Qādir al-Khaṭīb (Beirut: Muʾassasat al-Risāla, 2000).

Al-Bukhārī, Muḥammad b. Ismāʿīl, *Ṣaḥīḥ al-Bukhārī*, 3 vols (Vaduz: Thesaurus Islamicus Foundation, 2000).

Al-Çūrī, Ḥasan b. al-Sayyid, *Ḥāshiyat al-Çūrī ʿālā sharḥ al-ʿaqāʾid* (Beirut: Dār al-Kutub al-ʿIlmiyya, 2017).

Al-Dānī, Abū ʿAmr, *Al-Aḥruf al-sabʿa li-l-qurʾān*, ed. ʿAbd al-Muhaymin Ṭaḥḥān (Jeddah: Dār al-Manāra, 1997).

Ibn Fūrak, Muḥammad b. al-Ḥasan, *Maqālāt al-shaykh Abī al-Ḥasan al-Ashʿarī*, ed. Daniel Gimaret (Beirut: Dār al-Mashriq, 1987).

Ibn Ḥanbal, Aḥmad, *Al-Radd ʿalā al-zanādiqa wa-l-jahmiyya*, ed. Daghash b. Shabīb al-ʿAjamī (Kuwait: Gharās, 2005).

Ibn Khaldūn, ʿAbd al-Raḥmān, *Muqaddimat Ibn Khaldūn*, ed. Majdī Fatḥī al-Sayyid (Cairo: Dār al-Tawfīqiyya li-l-Turāth, 2010).

Ibn Khuzayma, Abū Bakr, *Kitāb al-tawḥīd wa-ithbāt ṣifāt al-rabb ʿazza wa-jalla*, ed. ʿAbd al-ʿAzīz al-Shahwān (Riyadh: Dār al-Rushd, 1988).

Ibn Saʿd, Muḥammad, *Kitāb al-ṭabaqāt al-kabīr*, ed. ʿAlī Muḥammad ʿAmr, 11 vols (Cairo: Maktabat al-Khānjī, 2001).

Al-Jurjānī, ʿAbd al-Qāhir, *Dalāʾil al-iʿjāz*, ed. Maḥmūd Muḥammad Shākir (Cairo: Maktabat al-Khānjī, 2004).

Al-Jurjānī, al-Sayyid al-Sharīf, *Sharḥ al-mawāqif* (Istanbul: Maṭbaʿat al-Ḥājj Muḥarram Afandī al-Būsnawī, 1869).

Al-Juwaynī, Abū al-Maʿālī, *Al-Shāmil fī uṣūl al-dīn*, ed. ʿAlī Sāmī al-Nashshār (Alexandria: Al-Manshūʾat al-Maʿārif, 1969).

Al-Kaʿbī, Abū al-Qāsim al-Balkhī, *ʿUyūn al-masāʾil wa-l-jawābāt*, ed. Rājiḥ al-Kurdī, ʿAbd al-Ḥamīd Kurdī and Ḥusayn Khānṣū (Amman: Dār al-Ḥāmid, 2014).

Al-Kalabadhī, Abū Bakr, *Kitāb al-taʿarruf li-madhhab ahl al-taṣawwuf* (Cairo: Maktabat al-Khānjī, 1994).

Al-Kāsānī, Abū Bakr, *Badāʾiʿ al-ṣanāʾiʿ fī tartīb al-sharāʾiʿ*, eds. ʿAlī Muḥammad Muʿawwaḍ and ʿĀdil Aḥmad ʿAbd al-Mawjūd, 10 vols (Beirut: Dār al-Kutub al-ʿIlmiyya, 2003).

Al-Kharpūtī, ʿAbd al-Laṭīf, *Tanqiḥ al-kalām fī ʿaqāʾid ahl al-islām* (Durr Saʿāda, 1912).

Al-Khaṭīb al-Baghdādī, *Tārīkh madīnat al-salām*, ed. Bashār ʿAwwād Maʿrūf, 17 vols (Beirut: Dār al-Gharb al-Islāmī, 2001).

Al-Kindī, Yaʿqūb b. Isḥāq, *Rasāʾil al-Kindī al-falsafiyya*, ed. Muḥammad ʿAbd al-Hādī Abū Rayda, 2 vols (Cairo: Dār al-Fikr al-ʿArabī, 1950).

Al-Kirmānī, Ḥarb b. Ismāʿīl, *Kitāb al-sunna*, ed. Abū ʿAbd Allāh ʿĀdil b. ʿAbd Allāh Āl Ḥamdān (Beirut: Dār al-Luʾluʾa, 2014).

Al-Lāmishī, Abū al-Thanāʾ, *Kitab al-tamhīd li-qawāʿid al-tawḥīd*, ed. ʿAbd al-Majīd Turkī (Beirut: Dār al-Gharb al-Islāmī, 1995).

Al-Māturīdī, Abū Manṣūr, *Kitāb al-tawḥīd*, ed. Fathalla Kholeif (Alexandria: Dār al-Jāmiʿāt al-Miṣriyya, 1970).

Al-Māturīdī, Abū Manṣūr, *Taʾwīlāt al-qurʾān*, eds. Ertuğrul Boynukalın and Bekir Topaloğlu, 18 vols (Istanbul: Dār al-Mīzān, 2006).

Al-Māturīdī, Abū Manṣūr, *Kitāb al-tawḥīd*, ed. Bekir Topaloğlu and Muḥammad Aruçi, 2nd edn (Istanbul: Maktabat al-Irshād, 2010).

Al-Nasafī, Abū al-Barakāt, *Sharḥ al-ʿumda fī ʿaqīdat ahl al-sunna wa-l-jamāʿa*, ed. ʿAbd Allāh Muḥammad ʿAbd Allāh Ismāʿīl (Cairo: Al-Maktaba al-Azhariyya li-l-Turāth, 2011).

Al-Nasafī, Abū Ḥafṣ, *Al-Qand fī dhikr ʿulamāʾ al-Samarqand*, ed. Naẓar Muḥammad al-Fārayābī (Riyadh: Maktabat al-Kawthar, 1991).

Al-Nasafī, Abū Ḥafṣ, 'Matn al-ʿaqīda al-Nasafiyya', in *Thamāniya mutūn fī al-ʿaqīda wa-l-tawḥīd* (Amman: RISSC, 2013), pp. 51–59.

Al-Nasafī, Abū al-Muʿīn, *Baḥr al-kalām*, ed. Walī al-Dīn al-Farfūr (Damascus: Dār al-Farfūr, 2000).

Al-Nasafī, Abū al-Muʿīn, *Al-Tamhīd fī uṣūl al-dīn aw al-tamhīd li-qawāʿid al-tawḥīd*, ed. Muḥammad ʿAbd al-Raḥmān al-Shāghūl (Cairo: Al-Maktaba al-Azhariyya li-l-Turāth, 2006).

Al-Nasafī, Abū al-Muʿīn, *Tabṣirat al-adilla fī uṣūl al-dīn*, ed. Muḥammad al-Anwar Ḥāmid ʿĪsā (Cairo: Al-Maktaba al-Azhariyya li-l-Turāth, 2011).

Al-Nasafī, Abū Muṭīʿ Makḥūl, *Kitāb al-radd ʿalā ahl al-bidaʿ wa-l-ahwāʾ*, in Marie Bernand, 'Le *Kitāb al-radd ʿalā l-bidaʿ* d'Abū Muṭīʿ Makḥūl al-Nasafī', *Annales Islamologiques*, 16 (1980), pp. 39–126.

Al-Nāṭifī, Aḥmad b. Muḥammad, *Al-Ajnās fī furū ʿ al-fiqh al-Ḥanafī*, 2 vols (Cairo: Dār al-Maʾthūr, 2016).
Al-Qārī, Mullā ʿAlī, *Sharḥ kitāb al-fiqh al-akbar* (Cairo: Dār al-Kutub al-ʿArabiyya al-Kubrā, 1909).
Al-Qudūrī, Aḥmad b. Muḥammad, *Al-Tajrīd*, ed. Muḥammad Aḥmad Sirāj and ʿAlī Jumuʿa Muḥammad, 12 vols (Cairo: Dār al-Salām, 2004).
Al-Rāzī, ʿAbd al-Qādir, *Mukhtār al-ṣiḥāḥ* (Beirut: Maktaba Lubnān Nāshirūn, 2007).
Al-Rāzī, Abū Bakr, *Rasāʾil falsafiyya*, ed. P. Krauss (Cairo: Jāmiʿat Fuʾād al-Awwal, 1939).
Al-Ṣābūnī, Nūr al-Dīn, *Al-Kifāya fī al-hidāya*, ed. Muḥammad Aruçi (Istanbul: İSAM, 2014).
Al-Ṣābūnī, Nūr al-Dīn, *Al-Bidāya fī uṣūl al-dīn*, ed. and trans. Bekir Topaloğlu, 18th edn (Istanbul: M. Ü. İlāhiyat Fakültesi Vakfı Yayınları, 2018).
Al-Ṣaffār, Abū Isḥāq, *Talkhīṣ al-adilla li-qawāʾid al-tawḥīd*, ed. Angelika Brodersen, 2 vols (Beirut: Orient-Institut Beirut, 2011).
Al-Salimi, Abdulrahman and Wilferd Madelung (eds), *Early Ibāḍī Theology: Six* kalām *texts by ʿAbd Allāh b. Yazīd al-Fazārī* (Leiden: Brill, 2014).
Al-Sālimī, Abū Shakūr, *Al-Tamhīd fī bayan al-tawḥīd*, ed. ʿUmur Turkmān (Istanbul: Markaz İSAM, 2017).
Al-Sālimī, Abū Shakūr, 'Al-Tamhīd fī bayan al-tawḥīd', in Angelika Brodersen, *Zwischen Māturīdīya und Ashʿarīya: Abū Shakūr as-Sālimī und sein* Tamhīd fī bayan at-tauḥīd (Piscataway, NJ: Gorgias Press, 2018).
Al-Samarqandī, Abū al-Layth (pseudo), 'Sharḥ al-fiqh al-absaṭ', in Hans Daiber, *The Islamic Concept of Belief in the 4th/10th Century: Abū l-Laiṯ as-Samarqandī's Commentary on Abū Ḥanīfa (died 150/767) al-Fiqh al-absaṭ* (Tokyo: Institute for the Study of Languages and Cultures of Asia and Africa, 1995).
Al-Samarqandī, Abū Salama, 'Jumal uṣūl al-dīn', in Ahmet Saim Kılavuz, *Ebû Seleme es-Semerkandî ve Akâid Risâlesi* (Istanbul: n. p., 1989).
Al-Samarqandī, Abū Salama, *Jumal min uṣūl al-dīn wa-yalīhu sharḥuhu*, ed. Ilhām Qāsimī (Beirut: Dār al-Kutub al-ʿIlmiyya, 2015).
Al-Samarqandī, ʿAlāʾ al-Dīn, *Mīzān al-uṣūl fī natāʾij al-ʿuqūl*, ed. ʿAbd al-Malik ʿAbd al-Raḥmān al-Saʿdī, 2 vols (Mecca: Jāmiʿat Umm al-Qurā, 1984).
Al-Samarqandī, Shams al-Dīn, *Al-Ṣaḥāʾif al-ilāhiyya*, ed. Aḥmad ʿAbd al-Raḥmān al-Sharīf (Cairo: Maktabat al-Falāḥ li-l-Nashr wa-l-Tawzīʿ, 1985).
Al-Sarakhsī, Muḥammad b. Aḥmad, *Al-Mabsūṭ*, 31 vols (Beirut: Dār al-Maʿrifa, 1989).
Al-Shaybānī, Muḥammad b. al-Ḥasan, *Kitāb al-āthār*, ed. Khālid al-ʿAwwād, 2 vols (Kuwait: Waqfiyyat al-Muzīnī, 2008).
Al-Shaybānī, Muḥammad b. al-Ḥasan, *Al-Aṣl*, ed. Muḥammad Boynukalin, 12 vols (Doha: Wizārat al-Awqāf wa'l-Shuʾūn al-Islāmiyya, 2012).
Shaykhzāde, ʿAbd al-Raḥmān, *Kitāb naẓm al-farāʾid* (Cairo: Al-Maṭbaʿa al-Adabiyya, 1899).
Al-Sighnāqī, Ḥusām al-Dīn, 'Al-Tasdīd fī sharḥ al-tamhīd', in Rassim Chelidze, *Husameddin es-Siğnaki ve et-Tesdid fi Şerhi't-Temhid Adlı Eseri (Tahkik İnceleme)*, PhD thesis (Bursa: Uludağ University, 2015).

Al-Subkī, Tāj al-Dīn, *Al-Sayf al-mashhūr fī sharḥ ʿaqīdat Abī Manṣūr*, ed. Mustafa Saim Yeprem (Ankara: Türkiye Diyanet Vakfı, 2011).

Al-Taftāzānī, Saʿd al-Dīn, *Sharḥ al-ʿaqīda al-Nasafiyya*, ed. Muṣṭafā Marzūqī (Ain M'lila: Dār al-Hudā, 1998).

Al-Taftāzānī, Saʿd al-Dīn, *Sharḥ al-maqāṣid*, ed. ʿAbd al-Raḥmān ʿUmayra, 5 vols (Beirut: ʿĀlam al-Kutub, 1998).

Al-Ṭaḥāwī, Abū Jaʿfar, *Sharḥ mushkil al-āthār*, ed. Shuʿayb al-Arnāʾūṭ, 16 vols (Beirut: Muʾassasat al-Risāla, 1994).

Al-Ṭaḥāwī, Abū Jaʿfar, *Matn al-ʿaqīda al-Ṭaḥāwiyya* (Beirut: Dār Ibn Ḥazm, 1995).

Al-Tamīmī, Abū al-Faḍl, *Iʿtiqād al-imām al-munabbal Abī ʿAbd Allāh Aḥmad b. Ḥanbal*, ed. Abū al-Mundhir al-Naqqāsh (Beirut: Dār al-Kutub al-ʿIlmiyya, 2001).

Al-Usmandī, ʿAlāʾ al-Dīn, *Lubāb al-kalām aw kitāb taṣḥīḥ al-iʿtiqād fī uṣūl al-dīn*, ed. M. Sait Özervarlı (Istanbul: İSAM, 2019).

al-Ustawāʾī, Abū al-ʿAlā, *Kitāb al-iʿtiqād*, ed. Sayyid Bāghjawān (Beirut: Dār al-Kutub al-ʿIlmiyya, 2005).

Al-Wafī, Ibrāhīm Ḥilmī, *Salām al-aḥkam ʿalā sawād al-aʿẓam* (Durr Saʿāda, 1895).

III. Other Sources

Abbott, Nabia, *Studies in Arabic Literary Papyri II: Qurʾānic Commentary and Tradition* (Chicago: University of Chicago Press, 1967).

ʿAbd al-Jalīl, 'Ẓāhirat al-ibdāl fī qirāʾāt ʿAbd Allāh b. Masʿūd wa-qīmatuhā al-tafsīriyya', *Journal of Qur'anic Studies* 15/1 (2013), pp. 168–213.

Abdel Haleem, M. A. S., 'Early *kalām*', in Seyyed Hossein Nasr and Oliver Leaman, *History of Islamic Philosophy* (London: Routledge, 1996), pp. 71–88.

Abdel Haleem, M. A. S., *The Qur'an: English Translation and Parallel Arabic Text* (Oxford: Oxford University Press, 2010).

Abdel Haleem, M. A. S., 'The Role of Context in Interpreting and Translating the Qur'an', *Journal of Qur'anic Studies*, 20/1 (2018), pp. 47–66.

Abdelsater, Hussein Ali, *Shiʿi Doctrine, Muʿtazili Theology: al-Sharīf al-Murtaḍā and Imami Discourse* (Edinburgh: Edinburgh University Press, 2017).

Abderrahmane, Taha, *Suʾāl al-lugha wa-l-manṭiq: ḥiwār maʿ Taha Abderrahmane* (Abu Dhabi: Tabah Foundation, 2010).

Abu Zayd, Nasr Hamid, *Naqd al-khiṭāb al-dīnī*, 2nd edn (Cairo: Sīnā li-l-Nashr, 1994).

Abu Zayd, Nasr Hamid, *Al-Naṣṣ al-sulṭa al-ḥaqīqa: al-fikr al-dīnī bayna irāda al-maʿrifa wa-irādat al-haymana* (Beirut: Al-Markaz al-Thaqāfī al-ʿArabī, 1995).

Abu Zayd, Nasr Hamid, 'The Dilemma of the Literary Approach to the Qur'an', *Alif: Journal of Comparative Poetics*, 23 (2003), pp. 8–47.

Acar, Rahim, *Talking about God and Talking about Creation: Avicenna's and Thomas Aquinas' Positions* (Leiden: Brill, 2005).

Adamson, Peter, 'Al-Kindī and the Muʿtazila: Divine Attributes, Creation and Freedom', *Arabic Sciences and Philosophy*, 13 (2003), pp. 45–77.

Adamson, Peter, *Al-Kindī* (Oxford: Oxford University Press, 2007).

Adamson, Peter, 'The Theology of Aristotle', in Edward N. Zalta (ed.), *The Stanford Encyclopedia of Philosophy* (Summer 2017 Edition), <https://plato.stanford.edu/archives/sum2017/entries/theology-aristotle/>.

Adamson, Peter, and Peter E. Pormann, *The Philosophical Works of al-Kindī* (Karachi: Oxford University Press, 2012).

Ahmad, Najah Nadi, *Theorising the Relationship between* Kalām *and* Uṣūl al-Fiqh: *The Theological-Legal Epistemology of Saʿd al-Dīn al-Taftāzānī (d. 792/1390)*, PhD thesis (University of Oxford, 2018).

Akbar, Ali, *Contemporary Perspectives on Revelation and Qur'anic Hermeneutics: An Analysis of Four Discourses* (Edinburgh: Edinburgh University Press, 2019).

Aldosari, Ayedh S., *Ḥanafī Māturīdism: Trajectories of a Theological Legacy, with a Study and Critical Edition of al-Khabbāzī's* Kitāb al-Hādī (Sheffield: Equinox, 2020).

Ali, Ghazoan, *Substance and Things: Dualism and Unity in the Early Islamic Cultural Field*, PhD thesis (University of Exeter, 2012).

Allard, Michel, *Le Problème des Attributs Divins: Dans la Doctrine D'al-Ashʿarī et de ses Premiers Grands Disciples* (Beirut: Imprimerie Catholique, 1965).

Alston, William P., 'Does God Have Beliefs', *Religious Studies*, 22/3–4 (1986), pp. 287–306.

Alston, William P., *Divine Nature and Human Language: Essays in Philosophical Theology* (Ithaca, NY: Cornell University Press, 1989).

Altaie, Basil, *God, Nature, and the Cause: Essays on Islam and Science* (Abu Dhabi: Kalam Research & Media, 2016).

Anselm, *Basic Writings*, trans. Thomas Williams (Indianapolis, IN: Hackett Publishing, 2007).

Aquinas, Thomas, *The* 'Summa Theologica' *of St. Thomas Aquinas*, trans. Fathers of the English Dominican Province, 21 vols (London: R. & T. Washbourne, 1911–25).

Arıkaner, Yusuf, 'Şerhu Cümeli usûli'd-dîn'in Ebü'l-Hüseyin Muhammed b. Yahyâ el-Beşâğarî'ye Aidiyeti Meselesi', *Mevzu: Sosyal Bilimler Dergisi*, 4 (2020), pp. 37–63.

Aristotle, *Metaphysics, Volume I: Books 1–9*, trans. Hugh Tredennick (Cambridge, MA: Harvard University Press, 1933).

Aristotle, *Metaphysics*, trans. Hugh Lawson-Tancred (London: Penguin, 2004).

Arkoun, Mohammed, *The Unthought in Contemporary Islamic Thought* (London: Saqi Books, in association with The Institute of Ismaili Studies, 2002).

Armstrong, David M., *Universals: An Opinionated Introduction* (Boulder, CO: Westview Press, 1989).

Armstrong, David M., *A World of States of Affairs* (Cambridge: Cambridge University Press, 1997).

Aruçi, Muhammed, 'Rüstüfağnî', in *TDV İslâm Ansiklopedisi*, 46 vols (Istanbul: İSAM, 1988–2016).

Asad, Muhammad, *The Message of the Qur'ān* (Gibraltar: Dar al-Andalus, 1984).

Asad, Talal, 'The Idea of an Anthropology of Islam', *Qui Parle*, 17/2 (2009), pp. 1–30.

Bacon, John, *Universals and Property Instances: The Alphabet of Being* (Oxford: Blackwell, 1995).

Bacon, John, 'Tropes', in Edward N. Zalta (ed.), *The Stanford Encyclopedia of Philosophy* (Winter 2011 Edition), <https://plato.stanford.edu/archives/win2011/entries/tropes/>.

Bader, Ralf M., 'Real Predicates and Existential Judgements', *European Journal of Philosophy*, 26/3 (2018), pp. 1153–58.

Badiou, Alain, *Being and Event*, trans. Oliver Feltham (London: Continuum, 2005).

Badiou, Alain, *Theoretical Writings*, trans. Ray Brassier and Alberto Toscano (London: Bloomsbury, 2015).

Baggini, Julian and Peter S. Fosl, *The Philosopher's Toolkit: A Compendium of Philosophical Concepts and Methods*, 2nd edn (Chichester: Wiley-Blackwell, 2010).

Baki, Burhanuddin, *Badiou's* Being and Event *and the Mathematics of Set Theory* (London: Bloomsbury, 2015).

Barnes, Jonathan, 'Introduction', in Keimpe Algra, Jonathan Barnes, Jaap Mansfeld and Malcolm Schofield (eds), *The Cambridge History of Hellenistic Philosophy*, pp. 65–76.

Barrett, Jeffrey A., review of *The Wave Function: Essays on the Metaphysics of Quantum Mechanics*, by Alyssa Ney and David Z. Albert (eds), *Notre Dame Philosophical Reviews*, 3 August 2013, <https://ndpr.nd.edu/news/the-wave-function-essays-on-the-metaphysics-of-quantum-mechanics/>. Accessed 20 June 2019.

Beck, W. David, 'A Thomistic Cosmological Argument' in William Lane Craig, Francis Beckwith and J. P. Moreland (eds), *To Everyone an Answer* (Downers Grove, IL: IVP Academic, 2004), pp. 95–101.

Bell, Richard, *Introduction to the Qur'ān* (Edinburgh: Edinburgh University Press, 1953).

Bello, Angela Ales, *The Divine in Husserl and Other Explorations* (Dordrecht: Springer, 2009).

Bergson, Henri, *An Introduction to Metaphysics*, trans. T. E. Hulme (New York: The Knickerbocker Press, 1912).

Berruin, Mohammad M., *The Concept of Substance in the Philosophy of Ya ʿqūb al-Kindī and Avicenna (Ibn Sīnā)*, PhD thesis (Durham University, 1971).

Bin Ramli, Harith, 'The Predecessors of Ashʿarism: Ibn Kullāb, al-Muḥāsibī and al-Qalānisī', in Sabine Schmidtke (ed.), *The Oxford Handbook of Islamic Theology* (Oxford: Oxford University Press, 2016), pp. 215–24.

Birinci, Züleyha, 'Ebû Mutîʿ Rivâyetli *el-Fıkhü'l-ekber Şerhi*'nin Müellifi Meselesi', *M.Ü. İlâhiyat Fakültesi Dergisi*, 35/2 (2008), pp. 57–72.

Bohr, Niels, *Essays 1958–1962 on Atomic Physics and Human Knowledge* (New York: Interscience Publishers, 1963).

Booth, Anthony Robert, *Analytic Islamic Philosophy* (London: Palgrave Macmillan, 2017).

Bostrom, Nick, *Anthropic Bias: Observation Selection Effects in Science and Philosophy* (New York: Routledge, 2002).

Brockelmann, Carl, *History of the Arabic Written Tradition, Supplement Volume 1*, trans. Joep Lameer (Leiden: Brill, 2017).

Brodersen, Angelika, *Der unbekannte* kalam: *Theologische Positionen der frühen* Māturīdīya *am Beispiel der Attributenlehre* (Berlin: LIT Verlag, 2014).

Brodersen, Angelika (ed.), *Zwischen Māturīdīya und Ashʿarīya: Abū Shakūr as-Sālimī und sein* Tamhīd fī bayan at-tauḥīd (Piscataway, NJ: Gorgias Press, 2018).

Brodersen, Angelika, 'New Light on the Emergence of Māturīdism: Abū Shakūr al-Sālimī (Fifth/Eleventh Century) and his *Kitāb al-tamhīd fī bayan al-tawḥīd*', *Journal of Islamic Studies*, 31/3 (2020), pp. 329–57.

Brown, Jonathan, *The Canonization of al-Bukhārī and Muslim: The Formation and Function of the Sunnī Ḥadīth Canon* (Leiden: Brill, 2007).

Bruckmayr, Philipp, 'The Spread and Persistence of Māturīdī Kalām and Underlying Dynamics', *Iran and the Caucasus*, 13 (2009), pp. 59–92.

Brunschvig, Jacques, *Papers in Hellenistic Philosophy*, trans. Janet Lloyd (Cambridge: Cambridge University Press, 1994).

Bulgen, Mehmet, 'al-Māturīdī and Atomism', *ULUM*, 2/2 (2019), pp. 223–64.

Burrell, David B., *Towards a Jewish-Christian-Muslim Theology* (Chichester: Wiley-Blackwell, 2014).

Byrne, Alex and David R. Hilbert, 'Are Colors Secondary Qualities?', in Lawrence Nolan (ed.), *Primary and Secondary Qualities: The Historical and Ongoing Debate* (Oxford: Oxford University Press, 2011), pp. 339–61.

Calder, Norman, Jawid Mojaddedi and Andrew Rippin (eds), *Classical Islam: A Sourcebook of Religious Literature* (London: Routledge, 2003).

Campanini, Massimo, *An Introduction to Islamic Philosophy*, trans. Caroline Higgitt (Edinburgh: Edinburgh University Press, 2008).

Campbell, Keith, *Abstract Particulars* (Oxford: Blackwell, 1990).

Carter, Brandon, 'Large Number Coincidences and the Anthropic Principle in Cosmology', in Malcolm S. Longair (ed.), *Confrontation of Cosmological Theories with Observable Data* (Dordrecht: Springer, 1974), pp. 291–98.

Cassin, Barbara (ed.), *Dictionary of Untranslatables: A Philosophical Lexicon* (Princeton, NJ: Princeton University Press, 2014).

Centrone, Stefania, *Logic and Philosophy of Mathematics in the Early Husserl* (Dordrecht: Springer, 2010).

Cerić, Mustafa, *Roots of Synthetic Theology in Islam: A Study of the Theology of Abū Manṣūr al-Māturīdī (d. 333/944)* (Kuala Lumpur: International Institute of Islamic Thought and Civilization, 1995).

Chevally, Catherine, 'Niels Bohr's Words and the Atlantis of Kantianism', in Jan Faye and Henry J. Folse (eds), *Niels Bohr and Contemporary Philosophy* (Dordrecht: Springer, 1994), pp. 33–55.

Chittick, William C., *The Sufi Path of Knowledge: Ibn al-ʿArabi's Metaphysics of Imagination* (Albany, NY: State University of New York Press, 1989).

Choi, Sungho and Michael Fara, 'Dispositions', in Edward N. Zalta (ed.), *The Stanford Encyclopedia of Philosophy* (Fall 2018 Edition), <https://plato.stanford.edu/archives/fall2018/entries/dispositions/>.

Chowdhury, Safaruk Zaman, 'God, Gluts and Gaps: Examining an Islamic Traditionalist Case for a Contradictory Theology', *History and Philosophy of Logic* (2020), DOI: 10.1080/01445340.2020.1797449.

Coady, C. A. J., *Testimony: A Philosophical Study* (Oxford: Oxford University Press, 1992).

Cohen, S. Marc, 'Aristotle's Metaphysics', in Edward N. Zalta (ed.), *The Stanford Encyclopedia of Philosophy* (Winter 2016 Edition), <https://plato.stanford.edu/archives/win2016/entries/aristotle-metaphysics/>.

Cohen, Yishai, 'Endless Future: A Persistent Thorn in the *Kalām* Cosmological Argument', in Paul Copan and William Lane Craig (eds), *The* Kalām *Cosmological Argument: Philosophical Arguments for the Finitude of the Past* (London: Bloomsbury, 2018).

Cook, Michael, 'The Stemma of the Regional Codices of the Koran', in George K. Livadas (ed.), *Festschrift in Honour of V. Christides* (Athens: Institute for Graeco-Oriental and African Studies, 2004), pp. 89–104.

Copan, Paul, 'Introduction', in Paul Copan and William Lane Craig (eds), *The* Kalām *Cosmological Argument: Philosophical Arguments for the Finitude of the Past* (London: Bloomsbury, 2018).

Correa, Dale, 'The Vehicle of Tawātur in al-Māturīdī's Epistemology', in İlyas Çelebi (ed.), *Büyük Türk Bilgini İmâm Mâtürîdî ve Mâtürîdîlik: Milletlerarası Tartışmalı İlmî Toplantı* (Istanbul: M. Ü. İlâhiyat Fakültesi Vakfı Yayınları, 2016), pp. 377–91.

Cowling, Sam, 'Ideological Parsimony', *Synthese*, 190/17 (2013), pp. 3889–908.

Craig, William Lane, *The* Kalām *Cosmological Argument* (London: MacMillan, 1979).

Craig, William Lane, 'Must the Beginning of the Universe Have a Personal Cause? A Rejoinder', *Faith and Philosophy*, 19/1 (2002), pp. 94–105.

Craig, William Lane, 'Graham Oppy on the *Kalam* Cosmological Argument', <https://www.reasonablefaith.org/writings/scholarly-writings/the-existence-of-god/graham-oppy-on-the-kalam-cosmological-argument/>. Accessed 10 October 2019.

Craig, William Lane, 'Creation and Divine Action', in Chad Meister and Paul Copan (eds), *The Routledge Companion to Philosophy of Religion* (Abingdon: Routledge, 2007), pp. 318–28.

Craig, William Lane, 'Prof. Grünbaum on the "Normalcy of Nothingness" in the Leibnizian and *Kalām* Cosmological Arguments', in Paul Copan and William Lane Craig (eds), *The* Kalām *Cosmological Argument: Philosophical Arguments for the Finitude of the Past* (London: Bloomsbury, 2018), pp. 53–70.

Craig, William Lane, 'The *Kalām* Cosmological Argument', in Paul Copan and William Lane Craig (eds), *The* Kalām *Cosmological Argument: Philosophical Arguments for the Finitude of the Past* (London: Bloomsbury, 2018), pp. 302–17.

Creath, Richard, 'Logical Empiricism', in Edward N. Zalta (ed.), *The Stanford Encyclopedia of Philosophy* (Fall 2017 Edition), <https://plato.stanford.edu/archives/fall2017/entries/logical-empiricism/>.

Crone, Patricia, 'Post-Colonialism in Tenth-Century Iran', *Der Islam*, 83/1 (2006), pp. 2–38.

Crosilla, Laura, 'Set Theory: Constructive and Intuitionistic ZF', in Edward N. Zalta (ed.), *The Stanford Encyclopedia of Philosophy* (Summer 2015 Edition), <https://plato.stanford.edu/archives/sum2015/entries/set-theory-constructive/>.

Cross, Richard, *Duns Scotus* (Oxford: Oxford University Press, 1999).

Daccache, Salim, *Le Problème de la Création du Monde et son Contexte rationnel et historique dans la Doctrine d'Abū Manṣūr al-Māturīdī* (Beirut: Dar el-Machreq, 2008).

Daiber, Hans, 'Zur Erstausgabe von al-Māturīdī, *Kitāb al-Tauḥīd*', *Der Islam*, 52/2 (1975), pp. 299–319.

Daiber, Hans, *The Islamic Concept of Belief in the 4th/10th Century: Abū l-Laiṯ as-Samarqandī's Commentary on Abū Ḥanīfa (died 150/767) al-Fiqh al-absaṭ* (Tokyo: Institute for the Study of Languages and Cultures of Asia and Africa, 1995).

Daftary, Farhad, 'Carmatians', in Ehsan Yarshater (ed.), *Encyclopaedia Iranica*, <https:// http://www.iranicaonline.org/articles/carmatians-ismailis/>. Accessed 4 September 2019.

Dallal, Ahmad, *An Islamic Response to Greek Astronomy:* Kitāb taʿdīl hayʾat al-aflāk *of Ṣadr al-Sharīʿa* (Leiden: Brill, 1995).

Al-Damanhūrī, Aḥmad Saʿd, *Naẓariyyat al-maʿrifa ʿinda ahl al-sunna wa-l-jamāʿa: dirāsa mawḍūʿiyya naṣṣiyya min khilāl ārāʾ aʿlām al-madrasa al-Māturīdiyya* (Amman: Dār al-Nūr, 2018).

Al-Damanhūri, Aḥmad Saʿd, *Sadd al-thughūr bi-sīrat ʿalam al-hudā Abī Manṣūr al-Māturīdī* (Amman: Dār al-Nūr, 2018).

D'Ancona, Cristina, 'Greek Sources in Arabic and Islamic Philosophy', in Edward N. Zalta (ed.), *The Stanford Encyclopedia of Philosophy* (Winter 2017 Edition), <https://plato.stanford.edu/archives/win2017/entries/arabic-islamic-greek/>.

Dauphinais, Michael A., 'Loving the Lord Your God: The *Imago Dei* in Saint Thomas Aquinas', *The Thomist: A Speculative Quarterly Review*, 63/2 (1999), pp. 241–67.

David, Marian, 'The Correspondence Theory of Truth', in Edward N. Zalta (ed.), *The Stanford Encyclopedia of Philosophy* (Fall 2016 Edition), <https://plato.stanford.edu/archives/fall2016/entries/truth-correspondence/>.

Davidson, Herbert, *Proofs for Eternity, Creation, and the Existence of God in Medieval Islamic and Jewish Philosophy* (Oxford: Oxford University Press, 1987).

De Pierris, Graciela and Michael Friedman, 'Kant and Hume on Causality', in Edward N. Zalta (ed.), *The Stanford Encyclopedia of Philosophy* (Winter 2013 Edition), <https://plato.stanford.edu/archives/win2013/entries/kant-hume-causality/>.

De Smet, Daniel, 'Ismāʿīlī Theology', in Sabine Schmidtke (ed.), *The Oxford Handbook of Islamic Theology* (Oxford: Oxford University Press, 2016), pp. 313–24.

Demir, Abdullah, 'Māturīdī Theologian Abū Ishāq al-Zāhid al-Saffār's Vindication of the Kalām', *Cumhuriyet Theology Journal*, 20/1 (2016), pp. 445–502.

Deng, Natalja, *God and Time* (Cambridge: Cambridge University Press, 2019).

Dgheim, Samih, *Mawsūʿa muṣṭalaḥāt ʿilm al-kalām al-islāmī*, 2 vols (Beirut: Maktaba Lubnān Nāshirūn, 1998).

Dhanani, Alnoor, *The Physical Theory of Kalām: Atoms, Space, and Void in Basrian Muʿtazilī Cosmology* (Leiden: Brill, 1993).

Dhanani, Alnoor, 'Al-Māturīdī and al-Nasafī on Atomism and the Tabāʾiʿ', in İlyas Çelebi (ed.), *Büyük Türk Bilgini İmâm Mâtürîdî ve Mâtürîdîlik: Milletlerarası Tartışmalı İlmî Toplantı* (Istanbul: M. Ü. İlâhiyat Fakültesi Vakfı Yayınları, 2012), pp. 65–76.

Dillon, John M., *The Middle Platonists: 80 B. C. to A. D. 220* (Ithaca, NY: Cornell University Press, 1996).

Dorroll, Philip, *Modern by Tradition: Abū Manṣūr al-Māturīdī and the New Turkish Theology*, PhD thesis (Emory University, 2013).

Dorroll, Philip, 'Māturīdī Theology in the Ottoman Empire: Debating Human Choice and Divine Power', in O. Demir, V. Kaya, K. Gömbeyaz and U. M. Kılavuz (eds), *Osmanlı'da İlm-i Kelâm: Âlimler, Eserler, Meseleler* (Istanbul: İSAR Yayınları, 2016), pp. 219–38.

Dorroll, Philip, 'The Universe in Flux: Reconsidering Abū Manṣūr al-Māturīdī's Metaphysics and Epistemology', *Journal of Islamic Studies*, 27/2 (2016), pp. 119–35.

Dorroll, Philip, 'The Doctrine of the Nature of the Qur'ān in the Māturīdī Tradition', in M. Raşit Akpinar, Recep Tuzcu and Aslı Menekşe (eds), *Mâtürîdî Düşünce ve Mâtürîdîlik Literatürü* (Istanbul: Selçuk Üniversitesi, 2018), pp. 123–40.

Douven, Igor, 'Abduction', in Edward N. Zalta (ed.), *The Stanford Encyclopedia of Philosophy* (Summer 2017 Edition), <https://plato.stanford.edu/archives/sum2017/entries/abduction/>.

Drummond, John J., *Historical Dictionary of Husserl's Philosophy* (Lanham, MD: Scarecrow Press, 2008).

Dummett, Michael, *The Logical Basis of Metaphysics* (Cambridge, MA: Harvard University Press, 1991).

Earman, John, 'The SAP Also Rises: A Critical Examination of the Anthropic Principle', *American Philosophical Quarterly*, 24/2 (1987), pp. 307–17.

Ehring, Douglas, *Tropes: Properties, Objects, and Mental Causation* (Oxford: Oxford University Press, 2011).

Eichner, Heidrun, 'Essence and Existence. Thirteenth-Century Perspectives in Arabic-Islamic Philosophy and Theology: Fakhr al-Dīn al-Rāzī's *al-Mulakhkhaṣ fī al-ḥikma* and the Arabic Reception of Avicennian Philosophy', in Dag Nikolaus Hasse and Amos Bertolacci (eds), *The Arabic, Hebrew and Latin Reception of Avicenna's Metaphysics* (Berlin: De Gruyter, 2012), pp. 123–51.

El-Bizri, Nader, 'The Microcosm/Macrocosm Analogy: A Tentative Encounter Between Graeco-Arabic Philosophy and Phenomenology', in Anna-Teresa Tymieniecka (ed.), *Islamic Philosophy and Occidental Phenomenology on the Perennial Issue of Microcosm and Macrocosm* (Dordrecht: Springer, 2006), pp. 3–23.

El Omari, Racha, *The Theology of Abū l-Qāsim al-Balkhī/al-Kaʿbī (d. 319/931)* (Leiden: Brill, 2016).

El-Rouayheb, Khaled, 'Theology and Logic', in Sabine Schmidtke (ed.), *The Oxford Handbook of Islamic Theology* (Oxford: Oxford University Press, 2016), pp. 408–31.

El-Rouayheb, Khaled, *The Development of Arabic Logic (1200–1800)* (Basel: Schwabe Verlag, 2019).

El Shamsy, Ahmed, *Rediscovering the Islamic Classics: How Editors and Print Culture Transformed an Intellectual Tradition* (Princeton, NJ: Princeton University Press, 2020).

El-Tobgui, Carl Sharif, *Ibn Taymiyya on Reason and Revelation: A Study of Darʾ taʿāruḍ al-ʿaql wa-l-naql* (Leiden: Brill, 2020).
Emberley, Peter and Barry Cooper (eds), *Faith and Political Philosophy: The Correspondence Between Leo Strauss and Eric Voegelin, 1934–1964* (Columbia, MO: University of Missouri Press, 1993).
Endress, Gerhard, 'Reading Avicenna in the Madrasa: Intellectual Genealogies and Chains of Transmission of Philosophy and the Sciences in the Islamic East', in James E. Montgomery (ed.), *Arabic Theology, Arabic Philosophy: From the Many to the One: Essays in Celebration of Richard M. Frank* (Leuven: Peeters, 2006).
Erlwein, Hannah, *Arguments for God's Existence in Classical Islamic Thought: A Reappraisal of the Discourse* (Berlin: De Gruyter, 2019).
Fackenheim, Emil L., 'The Possibility of the Universe in al-Farabi, Ibn Sina and Maimonides', in Arthur Hyman (ed.), *Essays in Medieval Jewish and Islamic Philosophy* (New York: Ktav Publishing House, 1977), pp. 303–34.
Fakhry, Majid, *Islamic Occasionalism: And its Critique by Averroës and Aquinas* (London: Routledge, 2008).
Farahat, Omar, *The Foundation of Norms in Islamic Jurisprudence and Theology* (Cambridge: Cambridge University Press, 2019).
Favrholdt, David, 'Niels Bohr and Realism', in Jan Faye and Henry J. Folse (eds), *Niels Bohr and Contemporary Philosophy* (Dordrecht: Springer, 1994), pp. 77–96.
Faye, Jan, 'Copenhagen Interpretation of Quantum Mechanics', in Edward N. Zalta (ed.), *The Stanford Encyclopedia of Philosophy* (Fall 2014 Edition), <https://plato.stanford.edu/archives/fall2014/entries/qm-copenhagen/>.
Fazlıoğlu, İhsan, 'Between Reality and Mentality: Fifteenth Century Mathematics and Natural Philosophy Reconsidered', *Nazariyat Journal for the History of Islamic Philosophy and Sciences*, 1/1 (2014), pp. 1–39.
Ferreirós, José, *Labyrinth of Thought: A History of Set Theory and Its Role in Modern Mathematics*, 2nd edn (Basel: Birkhäuser Verlag AG, 2007).
Feser, Edward, *Aquinas: A Beginner's Guide* (Oxford: Oneworld, 2009).
Flint, Thomas P. and Michael C. Rea, 'Introduction', in Thomas P. Flint and Michael C. Rea (eds), *The Oxford Handbook of Philosophical Theology* (Oxford: Oxford University Press, 2009), pp. 1–7.
Foudeh, Saeed (ed.), *Masāʾil al-ikhtilāf bayna al-Ashāʿira wa-l-Māturīdiyya taʾlīf al-ʿalāma al-wazīr Ibn Kamāl Bāshā Shams al-Dīn Aḥmad b. Sulaymān wa-yalīhu arbaʿa mukhtaṣarāt fī al-ʿaqāʾid* (Beirut: Dār al-Dhakhāʾir, 2015).
Foudeh, Saeed and Bilāl al-Najjār (eds), *Al-Dalīl al-kawnī ʿalā wujūd Allāh taʿālā: maqālāt min al-buḥūth al-gharbiyya al-muʿāṣira fī falsafat al-dīn* (Abu Dhabi: Kalam Research & Media/Al-Aṣlayn, 2016).
Fowden, Garth, *Before and After Muḥammad: The First Millenium Refocused* (Princeton, NJ: Princeton University Press, 2014).
Fraenkel, Abraham. A., Yehoshua Bar-Hillel, and Azriel Levy, *Foundations of Set Theory*, 2nd edn (Amsterdam: Elsevier, 1973).
Franchella, Miriam, 'Philosophies of Intuitionism: Why We Need Them', *Teorema: Revista Internacional de Filosofía*, 26/1 (2007), pp. 73–82.
Frank, Richard M., 'The Kalām, an Art of Contradiction-Making or Theological Science? Some Remarks on the Question', *Journal of the American Oriental Society*, 88/2 (1968), pp. 295–309.

Frank, Richard M., 'Notes and Remarks on the Ṭabāʾiʿ in the Teaching of al-Māturīdī', in P. Salmon (ed.), *Mélanges d'Islamologie* (Leiden: Brill, 1974), pp. 137–49.

Frank, Richard M., 'Al-Ashʿarī's Conception of the Nature and Role of Speculative Reasoning in Theology', in F. Rundgren (ed.), *Proceedings of the VIth Congress of Arabic and Islamic Studies, Visby 13–16 August, Stockholm 17–19 August, 1972* (Stockholm, 1975), pp. 136–54.

Frank, Richard M., *Beings and Their Attributes: The Teaching of the Basrian School of the Muʿtazila in the Classical Period* (Albany, NY: State University of New York Press, 1978).

Frank, Richard M., '*Kalām* and Philosophy: A Perspective from One Problem', in Parviz Morewedge (ed.), *Islamic Philosophical Theology* (Albany, NY: State University of New York Press, 1979), pp. 71–95.

Frank, Richard M., 'Al-Ustādh Abū Isḥāḳ: An ʿAḳīda together with Selected Fragments', *Mélanges de l'Institut Dominicain d'Études Orientales*, 19 (1989), pp. 129–202.

Frank, Richard M., 'Elements in the Development of the Teaching of al-Ashʿarī', *Le Muséon*, 104/1–2 (1991), pp. 141–90.

Frank, Richard M., '"*Lam yazal*" as a Formal Term in Muslim Theological Discourse', *MIDEO*, 15 (1995), pp. 243–70.

Frank, Richard M., 'The Ashʿarite Ontology: I Primary Entities', *Arabic Sciences and Philosophy*, 9 (1999), pp. 163–231.

Freddoso, Alfred J., 'Introduction', in Alfred J. Freddoso (ed.), *The Existence and Nature of God* (Notre Dame, IN: University of Notre Dame Press, 1983), pp. 1–10.

Friederich, Simon, 'Fine-Tuning', in Edward N. Zalta (ed.), *The Stanford Encyclopedia of Philosophy* (Winter 2018 Edition), <https://plato.stanford.edu/archives/win2018/entries/fine-tuning/>.

Gadamer, Hans-Georg, *Truth and Method*, trans. Joel Weinsheimer and Donald G. Marshall (London: Bloomsbury, 2013).

Gardet, L., 'Allāh', in P. Bearman, Th. Bianquis, C. E. Bosworth, E. Van Donzel, and W. P. Heinrichs (eds), *The Encyclopaedia of Islam, New Edition*, 12 vols (Leiden: Brill, 1986–2004).

Genequand, Charles, 'Metaphysics', in Seyyed Hossein Nasr and Oliver Leaman (eds), *History of Islamic Philosophy* (London: Routledge, 1996), pp. 783–801.

Al-Ghursī, Muḥammad Ṣāliḥ b. Aḥmad, *Taḥqīq masāʾil muhimmāt min ʿilm al-tawḥīd wa-l-ṣifāt* (Amman: Dār al-Fatḥ, 2016).

Gimaret, Daniel, *La Doctrine d'al-Ashʿarī* (Paris: Cerf, 1990).

Glick, David, 'Against Quantum Indeterminacy', *Thought: A Journal of Philosophy*, 6/3 (2017), pp. 204–13.

Goff, Philip, William Seager and Sean Allen-Hermanson, 'Panpsychism', in Edward N. Zalta (ed.), *The Stanford Encyclopedia of Philosophy* (Winter 2017 Edition), <https://plato.stanford.edu/archives/win2017/entries/panpsychism/>.

Goldziher, Ignaz, *The Ẓāhirīs: Their Doctrine and their History. A Contribution to the History of Islamic Theology*, trans. Wolfgang Behn (Leiden: Brill, 2008).

Griffith, Sidney H., 'Faith and Reason in Christian Kalām: Theodore Abū Qurrah on Discerning the True Religion', in Samir Khalil Samir and Jørgen S. Nielsen (eds), *Christian Arabic Apologetics During the Abbasid Period (750–1258)* (Leiden: Brill, 1994), pp. 1–43.

Grim, Patrick, 'On Sets and Worlds: A Reply to Menzel', *Analysis*, 46/4 (1986), pp. 186–91.

Grim, Patrick, 'The Being that Knew Too Much', *International Journal for Philosophy of Religion*, 47/3 (2000), pp. 141–54.

Grim, Patrick, 'Problems with Omniscience', <https://www.pgrim.org/articles/omniscience9.pdf>. Accessed 2 March 2020.

Grünbaum, Adolf, 'A New Critique of Theological Interpretations of Physical Cosmology', in Paul Copan and William Lane Craig (eds), *The* Kalām *Cosmological Argument: Philosophical Arguments for the Finitude of the Past* (London: Bloomsbury, 2018), pp. 15–52.

Gutas, Dimitri, *Greek Thought, Arabic Culture: The Graeco-Arabic Translation Movement in Baghdad and Early ʿAbbāsid Society (2nd–4th/8th–10th centuries)* (London: Routledge, 1998).

Gutas, Dimitri, 'Avicenna and After: The Development of Paraphilosophy', in Abdelkader Al Ghouz (ed.), *Islamic Philosophy from the 12th to the 14th Century* (Göttingen: V&R unipress, 2018), pp. 19–72.

Gwynne, Rosalind Ward, *Logic, Rhetoric, and Legal Reasoning in the Qur'ān: God's Arguments* (Abingdon: Routledge, 2004).

Haack, Susan, *Deviant Logic: Some Philosophical Issues* (Cambridge: Cambridge University Press, 1974).

Haddock, Guillermo E. Rosado, 'Platonism, Phenomenology, and Interderivability', in Mirja Hartimo (ed.), *Phenomenology and Mathematics* (Dordrecht: Springer, 2010), pp. 23–46.

Haidar, Yahya Raad, *The Debates between Ash'arism and Māturīdism in Ottoman Religious Scholarship: A Historical and Bibliographical Study*, PhD thesis (Australian National University, 2016).

Hall, James, *Knowledge, Belief, and Transcendence: Philosophical Problems in Religion* (Boston: Houghton Mifflin Company, 1975).

Hallett, Michael, 'Zermelo's Axiomatization of Set Theory', in Edward N. Zalta (ed.), *The Stanford Encyclopedia of Philosophy* (Winter 2016 Edition), <https://plato.stanford.edu/archives/win2016/entries/zermelo-set-theory/>.

Hanafi, Hassan, 'Phenomenology and Islamic Philosophy', in Anna-Teresa Tymieniecka (ed.), *Phenomenology World-Wide: Foundations, Expanding Dynamics, Life-Engagements, A Guide for Research and Study* (Dordrecht: Springer, 2002), pp. 318–22.

Hanafi, Hassan, *Taʾwīl al-ẓāhiriyyāt: al-ḥāla al-rāhina li-l-manhaj al-ẓāhiriyyātī wa-taṭbīqihi fī ẓāhirat al-dīn* (Cairo: Maktaba Madbūlī, 2013).

Hanna, Robert, *Cognition, Content, and the A Priori: A Study in the Philosophy of Mind and Knowledge* (Oxford: Oxford University Press, 2015).

Hansu, Hüseyin, 'Notes on the Term *Mutawātir* and its Reception in *Hadīth* Criticism', *Islamic Law and Society*, 16/3–4 (2009), pp. 383–408.

Hare, John E., *God's Command* (Oxford: Oxford University Press, 2015).

Hart, David Bentley, *The Experience of God: Being, Consciousness, Bliss* (New Haven, CT: Yale University Press, 2013).

Hartshorne, Charles, *Anselm's Discovery: A Re-examination of the Ontological Proof for God's Existence* (La Salle, IL: The Open Court Publishing Company, 1965).

Hartshorne, Charles, *Omnipotence and Other Theological Mistakes* (Albany, NY: State University of New York Press, 1984).

Harvey, Ramon, 'The Legal Epistemology of Qur'anic Variants: The Readings of Ibn Masʿūd in Kufan *Fiqh* and the Ḥanafī *Madhhab*', *Journal of Qur'anic Studies* 19/1 (2017), pp. 72–101.

Harvey, Ramon, *The Qur'an and the Just Society* (Edinburgh: Edinburgh University Press, 2018).

Harvey, Ramon, 'The Revelation of Mercy in the Light of Islamic Theology', in Valentino Cottini, Felix Körner and Diego R. Sarrió Cucarella (eds), *Raḥma: Muslim and Christian Studies in Mercy* (Rome: Pontificio Instituto di Studi Arabi e d'Islamistica, 2018), pp. 49–56.

Harvey, Ramon, 'Al-Māturīdī on the Abrogation of the *Sharīʿa* in the Qur'an and Previous Scriptures', in Hatice K. Arpaguş, Mehmet Ümit and Bilal Kır (eds), *İmâm Mâtürîdî ve Te'vîlâtü'l-Kur'ân* (Istanbul: M. Ü. İlâhiyat Fakültesi Vakfı Yayınları, 2019), pp. 511–24.

Hasan, Ali and Richard Fumerton, 'Foundationalist Theories of Epistemic Justification', in Edward N. Zalta (ed.), *The Stanford Encyclopedia of Philosophy* (Winter 2016 Edition), <https://plato.stanford.edu/archives/win2016/entries/justep-foundational/>.

Heisenberg, Werner, *Physics and Philosophy: The Revolution in Modern Science* (New York: Harper and Brothers Publishers, 1958).

Henderson, Leah, 'The Problem of Induction', in Edward N. Zalta (ed.), *The Stanford Encyclopedia of Philosophy* (Spring 2019 Edition), <https://plato.stanford.edu/archives/spr2019/entries/induction-problem/>.

Heraclitus, *The Cosmic Fragments: A Critical Study*, trans. G. S. Kirk (London: Cambridge University Press, 1962).

Holtzman, Livnat, *Anthropomorphism in Islam: The Challenge of Traditionalism* (700–1350) (Edinburgh: Edinburgh University Press, 2018).

Hoover, Jon, 'Perpetual Creativity in the Perfection of God: Ibn Taymiyya's Hadith Commentary on the Creation of this World', *Journal of Islamic Studies*, 15/3 (2004), pp. 287–329.

Horn, Laurence R., 'Contradiction', in Edward N. Zalta (ed.), *The Stanford Encyclopedia of Philosophy* (Spring 2014 Edition), <https://plato.stanford.edu/archives/spr2014/entries/contradiction/>.

Husserl, Edmund, *Cartesian Meditations: An Introduction to Phenomenology*, trans. Dorion Cairns (The Hague: Martinus Nijhoff, 1960).

Husserl, Edmund, *Formal and Transcendental Logic*, trans. Dorion Cairns (The Hague: Martinus Nijhoff, 1969).

Husserl, Edmund, *The Crisis of European Sciences and Transcendental Phenomenology*, trans. David Carr (Evanston: Northwestern University Press, 1970).

Husserl, Edmund, *On the Phenomenology of the Consciousness of Internal Time (1893–1917)*, trans. John Barnett Brough (Dordrecht: Kluwer Academic Publishers, 1991).

Husserl, Edmund, *The Idea of Phenomenology: A Translation of* Die Idee der Phänomenologie *Husserliana II*, trans. Lee Hardy (Dordrecht: Springer, 1999).

Husserl, Edmund, *The Shorter Logical Investigations*, trans. J. N. Findlay (London: Routledge, 2001).

Husserl, Edmund, *The Basic Problems of Phenomenology*, trans. Ingo Farin and James G. Hart (Dordrecht: Springer, 2006).

Husserl, Edmund, *Ideas: General Introduction to Pure Phenomenology*, trans. W. R. Boyce Gibson (Abingdon: Routledge, 2012).

Hyde, Dominic and Diana Raffman, 'Sorites Paradox', in Edward N. Zalta (ed.), *The Stanford Encyclopedia of Philosophy* (Summer 2018 Edition), <https://plato.stanford.edu/archives/sum2018/entries/sorites-paradox/>.

Hye, M. Abdul, 'Ashʿarism', in M. M. Sharif (ed.), *A History of Muslim Philosophy*, 2 vols (Wiesbaden: Otto Harrassowitz, 1963), vol. 1, pp. 220–43.

Iblāgh, ʿInāyat Allāh, *Al-Imām al-aʿzam Abū Ḥanīfa al-mutakallim* (n. p.: Al-Majlis al-Aʿlā li-l-Shuʾūn al-Islāmiyya, 1971).

Ibrahim, Lutpi, 'Al-Māturīdī's Arguments for the Existence of God', *Hamdard Islamicus*, 3/4 (1980), pp. 17–22.

Iemhoff, Rosalie, 'Intuitionism in the Philosophy of Mathematics', in Edward N. Zalta (ed.), *The Stanford Encyclopedia of Philosophy* (Winter 2016 Edition), <https://plato.stanford.edu/archives/win2016/entries/intuitionism/>.

Iqbal, Muhammad, *The Reconstruction of Religious Thought in Islam* (Stanford, CA: Stanford University Press, 2013).

Al-Jābī, Bassām ʿAbd al-Wahhāb, *Al-Masāʾil al-khilāfiyya bayna al-Ashāʿira wa-l-Māturīdiyya* (Beirut: Dār Ibn Ḥazm, 2003).

Jackson, Sherman A., *On the Boundaries of Theological Tolerance in Islam: Abū Ḥāmid al-Ghāzalī's* Fayṣal al-Tafriqa Bayna al-Islām wa al-Zandaqa (Oxford: Oxford University Press, 2002).

Jackson, Sherman A., *Islam and the Problem of Black Suffering* (Oxford: Oxford University Press, 2009).

Johns, A. H., 'A Humanistic Approach to *Iʿjaz* in the Qur'an: The Transfiguration of Language', *Journal of Qur'anic Studies*, 13/1 (2011), pp. 79–99.

Kalaycı, Mehmet, 'Projections of Māturīdite-Ḥanafite Identity on the Ottomans', *Cumhuriyet Theology Journal*, 20/2 (2016), pp. 9–72.

Kant, Immanuel, *Critique of Pure Reason*, trans. Marcus Weigelt (London: Penguin, 2007).

Kaş, Murat, 'Mental Existence Debates in the Post-Classical Period of Islamic Philosophy: Problems of the Category and Essence of Knowledge', trans. Aykut Mustak, *Nazariyat*, 4/3 (2018), pp. 49–84.

Kastrup, Bernardo, *The Idea of the World: A Multi-disciplinary Argument for the Mental Nature of Reality* (Alresford: John Hunt Publishing, 2019).

Kaufman, Gordon D., *The Theological Imagination: Constructing the Concept of God* (Philadelphia, PA: The Westminster Press, 1981).

Al-Kayyālī, ʿĀṣim Ibrāhīm (ed.), *Al-Nafaḥāt al-rabbāniyya al-mushtamala ʿalā khams rasāʾil mīrghaniyya* (Beirut: Dār al-Kutub al-ʿIlmiyya, 1971).

Kennedy, Hugh, *An Historical Atlas of Islam*, 2nd edn (Leiden: Brill, 2001).

Kholeif, Fathalla, *A Study on Fakhr al-Dīn al-Rāzī and His Controversies in Transoxiana* (Beirut: Dar el-Machreq Éditeurs, 1966).

Kholeif, Fathalla, 'Muqaddima', in Abū Manṣūr al-Māturīdī, *Kitāb al-tawḥīd*, ed. Fathalla Kholeif (Alexandria: Dār al-Jāmiʿāt al-Miṣriyya, 1970), pp. 1–51.

Kholeif, Fathalla, 'Al-Imām Abū Manṣūr al-Māturīdī', *ʿĀlam al-fikr*, 11/1 (1980), pp. 233–58.

Kment, Boris, 'Varieties of Modality', in Edward N. Zalta (ed.), *The Stanford Encyclopedia of Philosophy* (Spring 2017 Edition), <https://plato.stanford.edu/archives/spr2017/entries/modality-varieties/>.

Knight, Kelvin, 'After Tradition? Heidegger *or* MacIntyre, Aristotle *and* Marx', *Analyse & Kritik* 30 (2008), pp. 33–52.

Koons, Robert C., 'A New Look at the Cosmological Argument', *American Philosophical Quarterly*, 34/2 (1997), pp. 193–211.

Koons, Robert C. and Timothy H. Pickavance, *The Atlas of Reality: A Comprehensive Guide to Metaphysics* (Chichester: Wiley Blackwell, 2017).

Kortooms, Toine, *Phenomenology of Time: Edmund Husserl's Analysis of Time Consciousness* (Dordrecht: Springer, 2002).

Kripke, Saul A., *Naming and Necessity* (Cambridge, MA: Harvard University Press, 1980).

Kuegelgen, Anke von and Ashirbek Muminov, 'Mâturîdî Döneminde Semerkand İlahiyatçıları (4/10. Asır)', in Sönmez Kutlu (ed.), *İmam Mâturîdî ve Maturidilik: Tarihî Arka Plan, Hayatı, Eserleri, Fikirleri ve Maturidilik Mezhebi* (Ankara: Otto, 2017), pp. 279–90.

Kuhn, Thomas S., *The Structure of Scientific Revolutions*, 3rd edn (Chicago: The University of Chicago Press, 1996).

Küng, Hans, *Islam: Past, Present and Future* (Oxford: Oneworld, 2007).

Kurt, Erkan M., *Creation: The Principle of Nature in Islamic Metaphysics* (New York: Blue Dome Press, 2012).

Kurzman, Charles, 'Introduction: Liberal Islam and Its Islamic Context', in Charles Kurzman (ed.), *Liberal Islam: A Sourcebook* (Oxford: Oxford University Press, 1998), pp. 3–26.

Laher, Suheil, *Twisted Threads: Genesis, Development and Application of the Term and Concept of Tawatur in Islamic Thought*, PhD thesis (Harvard University, 2014).

Lane, E. W., *Arabic–English Lexicon*, 2 vols (Cambridge: Islamic Texts Society, 2003).

Lange, Christian, 'Power, Orthodoxy, and Salvation in Classical Islamic Theology', in Léon Buskens and Annemarie van Sandwijk (eds), *Islamic Studies in the Twenty-first Century* (Amsterdam: Amsterdam University Press, 2016), pp. 135–59.

Larkin, Margaret, *The Theology of Meaning: ʿAbd al-Qāhir al-Jurjānī's Theory of Discourse* (New Haven, CT: American Oriental Society, 1995).

Laycock, Steven W., 'Actual and Potential Omniscience', *Philosophy of Religion*, 26 (1989), pp. 65–88.

Le Poidevin, Robin, 'The Experience and Perception of Time', in Edward N. Zalta (ed.), *The Stanford Encyclopedia of Philosophy* (Summer 2019 Edition), <https://plato.stanford.edu/archives/sum2019/entries/time-experience/>.

Leftow, Brian, 'Individual and Attribute in the Ontological Argument', *Faith and Philosophy*, 7/2 (1990), pp. 235–42.

Leftow, Brian, *Time and Eternity* (Ithaca, NY: Cornell University Press, 1991).

Leftow, Brian, 'Omnipotence', in Thomas P. Flint and Michael C. Rea (eds), *The Oxford Handbook of Philosophical Theology* (Oxford: Oxford University Press, 2009), pp. 167–98.

Leftow, Brian, 'Necessity', in Charles Taliaferro and Chad Meister (eds), *The Cambridge Companion to Christian Philosophical Theology* (Cambridge: Cambridge University Press, 2010), pp. 15–30.

Leftow, Brian, 'One Step Toward God', *Royal Institute of Philosophy Supplement*, 68 (2011), pp. 67–104.

Leftow, Brian, *God and Necessity* (Oxford: Oxford University Press, 2012).

Levine, Michael, 'God Speak', *Religious Studies*, 34/1 (1998), pp. 1–16.

Lewinstein, Keith, 'Notes on Eastern Ḥanafite Heresiography', *Journal of the American Oriental Society*, 114/4 (1994), pp. 583–98.

Lewis, David, 'Anselm and Actuality', *Noûs*, 4/2 (1970), pp. 175–88.

Lewis, David, *Parts of Classes* (Oxford: Basil Blackwell, 1991).

Lewis, Frank A., *Substance and Predication in Aristotle* (Cambridge: Cambridge University Press, 1991).

Lewis, Frank A., *How Aristotle Gets By in* Metaphysics Zeta (Oxford: Oxford University Press, 2013).

Lewis, Peter J., *Quantum Ontology: A Guide to the Metaphysics of Quantum Mechanics* (Oxford: Oxford University Press, 2016).

Lizzini, Olga, 'Ibn Sina's Metaphysics', in Edward N. Zalta, *The Stanford Encyclopedia of Philosophy* (Fall 2016 Edition), <https://plato.stanford.edu/archives/fall2016/entries/ibn-sina-metaphysics/>.

Locke, John, *An Essay Concerning Human Understanding, 1690* (London: Scolar Press, 1970).

Loux, Michael J., *Metaphysics: A Contemporary Introduction*, 3rd edn (New York: Routledge: 2006).

Lowe, E. J., *A Survey of Metaphysics* (Oxford: Oxford University Press, 2002).

MacDonald, D. B., 'Māturīdī', in M. Th. Houtsma, T. W. Arnold, R. Basset and R. Hartmann (eds), *Encyclopaedia of Islam, First Edition (1913–1936)*, 9 vols (Leiden: Brill, 1913–36).

Lurçat, Francois, 'Understanding Quantum Mechanics with Bohr and Husserl', in Luciano Boi, Pierre Kerszberg and Frédéric Patras (eds), *Rediscovering Phenomenology: Phenomenological Essays on Mathematical Beings, Physical Reality, Perception and Consciousness* (Dordrecht: Springer, 2007), pp. 229–58.

McGinn, Bernard, *Thomas Aquinas's* Summa theologiae (Princeton, NJ: Princeton University Press, 2014).

MacIntyre, Alasdair, 'Epistemological Crises, Dramatic Narrative and the Philosophy of Science', *The Monist*, 60/4 (1977), pp. 453–72.

MacIntyre, Alasdair, *Whose Justice? Which Rationality?* (London: Duckworth, 1988).

MacIntyre, Alasdair, *Three Rival Versions of Moral Enquiry: Encyclopaedia, Genealogy, and Tradition: Being Gifford Lectures Delivered in the University of Edinburgh in 1988* (London: Duckworth, 1990).

MacIntyre, Alasdair, 'Moral Relativism, Truth and Justification', in Kelvin Knight (ed.), *The MacIntyre Reader* (Notre Dame, IN: University of Notre Dame Press, 1998), pp. 202–20.

MacIntyre, Alasdair, 'Practical Rationalities as Forms of Social Structure', in Kelvin Knight (ed.), *The MacIntyre Reader* (Notre Dame, IN: University of Notre Dame Press, 1998), pp. 120–35.

MacIntyre, Alasdair, 'On Not Having the Last Word: Thoughts on Our Debts to Gadamer', in Jeff Malpas, Ulrich Arnswald and Jens Kertscher (eds), *Gadamer's Century: Essays in Honor of Hans-Georg Gadamer* (Cambridge, MA: The MIT Press, 2002), pp. 157–72.

MacIntyre, Alasdair, *Edith Stein: A Philosophical Prologue, 1913–1922* (Lanham, MD: Rowman & Littlefield, 2006).

MacIntyre, Alasdair, *The Tasks of Philosophy: Selected Essays, Volume 1* (Cambridge: Cambridge University Press, 2006).

MacIntyre, Alasdair, *God, Philosophy, Universities: A Selective History of the Catholic Philosophical Tradition* (Lanham, MD: Rowman & Littlefield Publishers, 2009).

Mackie, J. L., *The Miracle of Theism: Arguments for and Against the Existence of God* (New York: Oxford University Press, 1983).

Madelung, Wilferd, 'The Spread of Māturīdism and the Turks', in *Actas IV Congresso de Estudos Árabes e Islâmicos Coimbra-Lisboa 1968* (Leiden: Brill, 1971), pp. 109–68.

Madelung, Wilferd, 'The Early Murjiʾa in Khurāsān and Transoxania and the Spread of Ḥanafism', *Der Islam*, 59 (1982), pp. 32–39.

Madelung, Wilferd, review of *Kitāb al-tawḥīd*, by Abū Manṣūr al-Māturīdī, ed. Fathalla Kholeif, *Zeitschrift der Deutschen Morgenländischen Gesellschaft*, 124/1 (1974), pp. 149–51.

Madelung, Wilferd, 'The Origins of the Controversy Concerning the Creation of the Koran', in J. M. Barral (ed.), *Orientalia Hispanica: Sive Studia F. M. Pareja Octogenario Dicata, Volume 1: Arabica-Islamica* (Leiden: Brill, 1974), pp. 504–25.

Madelung, Wilferd, 'The Shiite and Khārijite Contribution to Pre-Ashʿarite *Kalām*', in Parviz Morewedge (ed.), *Islamic Philosophical Theology* (Albany, NY: State University of New York Press, 1979), pp. 120–39.

Madelung, Wilferd, *Religious Trends in Early Islamic Iran* (Albany, NY: Bibliotheca Persica, 1988).

Madelung, Wilferd, 'Abu l-Muʿīn al-Nasafī and Ashʿarī Theology', in Carole Hillenbrand (ed.), *Studies in Honour of Clifford Edmund Bosworth, Volume II: The Sultan's Turret, Studies in Persian and Turkish Culture* (Leiden: Brill, 2000), pp. 318–30.

Mall, R. A., 'The God of Phenomenology in Comparative Contrast to that of Philosophy and Theology', *Husserl Studies*, 8 (1991), pp. 1–15.

Mangera, Abdur-Rahman, *A Critical Edition of Abū 'l-Layth al-Samarqandī's* Nawāzil, PhD thesis (SOAS, University of London, 2013).

Markosian, Ned, 'Time', in Edward N. Zalta (ed.), *The Stanford Encyclopedia of Philosophy* (Fall 2016 Edition), <https://plato.stanford.edu/archives/fall2016/entries/time/>.

Martin, C. B., 'Substance Substantiated', *Australasian Journal of Philosophy*, 58/1 (1980), pp. 3–10.

Al-Māturīdī, Abū Manṣūr, *Kitāb al-tawḥīd*, trans. Bekir Topaloğlu (Istanbul: İSAM, 2013).

Al-Māturīdī, Abū Manṣūr, *The Book of Monotheism, Kitaab At-Tawheed: God and the Universe, A Manual of Sunni Theology*, trans. Sulaiman Ahmed (Sheffield: Māturīdī Publications, 2019).

Mavrodes, George I., *Revelation in Religious Belief* (Philadelphia, PA: Temple University Press, 1988).

Mayer, Toby, 'Ibn Sīnā's "Burhān al-Ṣiddīqīn"', *Journal of Islamic Studies*, 12/1 (2001), pp. 18–39.

Meillassoux, Quentin, *After Finitude: An Essay on the Necessity of Contingency*, trans. Ray Brassier (London: Continuum, 2008).

Melamed, Yitzhak Y., 'Hasdai Crescas and Spinoza on Actual Infinity and the Infinity of God's Attributes', in Steven Nadler (ed.), *Spinoza and Medieval Jewish Philosophy* (Cambridge: Cambridge University Press, 2014), pp. 204–15.

Melchert, Christopher, 'God Created Adam in His Image', *Journal of Qur'anic Studies*, 13/1 (2011), pp. 113–24.

Menzel, Christopher, 'Possible Worlds', in Edward N. Zalta (ed.), *The Stanford Encyclopedia of Philosophy* (Winter 2017 Edition), <https://plato.stanford.edu/archives/win2017/entries/possible-worlds/>.

Migliore, Daniel L., *Faith Seeking Understanding: An Introduction to Christian Theology*, 2nd edn (Grand Rapids, MI: William B. Eerdmans Publishing Company, 2004).

Miller, Adam S., review of *Being and Event*, by Alain Badiou, trans. Oliver Feltham, *Journal for Cultural and Religious Theory*, 8/1 (2006), pp. 121–27.

Miller, J. T. M., 'Are All Primitives Created Equal?', *The Southern Journal of Philosophy*, 56/2 (2018), pp. 273–92.

Moad, Edward, review of *The Qur'an and the Just Society*, by Ramon Harvey, *Journal of Islamic Studies* (2019), DOI: 10.1093/jis/etz037.

Momin, Abdur-Rahman, 'Imām Abū Hanīfa and the Doctrine of Khalq al-Qur'ān: A Rejoinder to Dr. Ziaul Haque', *Hamdard Islamicus*, 9/3 (1986), pp. 41–50.

Moran, Dermot and Joseph Cohen, *The Husserl Dictionary* (London: Continuum, 2012).

Morewedge, Parviz, 'A Third Version of the Ontological Argument in the Ibn Sīnian Metaphysics', in Parviz Morewedge (ed.), *Islamic Philosophical Theology* (Albany, NY: State University of New York Press, 1979), pp. 188–222.

Morris, Thomas V., *Our Idea of God: An Introduction to Philosophical Theology* (Vancouver: Regent College Publishing, 2002).

Morris, Thomas V. and Christopher Menzel, 'Absolute Creation', *American Philosophical Quarterly*, 23/4 (1986), pp. 353–62.

Morriston, Wes, 'Must the Beginning of the Universe Have a Personal Cause? A Critical Examination of the Kalam Cosmological Argument', *Faith and Philosophy*, 17/2 (2000), pp. 149–69.

Morriston, Wes, 'Causes and Beginnings in the Kalam Argument: A Reply to Craig', *Faith and Philosophy*, 19/2 (2002), pp. 233–44.

Morujão, Carlos, 'Is There a Place for God after the Phenomenological Reduction? Husserl and Philosophical Theology', *Revista Portuguesa de Filosofia*, 73/2 (2017), pp. 439–54.

Mueller, Ian, 'The Completeness of Stoic Propositional Logic', *Notre Dame Journal of Formal Logic*, 20/1 (1979), pp. 201–15.

Muhtaroglu, Nazif, 'Al-Māturīdī's View of Causality', in Nazif Muhtaroglu (ed.), *Occasionalism Revisited: New Essays from the Islamic and Western Philosophical Traditions* (Abu Dhabi: Kalam Research & Media, 2017), pp. 3–21.

Mulligan, Kevin, Peter Simons and Barry Smith, 'Truth-Makers', *Philosophy and Phenomenological Research*, 44/3 (1984), pp. 287–321.

Murray, Michael J. and Michael Rea, 'Philosophy and Christian Theology', in Edward N. Zalta (ed.), *The Stanford Encyclopedia of Philosophy* (Winter 2016 Edition), <https://plato.stanford.edu/archives/win2016/entries/christiantheology-philosophy/>.

Nagasawa, Yujin, *Maximal God: A New Defence of Perfect Being Theism* (Oxford: Oxford University Press, 2017).

Al-Najjār, Aḥmad, *Tabriʾat al-imām Aḥmad bin Ḥanbal min kitāb al-radd ʿalā al-zanādiqa wa-l-jahmiyya* (Baghdad: Maktaba Alwān, 2018).

Nelson, Michael, 'Existence', in Edward N. Zalta (ed.), *The Stanford Encyclopedia of Philosophy* (Spring 2019 Edition), <https://plato.stanford.edu/archives/spr2019/entries/existence/>.

Nesteruk, Alexei V., 'A "Participatory Universe" of J. A. Wheeler as an Intentional Correlate of Embodied Subjects and an Example of Purposiveness in Physics', *Journal of Siberian Federal University: Humanities and Social Sciences*, 6/3 (2013), pp. 415–37.

Netton, Ian Richard, *Allāh Transcendent: Studies in the Structure and Semiotics of Islamic Philosophy, Theology and Cosmology* (London: Routledge, 1989).

Neuwirth, Angelika, *The Qur'an and Late Antiquity: A Shared Heritage* (Oxford: Oxford University Press, 2019).

Nicoll, Alexander, *Bibliothecæ Bodleianæ Codicum Manuscritorum Orientalium*, 2 vols (Oxford: Clarendon Press, 1835).

Nuʿmānī, Shiblī, *Imam Abu Hanifah: Life and Works*, trans M. Hadi Hussain (Karachi: Darul Ishaat, 2000).

Nuʿmānī, Shiblī, *ʿIlm al-kalām al-jadīd*, trans. Jalāl al-Saʿīd al-Ḥifnāwī (Cairo: Al-Markaz al-Qawmī li-l-Tarjama, 2012).

Oppy, Graham, 'Natural Theology', in Deane-Peter Baker (ed.), *Alvin Plantinga* (Cambridge: Cambridge University Press, 2007), pp. 15–47.

Oppy, Graham, 'Ontological Arguments', in Edward N. Zalta (ed.), *The Stanford Encyclopedia of Philosophy* (Spring 2019 Edition), <https://plato.stanford.edu/archives/spr2019/entries/ontological-arguments/>.

Özcan, Hanifi, *Matüridi'de Bilgi Problemi* (Istanbul: İFAV, 2012).

Özen, Şükrü, 'IV. (X.) Yüzyılda Mâverâünnehirʾde Ehl-i Sünnet-Muʿtezile Mücadelesi ve Bir Ehl-i Sūnnet Beyannamesi', *İslâm Araştırmaları Dergisi*, 9 (2003), pp. 49–85.

Özervarli, M. Sait, 'The Authenticity of the Manuscript of Māturīdī's Kitāb al-Tawḥ īd: A Re-examination', *İslâm Araştırmaları Dergisi*, 1 (1997), pp. 19–29.

Özervarli, M. Sait, 'Attempts to Revitalize *Kalām* in the Late 19th and Early 20th Centuries', *The Muslim World*, 89/1 (1999), pp. 90–105.

Pereboom, Derk, 'Kant's Transcendental Arguments', in Edward N. Zalta (ed.), *The Stanford Encyclopedia of Philosophy* (Spring 2019 Edition), <https://plato.stanford.edu/archives/spr2019/entries/kant-transcendental/>.

Pessagno, J. Meric, 'Intellect and Religious Assent: The View of Abū Manṣūr al-Māturīdī', *The Muslim World*, 69/1 (1979), pp. 18–27.

Pessagno, J. Meric, '*Irāda, Ikhtiyār, Qudra, Kasb*: The View of Abū Manṣūr al-Māturīdī', *Journal of the American Oriental Society*, 104/1 (1984), pp. 177–91.

Pessagno, J. Meric, 'The Reconstruction of the Thought of Muḥammad Ibn Shabīb', *Journal of the American Oriental Society*, 104/3 (1984), pp. 445–53.

Pessagno, J. Meric, 'The Uses of Evil in Maturidian Thought', *Studia Islamica*, 60 (1984), pp. 59–82.

Pessin, Sarah, 'Forms of Hylomorphism', in Richard C. Taylor and Luis Xavier López-Farjeat (eds), *The Routledge Companion to Islamic Philosophy* (Abingdon: Routledge, 2016), pp. 197–211.

Pietersma, Henry, 'Husserl's Concept of Existence', *Synthese*, 66/2 (1986), pp. 311–28.

Pike, Nelson, *God and Timelessness* (London: Routledge & Kegan Paul, 1970).

Pines, Shlomo, 'A Study of the Impact of Indian, mainly Buddhist, Thought on Some Aspects of Kalām Doctrines', *Jerusalem Studies in Arabic and Islam*, 17 (1994), pp. 182–203.

Pines, Shlomo, *Studies in Islamic Atomism*, trans. Michael Schwartz (Jerusalem: Magnes Press, The Hebrew University, 1997).

Plantinga, Alvin, *The Nature of Necessity* (Oxford: Oxford University Press, 1974).

Plantinga, Alvin, *Does God Have a Nature?* (Milwaukee, WI: Marquette University Press, 1980).

Plantinga, Alvin, 'Reason and Belief in God', in Alvin Plantinga and Nicholas Wolterstorff (eds), *Faith and Rationality: Reason and Belief in God* (Notre Dame, IN: University of Notre Dame Press, 1983).

Plantinga, Alvin, 'Two Concepts of Modality: Modal Realism and Modal Reductionism', *Philosophical Perspectives*, 1 (1987), pp. 189–231.

Plantinga, Alvin, 'Appendix: Two Dozen (or so) Theistic Arguments', in D. Baker (ed.), *Alvin Plantinga* (Cambridge: Cambridge University Press, 2007), pp. 203–28.

Plantinga, Alvin, *Where the Conflict Really Lies: Science, Religion, and Naturalism* (Oxford: Oxford University Press, 2011).

Plato, *Timaeus*, in Benjamin Jowett (trans.), *The Dialogues of Plato*, 5 vols (Oxford: Clarendon Press, 1892), vol. 3, pp. 339–515.

Potter, Michael, *Set Theory and its Philosophy* (Oxford: Oxford University Press, 2004).

Priest, Graham, 'Revising Logic', in Penelope Rush (ed.), *The Metaphysics of Logic* (Cambridge: Cambridge University Press, 2014).

Pugliese, Marc A., 'Quantum Mechanics and an Ontology of Intersubjectivity: Perils and Promises', *Open Theology*, 4 (2018), pp. 325–41.

Quinn, Philip L., 'Divine Conservation, Continuous Creation, and Human Action', in Alfred J. Freddoso (ed.), *The Existence and Nature of God* (Notre Dame, IN: University of Notre Dame Press, 1983), pp. 55–80.

Quinn, Philip L., 'Can God Speak? Does God Speak?', *Religious Studies*, 37/3 (2001), pp. 259–69.

Rahman, Fazlur, *Islam*, 2nd edn (Chicago: University of Chicago Press, 1976).

Rahman, Fazlur, 'Dhāt', in P. Bearman, Th. Bianquis, C. E. Bosworth, E. Van Donzel, and W. P. Heinrichs (eds), *The Encyclopaedia of Islam, New Edition*, 12 vols (Leiden: Brill, 1986–2004).

Rasmussen, Joshua, review of *God and Ultimate Origins: A Novel Cosmological Argument*, by Andrew Ter Ern Loke, *European Journal for Philosophy of Religion* 10/1 (2018), pp. 189–94.

Ratzsch, Del and Jeffrey Koperski, 'Teleological Arguments for God's Existence', in Edward N. Zalta (ed.), *The Stanford Encyclopedia of Philosophy* (Summer 2019 Edition), <https://plato.stanford.edu/archives/sum2019/entries/teleological-arguments/>.

Al-Raysūnī, Aḥmad, *Al-Tajdīd al-uṣūlī: nahw siyāgha tajdīdiyya li-ʿilm al-uṣūl al-fiqh* (Herndon, VA: The International Institute of Islamic Thought, 2015).

Reçber, Mehmet Sait, *Necessity, Logic and God*, PhD thesis (Kings College, University of London, 1998).

Reichenbach, Bruce, 'Cosmological Argument', in Edward N. Zalta (ed.), *The Stanford Encyclopedia of Philosophy* (Spring 2019 Edition), <https://plato.stanford.edu/archives/spr2019/entries/cosmological-argument/>.

Rescher, Nicholas, *Studies in Arabic Philosophy* (Pittsburgh, PA: University of Pittsburgh Press, 1968).

Reynolds, Gabriel Said, 'God has Spoken Before: On the Recitation of the Bible in Islamic Ritual Prayer', in Željko Paša (ed.), *Between the Cross and the Crescent: Studies in Honor of Samir Khalil Samir, S. J. on the Occasion of His Eightieth Birthday* (Rome: Pontificio Instituto Orientale, 2018), pp. 573–91.

Rizvi, Sajjad H., '"Only the Imam Knows Best": The Maktab-e Tafkīk's Attack on the Legitimacy of Philosophy in Iran', *Journal of the Royal Asiatic Society*, 22/3–4 (2012), pp. 487–503.

Rodriguez-Pereyra, Gonzalo, 'Nominalism in Metaphysics', in Edward N. Zalta (ed.), *The Stanford Encyclopedia of Philosophy* (Winter 2016 Edition), <https://plato.stanford.edu/archives/win2016/entries/nominalism-metaphysics/>.

Rolnick, Philip A., 'Realist Reference to God: Analogy or Univocity?' in William P. Alston (ed.), *Realism and Antirealism* (Ithaca, NY: Cornell University Press, 2002), pp. 211–37.

Rosenthal, Franz, *Knowledge Triumphant: The Concept of Knowledge in Medieval Islam* (Leiden: Brill, 2007).

Ross, James F., *Philosophical Theology*, 2nd printing (Indianapolis, IN: Hackett Publishing, 1969).

Ross, James F., 'Analogy as a Rule of Meaning for Religious Language', in Anthony Kenny (ed.), *Aquinas: A Collection of Critical Essays* (London: Palgrave Macmillan, 1969), pp. 93–138.

Ross, James F., 'Creation', *The Journal of Philosophy*, 77/10 (1980), pp. 614–29.

Ross, James F., 'Creation II', in Alfred J. Freddoso (ed.), *The Existence and Nature of God* (Notre Dame, IN: University of Notre Dame Press, 1983), pp. 115–41.

Roth, Brandon, *Experiencing Real Time: Husserl and the Debate About Tense*, PhD thesis (Stony Brook University, 2012).

Rudolph, Ulrich, 'Ratio und Überlieferung in der Erkenntnislehre al-Ashʿarī's und al-Māturīdī's', *Zeitschrift der Deutschen Morgenländischen Gesellschaft*, 142/1 (1992), pp. 72–89.

Rudolph, Ulrich, 'Reflections on al-Fārābī's *Mabādiʾ ārāʾ ahl al-madīna al-fāḍila*', in Peter Adamson (ed.), *In the Age of al-Fārābī: Arabic Philosophy in the Fourth/Tenth Century* (London/Turin: The Warburg Institute/Nino Aragno Editore, 2008), pp. 1–14.

Rudolph, Ulrich, *Al-Māturīdī and the Development of Sunnī Theology in Samarqand*, trans. Rodrigo Adem (Leiden: Brill, 2015).

Rudolph, Ulrich, 'Al-Māturīdī's Concept of God's Wisdom', in İlyas Çelebi (ed.), *Büyük Türk Bilgini İmâm Mâtürîdî ve Mâtürîdîlik: Milletlerarası Tartışmalı İlmî Toplantı* (Istanbul: M. Ü. İlâhiyat Fakültesi Vakfı Yayınları, 2016), pp. 47–55.

Rudolph, Ulrich, 'Ḥanafī Theological Tradition and Māturīdism', in Sabine Schmidtke (ed.), *The Oxford Handbook of Islamic Theology* (Oxford: Oxford University Press, 2016), pp. 280–96.

Russell, Bertrand, *History of Western Philosophy and its Connection with Political and Social Circumstances from the Earliest Times to the Present Day* (New Delhi: Popular Book Services, 1957).

Saeed, Abdullah, *Interpreting the Qur'an: Towards a Contemporary Approach* (New York: Routledge, 2005).

Al-Salimi, Abdulrahman and Wilferd Madelung (eds), *Early Ibāḍī Theology: Six* kalām *texts by ʿAbd Allāh b. Yazīd al-Fazārī* (Leiden: Brill, 2014).

Schacht, Joseph, 'New Sources for the History of Muhammadan Theology', *Studia Islamica*, 1 (1953), pp. 23–42.

Schöck, Cornelia, 'Jahm b. Ṣafwān (d. 128/745–6) and the 'Jahmiyya' and Ḍirār b. ʿAmr (d. 200/815)', in Sabine Schmidtke (ed.), *The Oxford Handbook of Islamic Theology* (Oxford: Oxford University Press, 2016), pp. 55–80.

Şeşen, Ramazan, *Fahras makhṭūṭāt maktaba Kūbrīlī*, 3 vols (Istanbul: Markaz al-Abḥāth li-l-Tārīkh wa-l-Funūn wa-l-Thaqāfa al-Islāmiyya, 1986).

Shannon, Nathan D., 'The Epistemology of Divine Conceptualism', *International Journal for Philosophy of Religion* (2014), DOI: 10.1007/s11153-014-9483-0.

Sharvy, Richard, 'Why a Class Can't Change Its Members', *Noûs*, 2/4 (1968), pp. 303–14.

Shihadeh, Ayman, 'Mereology in *Kalām*: A New Reading of the Proof from Accidents for Creation', *Oriens*, 48 (2020), pp. 5–39.

Sklare, David, 'Responses to Islamic Polemics by Jewish Mutakallimūn in the Tenth Century', in Hava Lazarus-Yafeh, Mark R. Cohen, Sasson Somekh and Sidney H. Griffith (eds), *The Majlis: Interreligious Encounters in Medieval Islam* (Wiesbaden: Harrassowitz Verlag, 1999), pp. 137–61.

Sklare, David, 'Muʿtazili Trends in Jewish Theology', *İslâmî İlimler Dergisi*, 12/2 (2017), pp. 145–78.

Smith, David Woodruff, '"Pure" Logic, Ontology, and Phenomenology', *Revue Internationale de Philosophie*, 224/2 (2003), pp. 21–44.

Smith, David Woodruff, *Husserl*, 2nd edn (Abingdon: Routledge, 2013).

Smith, David Woodruff, and Ronald McIntyre, *Husserl and Intentionality: A Study of Mind, Meaning, and Language* (Dordrecht: D. Reidel, 1982).

Smith, Wilfred Cantwell, 'Scripture as Form and Concept: Their Emergence for the Western World', in Miriam Levering (ed.), *Rethinking Scripture: Essays from a Comparative Perspective* (Albany, NY: State University of New York Press, 1989), pp. 29–57.

Sokolowski, Robert, *The Formation of Husserl's Concept of Constitution* (The Hague: Martinus Nijhoff, 1970).

Sokolowski, Robert, 'Identities in Manifolds: A Husserlian Pattern of Thought', *Research in Phenomenology*, 4 (1974), pp. 63–79.

Sokolowski, Robert, *The God of Faith and Reason: Foundations of Christian Theology* (Washington, D. C.: The Catholic University of America Press, 1995).

Sokolowski, Robert, *Introduction to Phenomenology* (Cambridge: Cambridge University Press, 2000).

Sommer, Benjamin D., *Revelation and Authority: Sinai in Jewish Scripture and Tradition* (New Haven, CT: Yale University Press, 2015).

Sorabji, Richard, *Time, Creation and the Continuum: Theories in Antiquity and the Early Middle Ages* (London: Duckworth, 1983).

Sorabji, Richard, *Matter, Space and Motion: Theories in Antiquity and Their Sequel* (London: Duckworth, 1988).

Soroush, Abdulkarim, *The Expansion of Prophetic Experience: Essays on Historicity, Contingency and Plurality in Religion*, trans. Nilou Mobasser (Leiden: Brill, 2009).

Soskice, Janet, *Metaphor and Religious Language* (Oxford: Oxford University Press, 1985).

Soskice, Janet, 'Naming God: A Study in Faith and Reason', in Paul J. Griffiths and Reinhard Hütter (eds), *Reason and the Reasons of Faith* (New York: T. & T. Clark International, 2005), pp. 241–54.

Spannaus, Nathan, *Preserving Islamic Tradition: Abū Naṣr Qūrṣāwī and the Beginnings of Modern Reformism* (Oxford: Oxford University Press, 2019).

Spevack, Aaron, 'The Qur'an and God's Speech According to the Later Ashʿarī-Māturīdī Verifiers', *Journal of Islamic Philosophy*, 11 (2019), pp. 45–94.

Staiti, Andrea, and Evan Clarke, 'Introduction', in Andrea Staiti and Evan Clarke (eds), *The Sources of Husserl's "Ideas I"* (Berlin: De Gruyter, 2018), pp. 1–10.

Stapp, Henry P., *Mindful Universe: Quantum Mechanics and the Participating Observer* (Berlin: Springer, 2007).

Steiner, Mark, 'Wittgenstein and the Covert Platonism of Mathematical Logic', in Penelope Rush (ed.), *The Metaphysics of Logic* (Cambridge: Cambridge University Press, 2014), pp. 128–44.

Stevenson, Angus (ed.), *Shorter Oxford English Dictionary*, 2 vols (Oxford: Oxford University Press, 2007).

Street, Tony, 'Arabic and Islamic Philosophy of Language and Logic', in Edward N. Zalta (ed.), *The Stanford Encyclopedia of Philosophy* (Spring 2015 Edition), <https://plato.stanford.edu/archives/spr2015/entries/arabic-islamic-language/>.

Sutanto, Nathaniel Gray, 'Two Theological Accounts of Logic: Theistic Conceptual Realism and a Reformed Archetype-ectype Model', *International Journal for Philosophy of Religion* (2015), DOI: 10.1007/s11153-015-9543-0.

Swinburne, Richard, *The Coherence of Theism*, revised edn (Oxford: Oxford University Press, 1993).

Swinburne, Richard, *The Christian God* (Oxford: Oxford University Press, 1994).
Swinburne, Richard, 'Philosophical Theism', in D. Z. Philips and Timothy Tessin (eds), *Philosophy of Religion in the 21st Century* (Basingstoke: Palgrave Macmillan, 2001), pp. 3–20.
Swinburne, Richard, *The Existence of God*, 2nd edn (Oxford: Oxford University Press, 2004).
Swinburne, Richard, *The Coherence of Theism*, 2nd edn (Oxford: Oxford University Press, 2016).
Al-Taftāzānī, Saʿd al-Dīn, *A Commentary on the Creed of Islam*, trans. Earl Edgar Elder (New York: Columbia University Press, 1950).
Tanner, Kathryn, *God and Creation in Christian Theology: Tyranny or Empowerment* (Oxford: Basil Blackwell, 1988).
Taylor, C. C. W. and Mi-Kyoung Lee, 'The Sophists', in Edward N. Zalta (ed.), *The Stanford Encyclopedia of Philosophy* (Winter 2016 Edition), <https://plato.stanford.edu/archives/win2016/entries/sophists/>.
Taylor, Charles, *A Secular Age* (Cambridge, MA: The Belknap Press of Harvard University Press, 2007).
Thomas, David, *Christian Doctrines in Islamic Theology* (Leiden: Brill, 2008).
Thomasson, Amie, 'Categories', in Edward N. Zalta (ed.), *The Stanford Encyclopedia of Philosophy* (Spring 2018 Edition), <https://plato.stanford.edu/archives/spr2018/entries/categories/>.
Tieszen, Richard, 'Mathematical Realism and Transcendental Phenomenological Idealism', in Mirja Hartimo (ed.), *Phenomenology and Mathematics* (Dordrecht: Springer, 2010), pp. 1–22.
Treiger, Alexander, 'Origins of Kalām', in Sabine Schmidtke (ed.), *The Oxford Handbook of Islamic Theology* (Oxford: Oxford University Press, 2016), pp. 27–43.
Trenery, David, *Alasdair MacIntyre, George Lindbeck, and the Nature of Tradition* (Eugene, OR: Wipf and Stock Publishers, 2014).
van Atten, Mark, *Essays on Gödel's Reception of Leibniz, Husserl, and Brouwer* (Dordrecht: Springer, 2015).
van Atten, Mark, 'Luitzen Egbertus Jan Brouwer', in Edward N. Zalta (ed.), *The Stanford Encyclopedia of Philosophy* (Winter 2017 Edition), <https://plato.stanford.edu/archives/win2017/entries/brouwer/>.
van Atten, Mark and Göran Sundholm, 'L. E. J. Brouwer's "Unreliability of the Logical Principles": A New Translation, with an Introduction', *History and Philosophy of Logic* (2016), DOI: 10.1080/01445340.2016.1210986.
Van Cleve, James, 'Three Versions of the Bundle Theory', *Philosophical Studies: An International Journal for Philosophy in the Analytic Tradition*, 47/1 (1985), pp. 95–107.
van Dalen, Dirk, 'Intuitionistic Logic', in Dov M. Gabbay and Franz Guenthner (eds), *Handbook of Philosophical Logic, 2nd Edition, Volume 5* (Dordrecht: Springer, 2002), pp. 1–114.
van Ess, Josef, 'The Logical Structure of Islamic Theology', in G. E. von Grunebaum (ed.), *Logic in Classical Islamic Culture* (Wiesbaden: Otto Harrassowitz, 1970), pp. 21–50.

van Ess, Josef, review of *Kitāb al-tawḥīd*, by Abū Manṣūr al-Māturīdī, ed. Fathalla Kholeif, *Oriens*, 27/28 (1981), pp. 556–65.

van Ess, Josef, 'Early Development of *Kalām*', in G. H. A. Juynboll (ed.), *Studies on the First Century of Islamic Society* (Carbondale: Southern Illinois University Press, 1982), pp. 109–23.

van Ess, Josef, '60 Years After: Shlomo Pines's Beiträge and Half a Century of Research on Atomism in Islamic Theology', *Proceedings of the Israel Academy of Sciences and Humanities*, 8/2 (2002), pp. 1–23.

van Ess, Josef, *Theology and Society in the Second and Third Centuries of the Hijra, Volume 1*, trans. John O'Kane (Leiden: Brill, 2017).

van Ess, Josef, *Theology and Society in the Second and Third Centuries of the Hijra, Volume 2*, trans. Gwendolin Goldbloom (Leiden: Brill, 2017).

van Ess, Josef, *Theology and Society in the Second and Third Centuries of the Hijra, Volume 3*, trans. Gwendolin Goldbloom (Leiden: Brill, 2018).

van Ess, Josef, *Theology and Society in the Second and Third Centuries of the Hijra, Volume 4*, trans. Gwendolin Goldbloom (Leiden: Brill, 2018).

van Ess, Josef, 'Abu'l-Qāsim al-Kaʿbī', in Hinrich Biesterfeldt (ed.), Kleine Schriften *by Josef van Ess*, 3 vols (Leiden: Brill, 2018), vol. 2, pp. 1381–87.

van Ess, Josef, 'Disputationspraxis in der islamischen Theologie. Eine vorläufige Skizze', in Hinrich Biesterfeldt (ed.), Kleine Schriften *by Josef van Ess*, 3 vols (Leiden: Brill, 2018), vol. 2, pp. 911–47.

van Ess, Josef, 'Ibn Kullāb et la *Miḥna*', in Hinrich Biesterfeldt (ed.), Kleine Schriften *by Josef van Ess*, 3 vols (Leiden: Brill, 2018), vol. 2, pp. 1454–510.

van Ess, Josef, 'Kalām', in Hinrich Biesterfeldt (ed.), Kleine Schriften *by Josef van Ess*, 3 vols (Leiden: Brill, 2018), vol. 2, pp. 903–10.

van Ess, Josef, 'Verbal Inspiration? Language and Revelation in Islamic Theology', in Hinrich Biesterfeldt (ed.), Kleine Schriften *by Josef van Ess*, 3 vols (Leiden: Brill, 2018), vol. 3, pp. 1759–74.

van Putten, Marijn, '"The Grace of God" as Evidence for a Written Uthmanic Archetype: The Importance of Shared Orthographic Idiosyncrasies', *Bulletin of SOAS*, 82/2 (2019), pp. 271–88.

Vasalou, Sophia, 'The Miraculous Eloquence of the Qur'an: General Trajectories and Individual Approaches', *Journal of Qur'anic Studies*, 4/2 (2002), pp. 23–53.

Vishanoff, David R., *The Formation of Islamic Hermeneutics: How Sunni Legal Theorists Imagined a Revealed Law* (New Haven, CT: American Oriental Society, 2011).

von Grunebaum, Gustave, 'The Concept and Function of Reason in Islamic Ethics', *Oriens*, 15 (1962), pp. 1–17.

von Grunebaum, Gustave, 'The Sources of Islamic Civilization', *Der Islam*, 46 (1970), pp. 1–54.

Wainwright, William J., 'God's Body', in Thomas V. Morris (ed.), *The Concept of God* (Oxford: Oxford University Press, 1987), pp. 72–87.

Walbridge, John, *God and Logic in Islam: The Caliphate of Reason* (Cambridge: Cambridge University Press, 2011).

Wang, Yuan, *The Goldbach Conjecture*, 2nd edn (Singapore: World Scientific Publishing, 2002).

Watt, William Montgomery, 'Early Discussions about the Qur'ān', *The Muslim World*, 40/1 (1950), pp. 27–40.

Watt, William Montgomery, *Islamic Revelation in the Modern World* (Edinburgh: Edinburgh University Press, 1969).

Watt, William Montgomery (trans.), *Islamic Creeds: A Selection* (Edinburgh: Edinburgh University Press, 1994).

Watt, William Montgomery, *The Formative Period of Islamic Thought* (London: Oneworld, 2008).

Weatherson, Brian, 'David Lewis', in Edward N. Zalta (ed.), *The Stanford Encyclopedia of Philosophy* (Winter 2016 Edition), <https://plato.stanford.edu/archives/win2016/entries/david-lewis/>.

Wensinck, A. J., *The Muslim Creed* (Cambridge: Cambridge University Press, 1932).

Westphal, Merold, 'On Reading God the Author', *Religious Studies*, 37/3 (2001), pp. 271–91.

Wheeler, John Archibald, 'Genesis and Observership', in Robert E. Butts and Jaako Hintikka (eds), *Foundational Problems in the Special Sciences: Part Two of the Proceedings of the Fifth International Congress of Logic, Methodology and Philosophy of Science, London, Ontario, Canada–1975* (Dordrecht: D. Reidel, 1977), pp. 3–33.

Wheeler, John Archibald, 'Beyond the Black Hole', in Harry Woolf (ed.), *Some Strangeness in the Proportion: A Centennial Symposium to Celebrate the Achievements of Albert Einstein* (Reading, MA: Addison-Wesley, 1980), pp. 341–75.

Wielandt, Rotraud, 'Main Trends of Islamic Theological Thought from the Late Nineteenth Century to the Present Times', in Sabine Schmidtke (ed.), *The Oxford Handbook of Islamic Theology* (Oxford: Oxford University Press, 2016), pp. 707–64.

Wierenga, Edward R., 'Timelessness out of Mind: On the Alleged Incoherence of Divine Timelessness', in Gregory E. Ganssle and David M. Woodruff, *God and Time: Essays on the Divine Nature* (Oxford: Oxford University Press, 2002), pp. 153–64.

Wierenga, Edward R., 'Omniscience', in Thomas P. Flint and Michael C. Rea (eds), *The Oxford Handbook of Philosophical Theology* (Oxford: Oxford University Press, 2009), pp. 129–44.

Williams, A. N., 'Is Aquinas a Foundationalist?', *New Blackfriars*, 91/1031 (2010), pp. 20–45.

Williams, Rowan, *On Christian Theology* (Oxford: Blackwell, 2000).

Williams, Rowan, *The Edge of Words: God and the Habits of Language* (London: Bloomsbury, 2014).

Wisnovsky, Robert, *Avicenna's Metaphysics in Context* (Ithaca, NY: Cornell University Press, 2003).

Wisnovsky, Robert, 'One Aspect of the Avicennian Turn in Sunnī Theology', *Arabic Sciences and Philosophy*, 14 (2004), pp. 65–100.

Wisnovsky, Robert, 'Essence and Existence in the Eleventh- and Twelfth-Century Islamic East (*Mashriq*): A Sketch', in Dag Nikolaus Hasse and Amos Bertolacci (eds), *The Arabic, Hebrew and Latin Reception of Avicenna's Metaphysics* (Berlin: De Gruyter, 2012), pp. 27–50.

Wisnovsky, Robert, 'On the Emergence of Maragha Avicennism', *Oriens*, 46 (2018), pp. 263–301.

Wolfson, Harry Austryn, *The Philosophy of the Kalam* (Cambridge, MA: Harvard University Press, 1976).

Wolterstorff, Nicholas, *On Universals: An Essay in Ontology* (Chicago: The University of Chicago Press, 1970).

Wolterstorff, Nicholas, 'Divine Simplicity', *Philosophical Perspectives*, 5, Philosophy of Religion (1991), pp. 531–52.

Wolterstorff, Nicholas, *Divine Discourse: Philosophical Reflections on the Claim that God Speaks* (Cambridge: Cambridge University Press, 1995).

Wolterstorff, Nicholas, 'Reformed Epistemology', in D. Z. Philips and Timothy Tessin (eds), *Philosophy of Religion in the 21st Century* (Basingstoke: Palgrave Macmillan, 2001), pp. 39–63.

Wolterstorff, Nicholas, 'Response to Helm, Quinn, and Westphal', *Religious Studies*, 37/3 (2001), pp. 293–306.

Wolterstorff, Nicholas, 'How Philosophical Theology Became Possible within the Analytic Tradition of Philosophy', in Oliver D. Crisp and Michael C. Rea (eds), *Analytic Theology: New Essays in the Philosophy of Theology* (Oxford: Oxford University Press, 2009), pp. 155–68.

Wright, Crispin, 'How High the Sky? Rumfitt on the (Putative) Indeterminacy of the Set-Theoretic Universe', *Philosophical Studies*, 175/8 (2018), pp. 2067–78.

Wykstra, Stephen J., 'On Behalf of the Evidentialist – a Response to Wolterstorff', in D. Z. Philips and Timothy Tessin (eds), *Philosophy of Religion in the 21st Century* (Basingstoke: Palgrave Macmillan, 2001), pp. 64–84.

Xiuyuan, Dong, 'The Presence of Buddhist Thought in Kalām Literature', *Philosophy East and West*, 68/3 (2018), pp. 944–73.

Yandell, Keith E., 'Divine Necessity and Divine Goodness', in Thomas V. Morris (ed.), *Divine and Human Action: Essays in the Metaphysics of Theism* (Ithaca, NY: Cornell University Press, 1988), pp. 313–44.

Yavuz, Yusuf Şevki, 'İmâm Mâtürîdî'nin Tabiat ve İlliyete Bakişi', in İlyas Çelebi (ed.), *Büyük Türk Bilgini İmâm Mâtürîdî ve Mâtürîdîlik: Milletlerarası Tartışmalı İlmî Toplantı* (Istanbul: M. Ü. İlâhiyat Fakültesi Vakfı Yayınları, 2016), pp. 56–66.

Zadeh, Travis, *The Vernacular Qur'an: Translation and the Rise of Persian Exegesis* (Oxford: Oxford University Press, in association with the Institute of Ismaili Studies, 2012).

Zagzebski, Linda, 'Omniscience', in Chad Meister and Paul Copan (eds), *The Routledge Companion to Philosophy of Religion* (Abingdon: Routledge, 2007), pp. 261–70.

Zahavi, Dan, 'Husserl's Intersubjective Transformation of Transcendental Philosophy', in Donn Welton (ed.), *The New Husserl: A Critical Reader* (Bloomington, IN: Indiana University Press, 2003), pp. 233–51.

Zahavi, Dan, *Husserl's Legacy: Phenomenology, Metaphysics, and Transcendental Philosophy* (Oxford: Oxford University Press, 2017).

Al-Zayd, Zayd b. ʿAbd al-Muḥsin (ed.), *Fahras al-makhṭūṭāt fī markaz al-malik Fayṣal li-l-buḥūth wa-l-dirāsa al-islāmiyya*, 8 vols (Riyadh: Markaz al-malik Fayṣal li-l-buḥūth wa-l-dirāsa al-islāmiyya, 1994).

Zenker, Julius (ed.), 'Kitāb Aristūṭālis al-musammā qāṭīghūriyyā ay al-maqūlāt', in Julius Zenker (ed.), *Aristotelis Categoriae: Graece cum Versione Arabica* (Leipzig: Engelmann, 1846).

Zolghadr, Behnam, 'The Sufi Path of Dialetheism: Gluon Theory and Wahdat al-Wujud', *History and Philosophy of Logic*, 39/2 (2018), pp. 99–108.

Zysow, Aron, 'Muʿtazilism and Māturīdism in Ḥanafī Legal Theory' in Bernard G. Weiss (ed.), *Studies in Islamic Legal Theory* (Leiden: Brill, 2002), pp. 223–65.

Zysow, Aron, *The Economy of Certainty: An Introduction to the Typology of Islamic Legal Theory* (Atlanta: Lockwood Press, 2013).

Index

Ash'arism (*cont.*)
on divine command theory, 216, 233
on essence and existence, 77–78, 226
on God's attributes, 124*n*1, 141, 146–47, 149, 150, 183–84, 188–89, 197, 227, 233
on God's speech, 196
on God's wisdom, 159, 161
on the Qur'an, 206–10, 228
on *takwīn*, 175, 180–83
'Aṭā' b. 'Alī al-Jūzjānī, 32*n*114
A-theory and B-theory of time (Leftow), 128–29, 131–32, 190, 231
atomism, 87, 88–89; *see also* concrete particulars (a'*yān*/*jawāhir*)
Atten, Mark van, 81–82, 117
attributes (*ṣifāt*) of God, 30–31, 33–34, 141–58, 227
ḥikma (wisdom), 45, 71, 119–20, 159–66, 172–4, 188, 216–18, 224, 232, 233
'*ilm* (omniscience), 70, 132, 147–48, 159–74, 188–89, 227, 231
kalām (speech), 152, 176*n*5, 181, 191–221, 224, 227–28, 232
takwīn (creative action), 47, 159, 165, 175–90, 221, 224, 227, 232
see also God
Avicenna (Ibn Sīnā), 41–42, 77–78, 106, 128, 130, 132–33, 147, 187–88, 226
'*ayān*/*jawāhir see* concrete particulars (a'*yān*/*jawāhir*)

Bacon, John, 85
Badiou, Alain, 85–87, 95, 137, 229
Baghdad, 34, 163
al-Baghdādī, 'Abd al-Qāhir, 147
al-Balkhī, Abū Muṭī', 30*n*102, 31, 32*n*114, 176*n*4, 177*n*10, 194
baqā' (endurance), 90, 100
al-Bāqillānī, Abū Bakr, 110, 147, 205*n*73, 206, 208, 218
Basra, 34, 88
al-Bayāḍī, Kamāl al-Dīn, 44–45
al-Bazdawī, 'Abd al-Karīm, 39*n*154
al-Bazdawī, Abū al-Yusr, 40, 126
on eternality, 128, 226
on God's knowledge, 147–48
on God's speech, 184*n*58, 206–7
on God's wisdom, 165
on *takwīn*, 176*n*5, 180–81
Bell, Richard, 211*n*110
Bin Ramli, Harith, 42*n*183
Birinci, Züleyha, 32*n*114
bivalence, 80–81, 136, 166, 229, 231
bodies (*ajsām*, sing. *jism*), 61, 75, 87–92, 101, 189, 223
Bohr, Niels, 60*n*24, 67–69, 71–72, 113, 169–70
Bolzano, Bernard, 50
bracketing process (Husserl), 50, 58, 64–65, 79, 118
Brodersen, Angelika, 146, 182
Brouwer, L. E. J., 81, 82, 114, 116, 118
Buddhism, 32
'buffered self' (Taylor), 66
Bulgen, Mehmet, 90*n*217
bundle theory, 88, 89–93, 97, 98–101, 150, 223, 229–30

Cairo, 46
Campbell, Keith, 96–97, 99*n*268, 229–30
Cantor, Gregor, 84, 86, 114, 116, 168–69
Cantor's Theorem, 168–69
Carter, Brandon, 71–72
categorial entities, knowledge of, 65, 73–87, 98, 113, 117, 137, 157, 171, 229
Categories (Aristotle), 34–37
causation, intuitions of, 112–13
Cerić, Mustafa, 15, 49, 108*n*27, 144*n*103
Chevally, Catherine, 68–69
choice sequences, 116
Christianity, 4, 32, 33*n*123, 57*n*10, 104, 141–42, 185–86, 187, 211, 216
Cohen, Yishai, 115–16

colour, concept of, 90–91*n*218, 96–97, 98–101, 134, 199
complementarity (Bohr), 60*n*24, 169–70
composition (*naẓm*), 204, 205*n*74, 207, 208
concept nominalism, 154, 198–99
concordance (*muwāfaqa*), 201, 220, 224
concrete and mental existence, 78–79
concrete particulars (*aʿyān/jawāhir*), 58, 74–75, 89, 198–99, 230
  in the *Categories*, 35–36
  and nature of God, 143, 150, 153–57
  in ontology, 98–101
  and temporality, 109
concurrentism, 93*n*235
consciousness, centrality of, 69–72, 130–32, 223, 229
consensus (*ijmāʿ*), 22–23, 25–26
contingency of the world
  and existence of God, 76, 86, 99, 106–10, 128, 133–34, 139–40
  God's transcendence over, 149, 156–57, 171, 214, 223, 224, 226, 227
contingent history, 51–54
Copenhagen interpretation, 58, 67–69, 71–72, 113, 169–70, 230; *see also* quantum mechanics
Correa, Dale, 23
correspondence theory of truth, 79–87, 98
cosmological arguments, 47–48, 128, 132
  kalām (KCA), 107–22, 129, 230
  Leibnizian, 107, 133
  Thomistic, 107
counterpart theory, 100, 101
Craig, William Lane, 110, 111–14, 115–16, 189, 230
creation
  ex nihilo, 126, 160–61, 189–90, 232
  and the existence of God, 47–48, 93
  and God's wisdom, 161–65
  khalq al-qurʾān controversy, 192–94
  and necessity, 27
  see also natures (*ṭabāʾiʿ*); *takwīn* (creative action)
Crosilla, Laura, 169
Cross, Richard, 141–42
al-Çūrī, Ḥassan b. al-Sayyid, 20*n*45, 44

Daccache, Salim, 176*n*6
Daiber, Hans, 32*n*114
dalālat al-shāhid ʿalā al-ghāʾib (al-Māturīdī), 59–60, 75, 117, 118, 126
al-Damanhūrī, Aḥmad Saʿd, 25*n*77
David, Prophet, 26*n*78
Davidson, Herbert, 110
de dicto and *de re* necessity, 133, 134
deduction, 29, 62*n*31, 68, 71, 108, 118, 121–22, 197; *see also kalām* cosmological argument (KCA)
deity theories, 139, 154–55, 157
demonstration (*burhān*), 42–43, 47, 108, 225
Descartes, René, 104, 106
Devil, the, 211*n*110
Dhanani, Alnoor, 90*n*217, 142*n*90
dhāt (essence), 60*n*21, 76–78, 142–48, 150–54, 223, 226–27
dialectics, 41–43, 59*n*19, 108, 225
Ḍirār b. ʿAmr, 75*n*119, 88, 89–90
dispositions (*ṭabāʾiʿ*), 89, 90–93, 101–2, 160, 223, 230
divine command theory, 215–16, 219, 233
divine simplicity, 33, 141–42, 145, 154, 156–57, 186, 198, 213–14
Dorroll, Philip, 44, 57, 61, 204
Dummett, Michael, 80, 81*n*160

Earman, John, 72
Ehring, Douglas, 96–97, 99*n*268, 100–1
Eichner, Heidrun, 77
El-Bekri, Hamza, 44*n*193
endurance (*baqāʾ*), 90, 100
Enlightenment, the, 46, 51, 52
enquiry (*naẓar*), 20, 26–28
  in contemporary thought, 51, 52–55
  use of the term, 4*n*20

epistemology, 5, 8, 11–29, 42, 60, 67–69, 98, 108, 127, 169–71, 213–14, 229
epoché (bracketing process, Husserl), 50, 58, 64–65, 79, 118
Erlwein, Hannah, 103*n*1
essence (*dhāt*), 60*n*21, 76–78, 142–48, 150–54, 223, 226–27
eternality
  of God, 125–32, 145–47, 148–50, 226
  of God's actions, 176, 177–78, 183–84, 188–89, 197–200, 224, 233–34
  of God's omniscience, 167
  of God's speech and the Qur'an, 197–200, 203–4, 219, 220–21
  of the Law, 33
  of prime matter, 35–37
  takwīn-mukawwan distinction, 179–81, 227
  and the world, 63, 108–9, 126–32, 188
ethics, 8, 27, 232
evidentialism, 11, 14–17, 61, 82–3, 222
evil, existence of, 111, 176–77
ex nihilo creation, 126, 160–61, 189–90, 232
existence, mental and concrete, 78–79
existence of God, arguments for, 47–48, 93, 103–23, 137–40, 142–44, 229
Exodus, Book of, 191

facticity (isness), 79*n*146
falāsifa (philosophers), 60–61, 87*n*198, 91–92, 126, 175; *see also ḥukamāʾ* (philosophers)
fallibilism, 24, 25
fanāʾ (perishing), 70–71
al-Fārābī, 16, 77
Farahat, Omar, 210
Feser, Edward, 112*n*42
finite past and infinite future, arguments for, 115–17
Al-Fiqh al-akbar (Al-Fiqh al-absaṭ) (al-Balkhī), 30*n*102, 31, 32*n*114, 176*n*4, 177*n*10, 194
Al-Fiqh al-akbar II (Abū Ḥanīfa), 31–32, 192, 194, 224
Foudeh, Saeed, 114*n*57, 183, 227
foundationalism, 4, 5, 47
  in *Al-ʿAqīda al-Nasafiyya*, 11
  and contemporary thought, 53–55
  non-foundationalism of al-Māturīdī, 12, 17–18, 27–28, 108, 222–23
  and Reformed Epistemology, 17
Fowden, Garth, 2*n*3
Frank, Richard M., 17*n*26, 89, 90*n*218, 92*n*233, 142*n*90
free will, 188
Frege, Gottlob, 105
fusion, 83

Gadamer, Hans-Georg, 5, 51–52, 54, 79*n*146
Genesis, Book of, 57*n*10
al-Ghazālī, Abū Ḥāmid, 2*n*4
al-Ghursī, Muḥammad Ṣāliḥ, 3*n*11, 147, 219*n*153
Glick, David, 169–70
God
  arguments for the existence of, 47–48, 93, 103–23, 137–40, 142–44, 229
  divine simplicity, 33, 141–42, 145, 154, 156–57, 198, 213–14
  eternality of, 125–32, 145–47, 148–50, 226
  the mind, the world and, 59–73
  nature of, 141–58
  and necessity of the world's creation, 27, 47–48, 93
  properties of, 153–56
  relationship to evil, 111, 176–77
  relationship to logic, 128, 132–33, 135–40, 168–71
  relationship with creation, 184–85
  tawḥīd (unicity of), 33, 35, 74, 91*n*221, 120–1, 156–7, 231
  and tropes, 87, 153–54, 157, 186, 214, 221, 231
  use of the term, 3*n*8
  whatness (*māʾiyya*) of, 74–76, 143, 144
  see also attributes of God

Goldbach Conjecture, 81
good, knowledge of, 19–20
goodness of God, 233
Gorgias, 21*n*52
Grim, Patrick, 168–69
Grünbaum, Adolf, 119*n*89
Gutas, Dimitri, 1*n*2, 34

Hackett, Stuart, 112
al-Ḥakam, Hishām b., 88
Hanafi, Hassan, 57–58, 139, 140
'Ḥanafī-Māturīdī', use of the term, 7
Ḥanafism, 29–32, 37, 41–42, 133, 175–76, 193, 202–3, 224
Ḥanbalism, 141, 124*n*1, 219
Hanna, Robert, 62*n*31, 134*n*60
Hansu, Hüseyin, 24*n*72
Hart, David Bentley, 138
Hartshorne, Charles, 106, 171, 230
hastiyya (isness), 60, 73–76, 79*n*146, 97*n*259, 223
Heidegger, Martin, 51, 52
Heisenberg, Werner, 60*n*24, 67, 69–70
Hellenism, 29, 33, 34
Heraclitus, 56–57
hermeneutics, 51–52, 80, 215, 218
ḥikāya (imitation), 206, 207
ḥikma (wisdom) of God, 45, 71, 119–20, 159–66, 172–74, 224, 232, 233
  and free will, 188
  and morality, 216–18
Hilbert, David, 114
Hinduism, 60*n*23
howness (*kayfiyya*), 60–61, 63, 117
ḥukamāʾ (philosophers), 18, 28, 47; *see also falāsifa* (philosophers)
Hume, David, 61–62, 113
Husserl, Edmund, 2*n*7, 50–51, 56*n*1, 57–59, 64–72, 79–85, 95, 99, 105, 117–19, 129, 137, 170–71, 229–30

Ibāḍism, 141
ʿibāra (expression), 196, 206, 207, 220, 228
Iblāgh, ʿInāyat Allāh, 31*n*113
Ibn Fūrak, 206, 209–10
Ibn Ḥanbal, Aḥmad, 146, 194, 202*n*61
Ibn Kamāl Bāshā, 43, 175*n*2
Ibn Karrām, 31
Ibn Khaldūn, 18
Ibn Khuzayma, 176*n*5
Ibn Kullāb, ʿAbd Allāh, 196, 206, 228
  Kullābī formula, 149, 151–52, 157, 202*n*61, 210, 231
Ibn Masʿūd, ʿAbd Allāh, 196
Ibn Mubashshir, Jaʿfar, 206
Ibn Saʿdī, 15*n*18
Ibn Shabīb, 23
Ibn Shujāʿ al-Thaljī, 23
Ibn Sīnā (Avicenna), 41–42, 77–78, 106, 128, 130, 132–33, 147, 187–88, 226
Ibn Sulaymān, ʿAbbād, 146*n*118
Ibn Taymiyya, 61*n*25, 175*n*1
Ibn Yaḥyā al-Bashāgharī, 39–40, 93, 176–77, 178, 204–5
idealism, 64–6, 70, 81–2, 100
iʿjāz (inimitability) of the Qur'an, 16, 204–5, 207, 208, 228
ijmāʿ (consensus), 22–23, 25–26
ijtihād (exhaustive legal enquiry), 25–26
ilhām (spiritual insight), 19–20
ʿilm (omniscience) of God, 70, 132, 147–48, 159–74, 188–89, 227, 231
imago dei (image of God), 57*n*10
imitation (*ḥikāya*), 206, 207
incarnation analogy, 191
indeterminacy, 70, 72, 113, 136, 167–71, 231
induction, 61–62, 81, 97, 113, 122
infinite and finite beings, 85–87
infinity arguments, 114–16, 153
inimitability (*iʿjāz*) of the Qur'an, 16, 204–5, 207, 208, 228
intentionality, theory of (Husserl), 50, 65
intuitionism, 68, 81–87, 98–101, 105–6, 109, 111–19, 137–40, 151–53, 157, 169–71, 229, 231
Iqbal, Muhammed, 3, 86, 112*n*45
Isaacson, Daniel, 84

al-Isfarāyīnī, Abū Isḥāq, 147
ʿiṣma (protection from error), 24
Ismāʿīlism, 125
isness (*hastiyya*), 60, 73–76, 79*n*146, 97*n*259, 223
ithbāt (affirmation) *see taḥqīq* (verification of attributes)
al-ʿIyāḍī, Abū Aḥmad, 39
al-ʿIyāḍī, Abū Bakr, 146, 204
al-ʿIyāḍī, Abū Naṣr, 39
al-Izmīrī, Muḥammad b. Walī al-Qirshahrī, 43

Jackson, Sherman A., 10, 28*n*93
al-Jāḥiẓ, Abū ʿUthmān, 152
Jahm b. Ṣafwān, 34, 125, 145, 193–94
Jahmī/Jahmiyya, 193–94
jawhar see concrete particulars (*aʿyān/jawāhir*)
al-Jawnī, Abū al-Jald, 195
Jesus, Prophet, 191
jinn possession, 66*n*60, 164*n*35
jism see bodies (*ajsām*, sing. *jism*)
Johns, Anthony, 212
Judaism, 33, 195, 196, 210–11
al-Jurjānī, ʿAbd al-Qāhir, 208
al-Jurjānī, al-Sayyid al-Sharīf, 42, 79
justification of truth claims, 14–17, 19–20
  in contemporary thought, 52–54
  and foundationalism, 4, 5, 11–12
al-Juwaynī, Abū al-Maʿālī, 110, 147

al-Kaʿbī, Abū al-Qāsim, 30, 90*n*217, 151, 163, 172, 176, 197–98
kalām, definitions of, 1–2, 9
kalām cosmological argument (KCA), 107–22, 129, 230
kalām jadīd movement, 3, 5, 7, 45–49, 226, 234
Kant, Immanuel, 49–50, 51, 63–65, 104–5, 107, 112, 119
Karrāmiyya, 179, 180
Kaş, Murat, 78
al-Kāsānī, 195
Kastrup, Bernardo, 66
kayfiyya (howness), 60–61, 63, 117
khalq al-qurʾān (creation of the Qur'an) controversy, 192–94
al-Kharpūtī, ʿAbd al-Laṭīf, 46–48
khilāf (transcendence), 60, 63, 86–87, 126, 144; *see also* contingency of the world
Kholeif, Fathalla, 15*n*21, 111*n*38, 161*n*15, 182–83, 184, 227
al-Kindī, 18*n*35, 34, 35, 73, 75*n*118, 128, 175*n*1
Kirk, G. S., 56–57
Kitāb al maqālāt (al-Māturīdī), 75
Kitāb al-ʿālim wa-l-mutaʿallim (Abū Ḥanīfa), 31, 192–93
Kitāb al-tawḥīd (al-Māturīdī), manuscript source for, 12–13, 46
Kitāb al-waṣiyya (Abū Ḥanīfa), 31, 192, 194
knowledge, God's *see* omniscience (*ʿilm*) of God
knowledge, human
  of good, 19–20
  of material and categorial 'things', 73–87
  al-Māturīdī's theory of, 19–24, 73, 166
Kufa, 34
Kuhn, Thomas, 52, 52*n*240, 150*n*143
Kullābī formula, 149, 151–52, 157, 202*n*61, 210, 231
Kurt, Erkan, 108–9, 217*n*142

al-Lāmishī, Abū Thanāʾ, 165
Lange, Christian, 1*n*2
language and the Qur'an, 194–96, 201–2, 205, 207, 208, 218–21, 228
Law of Identity, 83
Law of Non-contradiction, 83, 136
Law of Excluded Middle (LEM), 37, 80–84, 136, 151–2, 169, 229
Laycock, Steven, 170–71
Leftow, Brian, 130–31, 134*n*60, 139–40, 153–57, 185–86, 231
Leibniz, Gottfried Wilhelm, 104, 107, 110, 133

Leibniz's Law (the Indiscernibility of Identicals), 99
Levine, Michael, 211*n*111
Lewinstein, Keith, 75*n*120
Lewis, David, 83–84, 104–5, 134
Lewis, Frank A., 36
Liar's Paradox, 168–69
life-world (Husserl), 50–51, 56*n*1
Locke, John, 23*n*66, 98*n*263
logic
  and God's omniscience, 168–71
  impact on Māturīdī thought, 37, 42
  and intuitionism, 81–85
  Kullābī formula, 149, 151–52, 157, 202*n*61, 210, 231
  on the necessity and eternality of God, 128, 132–33, 135–40
  Stoicism, 152
logos, 56–57, 191
lots, drawing of, 19, 20
Lowe, E. J., 96*n*253
Lucknow, 46
luṭf (kindness or grace of God), 22

MacDonald, Duncan, 226
MacIntyre, Alasdair, 4*n*20, 5, 6, 52–55, 119, 228
McTaggart, J. M. E., 128
Madelung, Wilferd, 40*n*168, 193
al-Maḥbūbī, Ṣadr al-Sharīʿa, 42, 133
māʾiyya (whatness), 60–61, 73–76, 79*n*146, 97*n*259, 117, 223
  of God, 74–76, 143, 144
al-Maʿmūn, Caliph, 192
maʿnā (cause), 26
maʿnā (meaning of divine speech), 203, 205, 207–8, 219
maʿnā (substantive attribute), 147
manuscript sources, 12–13, 46
  lost treatises of al-Māturīdī, 12*n*10
Many Over One (trope theory), 96, 97–100, 156
al-Marīsī, Bishr, 26*n*78, 193–94
Mavrodes, George, 210
Mayer, Toby, 106
medieval period, use of the term, 1–2*n*3
Meillassoux, Quentin, 62*n*31
mental and concrete existence, 78–79
Menzel, Christopher, 140
message analogy, 220, 233
metaphor (*majāz*), 201, 204, 224
microcosm/macrocosm analogy, 18, 93
mind, the
  and natures (*ṭabāʾiʿ*), 93
  and necessity, 137–39
  on temporality and eternality, 125–27
  the world, God and, 59–73
mithl (analogy) *see* analogy (*mithl*)
Moad, Edward, 216–17
modality, categories of, 106, 132–40, 168, 231
Momin, Abdur-Rahman, 193*n*8
morality and divine wisdom, 216–18
Morris, Thomas V., 140
Morriston, Wes, 112–13, 115
Moses, Prophet, 173, 191, 201
Mueller, Ian, 37
Muḥammad, Prophet, 8, 16, 19, 21–22, 125*n*8, 179, 192, 196, 203, 211–13
mukawwan (created thing), 176–77, 178, 179–81
mutashābih (ambiguous) attributes, 124*n*1
Muʿtazilism, 29–30, 45, 224, 233–34
  al-maʿdūm shayʾ (the non-existent is a thing), 76–77
  on atomism, 88
  on divine knowledge, 148*n*129
  on God's nature, 145, 146, 154, 157
  on God's speech, 192, 197–200, 203, 205, 207, 217–18
  on God's wisdom, 160, 163–65
  on *takwīn*, 23–24, 176–77, 180

Nadwatul Ulema, Lucknow, 46
al-Najjār, al-Ḥusayn, 30, 88, 89, 163–64
al-Najjār, Bilāl, 114*n*57

prophecy, 19, 24; *see also* revelation
Pugliese, Marc, 68

al-Qalānisī, Abū al-ʿAbbās, 148–49
Qalānisīs, 182
al-Qārī, Mullā ʿAlī, 161
qiyās al-ghāʾib ʿalā al-shāhid principle, 59–63, 68*n*72, 75, 117, 118, 126, 144
quantum mechanics, 58, 66–73, 113–14, 122, 123, 169–70, 229–30
  complementarity (Bohr), 60*n*24, 169–70
  Heisenberg uncertainty principle, 169
  two-slit experiment, 170
qudra (God's power), 214, 227
  and God's action, 177, 178, 182–83, 184, 185–86, 187
  and God's speech, 214
  and *takwīn*, 181, 183
Quine, W. V., 62*n*31
Quinn, Philip, 189*nn*85–86, 216, 232
Qur'an, the
  and divine speech, 191–221, 211, 224, 227–28, 232
  inimitability (*iʿjāz*) of, 16, 204–5
  khalq al-qurʾān controversy, 192–94
  quotations from: 'Be! (*kun*)', 179, 224; on creation, 92, 127*n*14, 162; on God's omniscience and wisdom, 159–60; 'He ascended the throne', 124*n*1; on inexhaustibility of meanings of God's speech, 209; on Moses, 173, 191; on reasoned enquiry, 27; 'there is nothing like God', 74, 200; on unicity of God, 35, 121
  translation of, 194–96, 201–2, 205, 207, 208, 218–19
al-Qūrṣāwī, Abū Naṣr, 148*n*131

Rasmussen, Joshua, 114
Rayy, 163
al-Rāzī, Abū Bakr, 163
al-Rāzī, Abū Ḥātim, 163
al-Rāzī, Fakhr al-Dīn, 41, 42, 45, 77, 78, 225, 226
realism
  of mathematical objects, 84, 100–1, 140
  of morality, 217
  of physical objects, 21, 66, 229
  of time, 132
  of universals, 94, 154–55
Reçber, Mehmet, 134, 137
recitation, Qur'anic, 194–96
Reformed Epistemology, 17
Reichenbach, Bruce, 107, 113
relativism, 14–15, 54
reports, 20, 61*n*25
  mutawātir (mass-transmitted), 21–26
  in relation to *ijmāʿ* (consensus), 22–23, 25–26
revelation, 17*n*26
  and divine speech, 210–11
  four stage model of, 211–13
  Ibn Taymiyya on, 61*n*25
  and *takwīn*, 179
  see also Qur'an
Reynolds, Gabriel, 195, 205*n*73
rigid designator, 100*n*272, 139*n*80
Rosenthal, Franz, 163
Ross, James F., 186, 190
Rudolph, Ulrich, 16*n*23, 20, 28*n*90, 30, 31, 32*n*114, 35*n*134, 38*n*153, 88, 90*n*217, 91*n*224, 108*n*27, 144*n*103, 161, 222–34
Russell, Bertrand, 105, 114
al-Rustughfanī, Abū al-Ḥasan, 31*n*113, 38, 39, 40, 164, 203–4, 225

sabʿat aḥruf (seven, or many, lections), 195–96
al-Ṣābūnī, Nūr al-Dīn, 41, 128, 148, 150, 208
al-Ṣaffār, Abū Isḥāq, 12, 148–49, 161, 166
al-Sālimī, Abū al-Shakūr, 36*n*139, 40, 127, 146, 148, 160, 164–65, 179–80, 206, 207, 226

ta'ṭīl (nullification of attributes), 74, 145, 185
tawātur (continuous mass narration), 17, 21–27, 223
tawhīd (unicity of God), 33, 35, 74, 91*n*221, 120–21, 156–57, 231
Ta'wīlāt al-qur'ān (al-Māturīdī), 26, 26*n*78, 74*n*114, 92, 127*n*14, 179, 201–2, 223, 225
Taylor, Charles, 66, 122*n*107
teleological arguments, 48, 51, 57, 70–72, 103*n*1, 104, 110, 119–22, 159–60, 229–30
temporality of the world, 60, 63, 108–10, 111–17
  and eternality of God, 126–32, 188
tensed and untensed time, 111–12, 115, 117, 128–32
theories
  bundle theory, 88, 89–93, 97, 98–101, 150, 223, 229–30
  correspondence theory of truth, 79–87, 98
  counterpart theory, 100, 101
  divine command theory, 215–16, 219, 233
  set theory, 83–86, 96, 98–101, 153, 157, 168–71, 229–30
  speech act theory, 213, 214–15, 220, 221, 232–33
  Stage Theory, 101
  A-theory and B-theory of time, 128–9, 131–32, 190, 231
  theory of intentionality, 50, 65
  theory of truth, 65–66, 79–80, 82–83, 87, 95
  trope theory, 87, 93–101, 97, 97–98, 98–101, 153–58, 161*n*14, 199, 229–30
  Worm Theory, 101
Theory of Everything, 121–22
'things', knowledge of, 73–87
thisness, 97
Thomas, David, 32–33
Thomistic cosmological argument, 107
Tieszen, Richard, 82*n*166
time, 125–32, 190, 231
  and God's omniscience, 167
  and *takwīn*, 178, 179–80
  tensed time, 111–12, 115, 117, 128–32
Topaloğlu, Bekir, 37*n*143
Torah, 195, 207
tradition and reason, 11–55, 119
traditionalism, 2*n*4, 10, 39–40, 50, 176, 193–96, 204–9, 220, 228
tradition-constituted enquiry (MacIntyre), 52–55, 119, 228
transcendence *see khilāf* (transcendence)
transcendental idealism, 64, 70
translation of the Qur'an, 194–96, 201–2, 205, 207, 208, 218–19
Transoxiana, 5*n*21
Treiger, Alexander, 1*n*1
Trenery, David, 3*n*10
triangles, as example of necessity, 133, 134, 135, 136, 139
trope theory, 87, 93–101, 153–58, 161*n*14, 199, 229–30
  bundle theory, 97, 98–101
  substrate-attribute theory, 97–98
truth, theory of, 65–66, 79–80, 82–83, 87, 95
truth claims
  in contemporary thought, 52–54
  correspondence theory of, 79–87
  and *tawātur*, 21–25, 223
truthbearers, 80, 87, 98
truthmakers, 80, 87, 99, 153, 155*n*172, 157
Turkey, 49, 234

uncertainty principle (Heisenberg), 60*n*24, 67, 69
unicity of God (*tawhīd*), 33, 35, 74, 91*n*221, 120–21, 156–57, 231
Uniformity Principle (UP), 61–62
universal experienceability, 2*n*7, 64, 130, 188

universals, 94–100, 154–55, 157, 161, 161*n*14, 230
al-Usmandī, ʿAlāʾ al-Dīn, 150, 151
ʿUthmanī *rasm* of the Qur'an, 22

van Ess, Josef, 13, 36*n*139, 59*n*19, 60*n*23, 61*n*28, 74*n*109, 142
van Putten, Marijn, 22*n*58
verification
  of attributes (*taḥqīq*), 44*n*193, 74–76, 185, 223, 229
  and God's omniscience, 166–68, 171
  Husserlian, 79–80, 98–99, 105, 156
Vishanoff, David, 218–19
visible and veiled, analogy of, 59–63, 68*n*72, 75, 117, 118, 126, 144
von Grunebaum, Gustave, 29, 34

waqf (suspension of judgement), 152, 193, 202, 204, 224
water, as example of necessity, 134, 139–40
Watt, William Montgomery, 31*n*113, 32
Wensinck, A. J., 31–32
Westphal, Merold, 213–14
whatness (*māʾiyya*), 60–61, 73–6, 79*n*146, 97*n*259, 117, 223
  of God, 74–76, 143, 144
Wheeler, John Archibald, 71–72, 123
Wielandt, Rotraud, 45
Williams, Rowan, 10, 73, 185
wisdom (*ḥikma*) of God, 45, 71, 119–20, 159–66, 172–74, 224, 232, 233
  and free will, 188
  and morality, 216–18
Wisnovsky, Robert, 74*n*112, 77, 149
Wittgenstein, Ludwig, 82*n*167
Wolfson, Harry, 33
Wolterstorff, Nicholas, 4, 54, 210*n*108, 213–16, 217, 220, 232–33
world, the
  the mind, God and, 59–73
  use of the term, 2*n*7
Worm Theory, 101
Wykstra, Stephen, 17, 222

Zadeh, Travis, 205, 205*n*74, 207–8
Zagzebski, Linda, 166, 172
Zahavi, Dan, 65
Ẓāhirīs, 125*n*8
Zermelo, Ernst, 84
Zysow, Aron, 23, 24*n*72, 26*n*78

EU representative:
Easy Access System Europe
Mustamäe tee 50, 10621 Tallinn, Estonia
Gpsr.requests@easproject.com

www.ingramcontent.com/pod-product-compliance
Lightning Source LLC
Chambersburg PA
CBHW051604230426
43668CB00013B/1969